AF606764

LONDON

FROM THE AIR

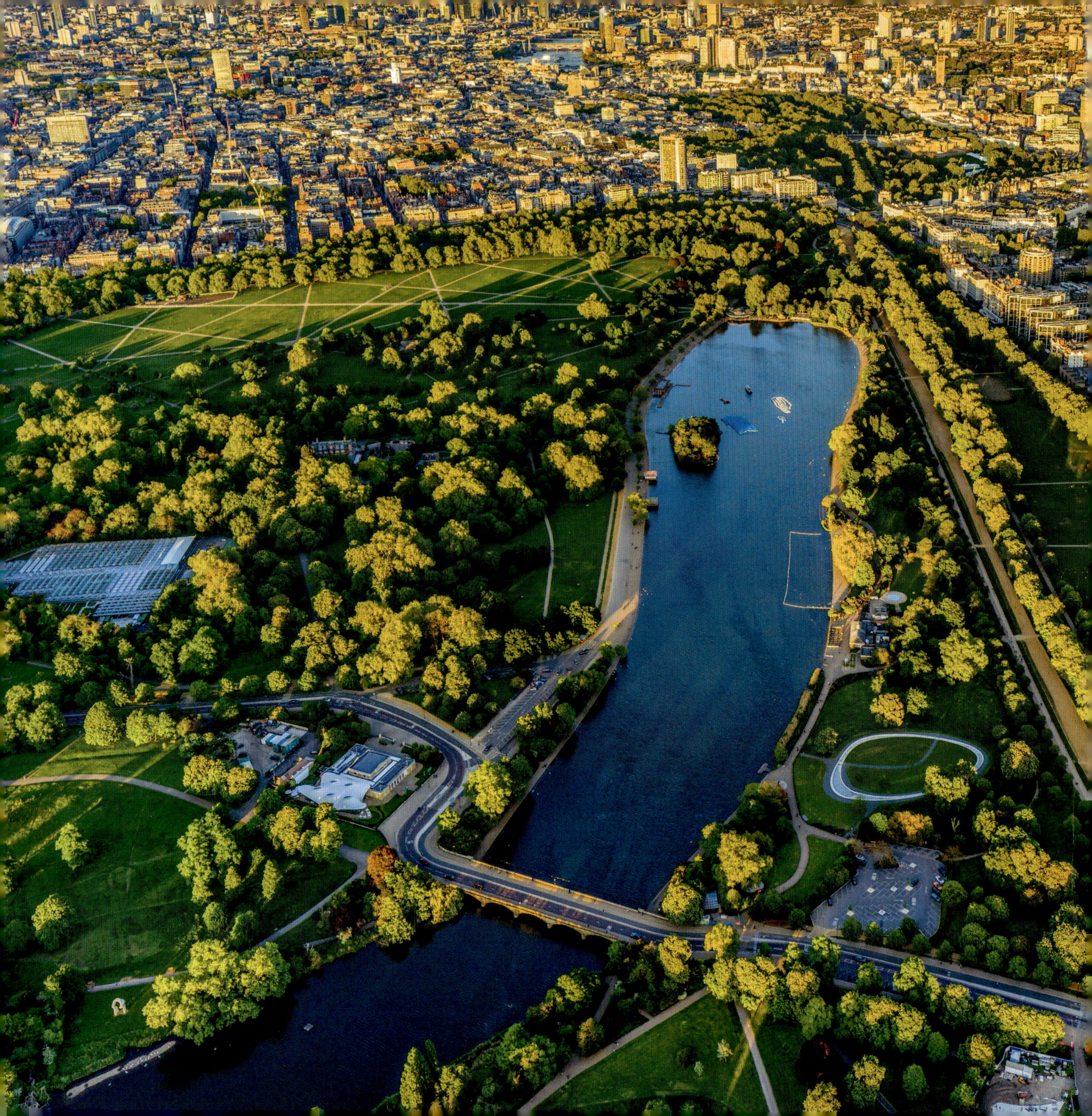

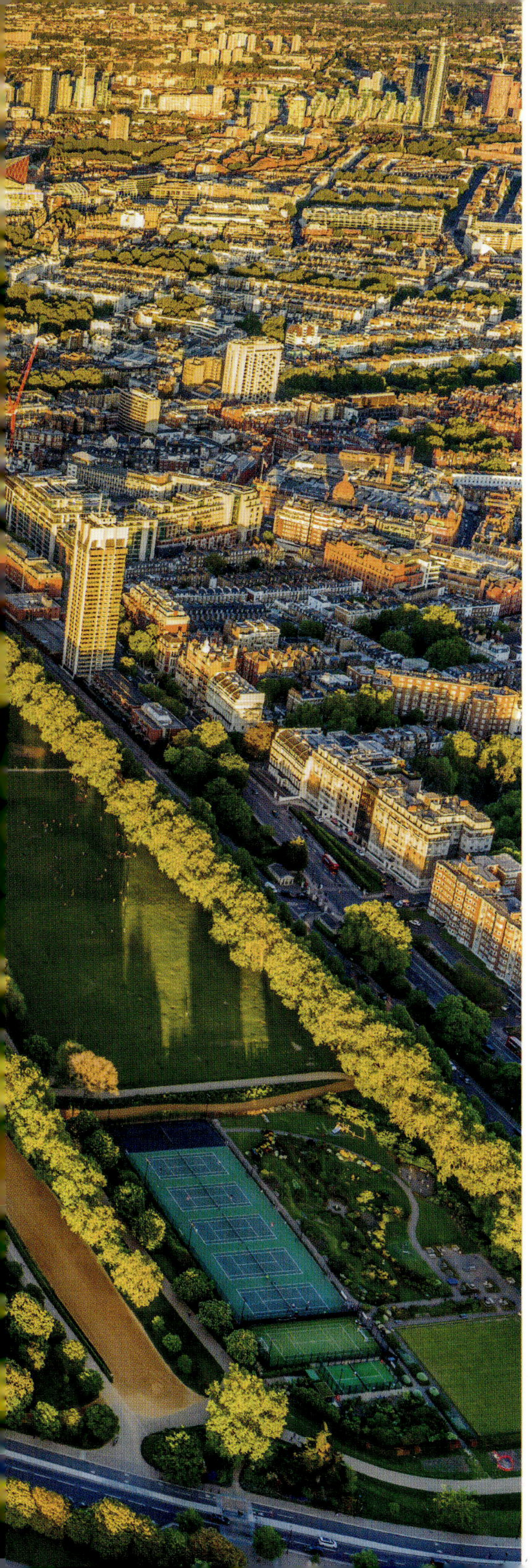

LONDON

FROM THE AIR

JEFFREY MILSTEIN

FOREWORD BY
SIR NORMAN FOSTER

INTRODUCTION & SELECTED NOTES BY
ROBERT MORTON

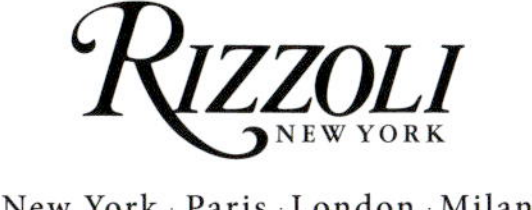

New York · Paris · London · Milan

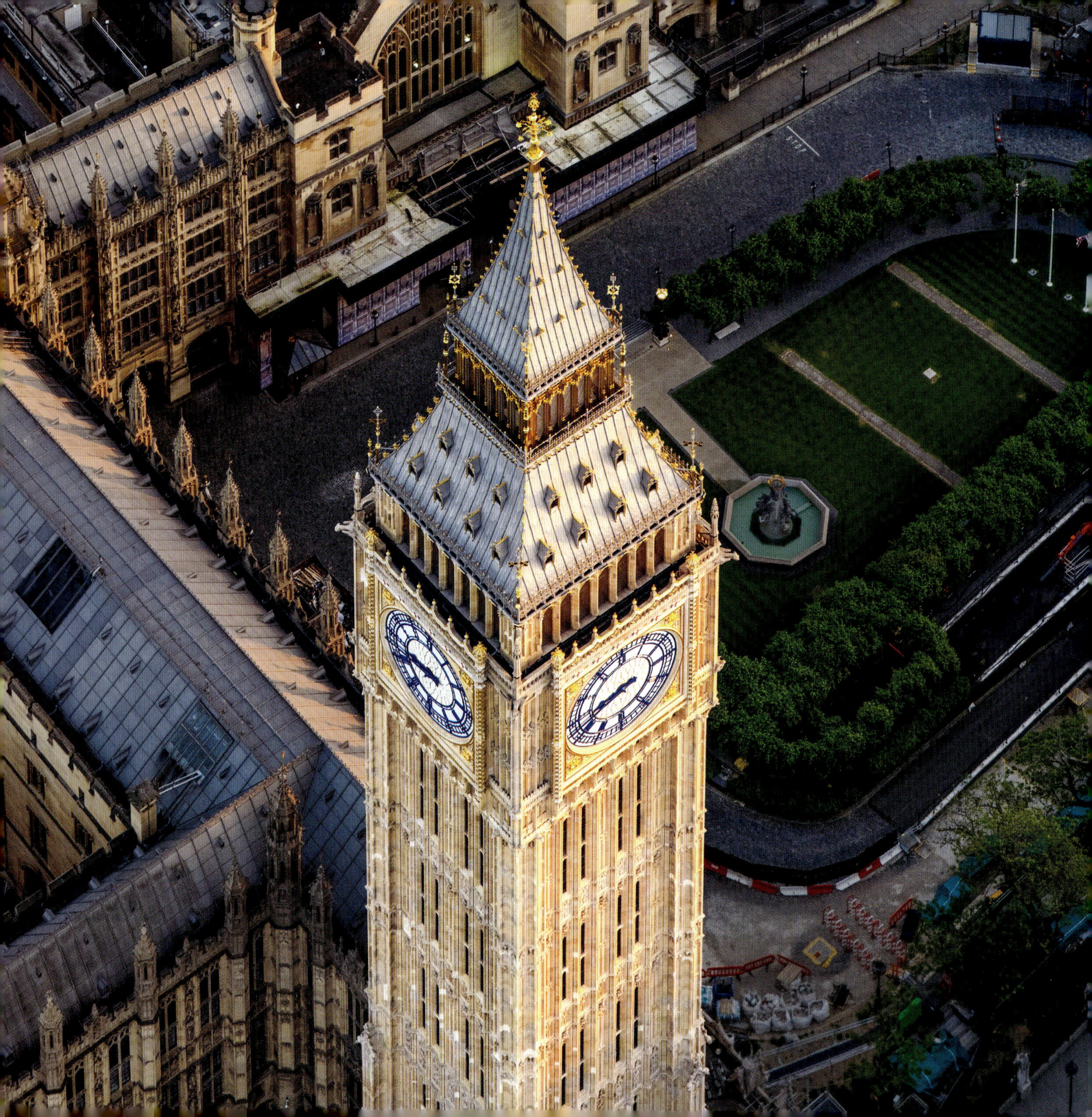

CONTENTS

Pages 2–3: Looking east over Hyde Park and the lake known as the Serpentine

Opposite: Elizabeth Tower, with the Great Clock of Westminster and the Great Bell, known as Big Ben

Pages 6–7: City of London, looking past the skyscraper nicknamed the Shard

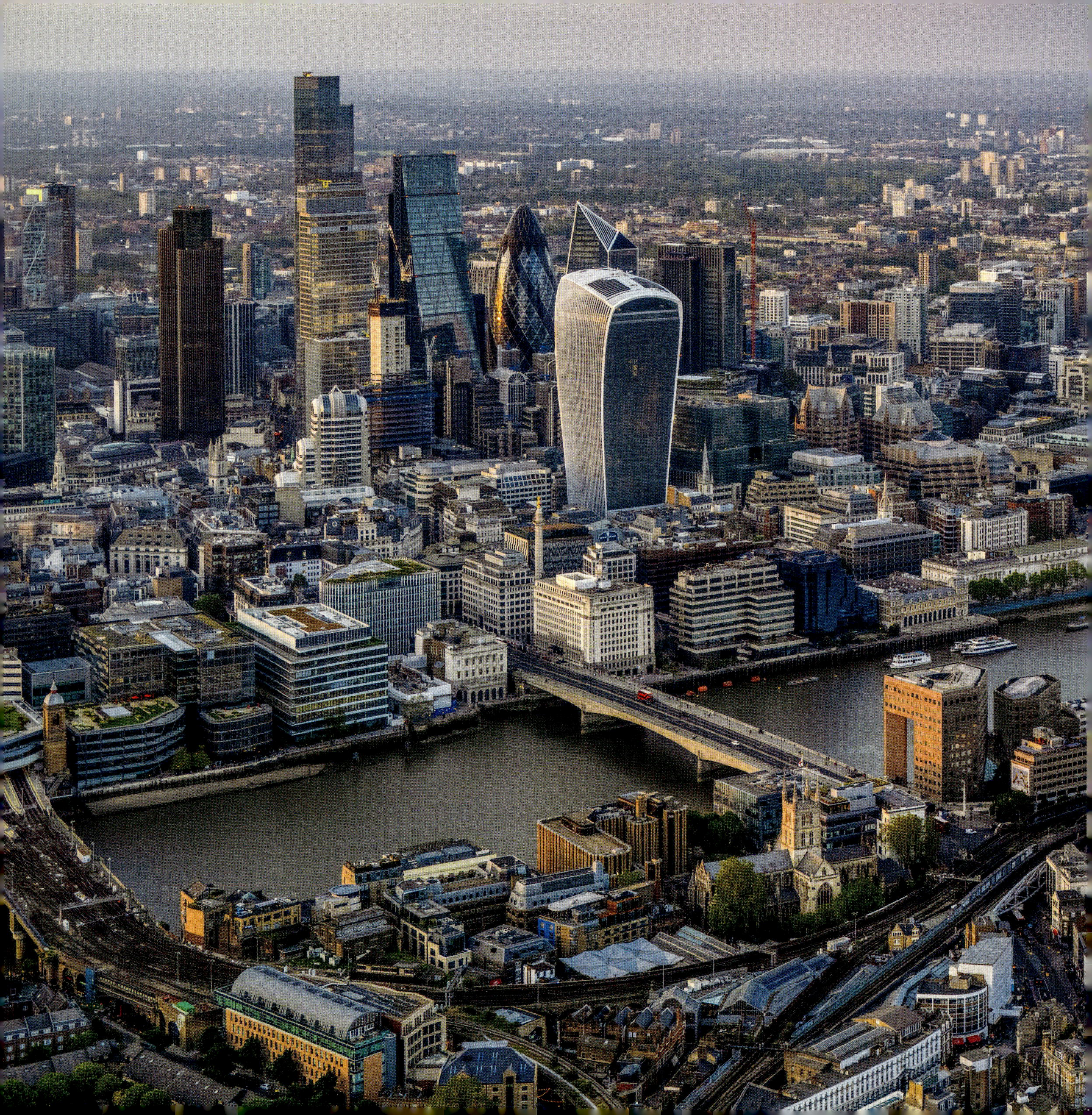

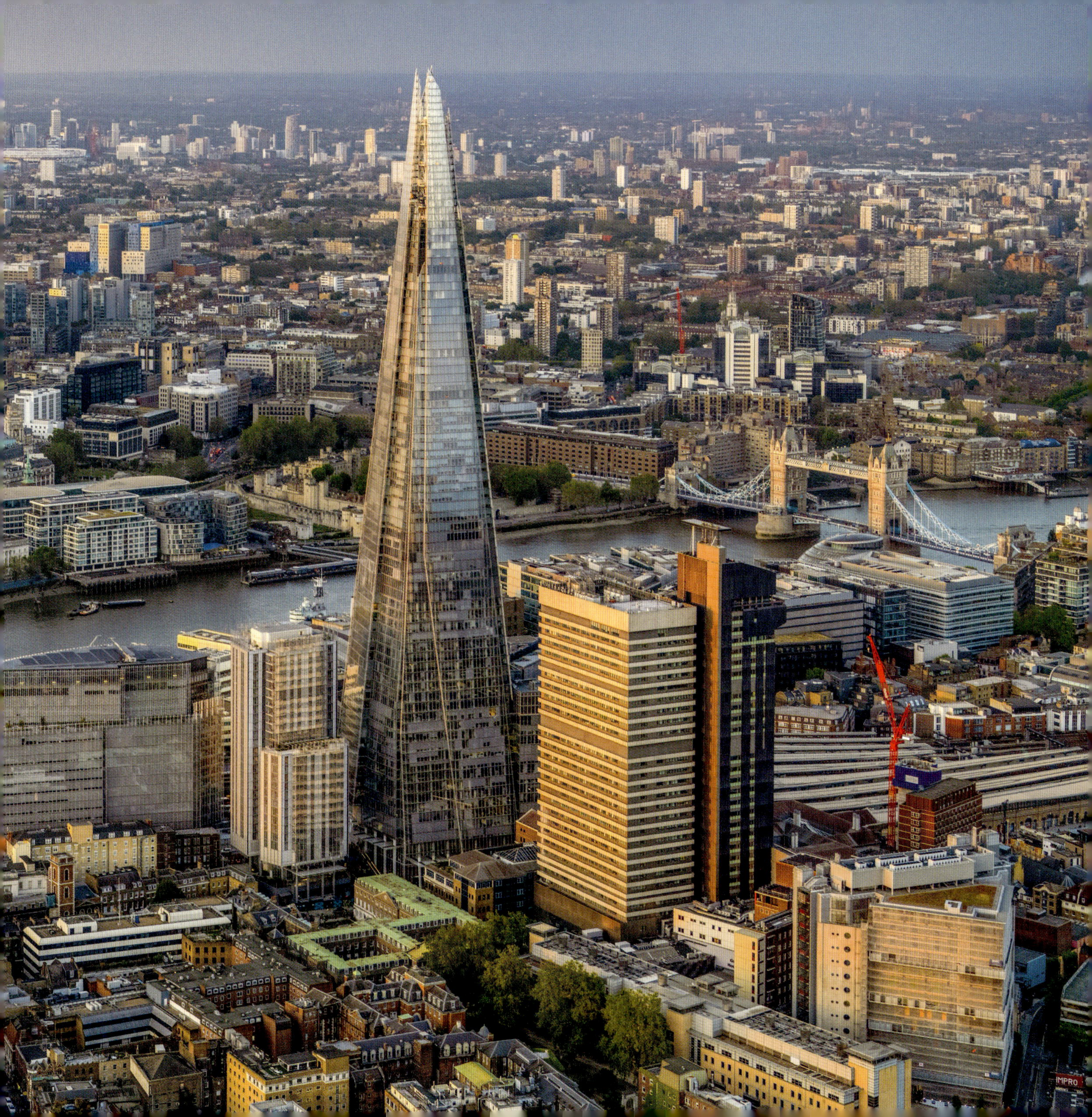

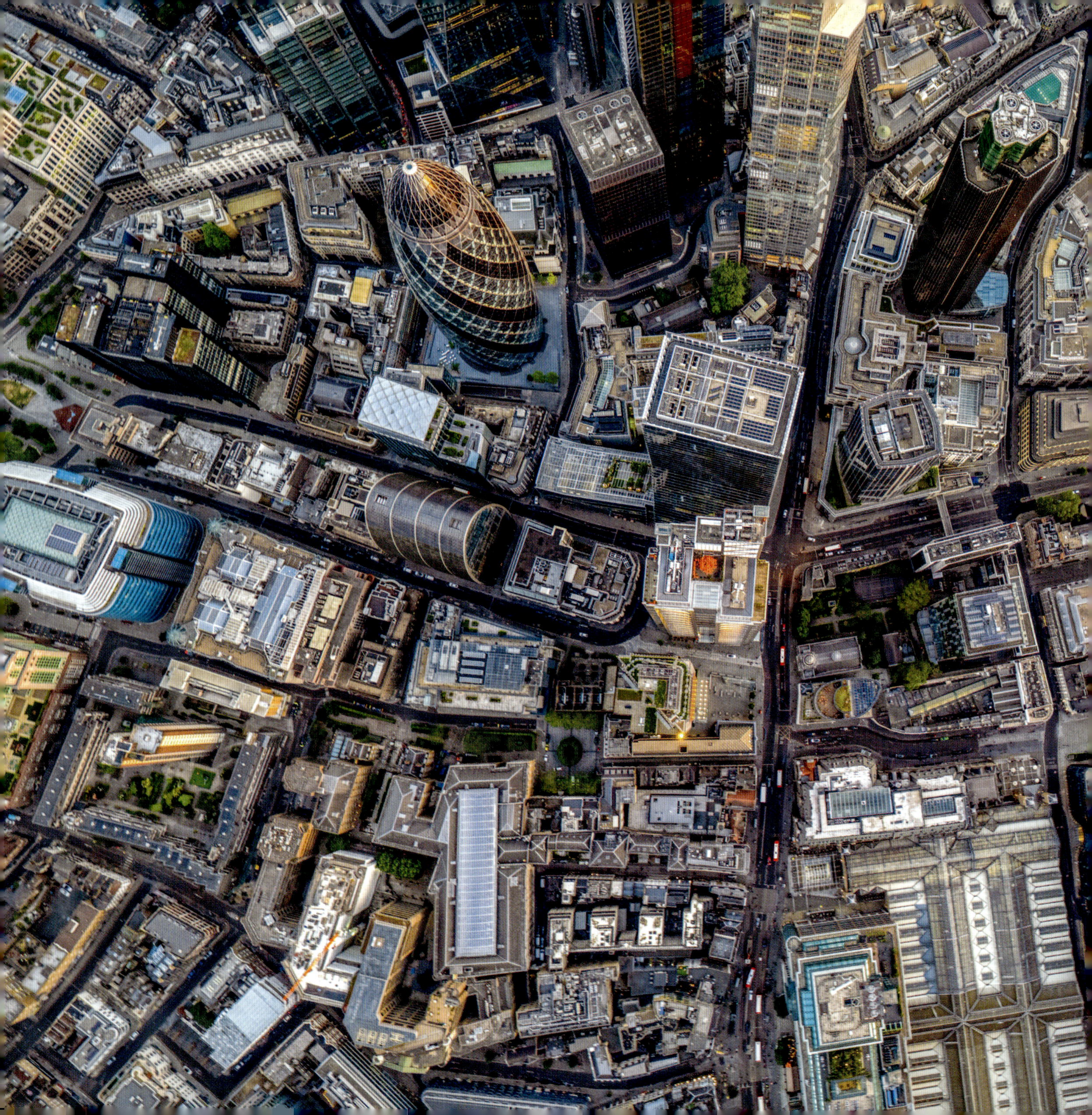

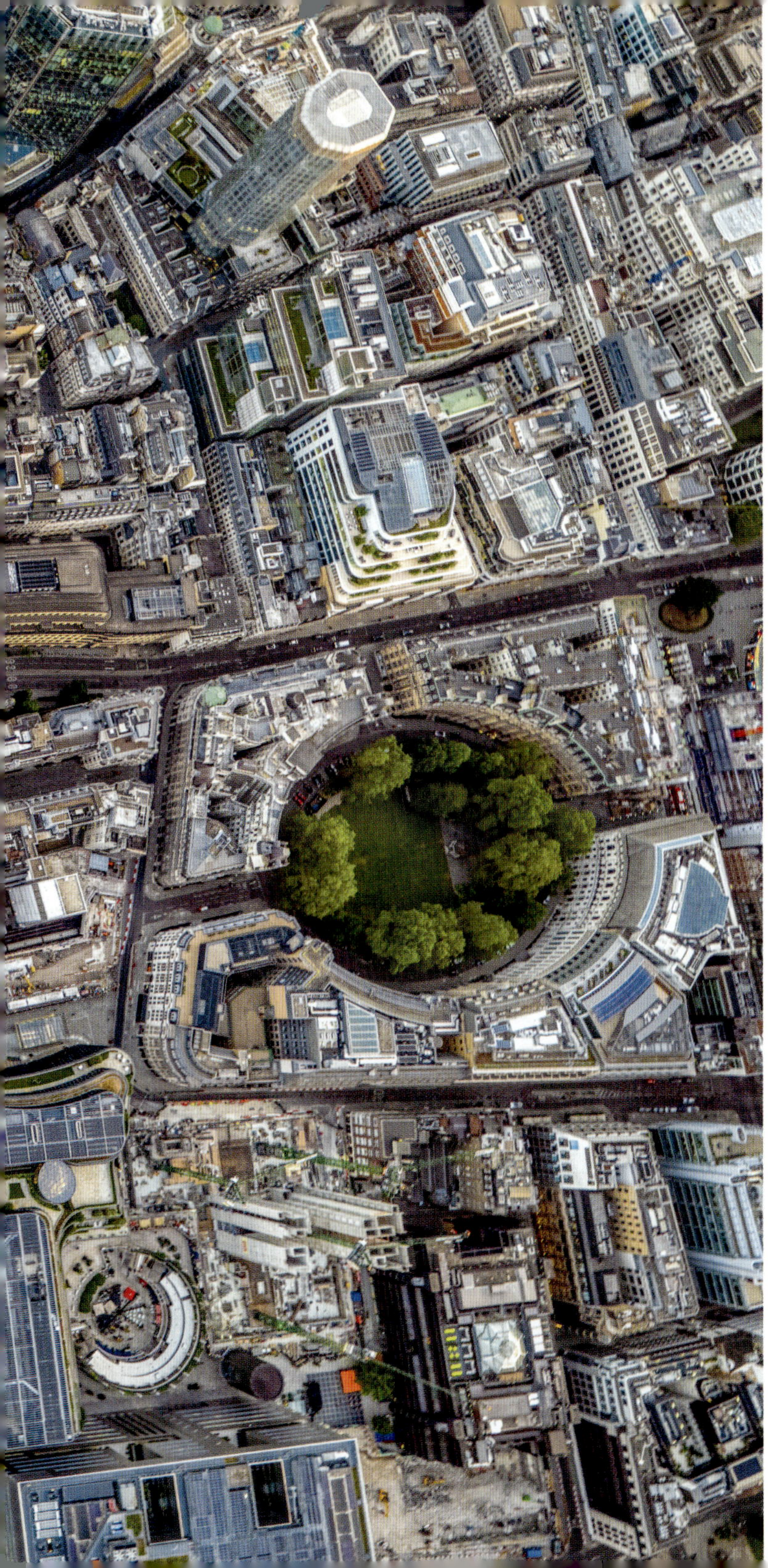

Looking down on the London Wall and Bishopsgate, with the skyscraper at 30 St. Mary Axe (nicknamed the Gherkin) at upper left and Finsbury Circus Gardens at right

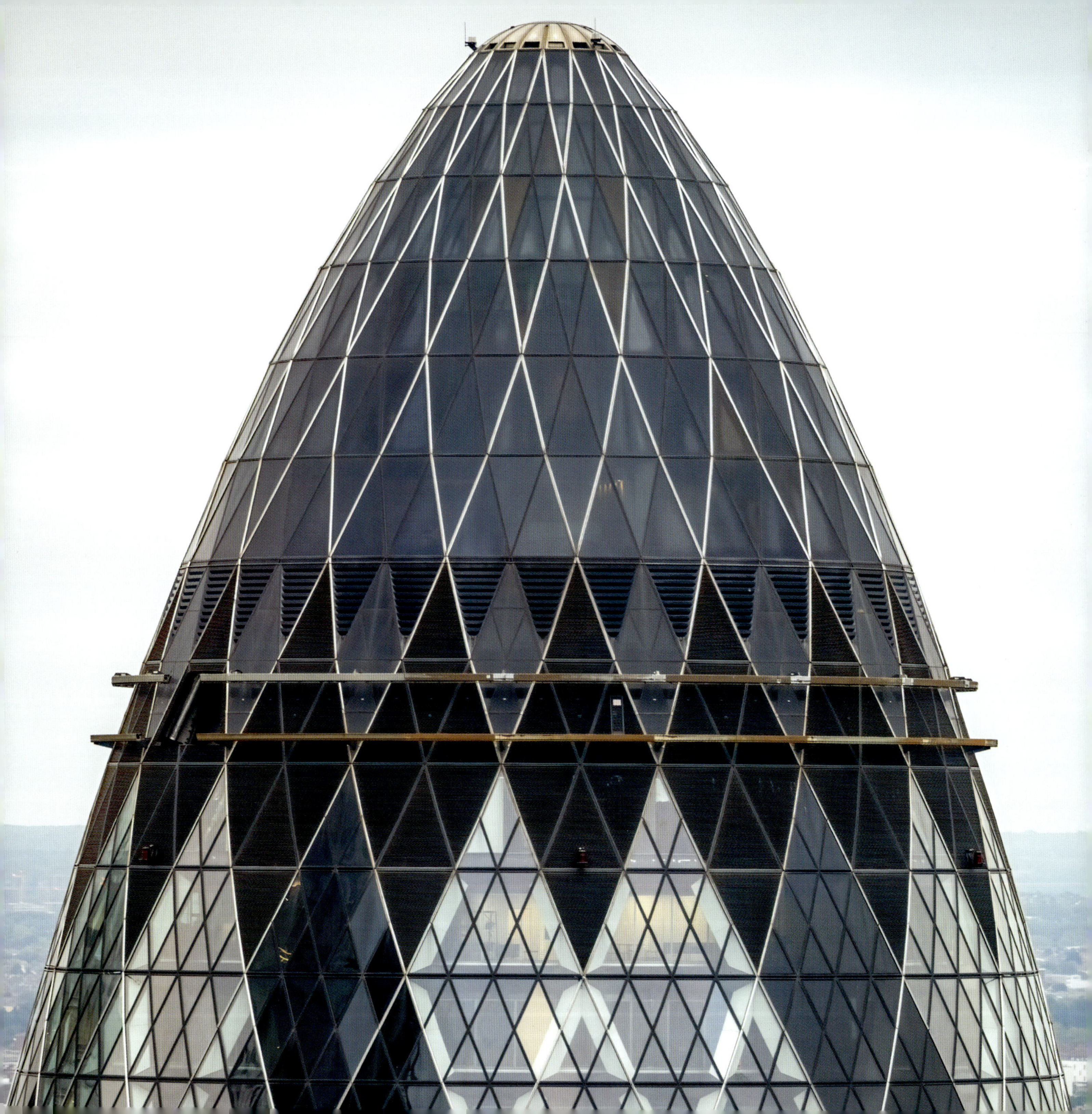

FOREWORD

Sir Norman Foster

Jeffrey Milstein's images of his chosen cities, seen from above, are pure feasts for the eyes. Whether taken in plan view, or with perspectives that stretch to the horizon, each image is picture-perfect. The expression "to have an eye" suggests a person's ability to discern and appreciate beauty. Milstein's selective eye, filtered through the lens of his camera, goes beyond the mere capturing of urban landscapes to create the most elegant aerial compositions.

For the visual reader, this book can delight at a purely aesthetic level and need go no further. But discerning viewers can also read much more into the photographs as they reveal the infrastructure of public spaces, parks, avenues of trees, streets, arteries of roads and railways, and airport terminals where the highways in the sky finally come down to earth. I have described this infrastructure of connectivity as the urban glue that binds together the architecture of individual buildings. It determines the identity or DNA of the city in question. Scanning this book from cover to cover is to see the London metropolis as an aggregation of village-like clusters, each with its own sense of place. It is this diversity that helps give London its own special character.

The upper floors of the Gherkin

For those who know London from walking, cycling, or driving, Milstein offers a complementary viewpoint, revealing underlying patterns that might otherwise lay hidden. This aerial perspective also enables the city to be seen in its wider regional setting and makes visible the benefits of the Green Belt that has protected London over many decades from unsustainable sprawl. It is also a timely reminder of the value of the enlightened master planning that has reinforced the concept of London's neighborhoods. These initiatives were embodied in the Greater London Plan conceived in 1943 at the height of World War II by Patrick Abercrombie and John Henry Forshaw.

London from the Air can provoke other insights into the past, such as the city's roots as a prime Roman river crossing or its more modern foundation following the rebuild after the Great Fire. These and other layers of history are brought to life by the vivid and beautiful record of Jeffrey Milstein's airborne journey across one of the greatest cities of the world.

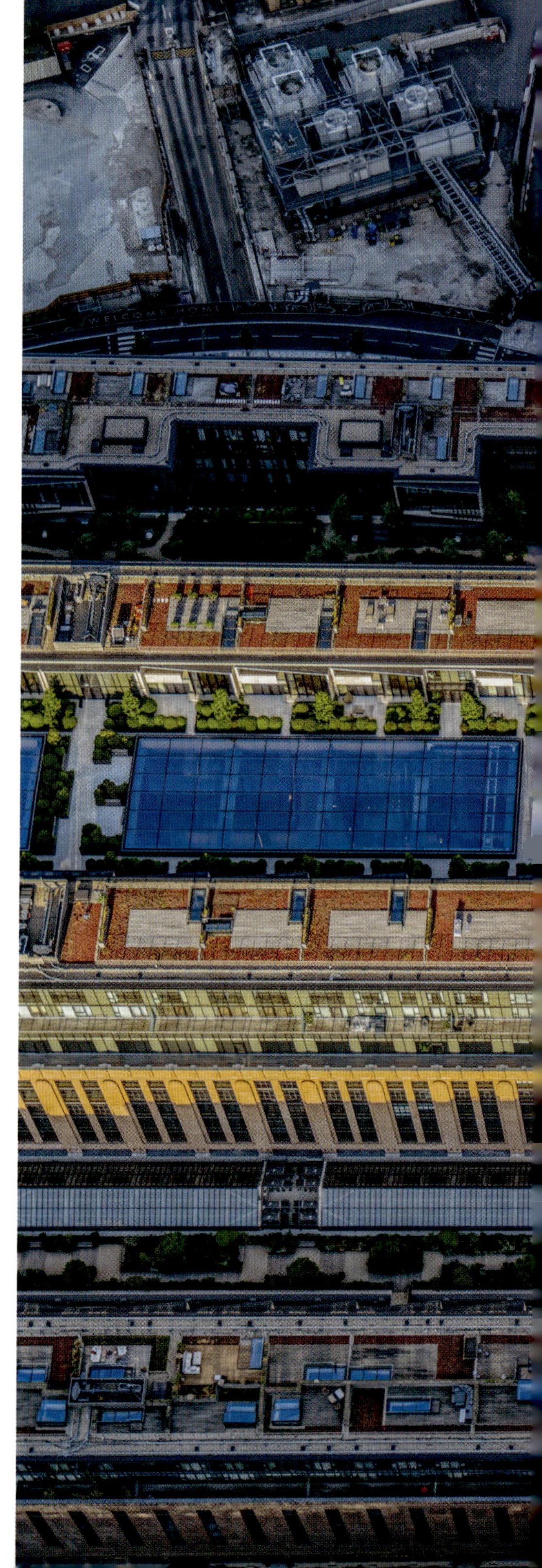

Battersea Power Station and the Foster + Partners–designed apartment complex with roof gardens along Electric Boulevard

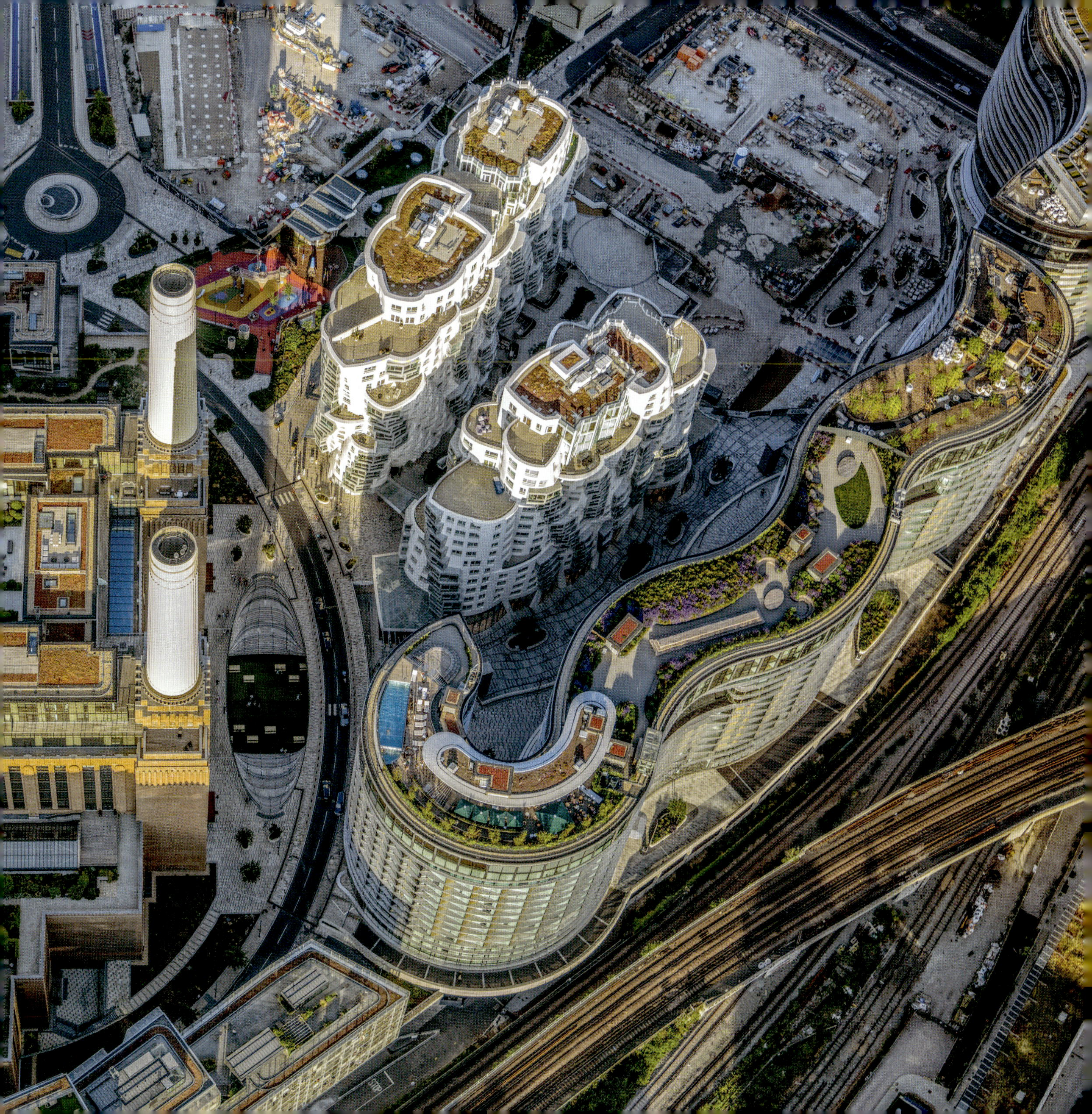

INTRODUCTION

Robert Morton

Defining London has never been easy despite its 2,000-year history, though most writers in Britain's long and distinguished literary heritage have either been born there, lived within its precincts, or visited for substantial periods of time. Even speaking geographically, London contradicts itself because what has historically been known as the City of London, and is still so called, is only a little more than one square mile in extent, whereas the modern city, now known as Greater London, extends more than 600 square miles and reaches as far as 14 miles west to include Heathrow Airport.

The City of London, still partly contained within an existing Roman wall, attests to the long occupation of Britain by the Roman Empire. After Julius Caesar invaded the island in AD 55, subsequent Roman emperors landed large quantities of warriors and established a variety of cities, mining the land for tin, gold, silver, and other metals and exporting agricultural products and seafood. With its easy access to the North Sea along the River Thames and several hills offering defensive positions above the shoreline, the site known as Londinium became the principal city of Roman Britain and remained so until AD 410, when the Romans withdrew. They left a significant legacy, however, including roads, aqueducts, towns, and forts. They left behind the Latin language that contributed to the evolution of English, the Christian religion, and a system of government that formed a model for today.

In AD 1066, at Londinium, another foreign invader, William the Conqueror of Normandy, established a castle and a fort with a white tower inside the Roman wall, a place known today as the Tower of London. Around the Royal Bastion, which eventually included two defensive walls and a moat, grew a warren of lanes and streets and thoroughfares. Their configuration and names were dictated more by the nature of the soil (some of which was marshy), the proximity of churches (including St. Paul's Cathedral, built on the site of a church that goes back to AD 604), and the occupations of inhabitants (particularly inns and public houses) than by any urban planner. The buildings lining these passages were made mainly of wood and roofed with thatch so that periodic fires wreaked havoc throughout the city from the early days until 1666, when the Great Fire gutted the area. Rebuilding occurred on much the same plan as before rather than being struck through with broad avenues that might have served firefighting better, so Central London's urban scheme, like most old cities, retains its original character.

There's no better way of seeing that character than from above, and Jeffrey Milstein has an unparalleled eye for such viewing. He was a passionate pilot from his teenage years in Los Angeles onward, and his later qualification as an architect and his professional work as a photographer combined to provide him with tools and a vision to explore urban design shared by no one else. In thousands of photographs, selections of which have been published in previous books, Milstein has made the unique contribution of the straight-down view, a precise 90-degree angle that graphically defines the pattern of streets, avenues, boulevards, monumental spaces, plazas, parks, and gardens of each city he flies over. With superior photographic equipment and his masterly eye, he creates images that no drone or casual aerial photographer can match.

And what does that show the viewer about London? First, despite dense development over many centuries, London remains the greenest of all the major cities in the world. It offers residents and visitors some 3,000 parks, gardens, squares, and crescents totaling about

18 percent of its entire living space. By contrast, Paris has fewer than 450 parks and gardens, with the largest—the Champ-de-Mars, across from the Eiffel Tower—covering only about 63 acres. In London, Regent's Park alone boasts 410 acres.

Most of London's parks and large garden squares were created by monarchs and aristocrats but made available to the people from the early days. Hyde Park, for example, was created in 1536 as a hunting preserve for Henry VIII, who took the land from the monks at Westminster Abbey. It was later linked to the east with the parkland of St. James's Palace and to the west under Queen Anne, who created Kensington Gardens, where William III and Mary II subsequently established Kensington Palace. Together with Green Park nearby and the gardens of Buckingham Palace, which are, of course, only occasionally open to the public, London's royal green heritage covers some 700 acres.

Among the major grassy squares, the two largest, Russell and Grosvenor (about six acres each), are owned by the dukes of Westminster and Bedford, who developed the bordering land for housing in

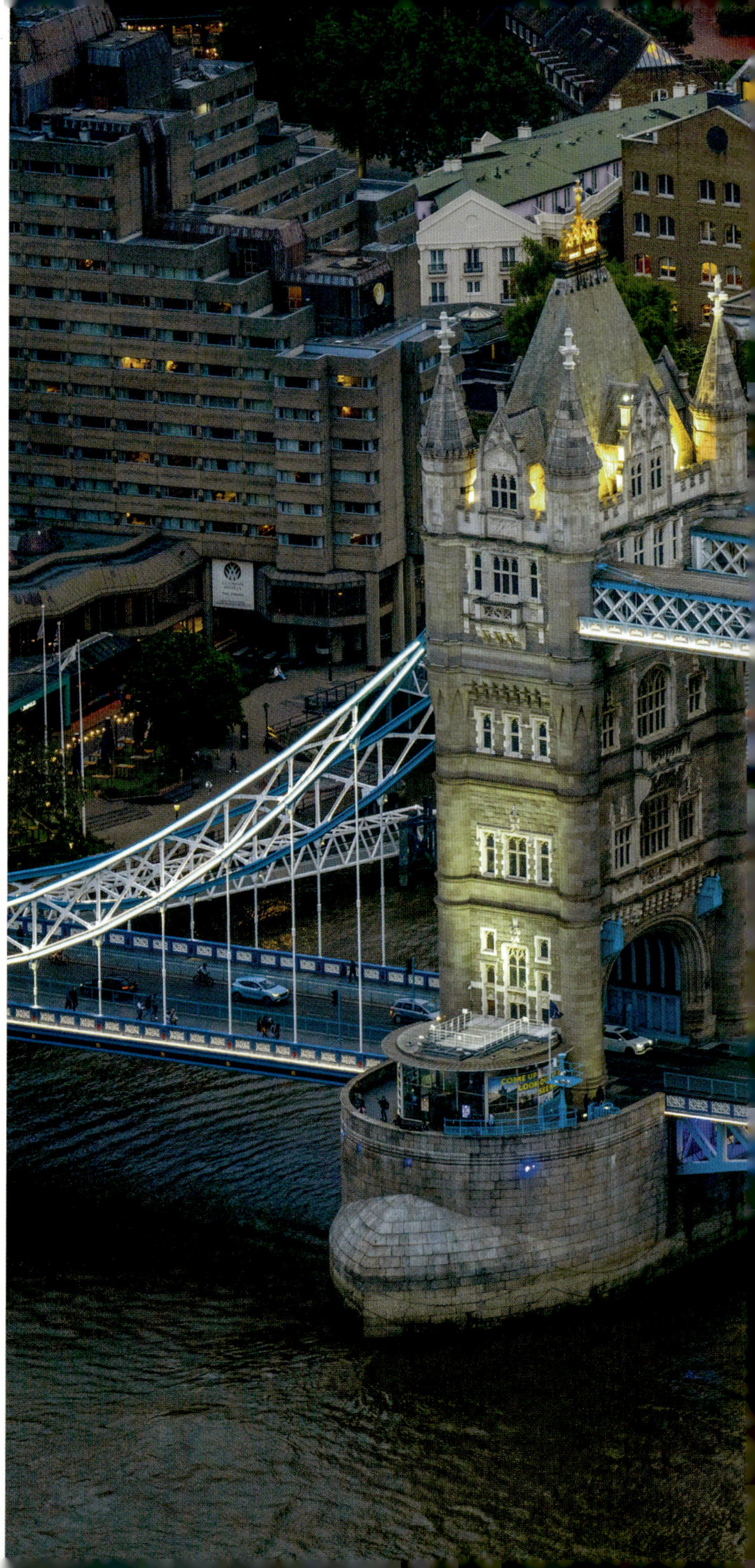

Tower Bridge

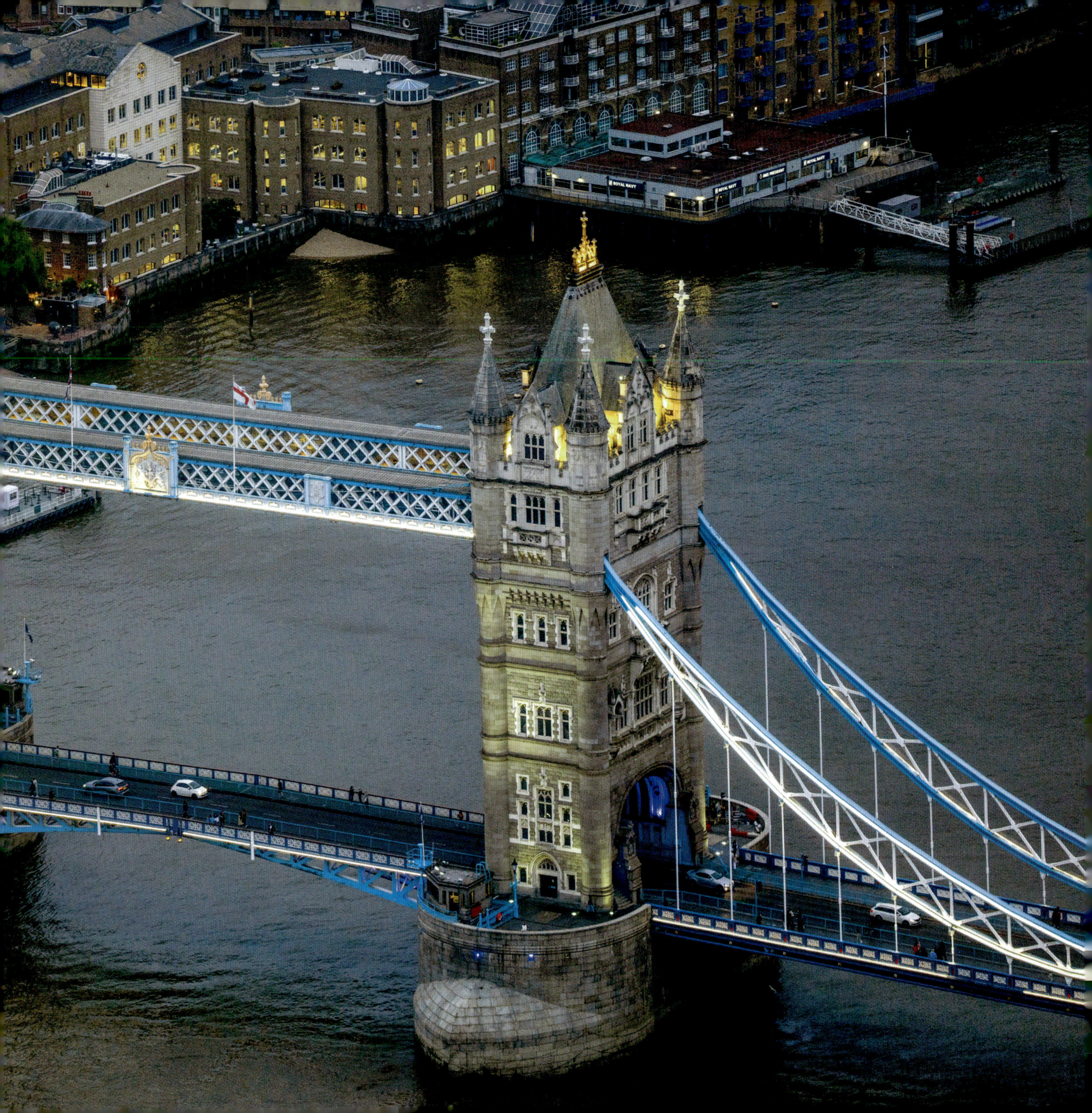

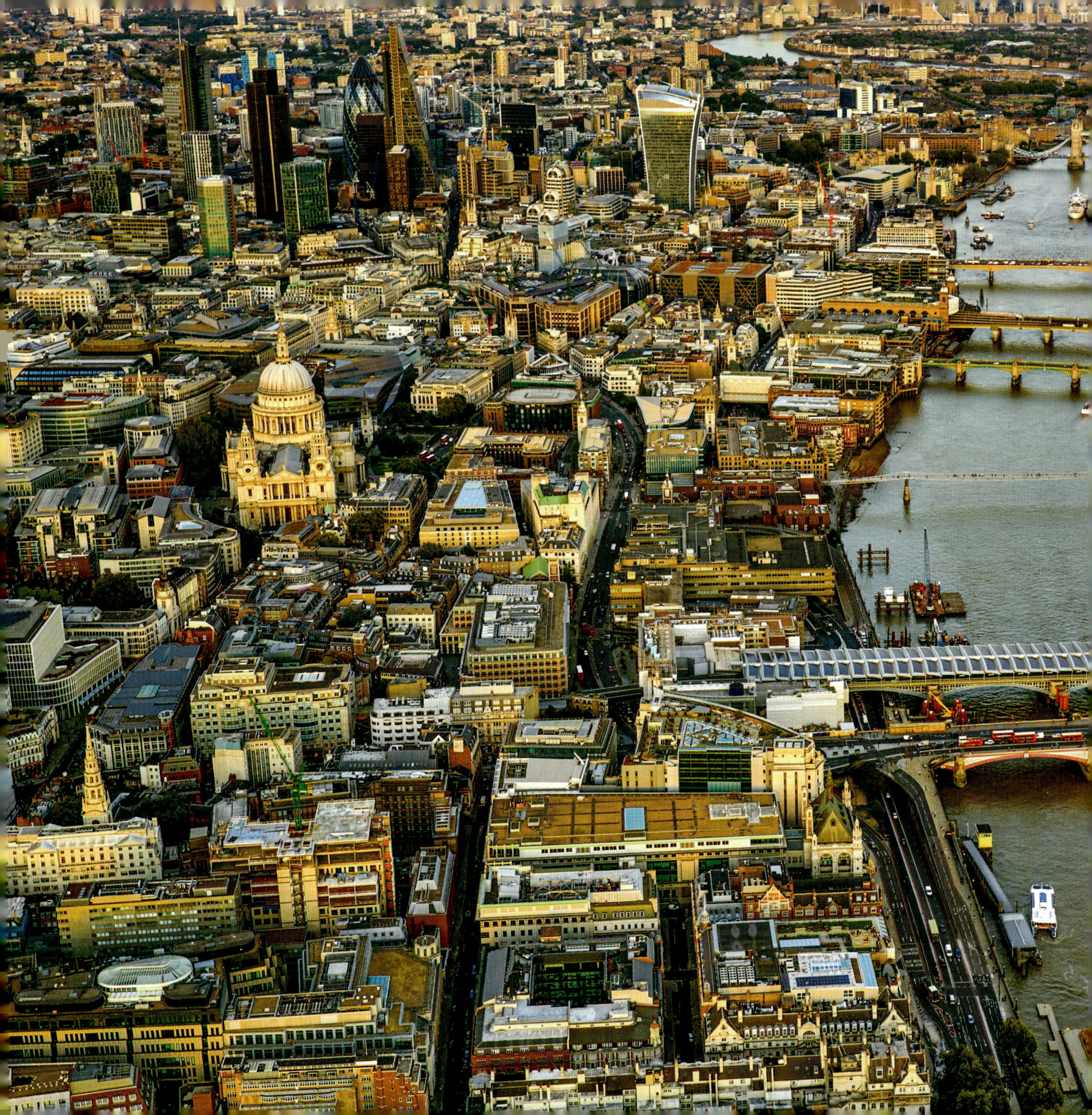

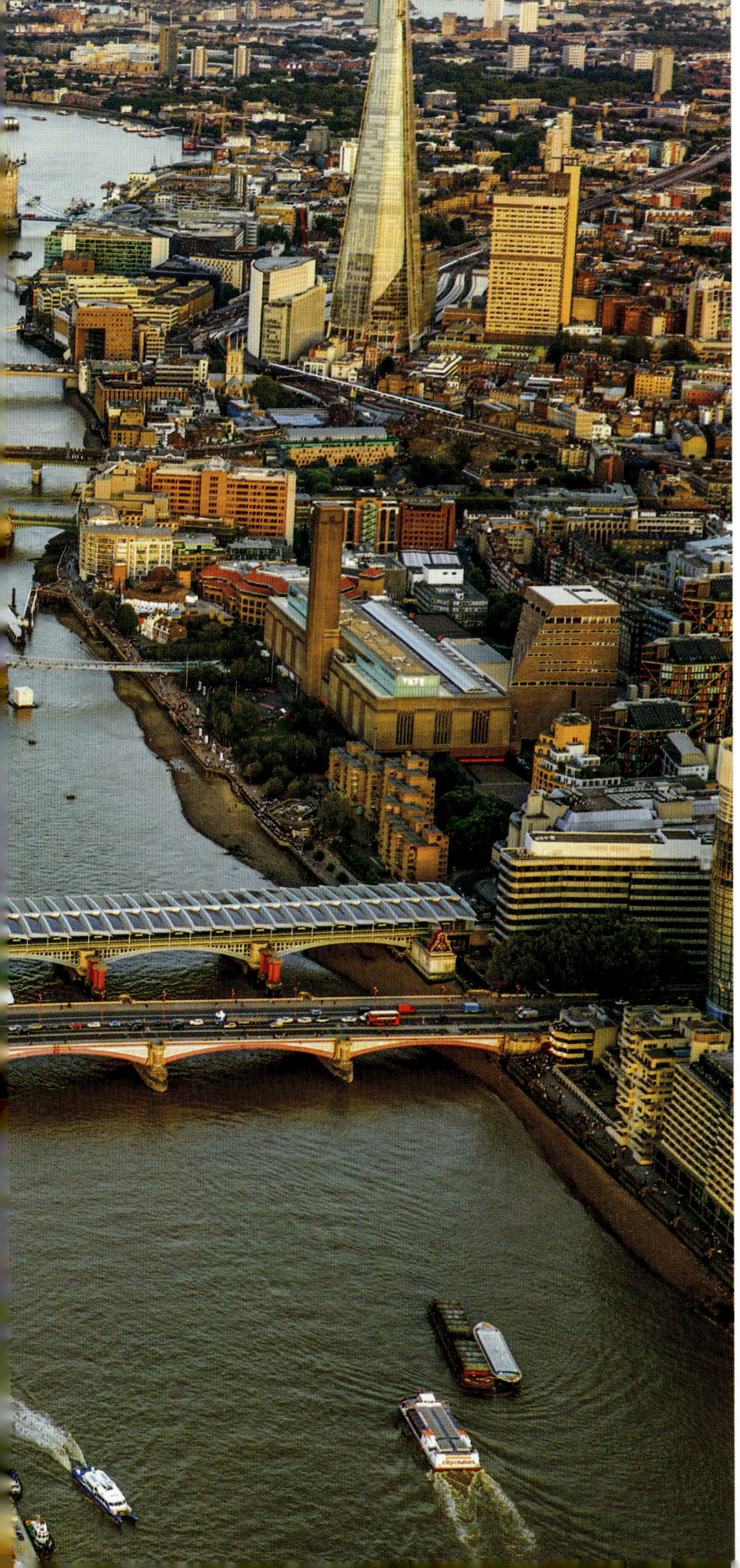

the 18th century but left the gardens as public spaces. (The Bedford Estate controls seven other squares in the Bloomsbury area alone.) Berkeley Square, about two-and-a-half acres in extent and owned by the Devonshire dukes since 1696, has been famous in song and story for many years and was a childhood home of Winston Churchill.

Equally impressive from above or at ground level are London's seats of government—the Houses of Parliament—with their impressive towers, giant clock, and enormous bell; the nearby abbey and churches; and the attendant office buildings and commonwealth departments. Along with London's huge array of museums, art galleries, specialist collections, and historic homes, which preserve and display unparalleled examples of the world's finest achievements, these are the things that define the city. It is a city that once caused Samuel Johnson to say in defense of his adopted home, "Sir, when a man is tired of London, he is tired of life; for there is in London all that life can afford."

Looking east along the Thames, with St. Paul's Cathedral on the left across from Tate Modern on the South Bank

20

GREEN LONDON

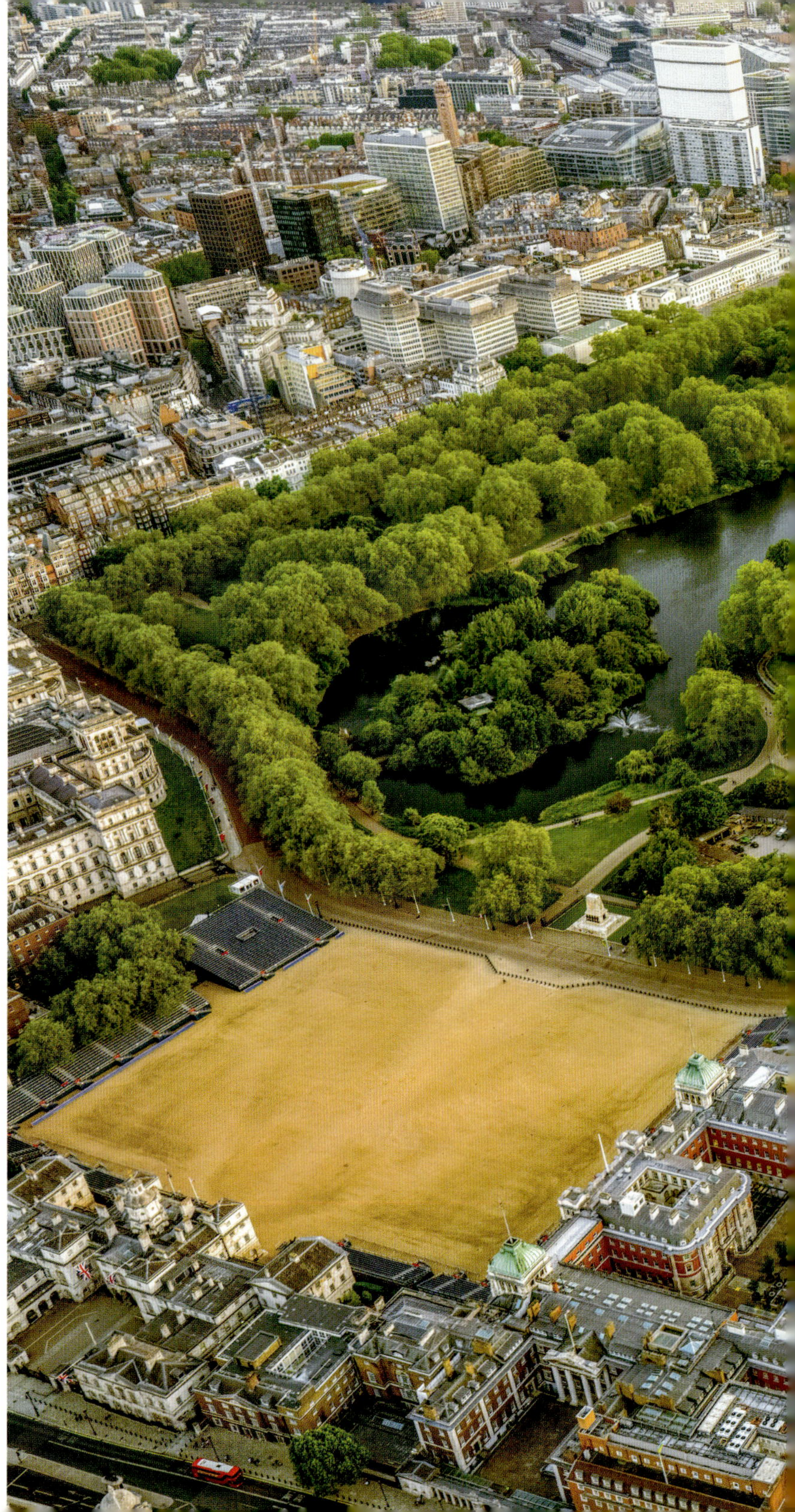

Looking along the Mall from Admiralty Arch to Buckingham Palace, with St. James's Park at left and Green Park at top

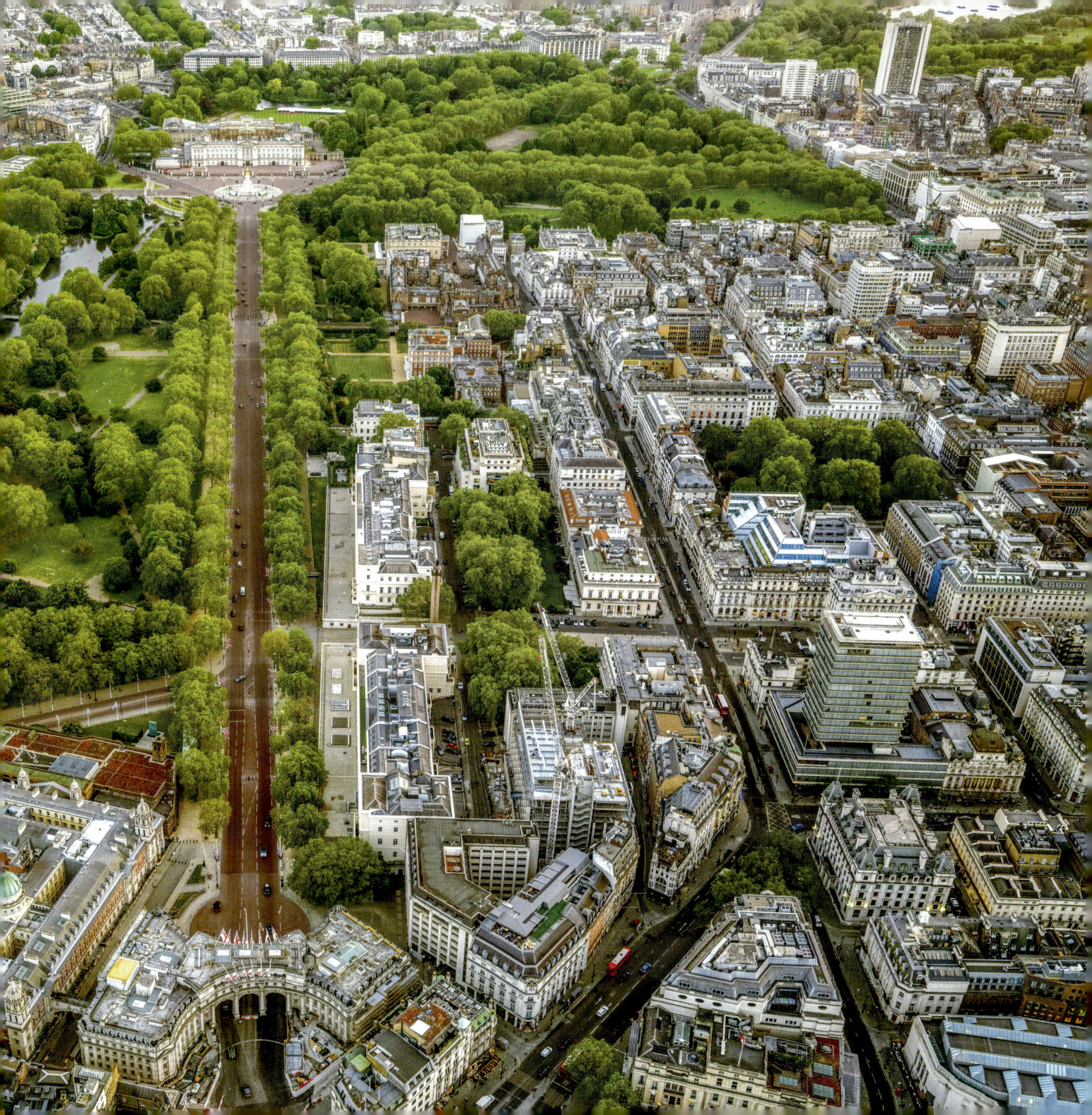

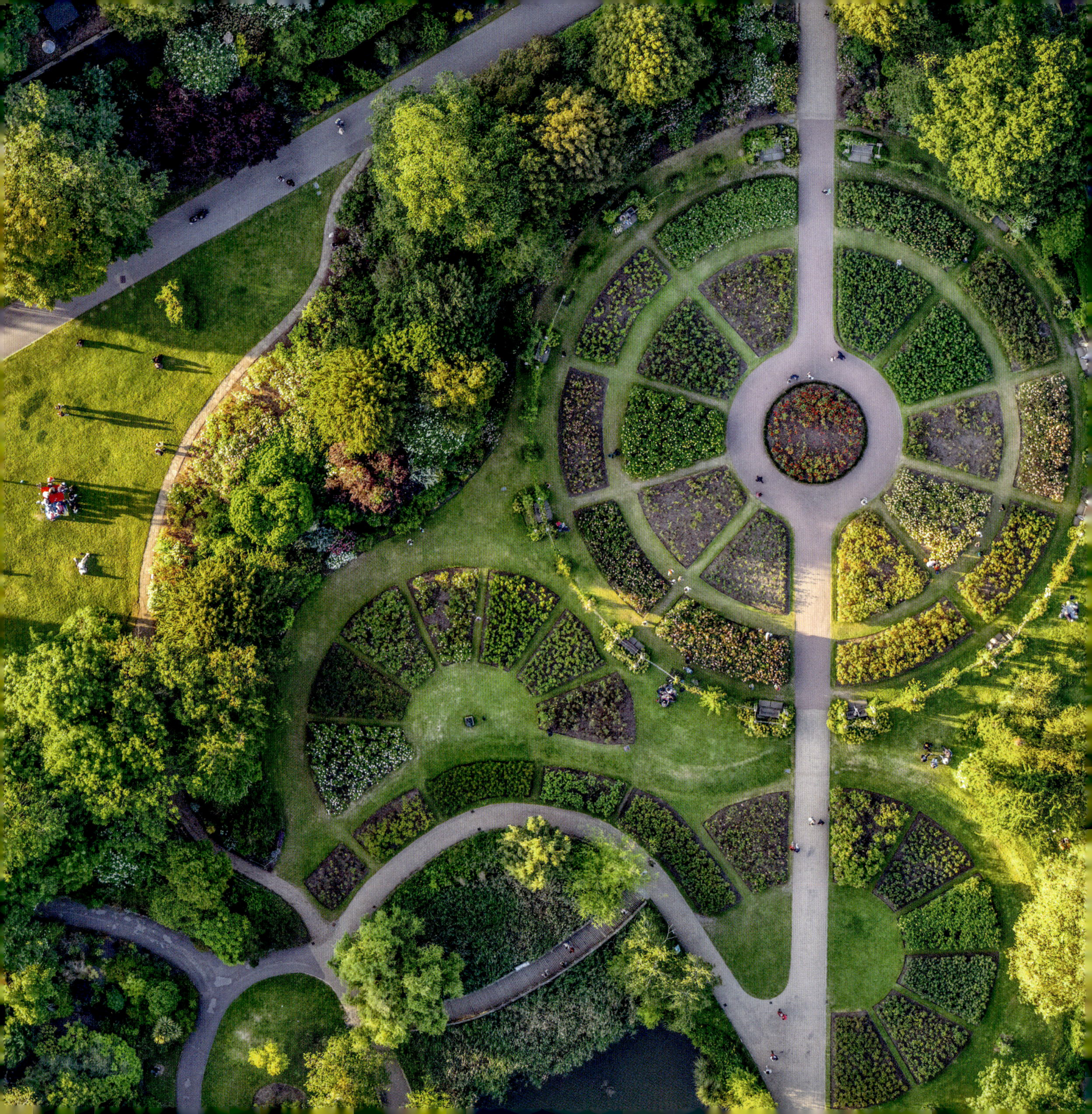

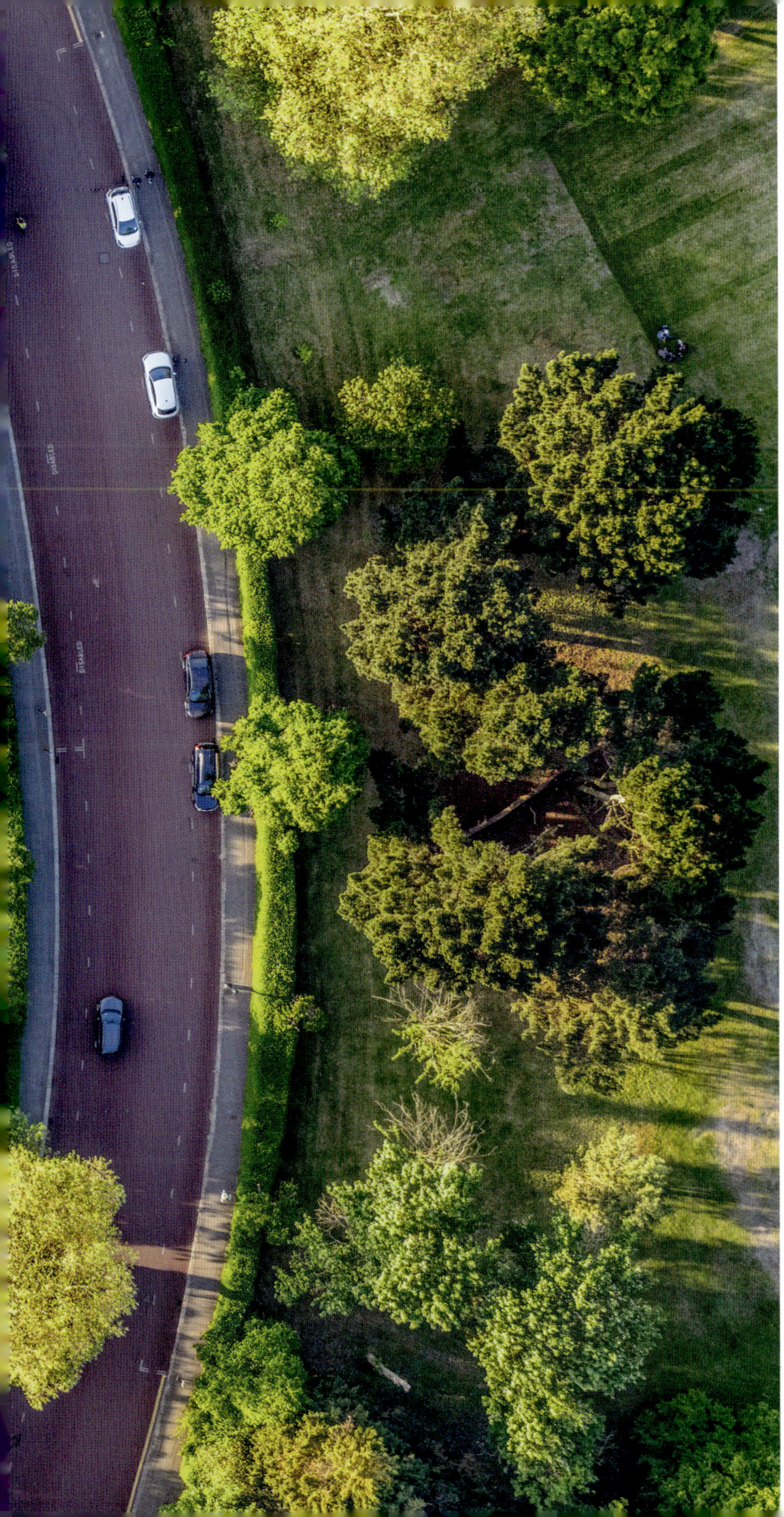

Opposite: Queen Mary's Gardens in Regent's Park

Page 24: Playing fields in Regent's Park

Page 25: Regent's Park, with Triton Fountain at top, the Open Air Theatre at upper left, and Queen Mary's Gardens at lower right

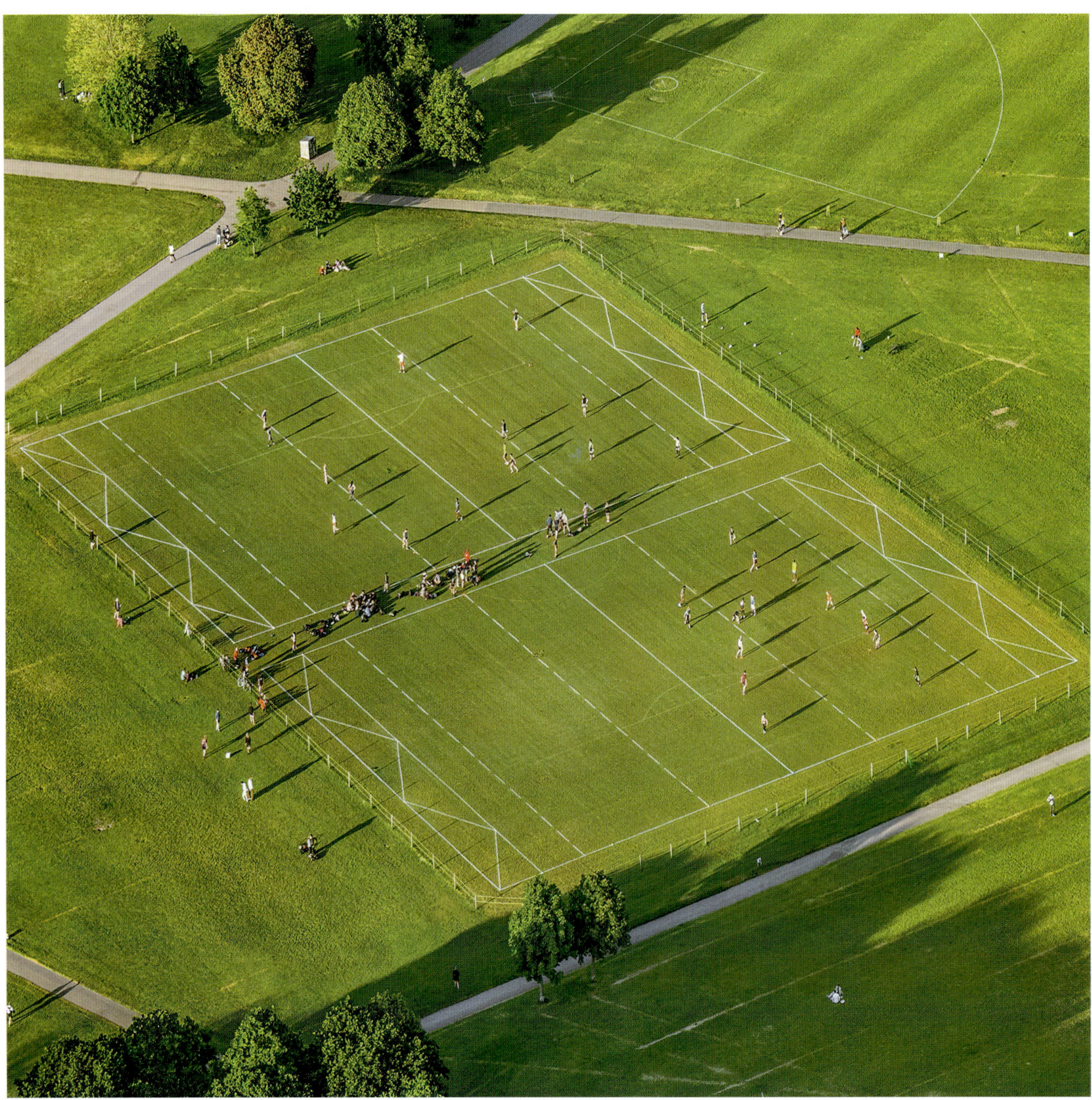

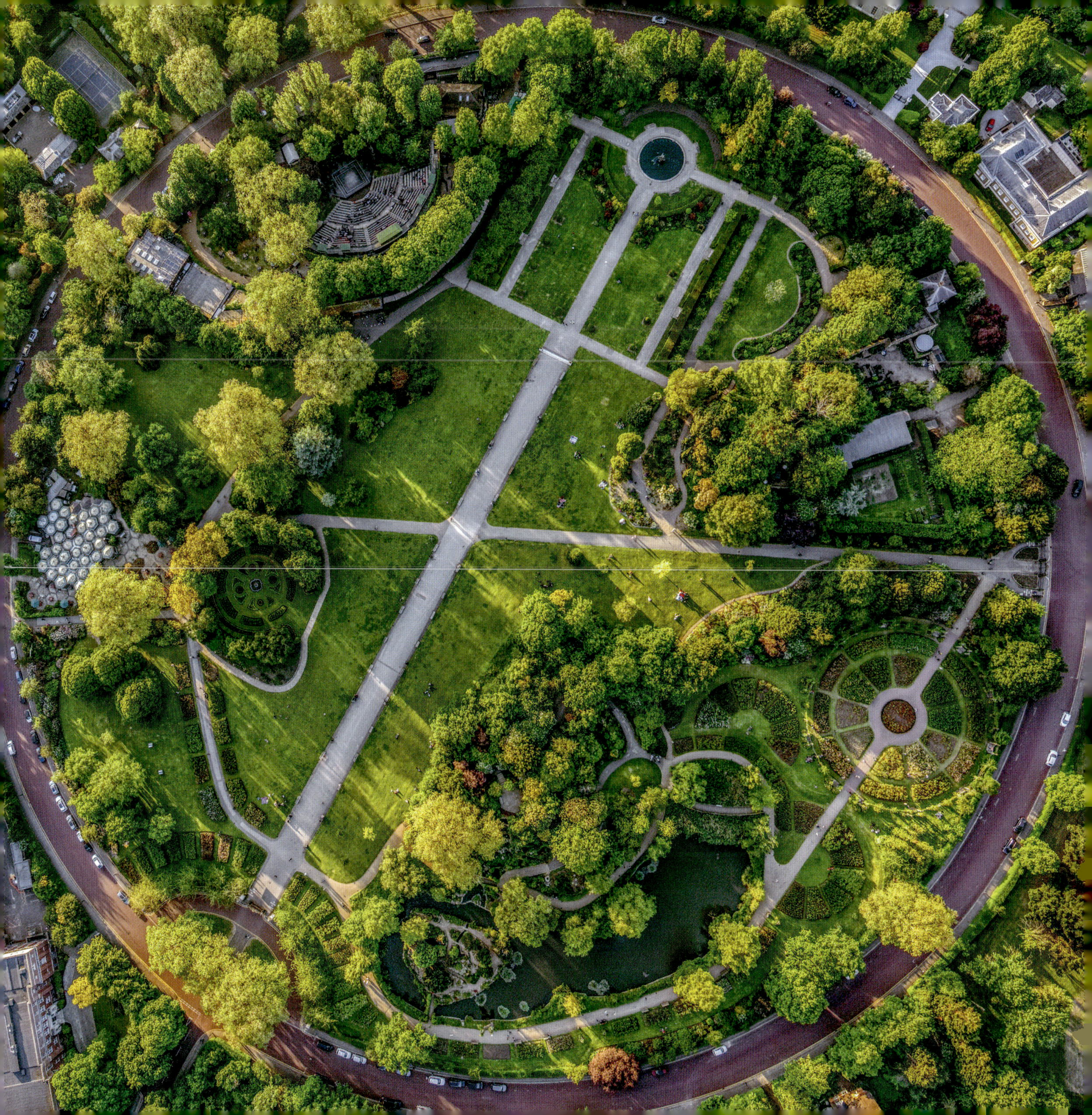

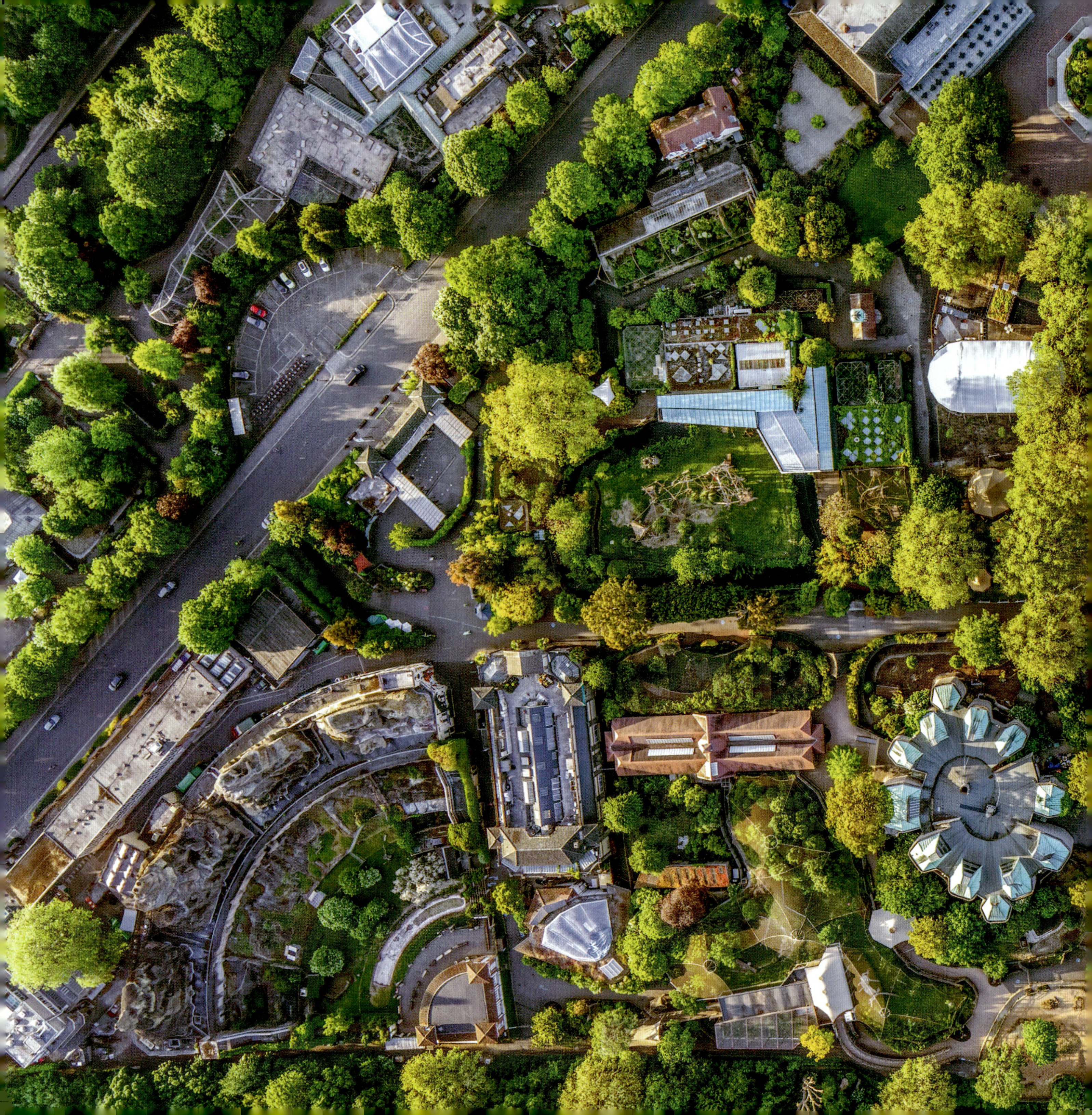

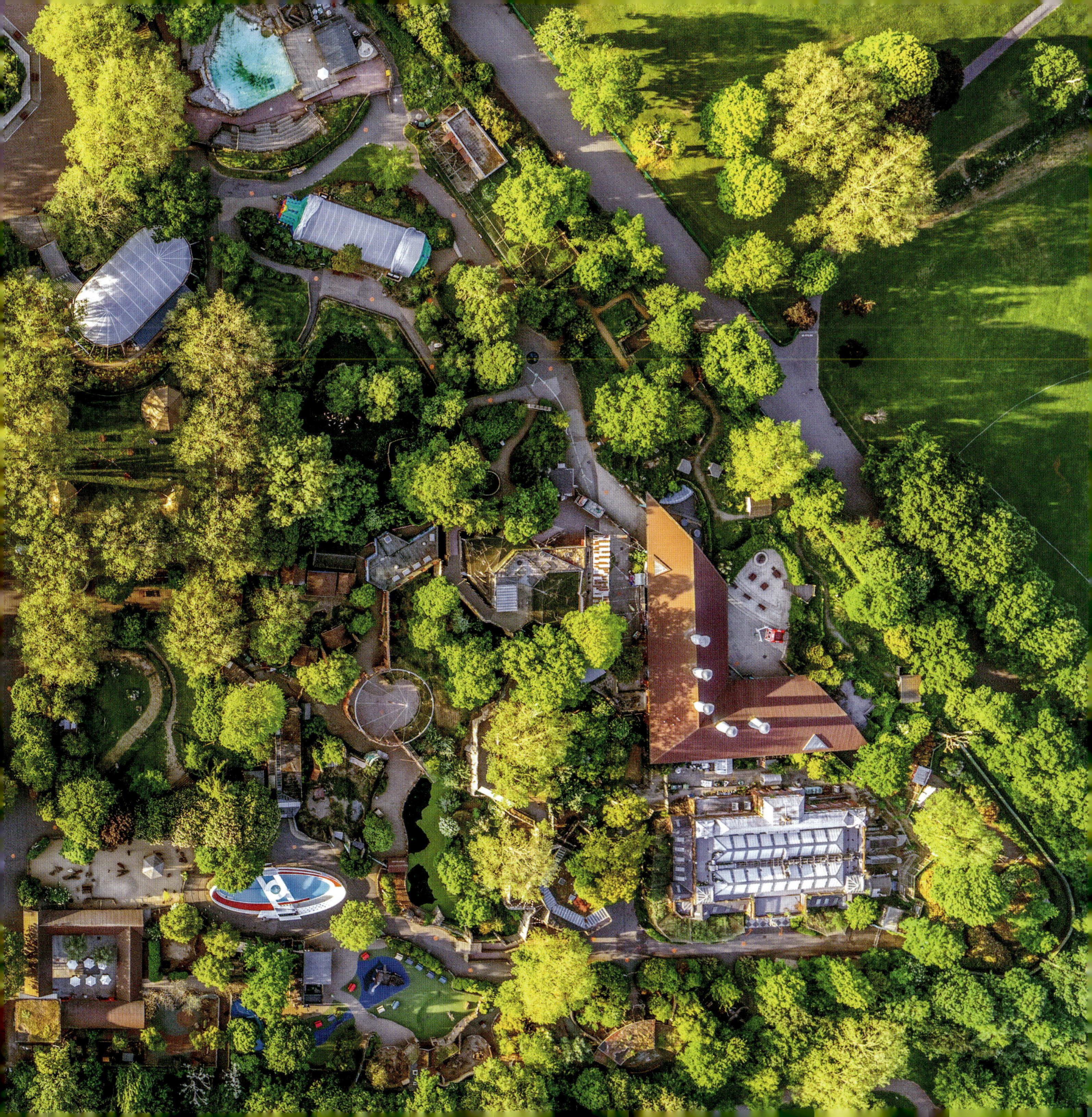

Pages 26–27: London Zoo in Regent's Park

Opposite: Kensington Palace Gardens and Round Pond

Pages 30 & 31: Two views of the Albert Memorial, with Royal Albert Hall across Kensington Road

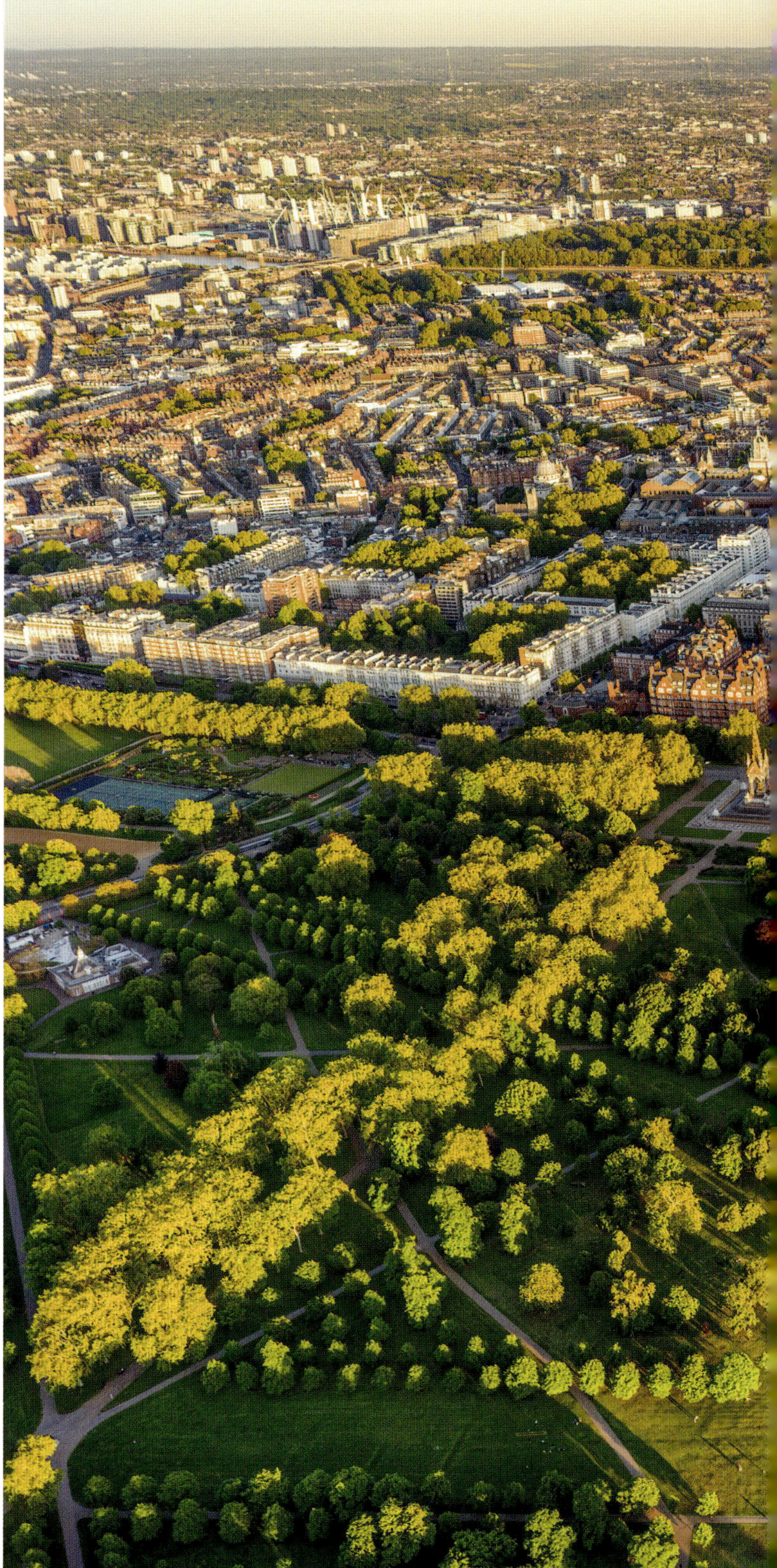

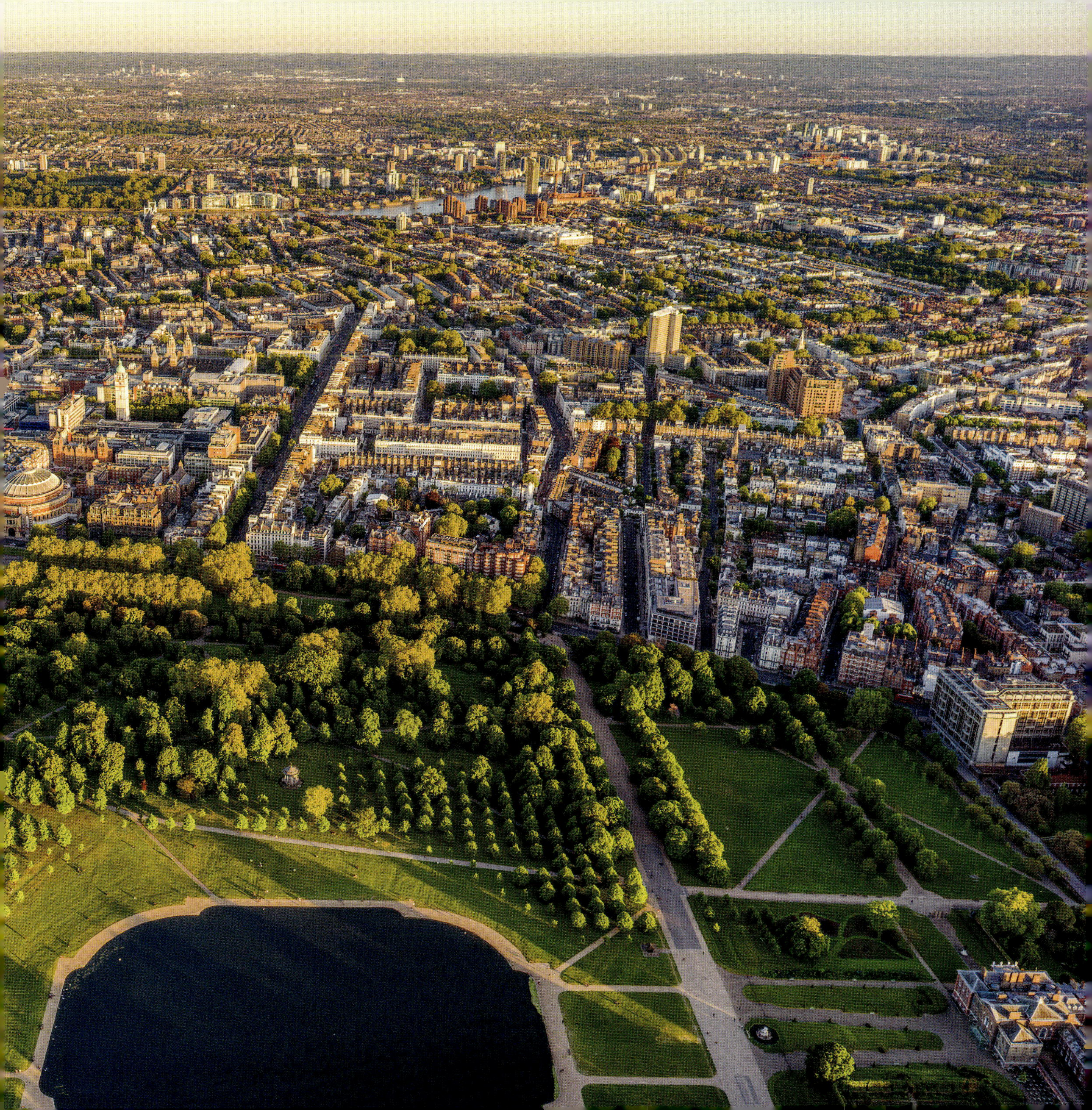

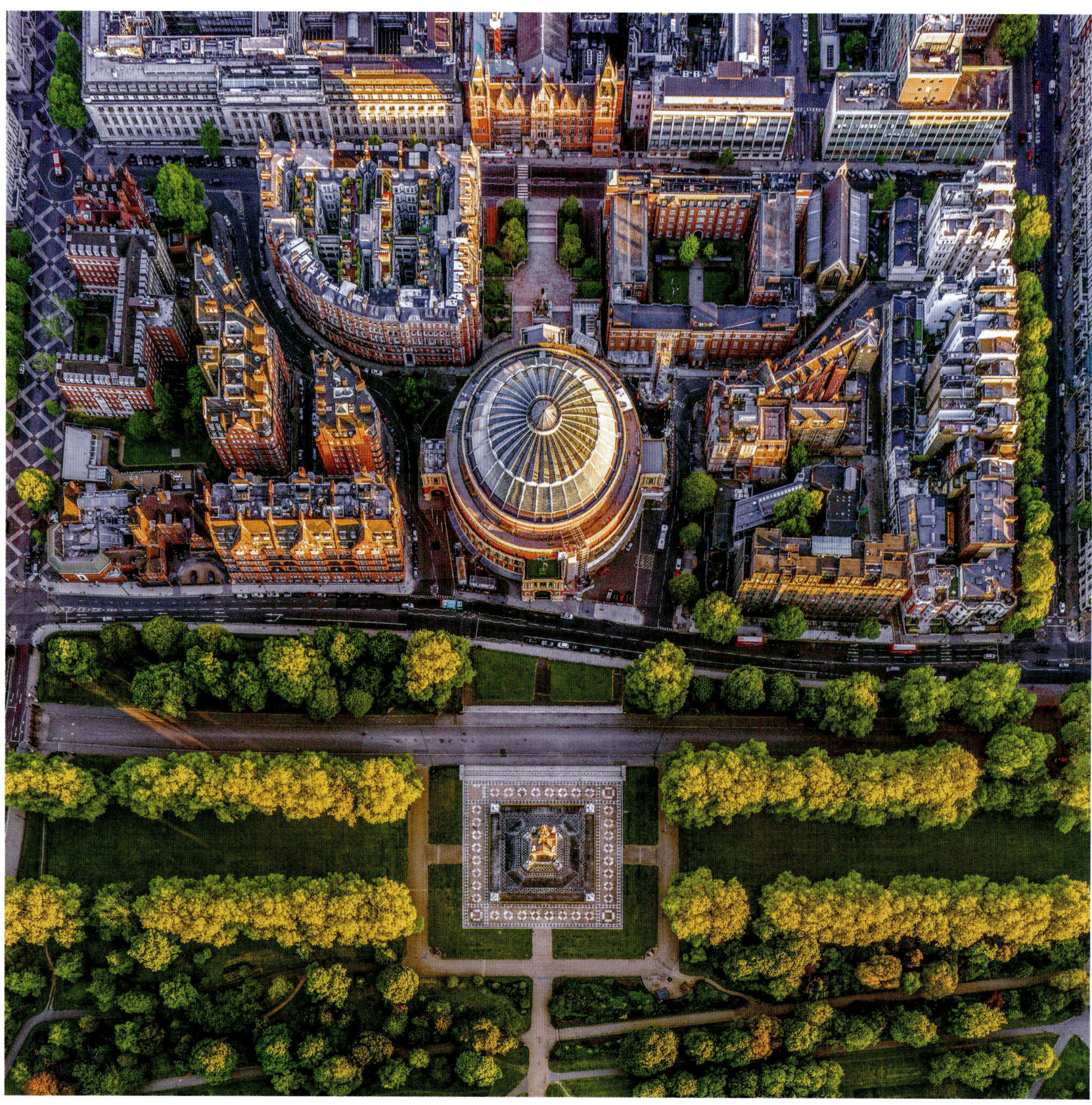

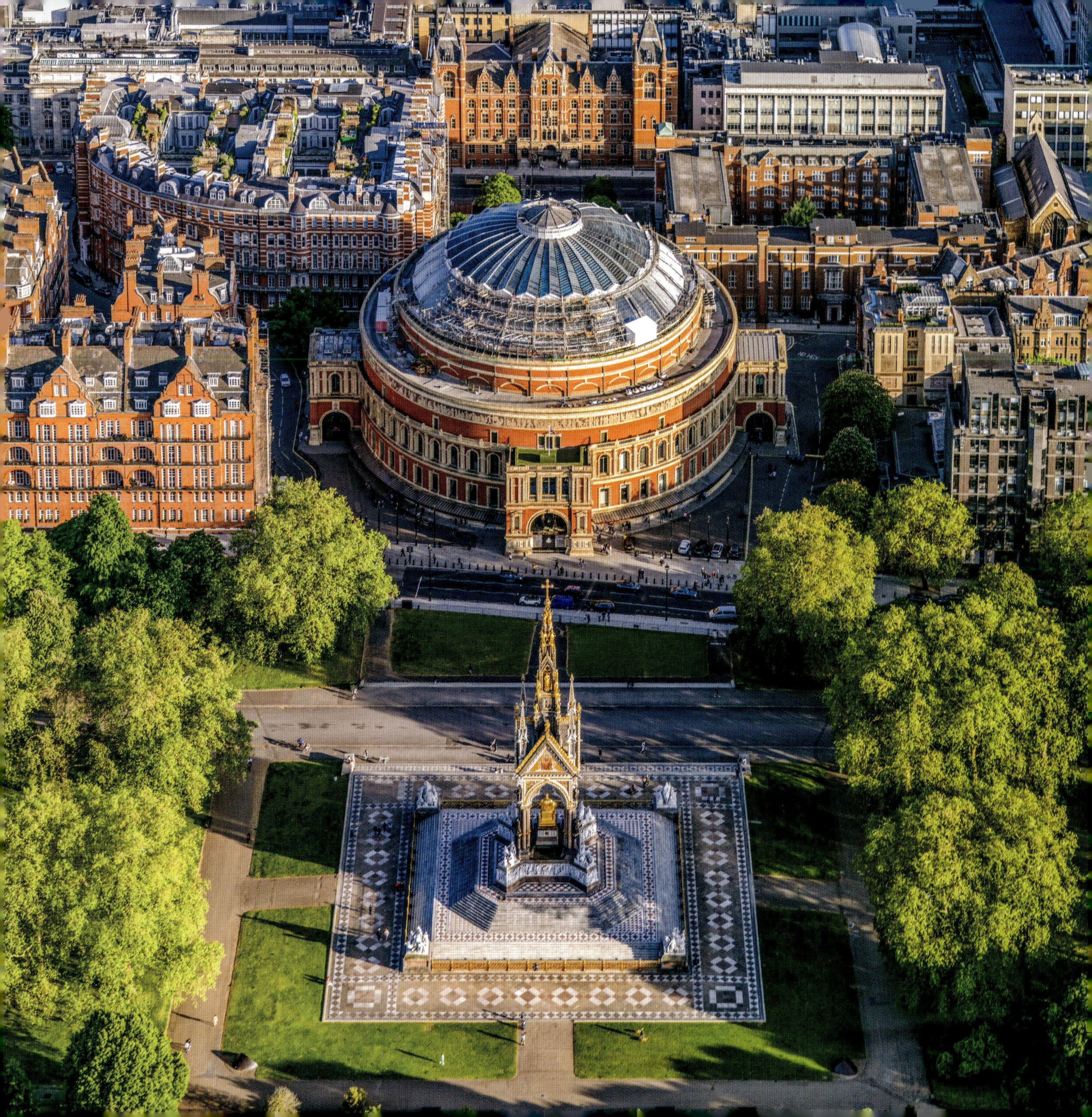

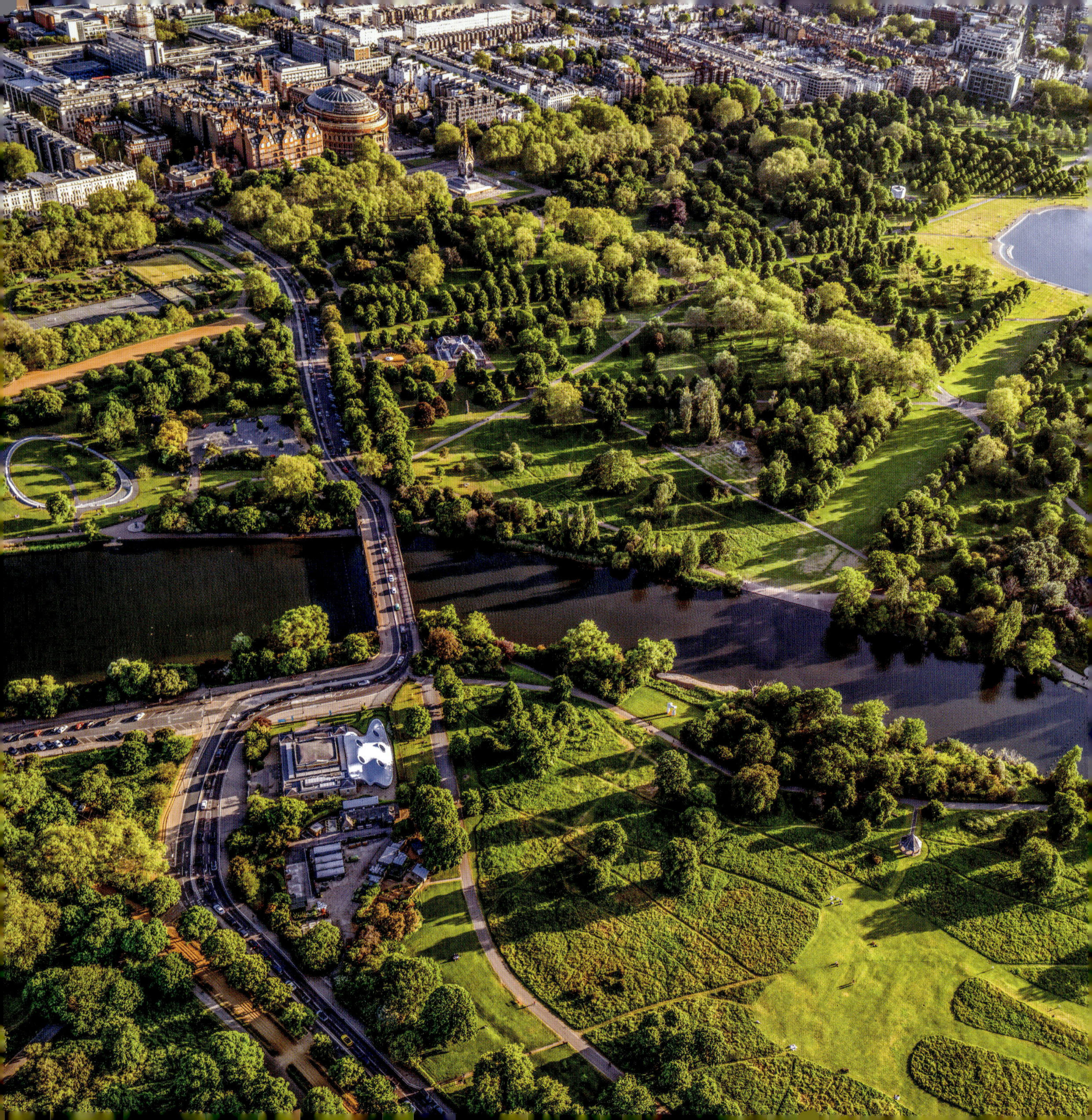

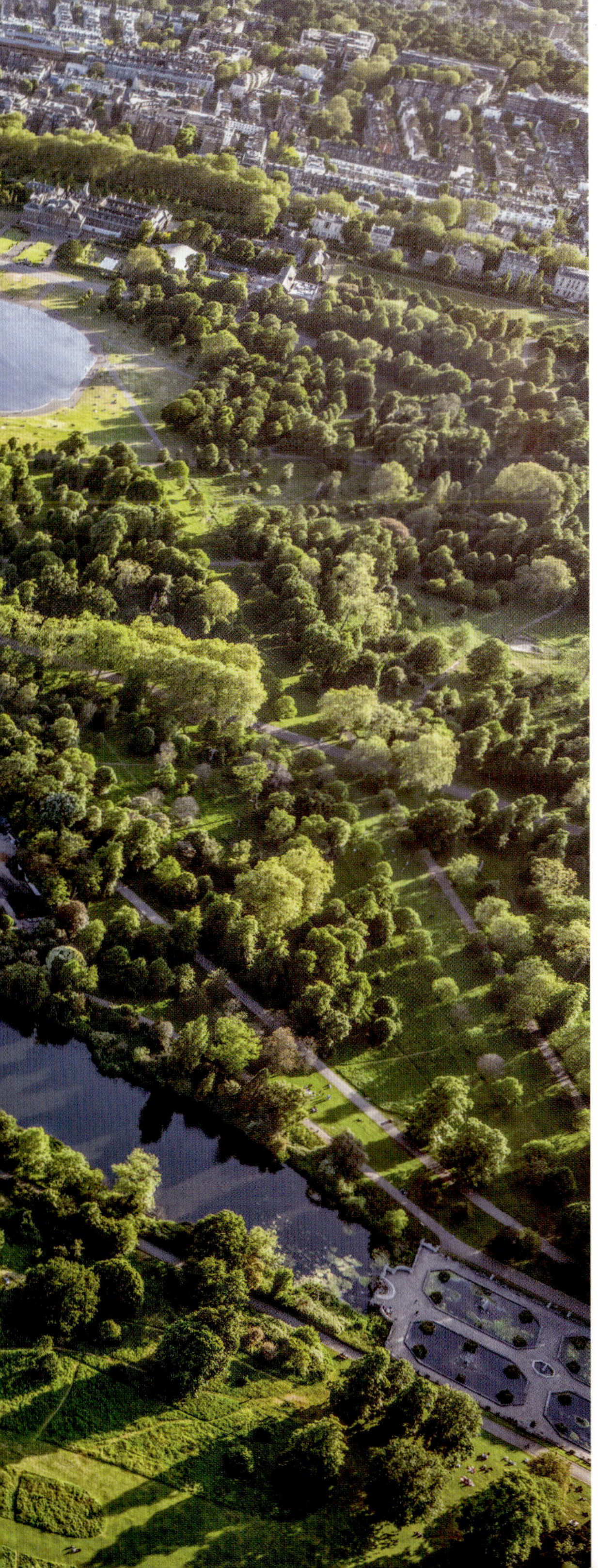

Looking over the Serpentine in Hyde Park toward
Round Pond in Kensington Gardens

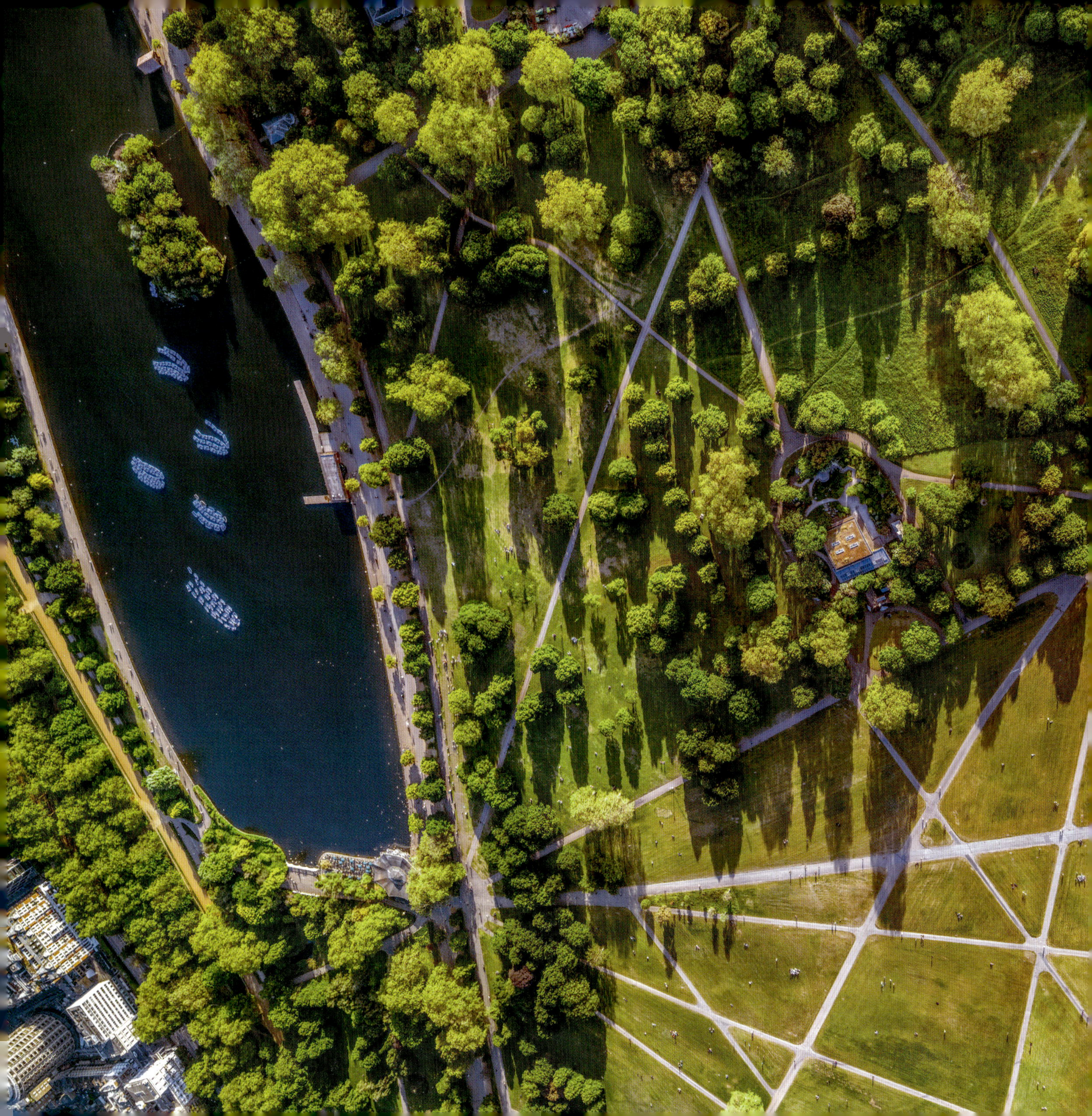

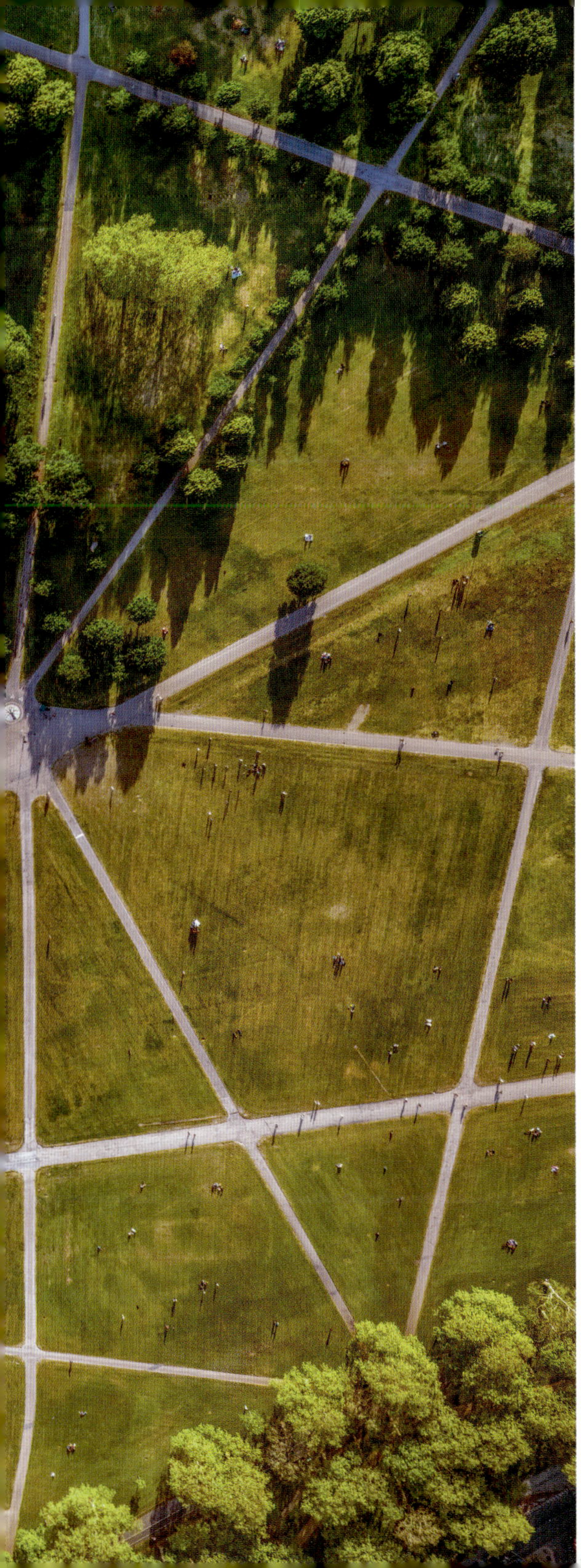

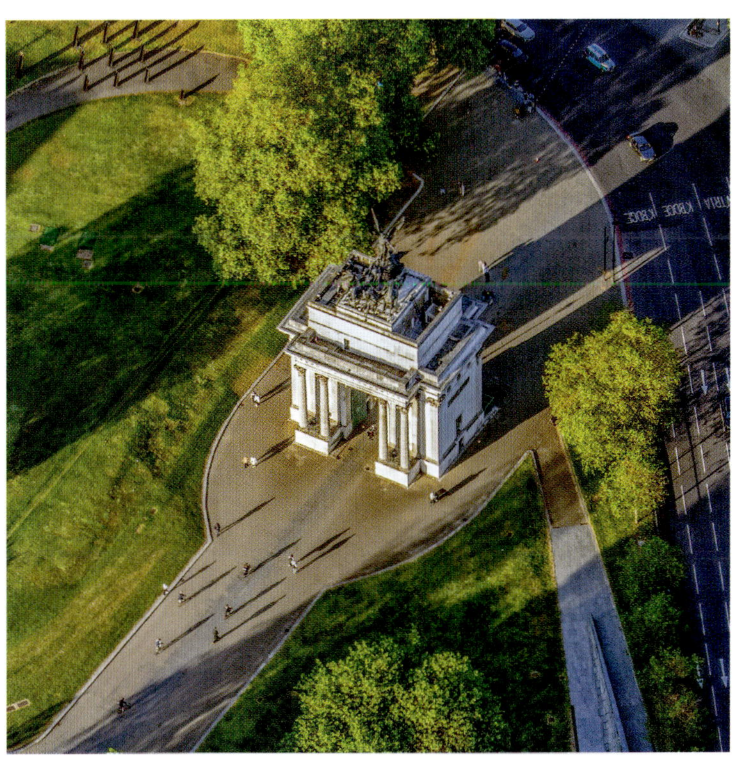

Opposite: A detail of fields in Hyde Park and the boating facility on the Serpentine

Above: Wellington Arch at the southeast corner of Hyde Park

Hyde Park corner, with Marble Arch at the junction of Oxford Street running east–west and Park Lane running south

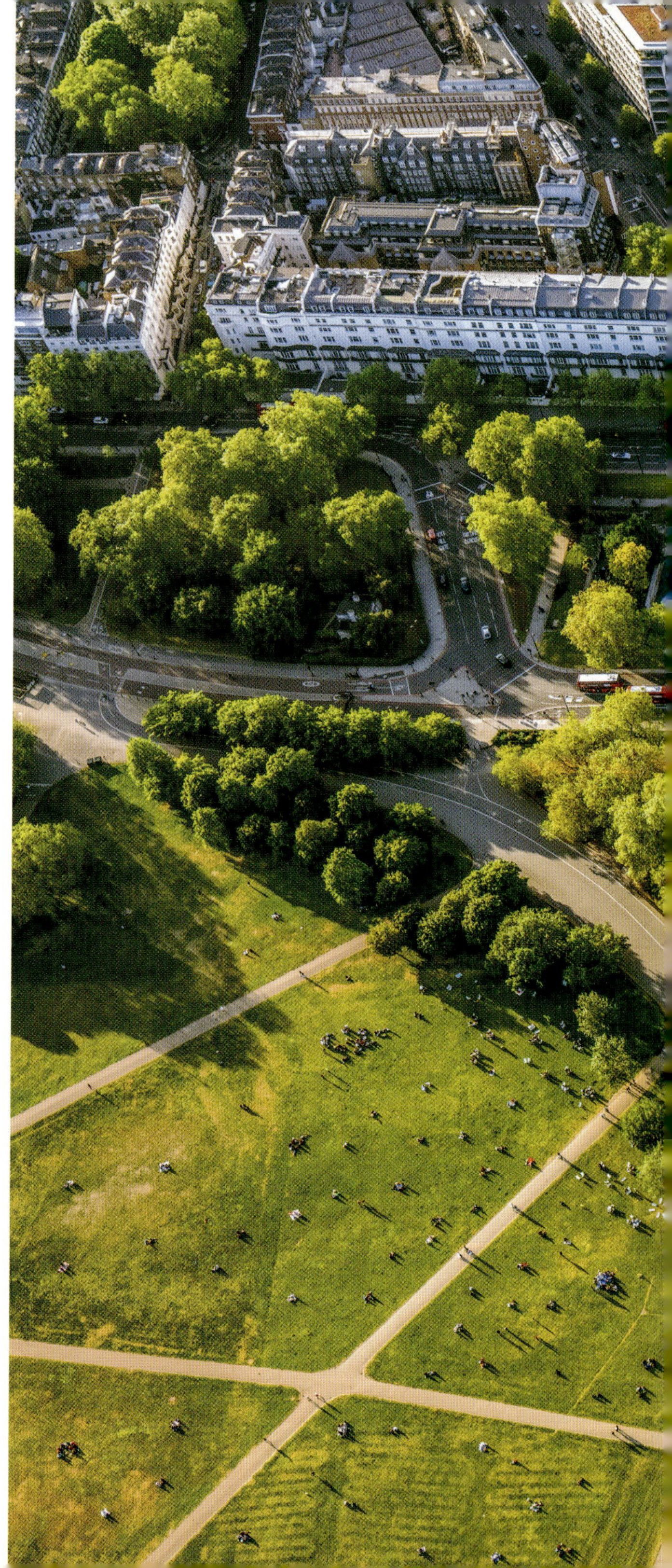

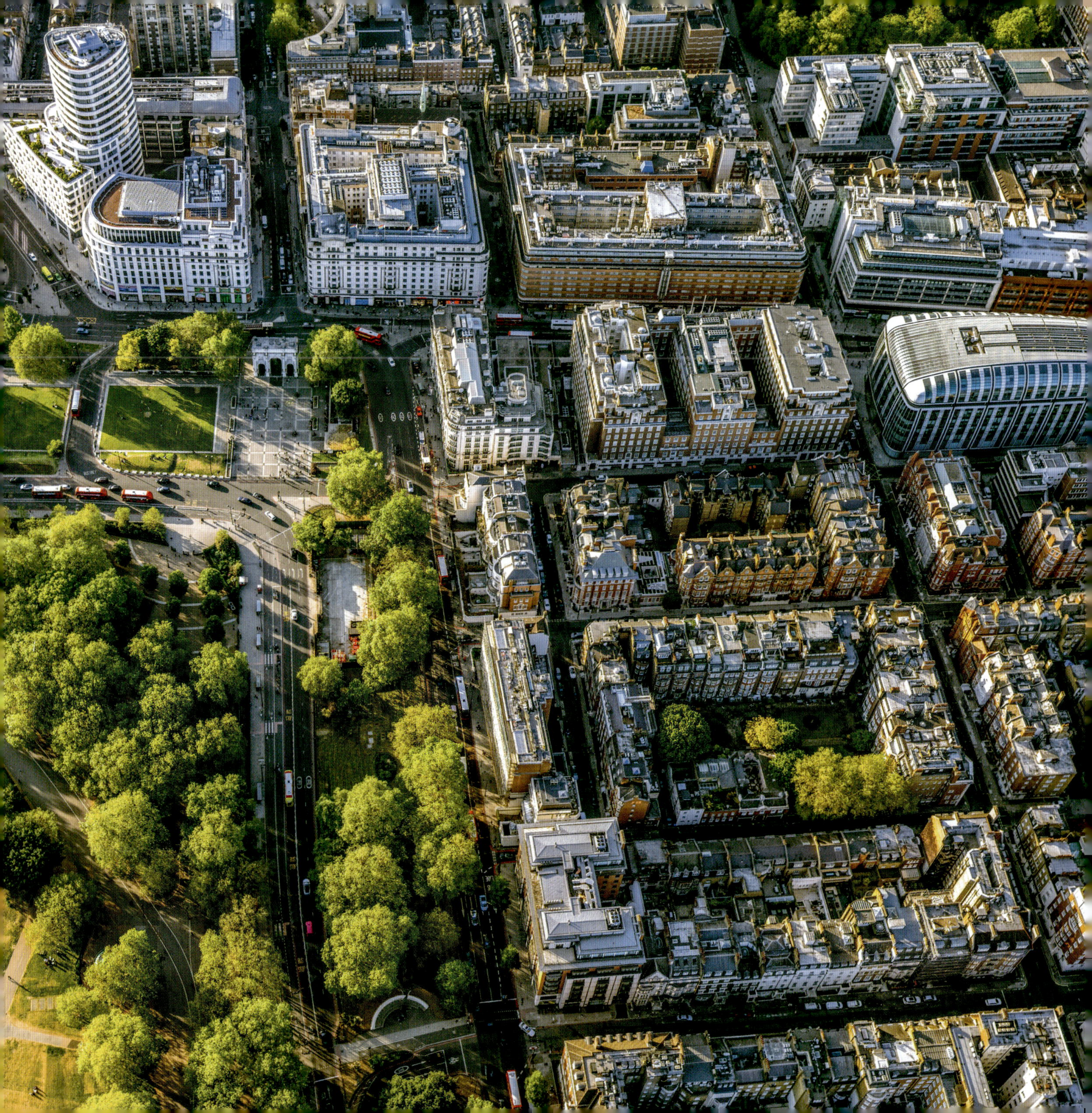

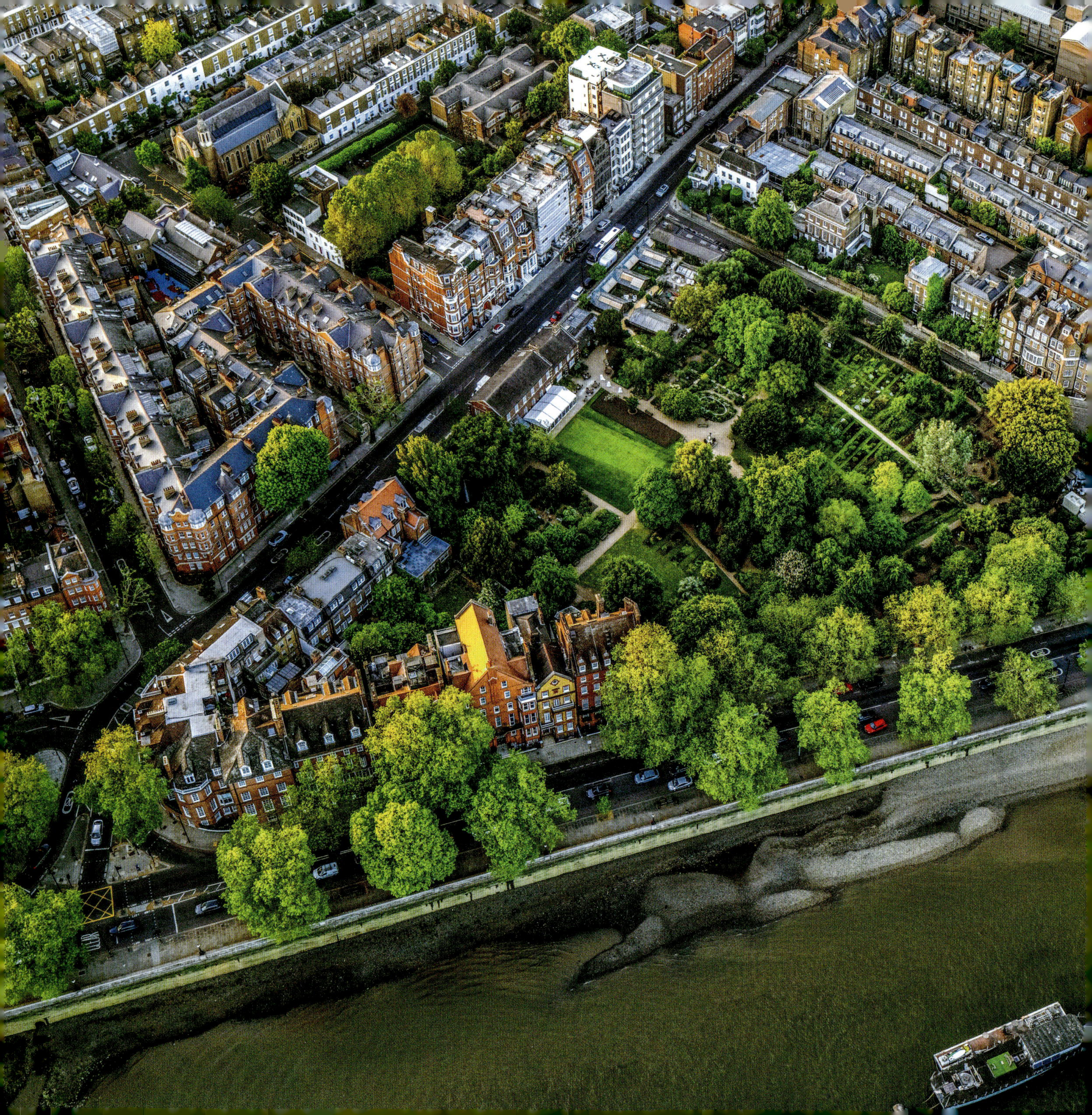

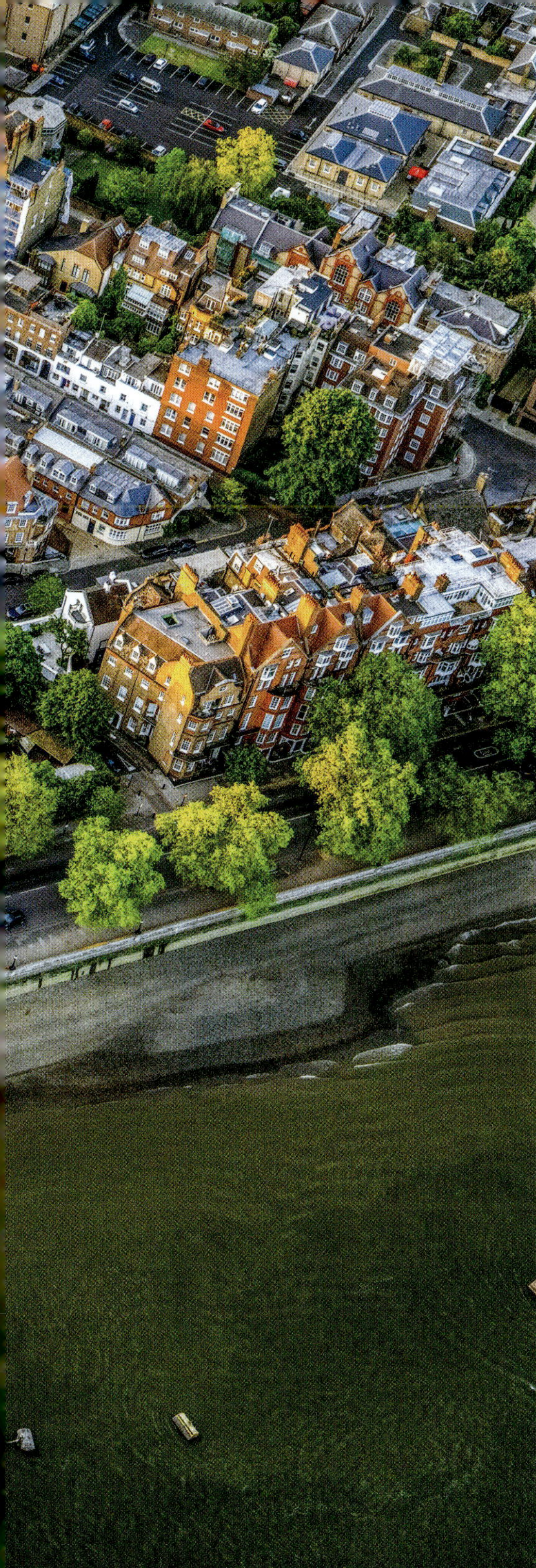

Opposite: Chelsea Physic Garden

Page 40: Royal Hospital Chelsea, with extensive gardens, site of the annual RHS Chelsea Flower Show

Page 41: Looking down on Royal Hospital Chelsea

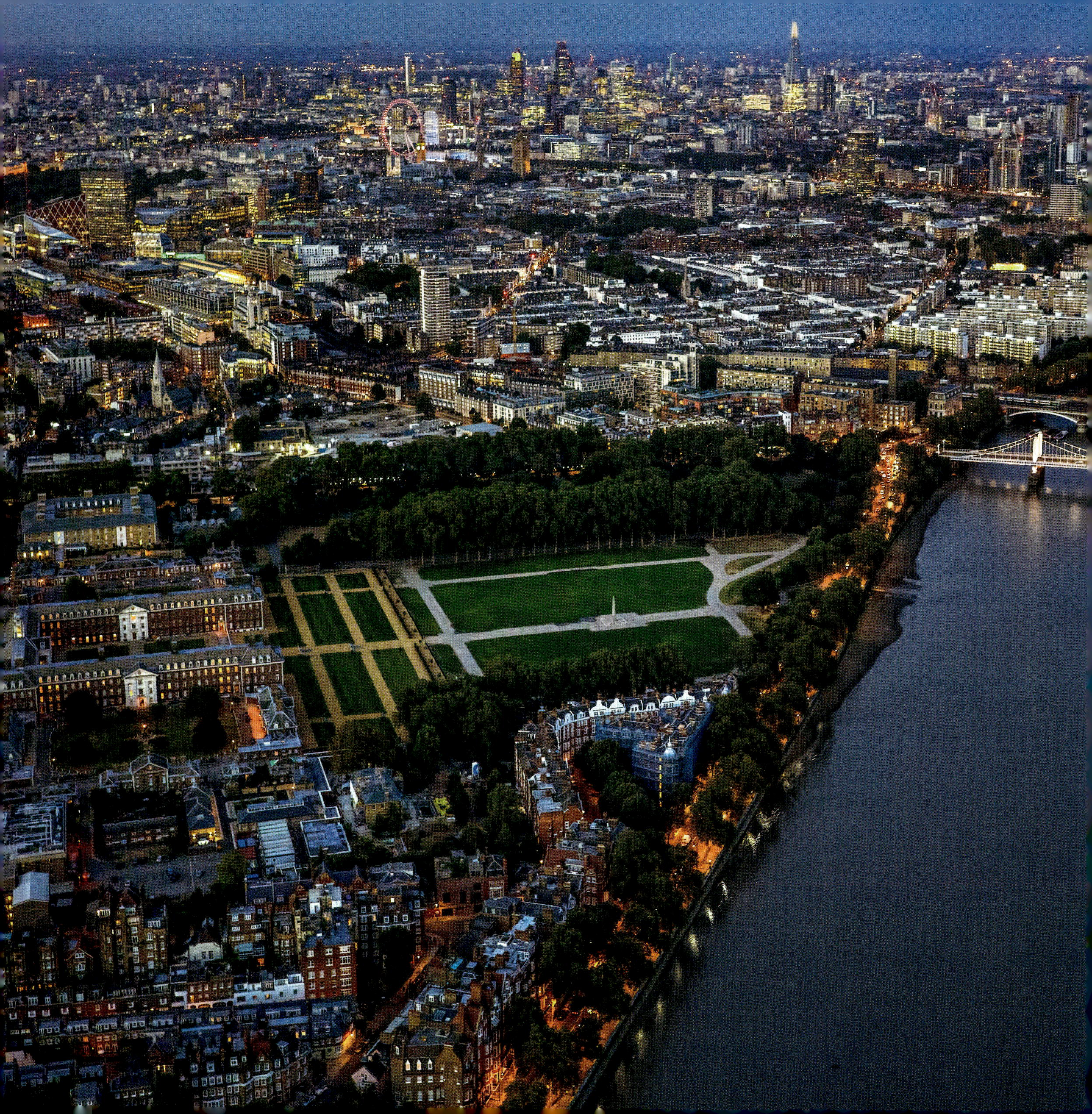

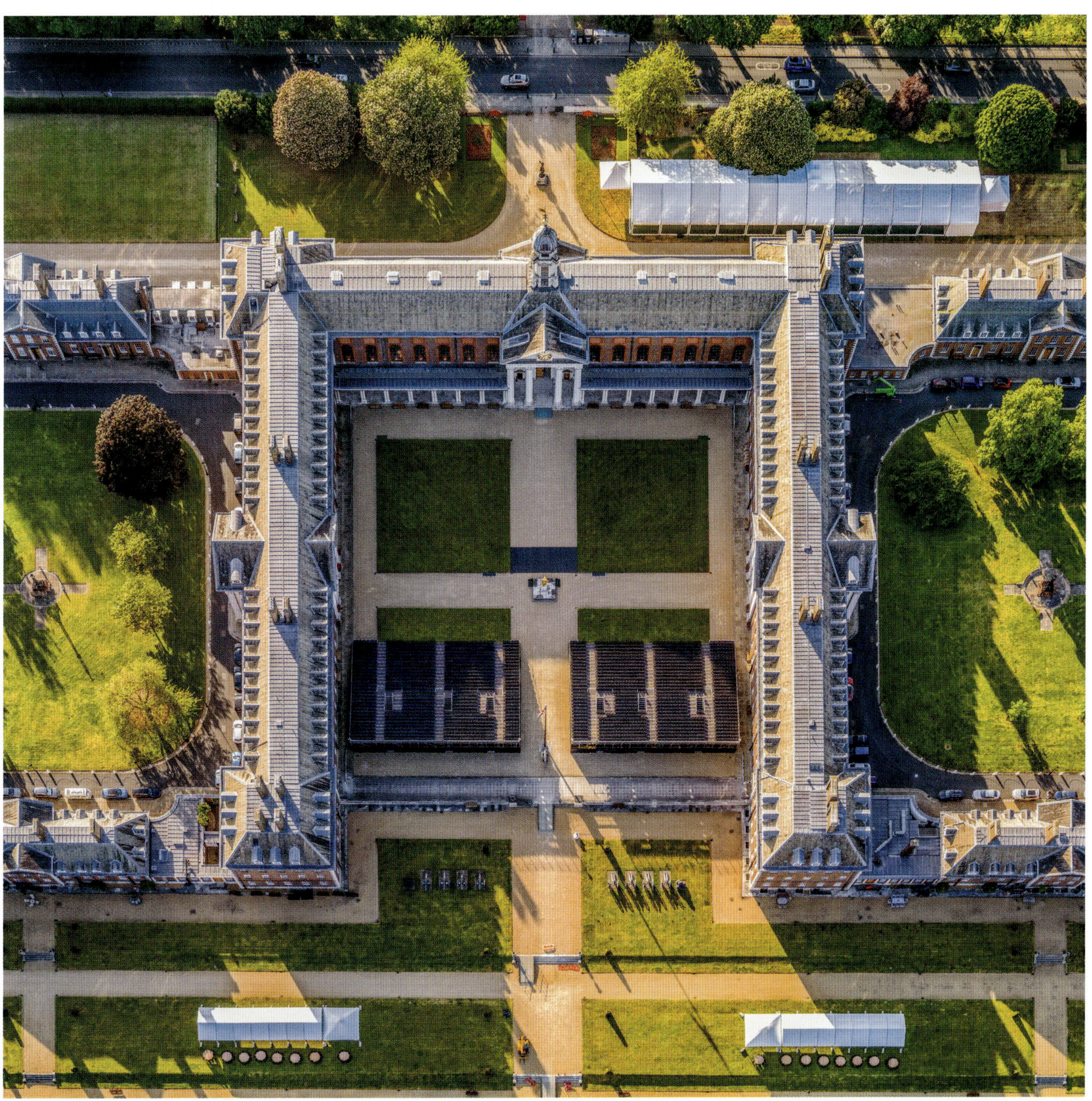

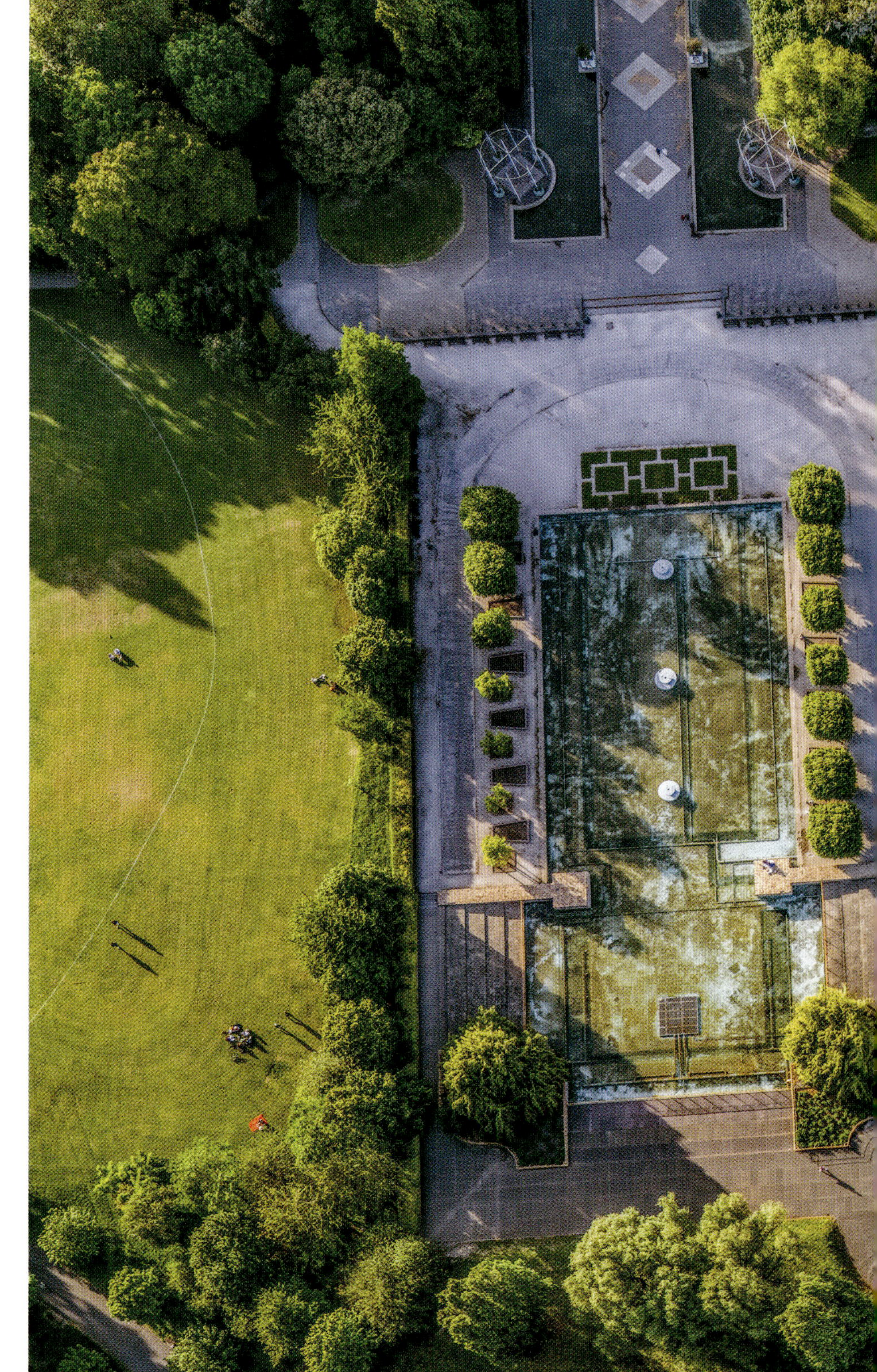

A detail of Battersea Park's gardens, directly across the Thames from Royal Hospital Chelsea and Chelsea Physic Garden

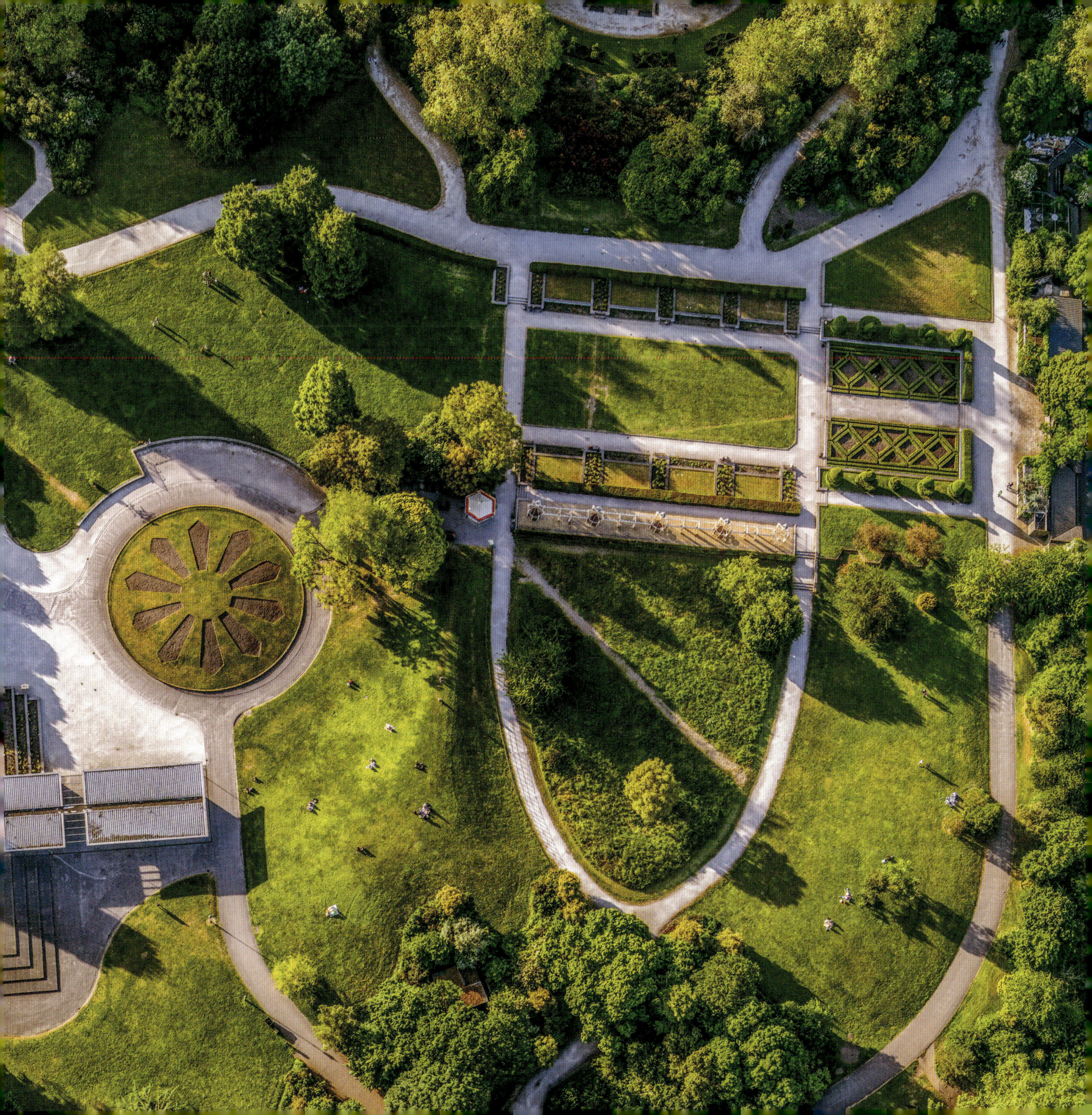

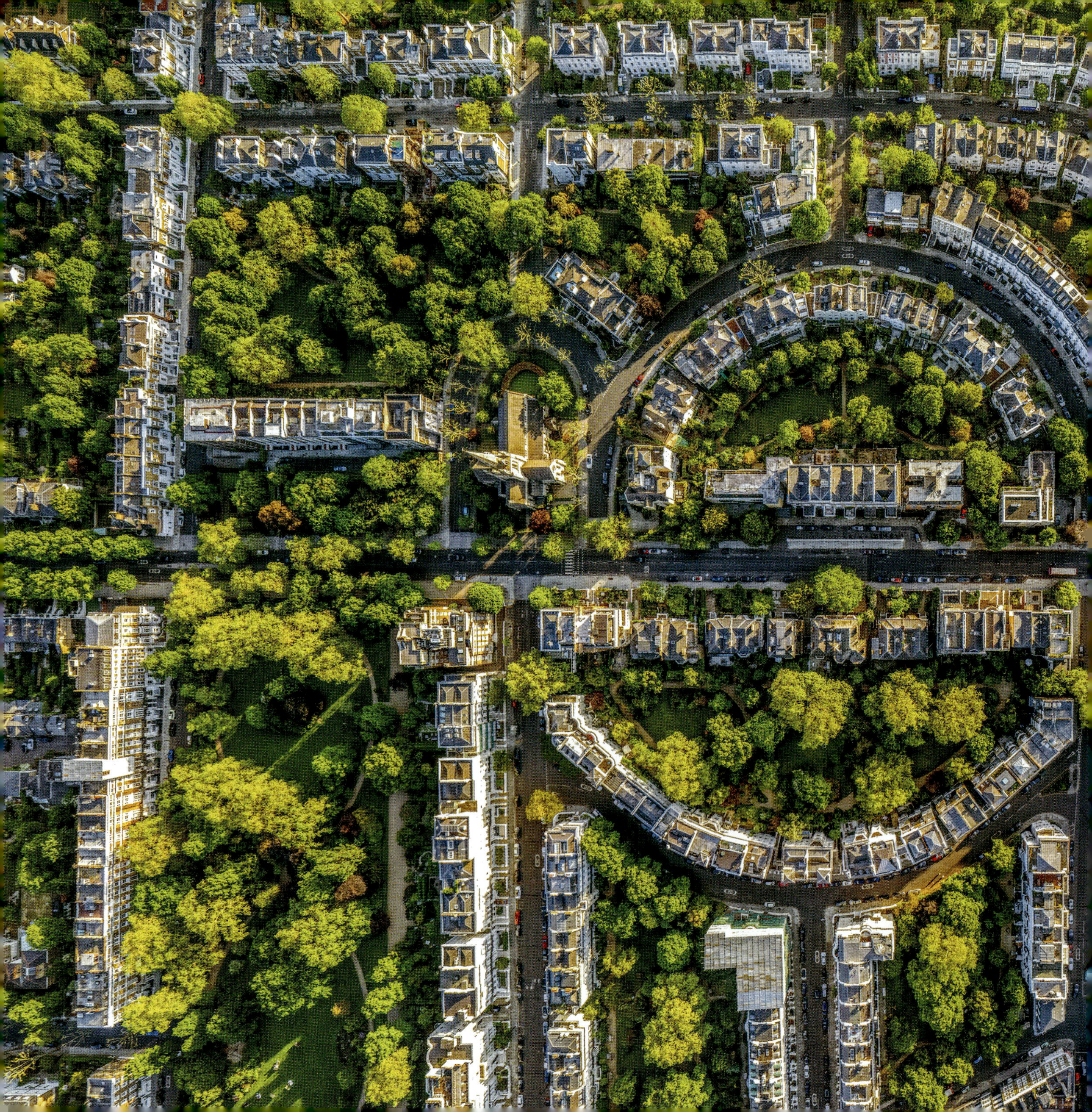

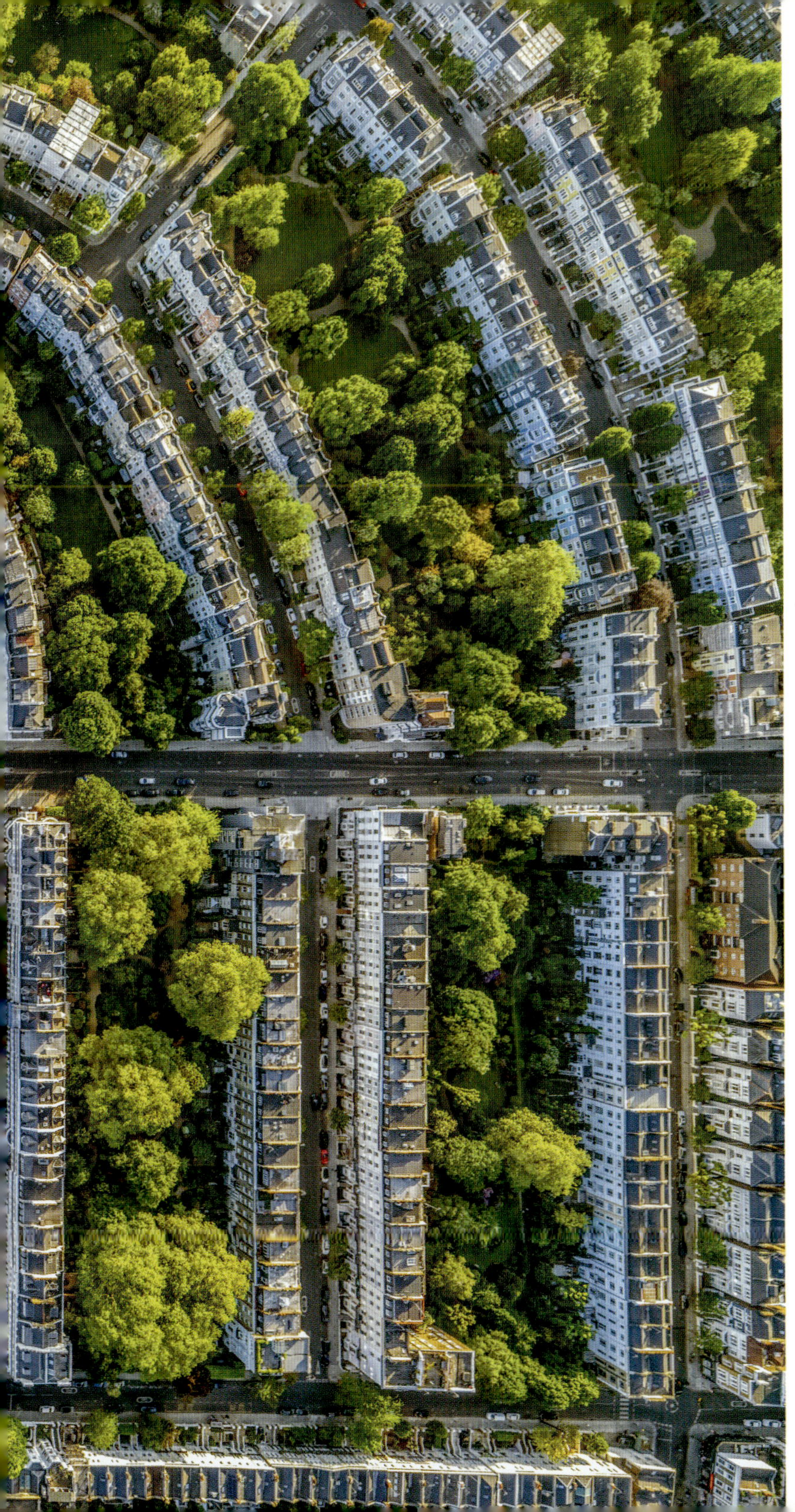

Lansdowne Crescent (at top) and Stanley Crescent, bisected by Ladbroke Grove in Notting Hill

46 # THE CITY

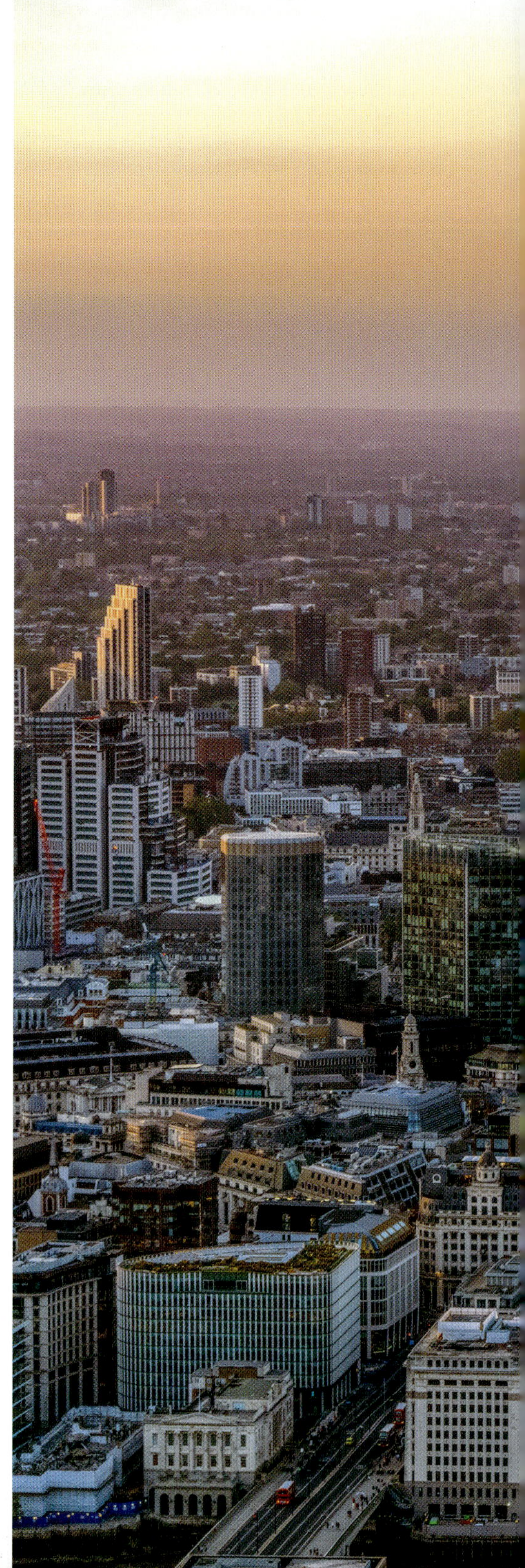

Looking north past the Shard toward a group of City of London skyscrapers, with the one nicknamed the Walkie-Talkie at center

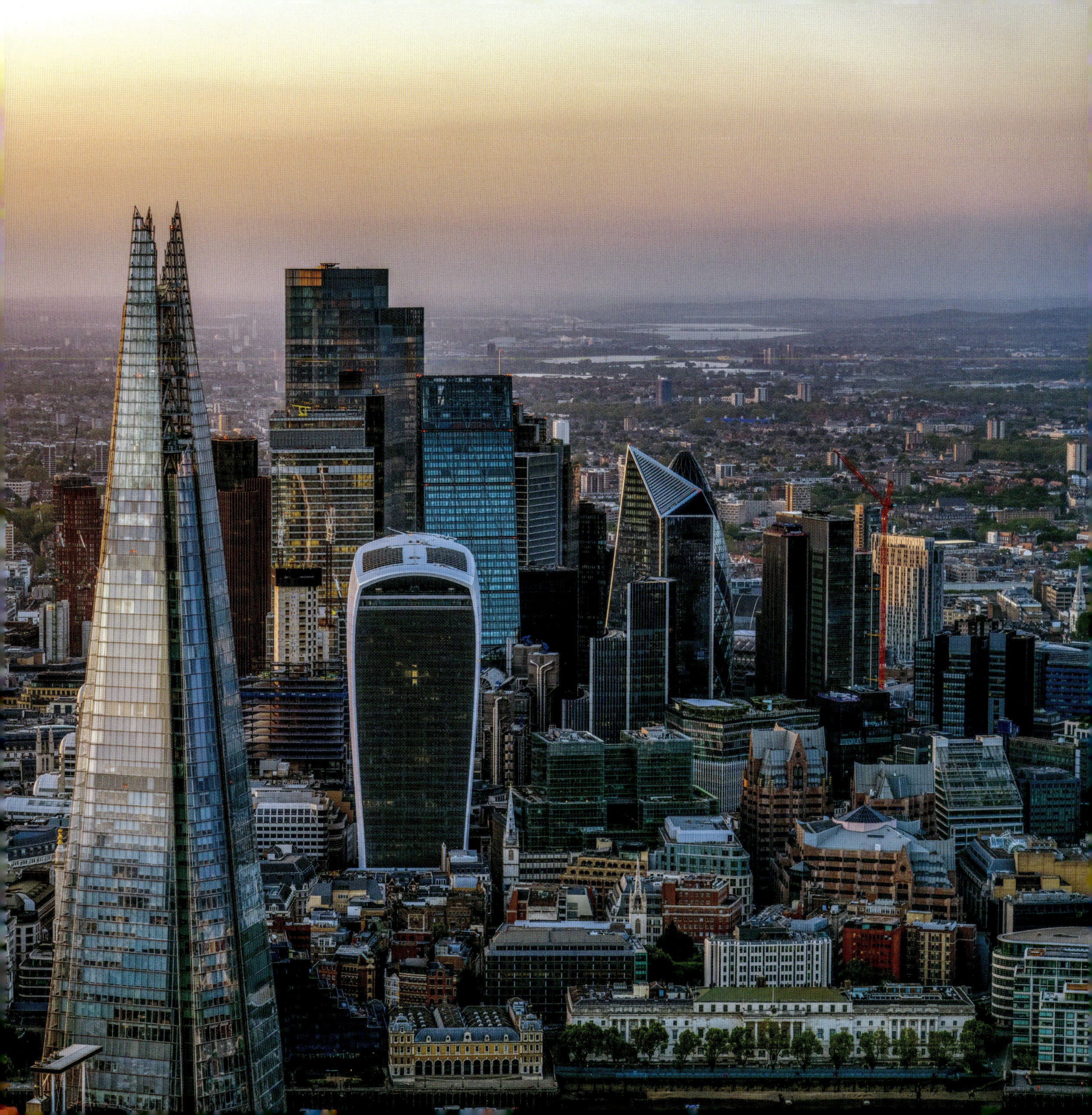

Opposite: Tower of London

Pages 50–51: Tower Bridge at night

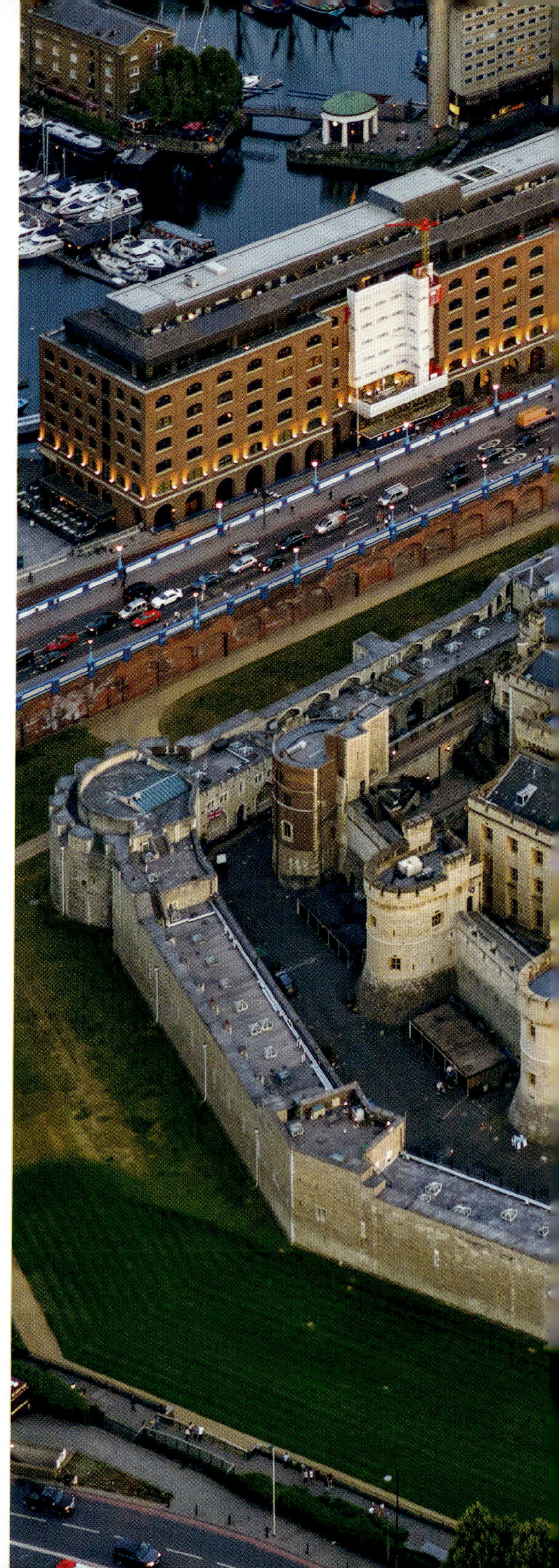

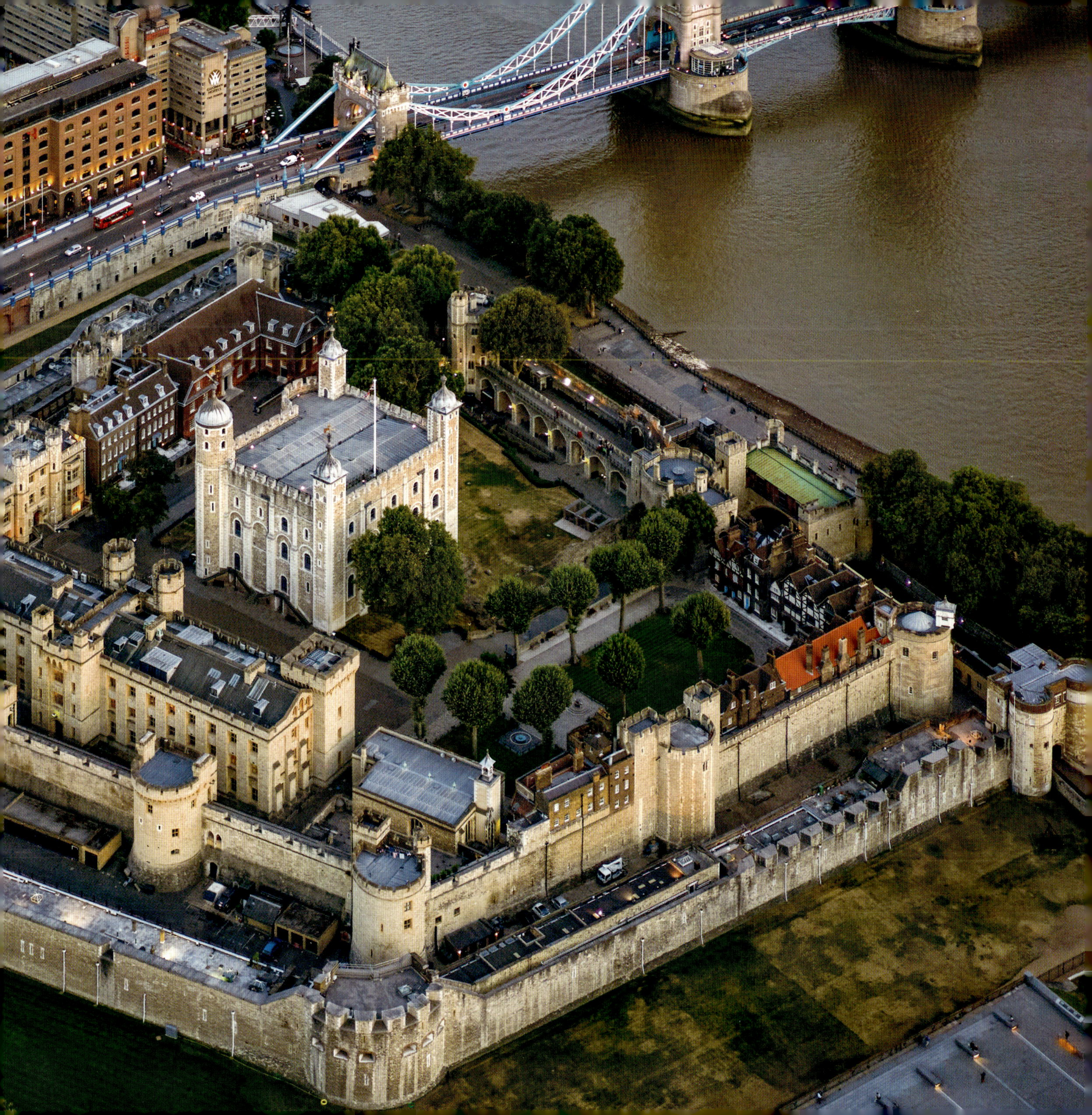

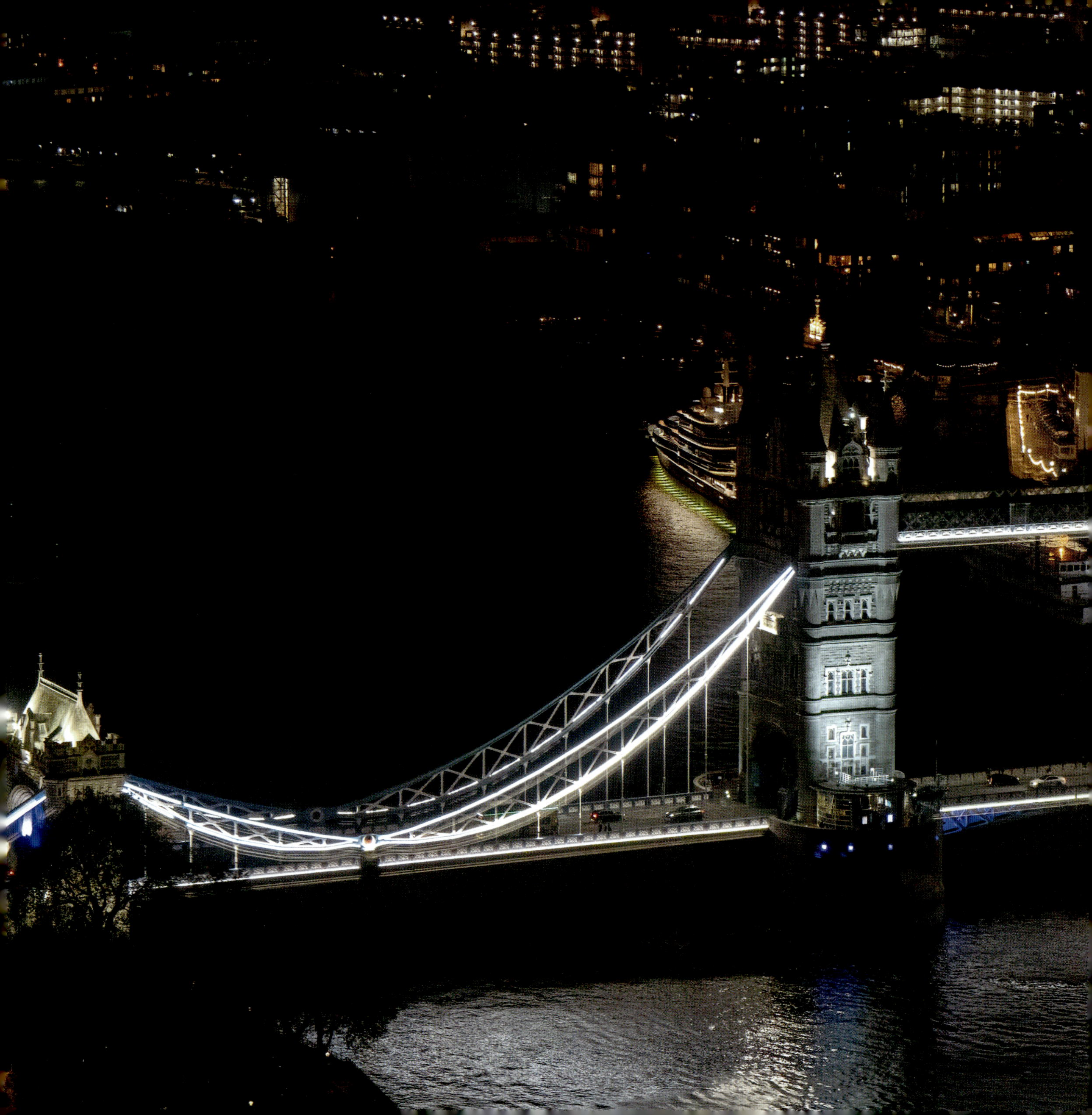

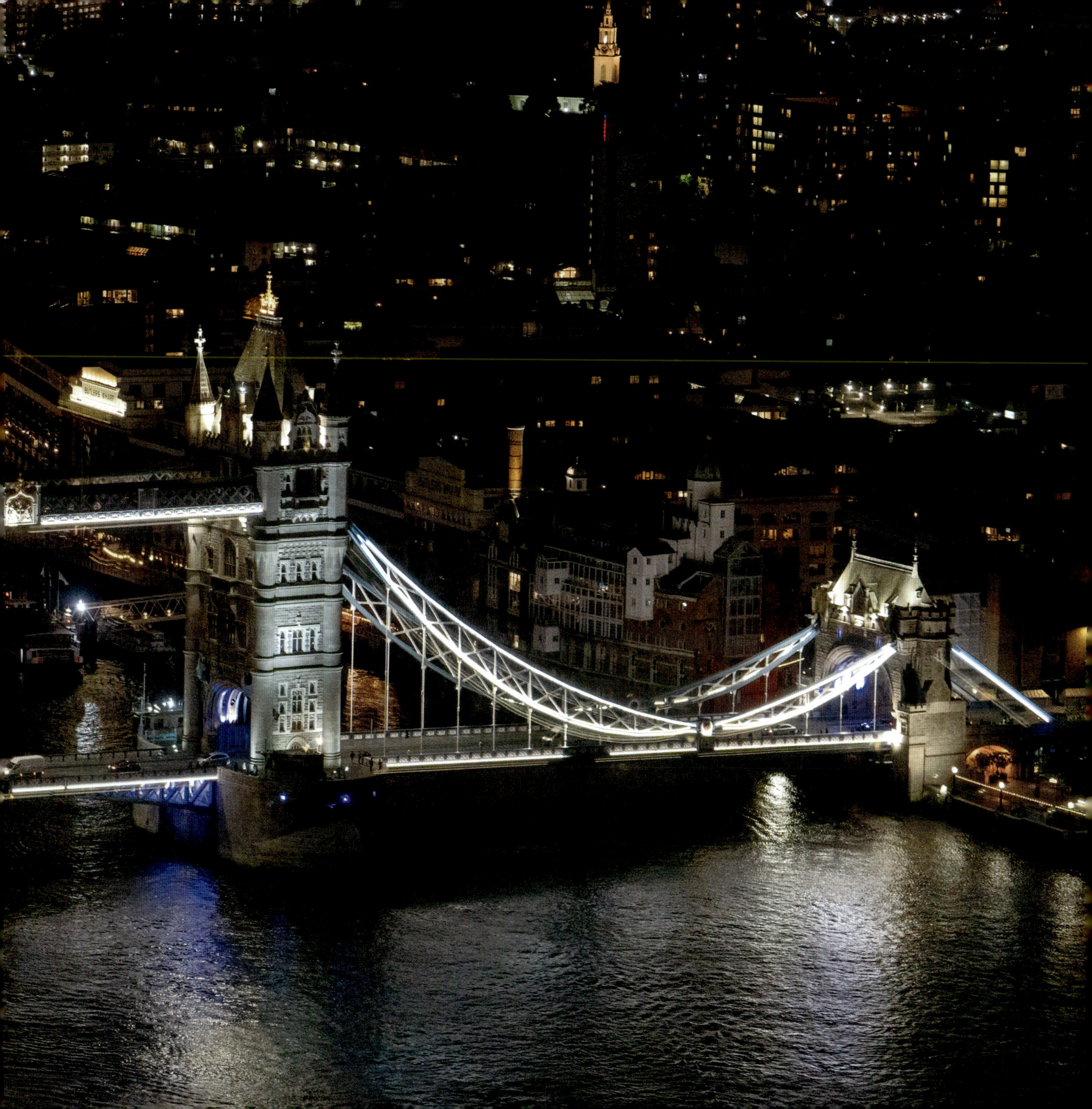

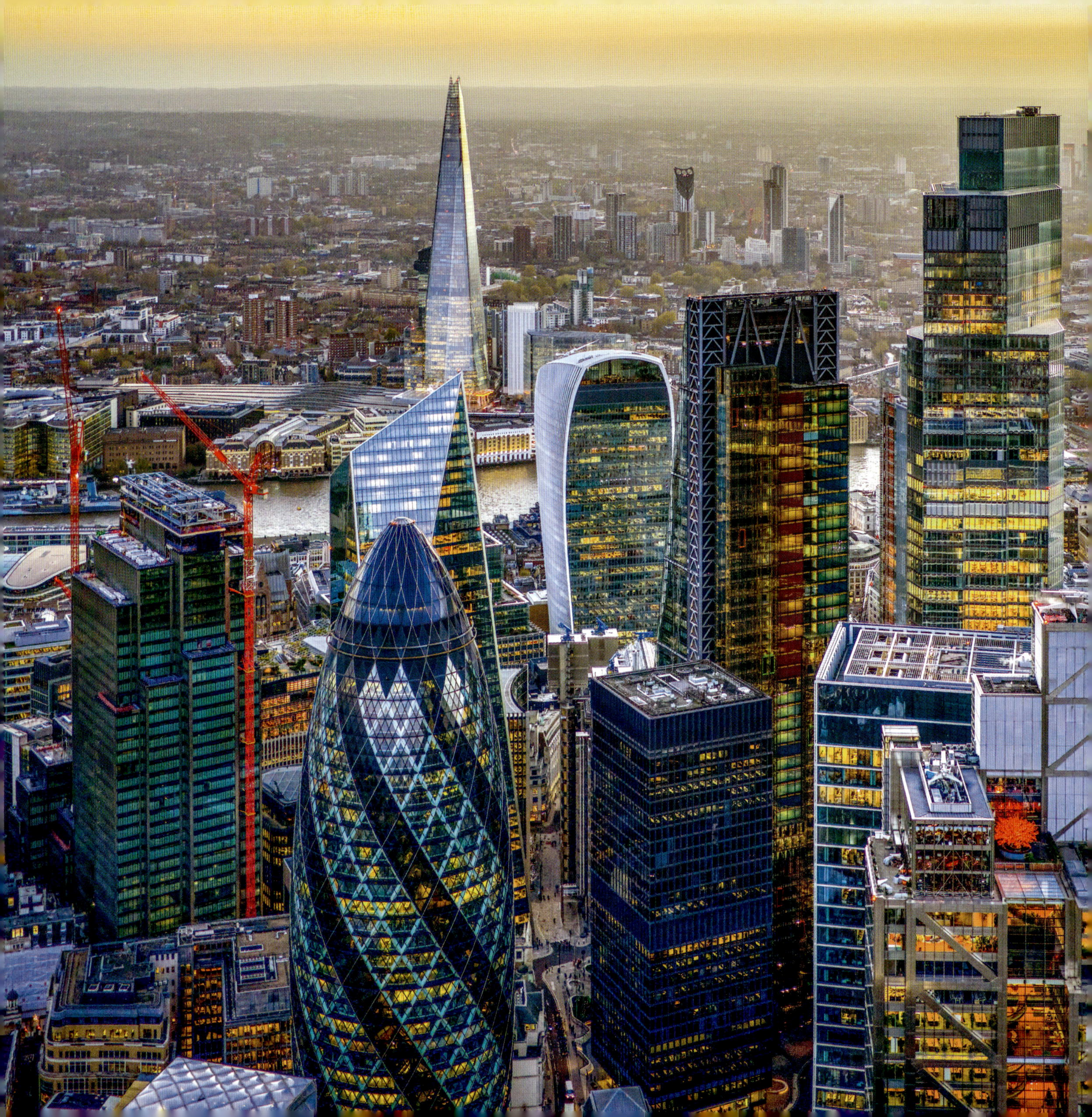

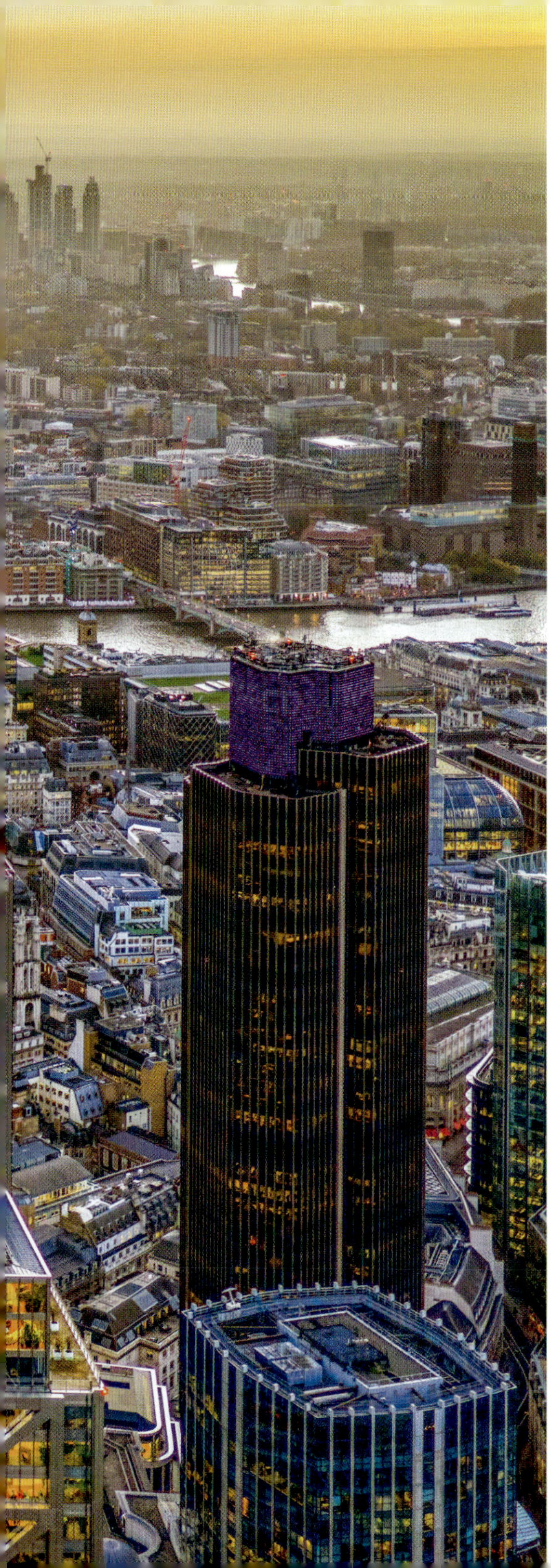

Looking south over the City of London, with
the Gherkin, the Walkie-Talkie, the Scalpel, and
the Cheesegrater prominent

Looking down on the Gherkin; the angled street at left is St. Mary Axe, named after a medieval parish and church demolished in 1561

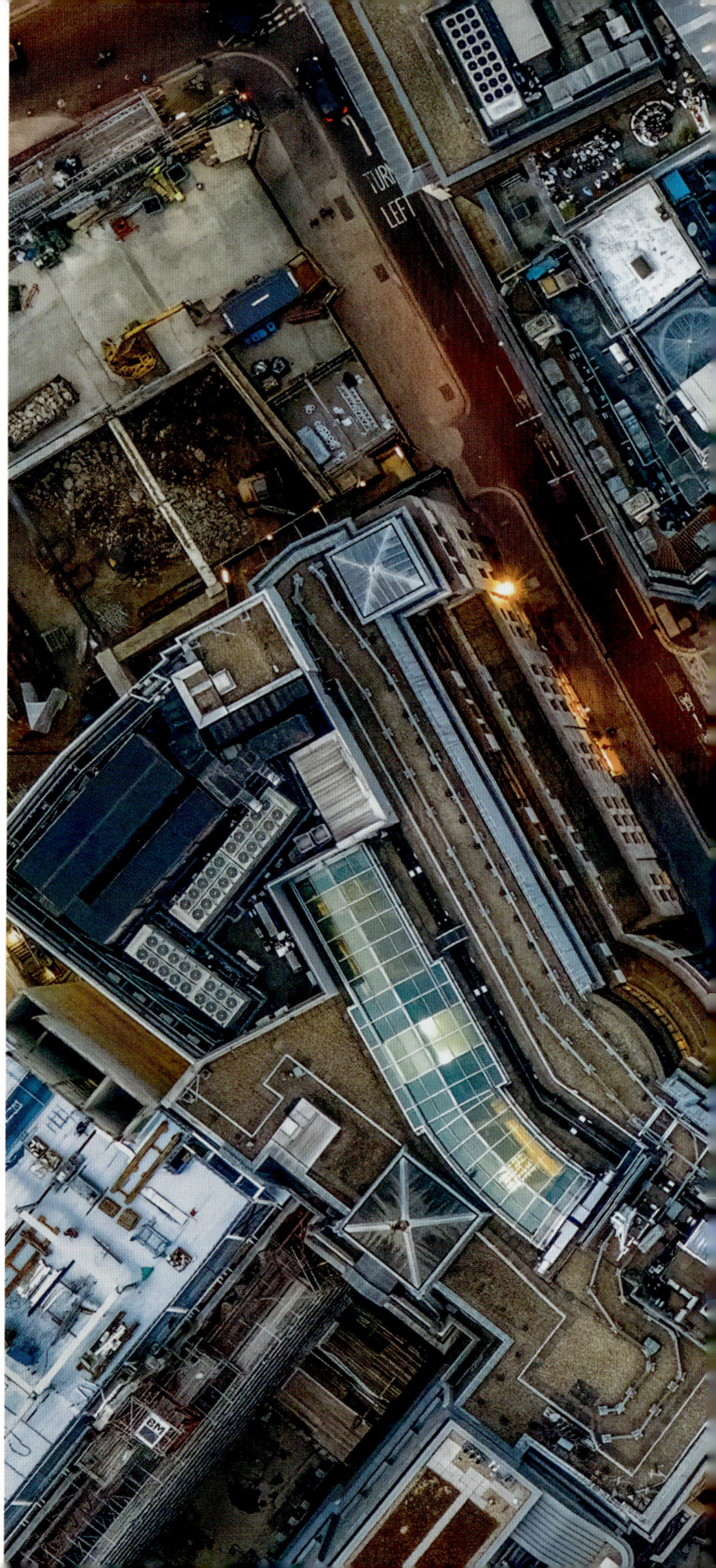

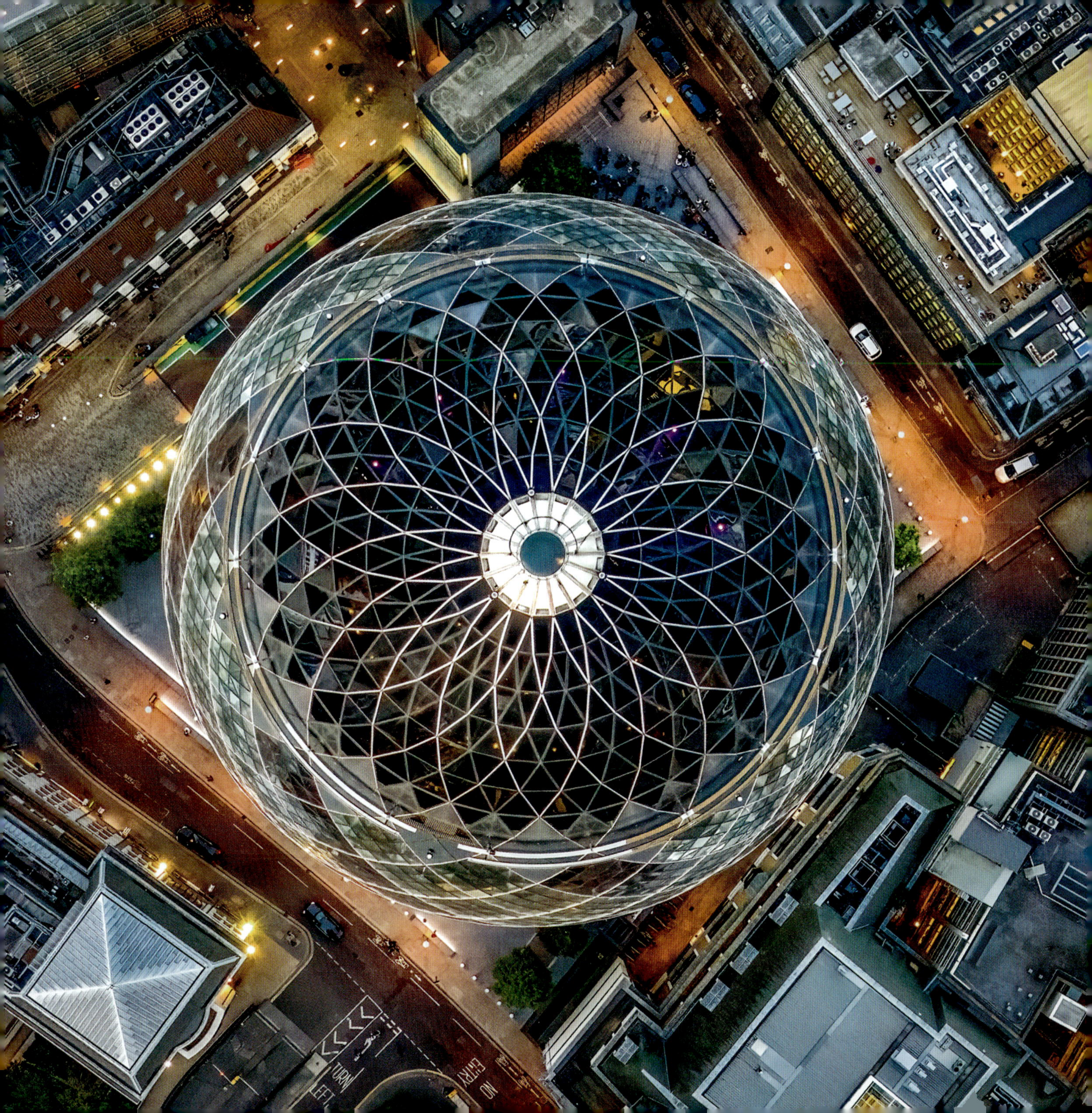
TURN
NO ENTRY

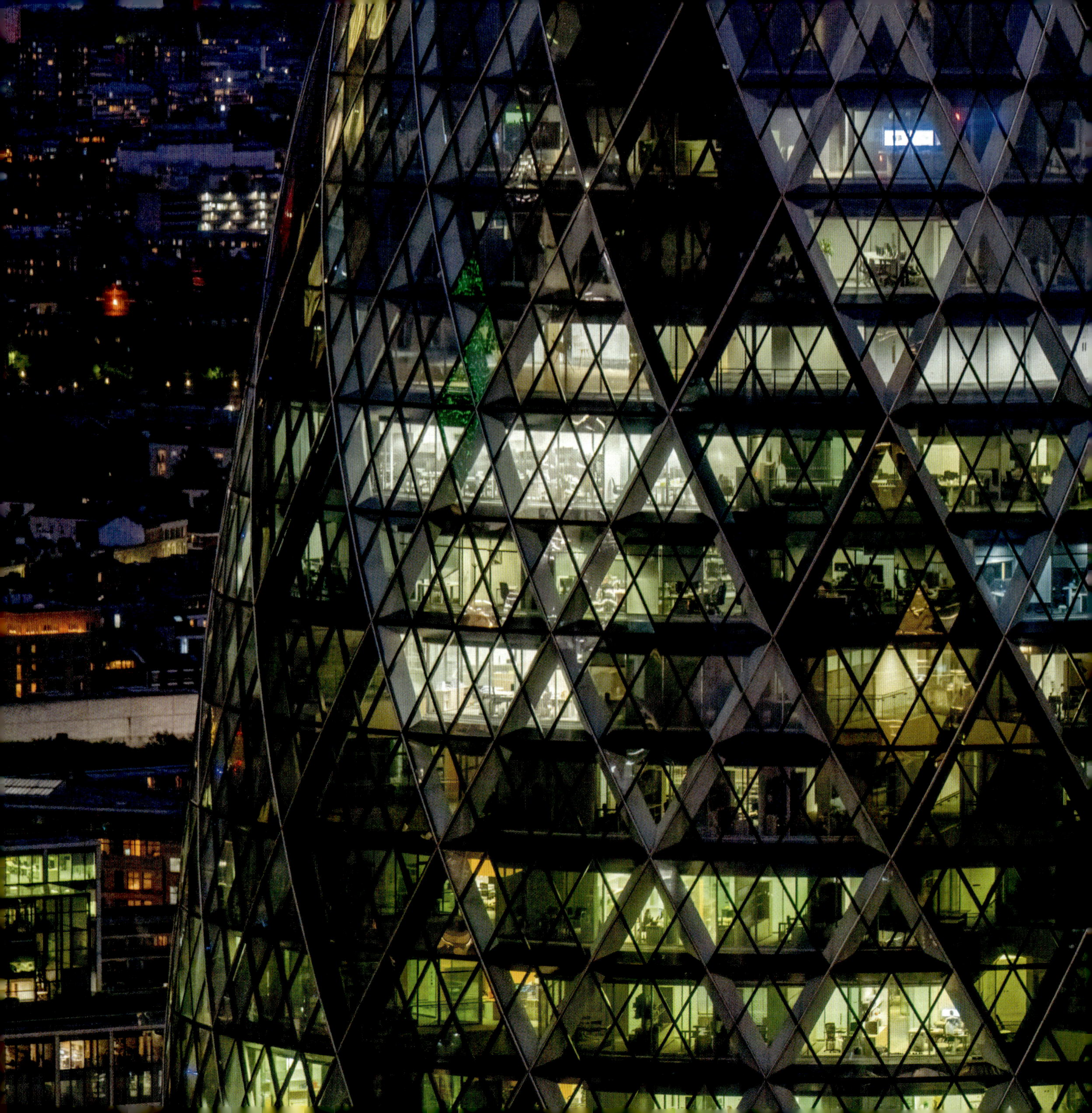

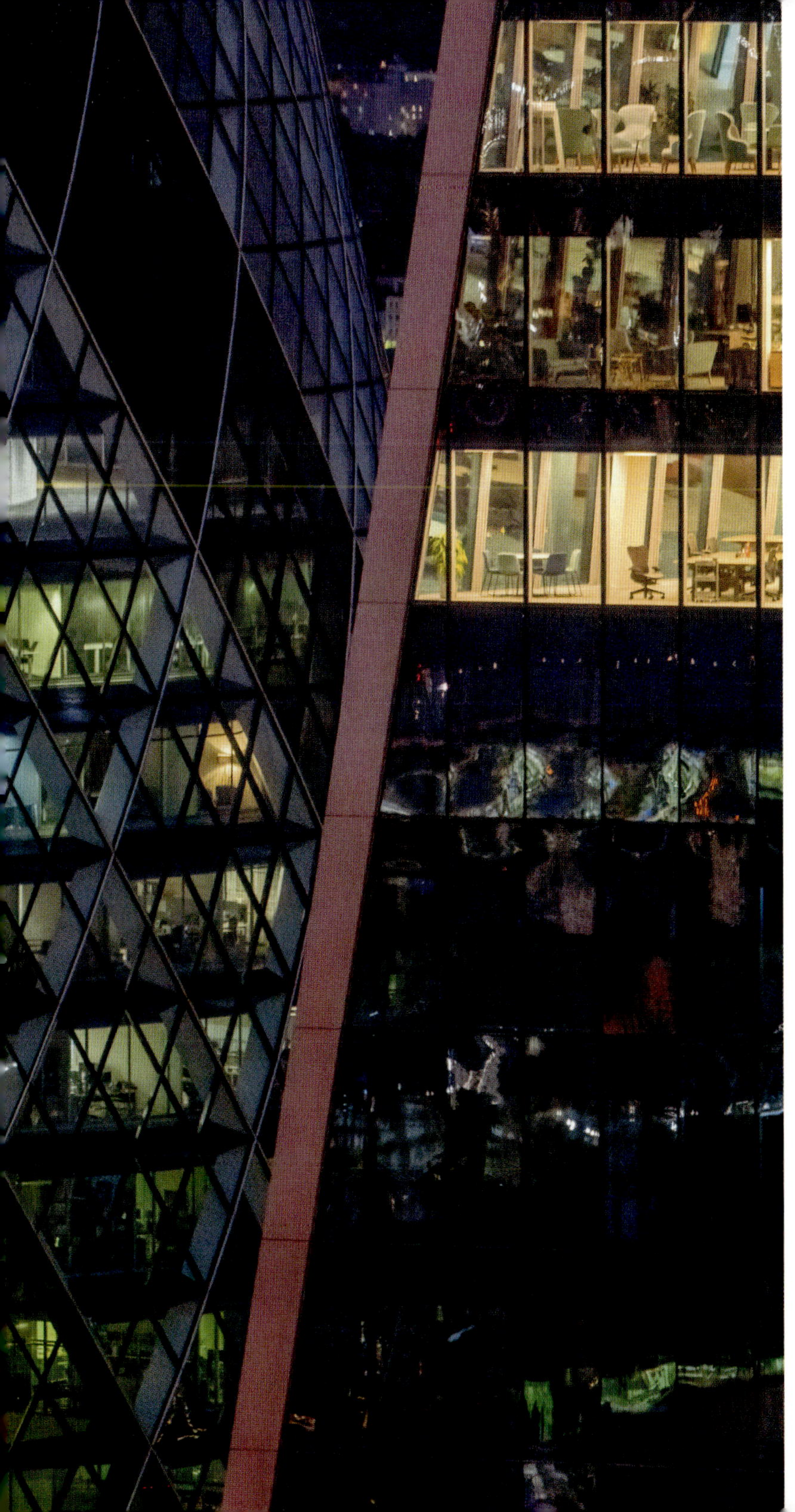

A view into the offices of the
Gherkin and the Scalpel

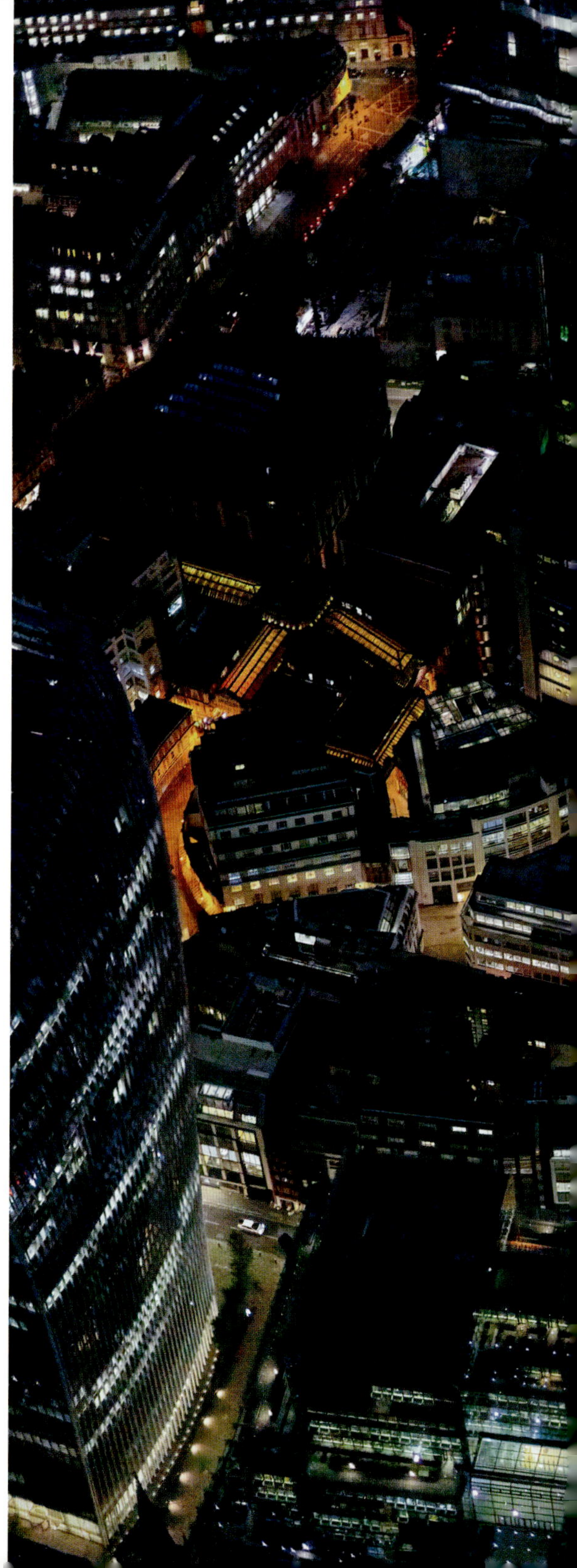

Looking down on Fenchurch Street, with the Garden at 120, a rooftop public garden maintained by the City of London, at center

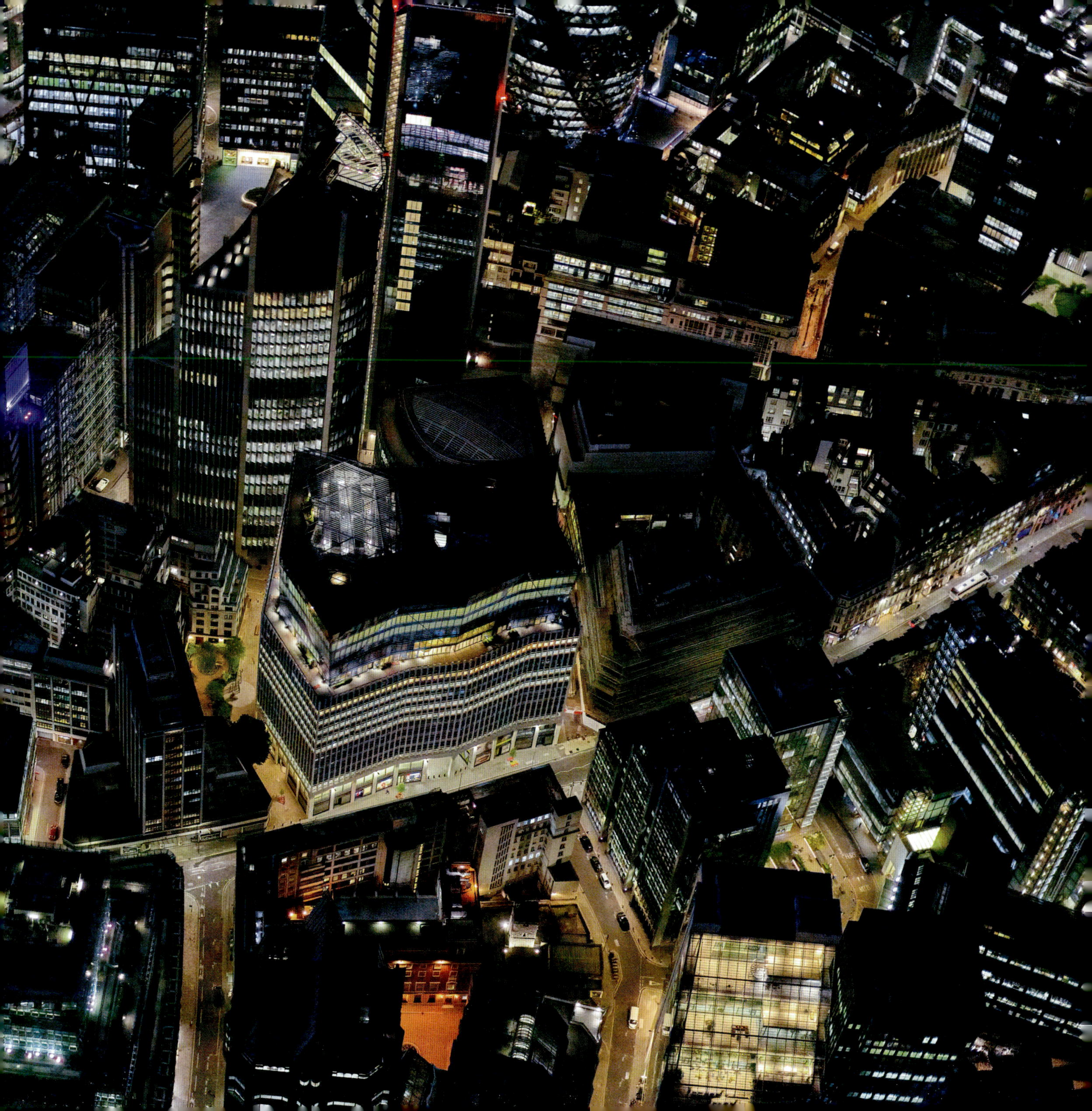

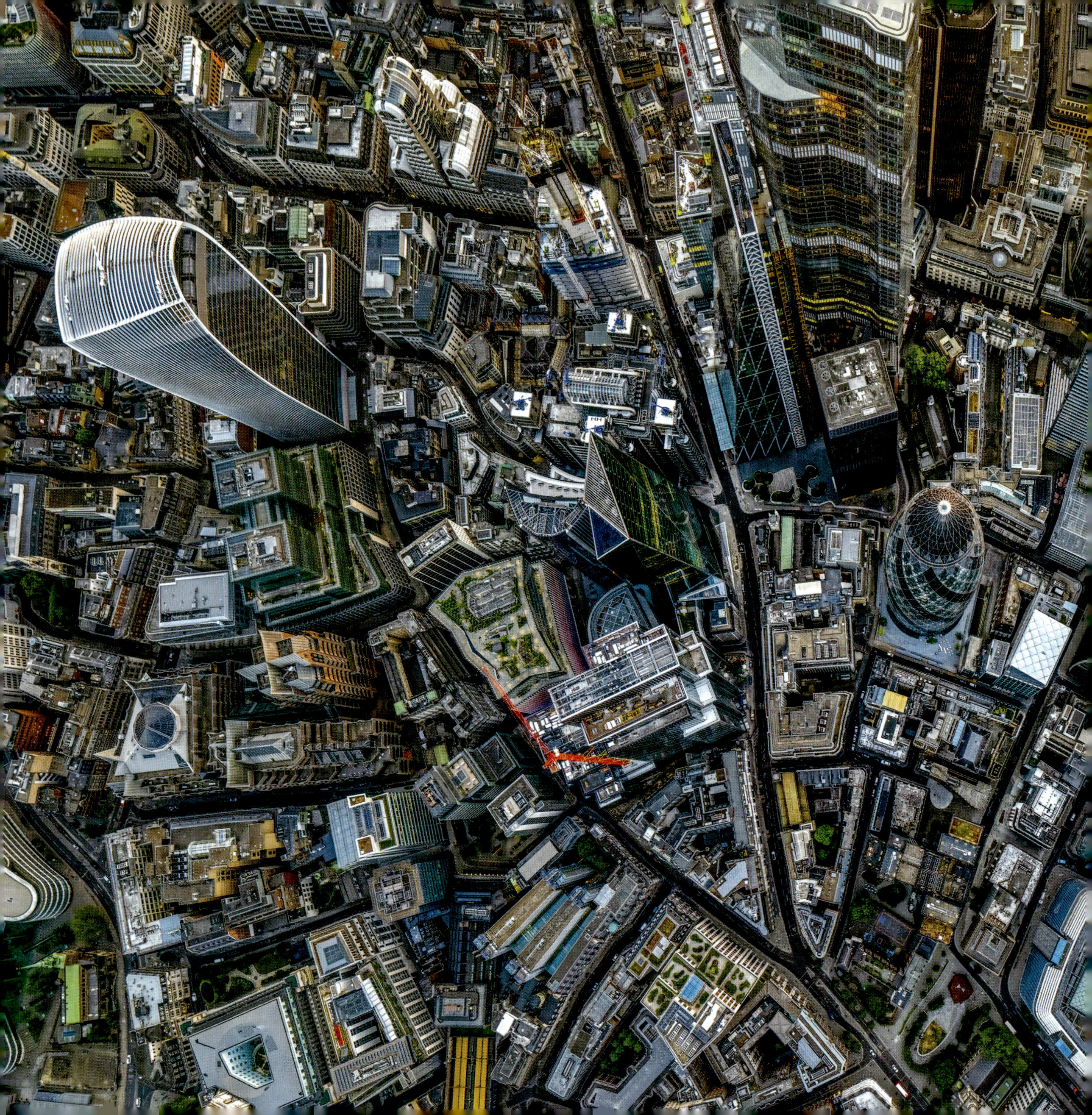

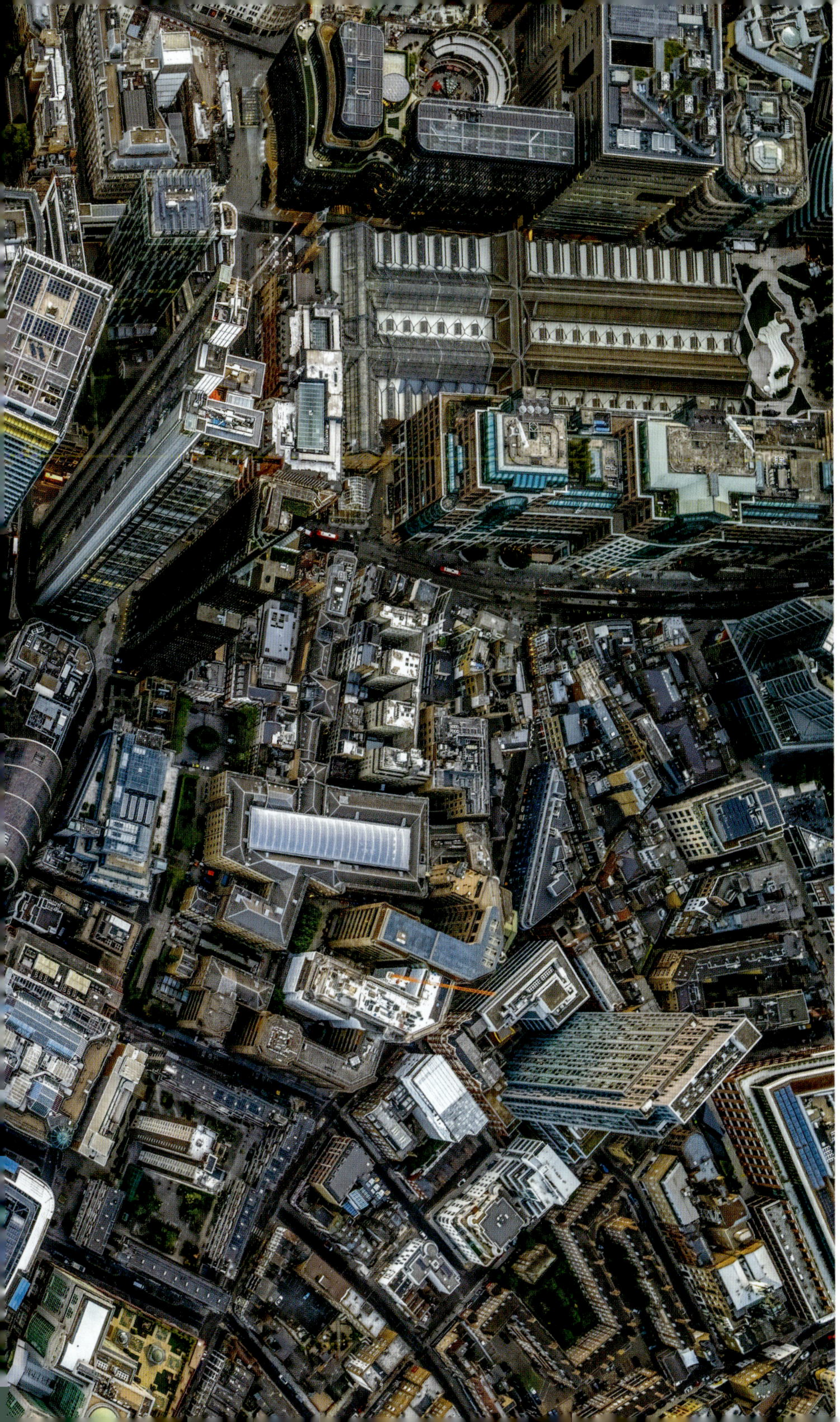

Looking down on the Financial District; the sharp-edged building between the Walkie-Talkie (at left) and the Gherkin (at right) is called the Scalpel

62 The Walkie-Talkie

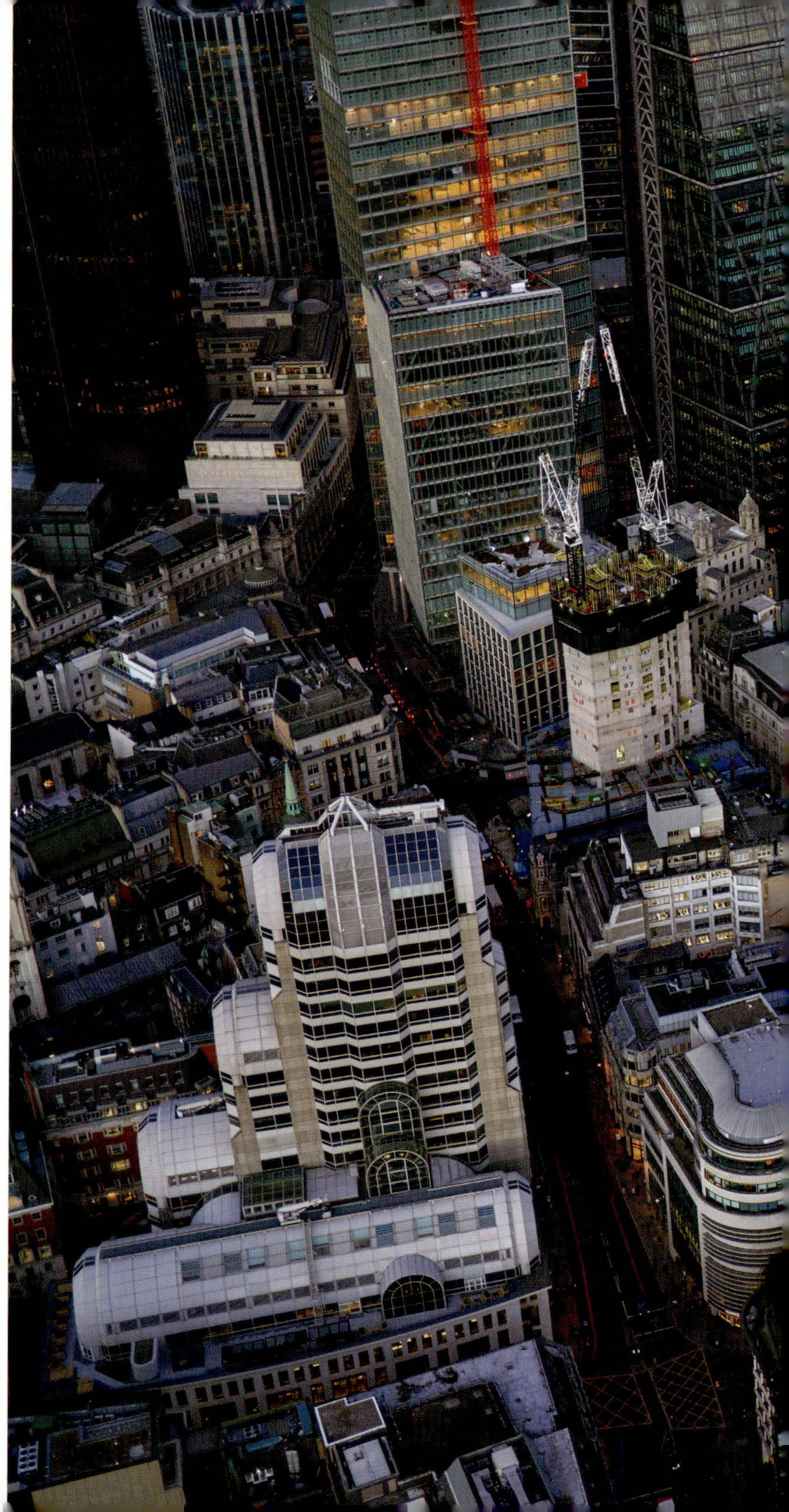

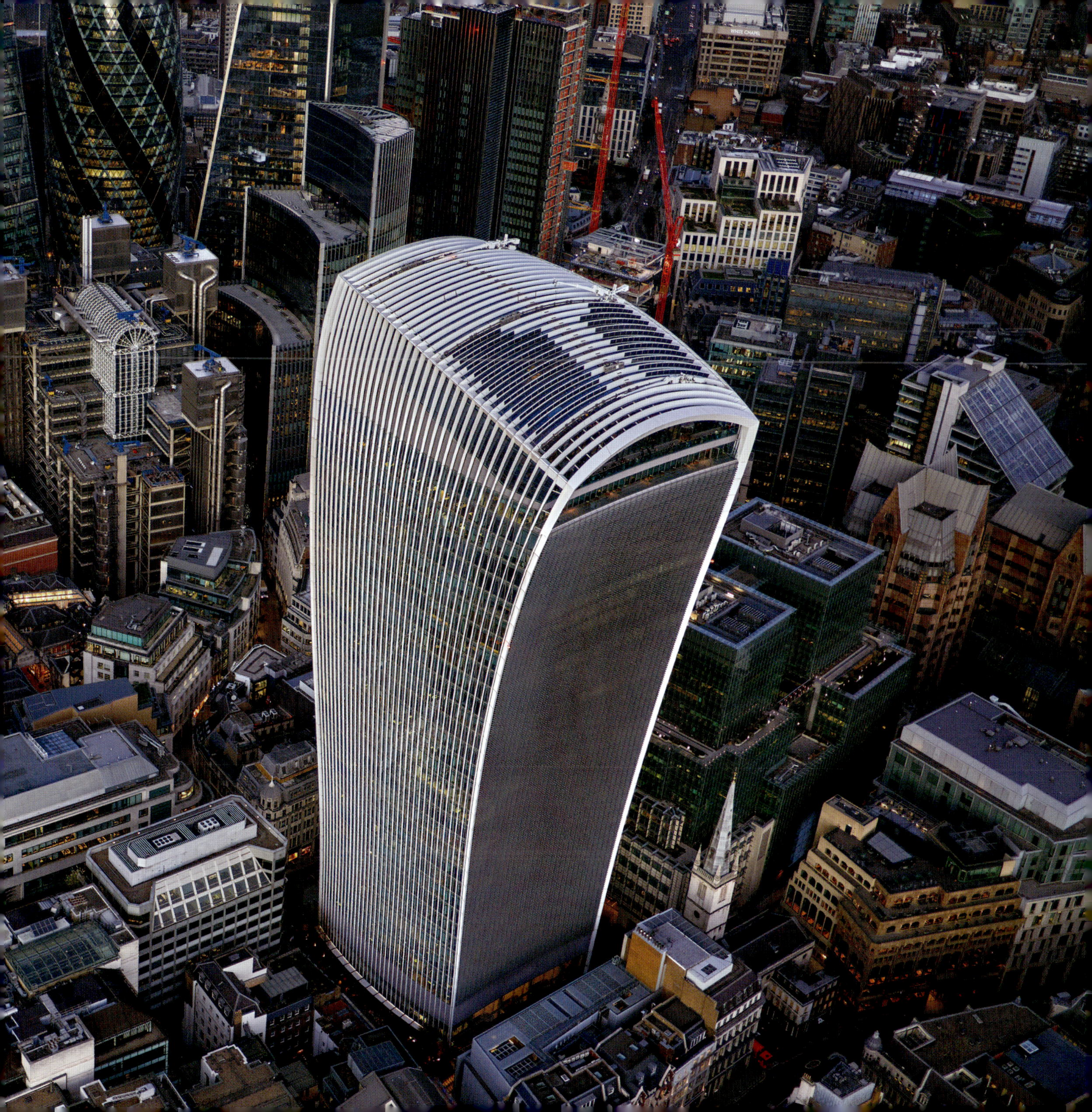
WHITE CHAPEL

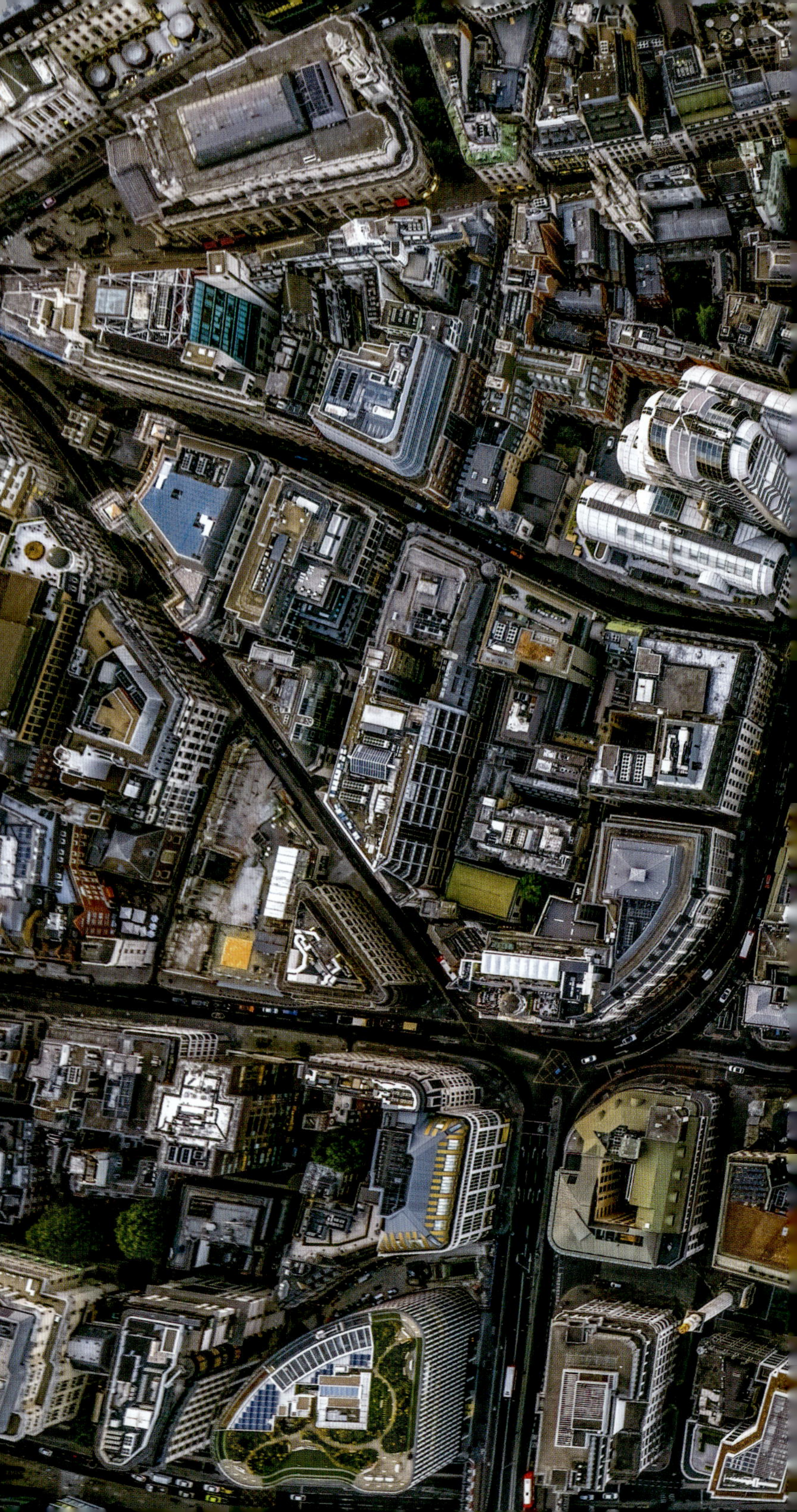

Looking down on the Walkie-Talkie; below, at lower right, Great Tower Street runs directly to the Tower of London

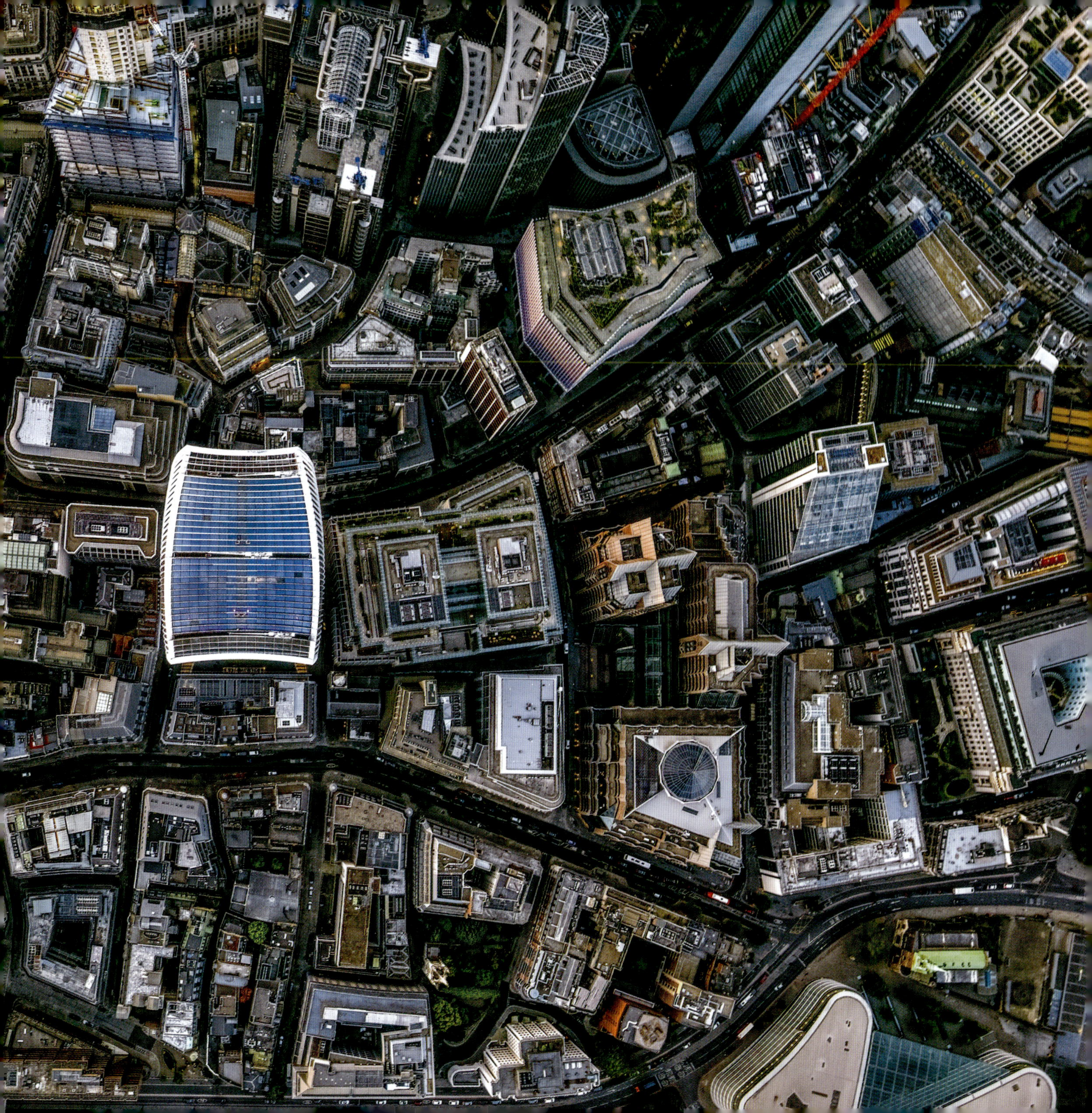

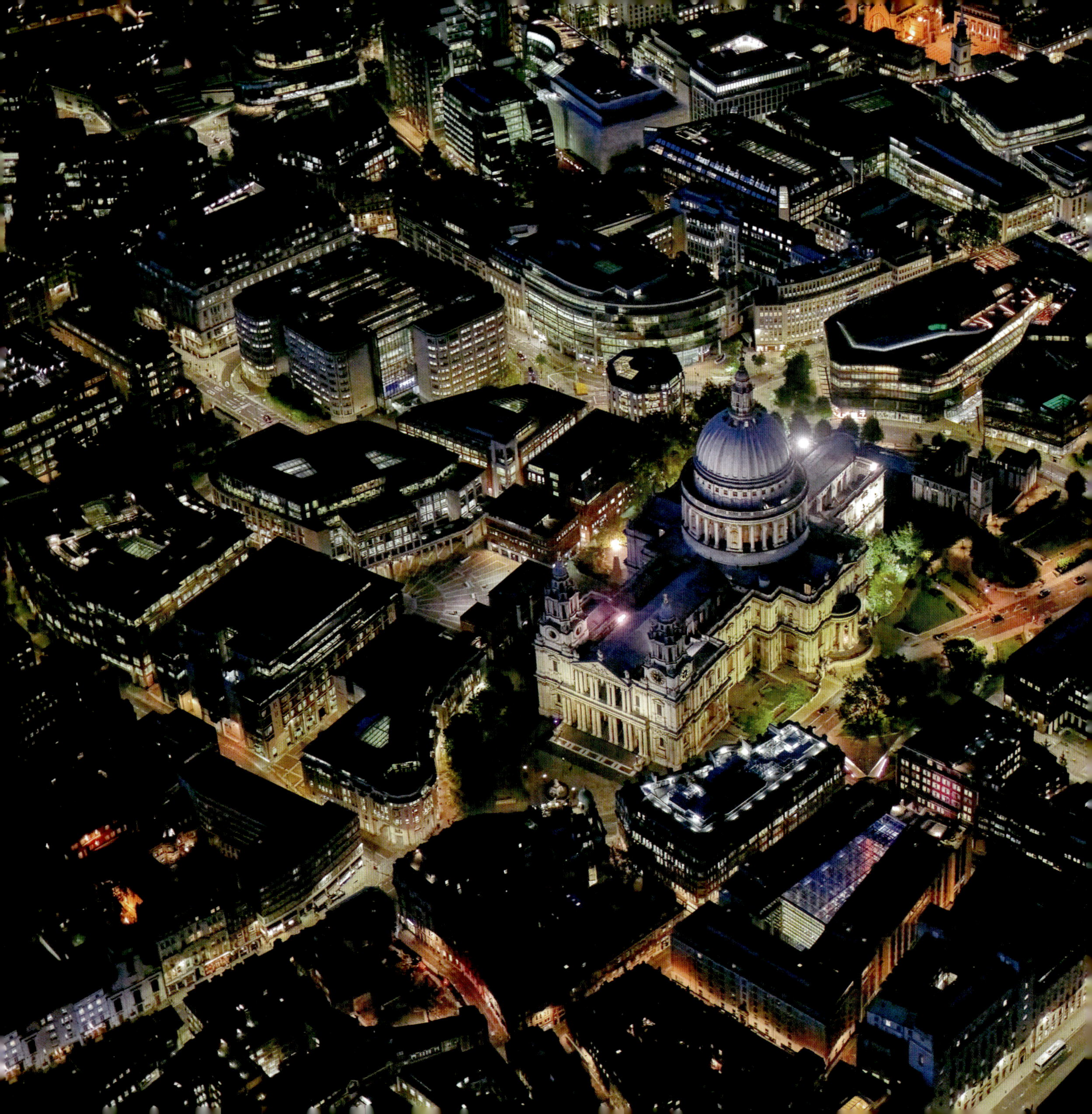

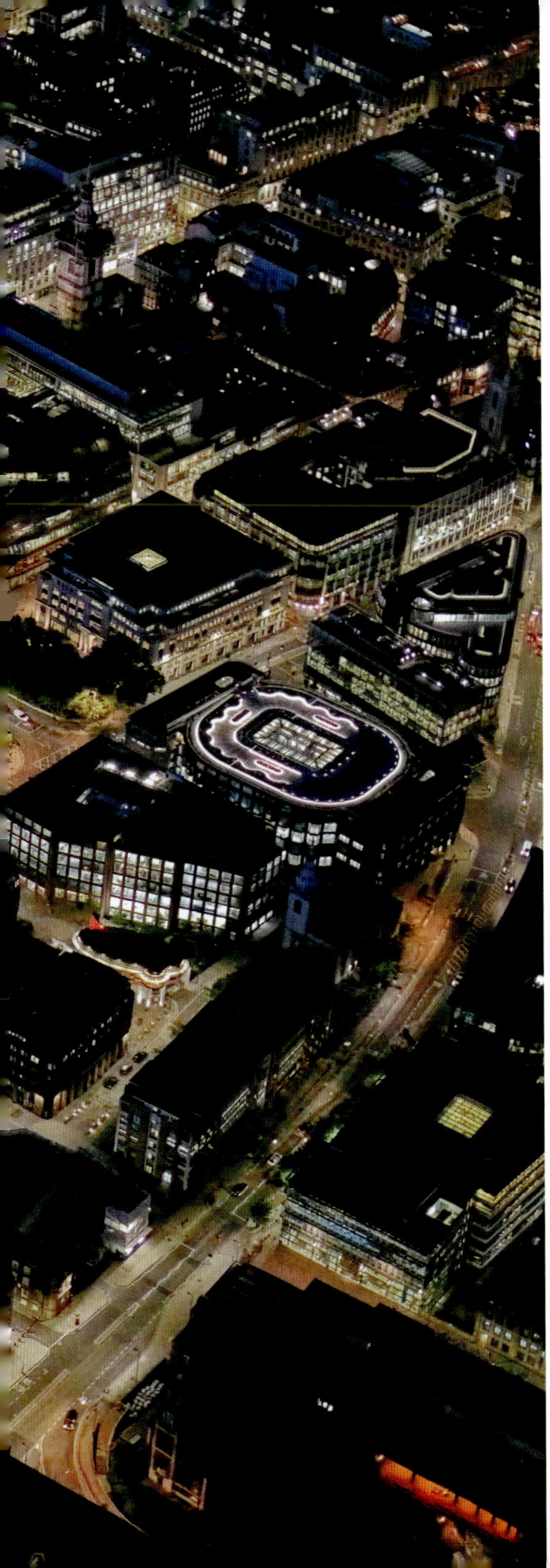

Opposite: St. Paul's Cathedral at night

Pages 68–69: The dome of St. Paul's Cathedral rising above the north transept semicircular entrance portico, with the west front and towers to the right

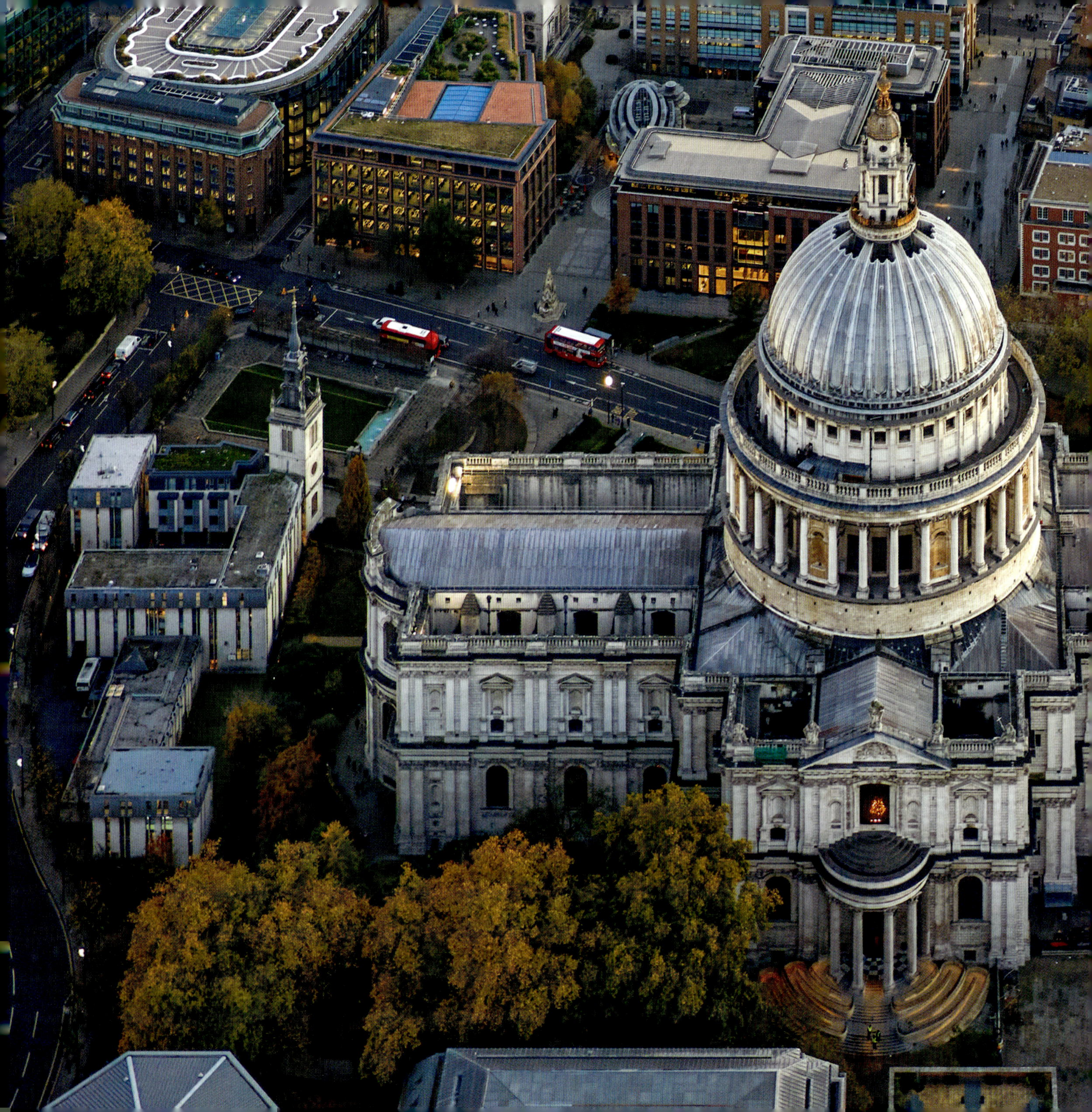

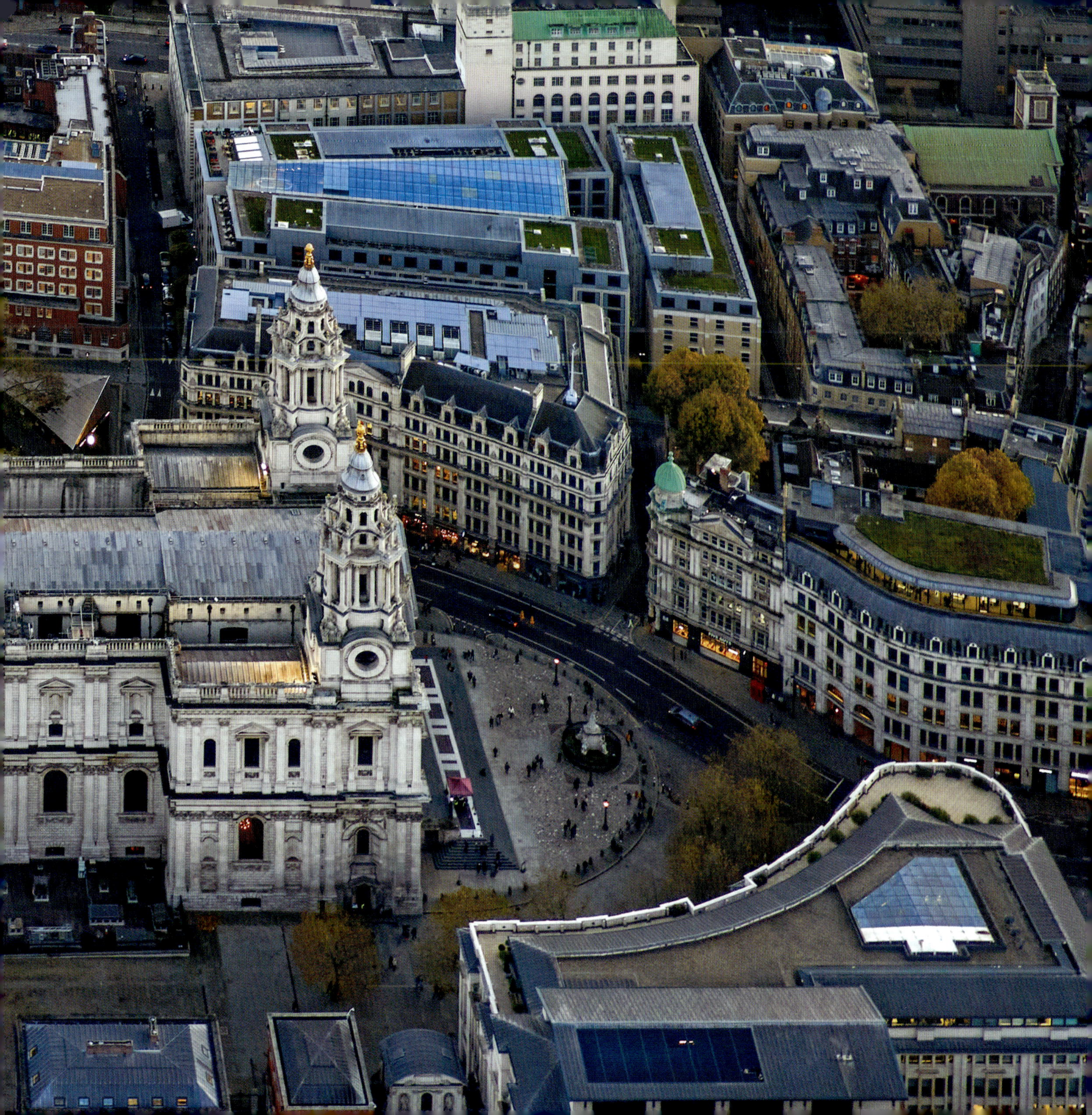

70 Looking down on St. Paul's Cathedral

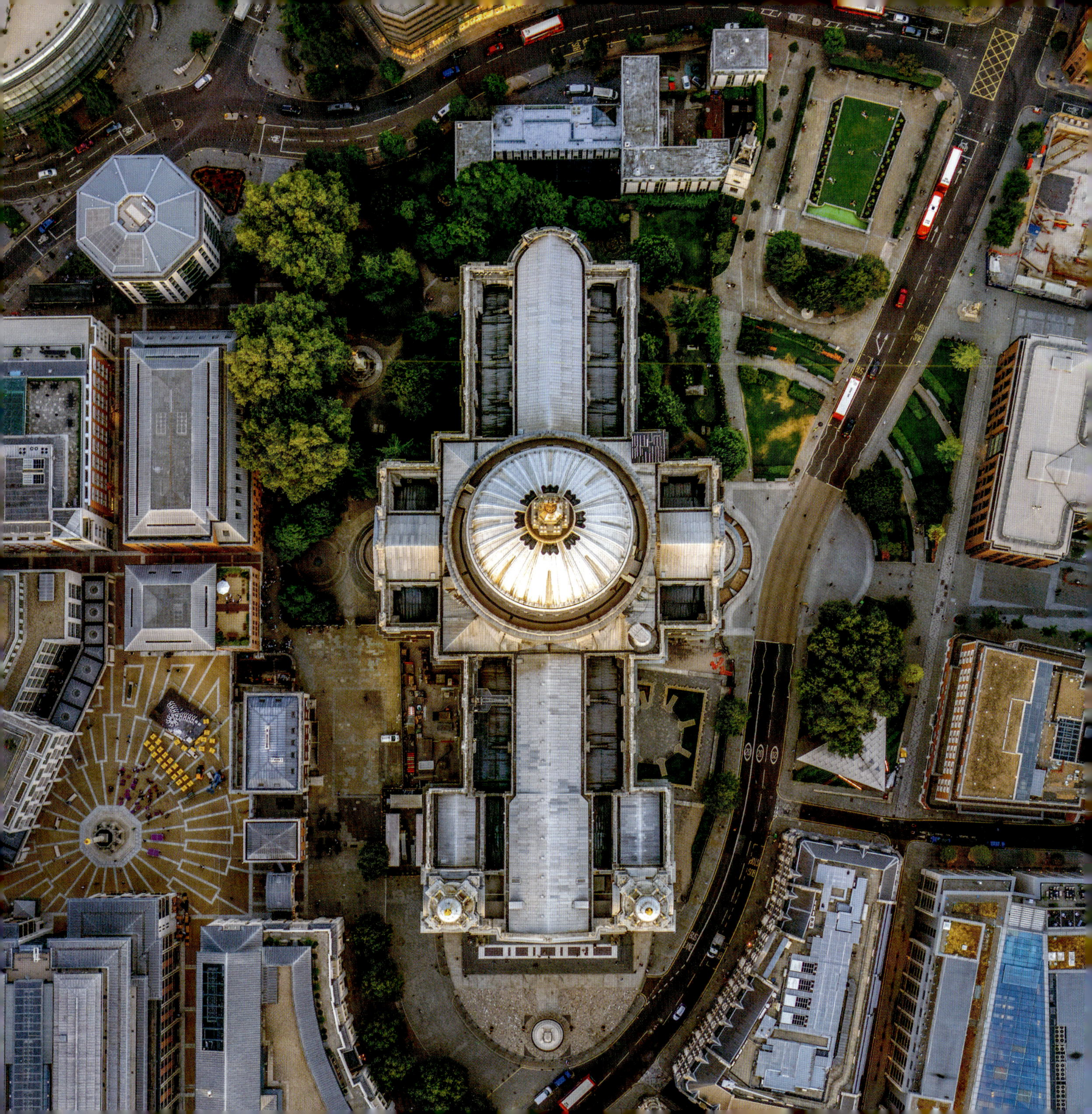

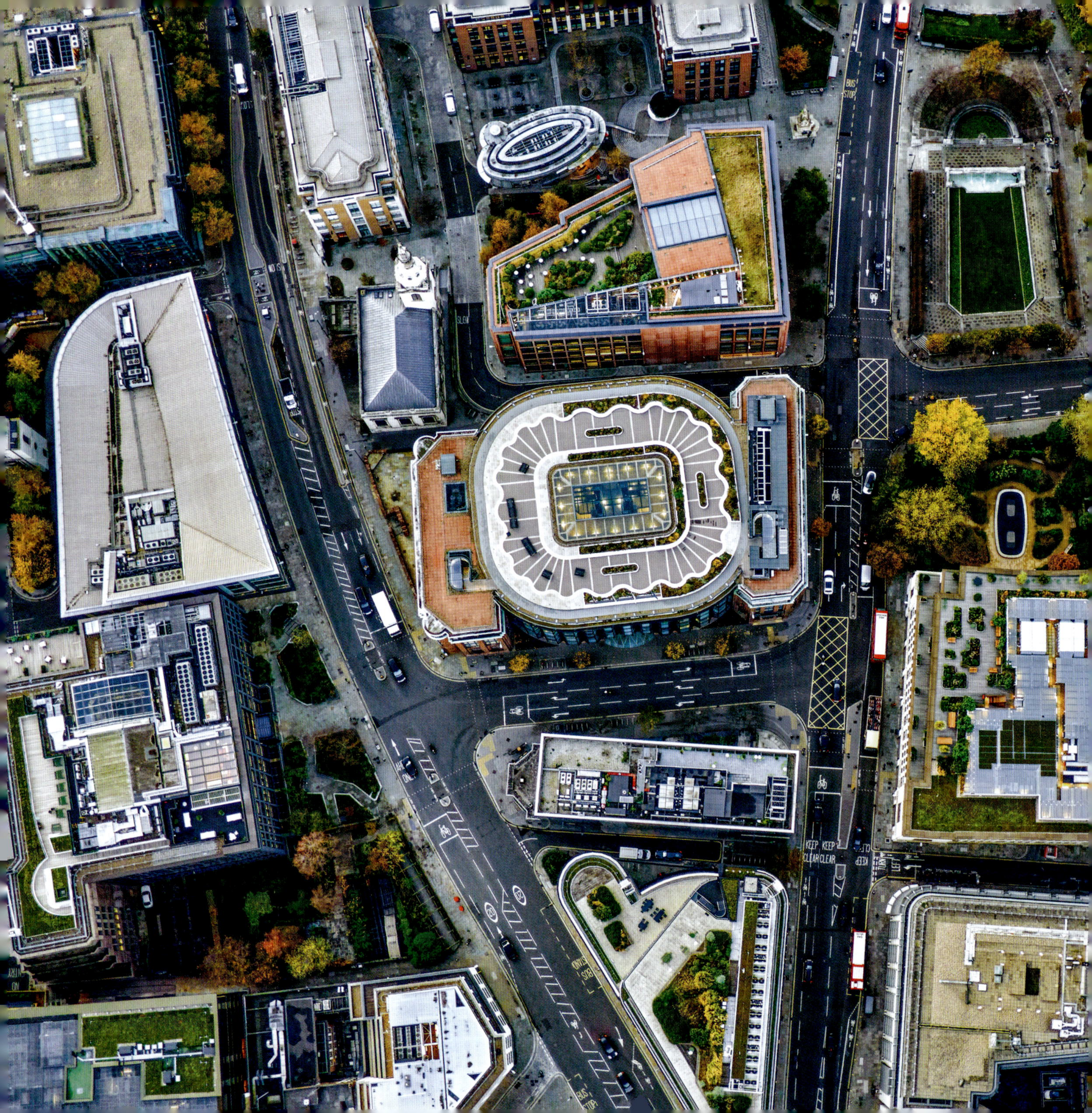

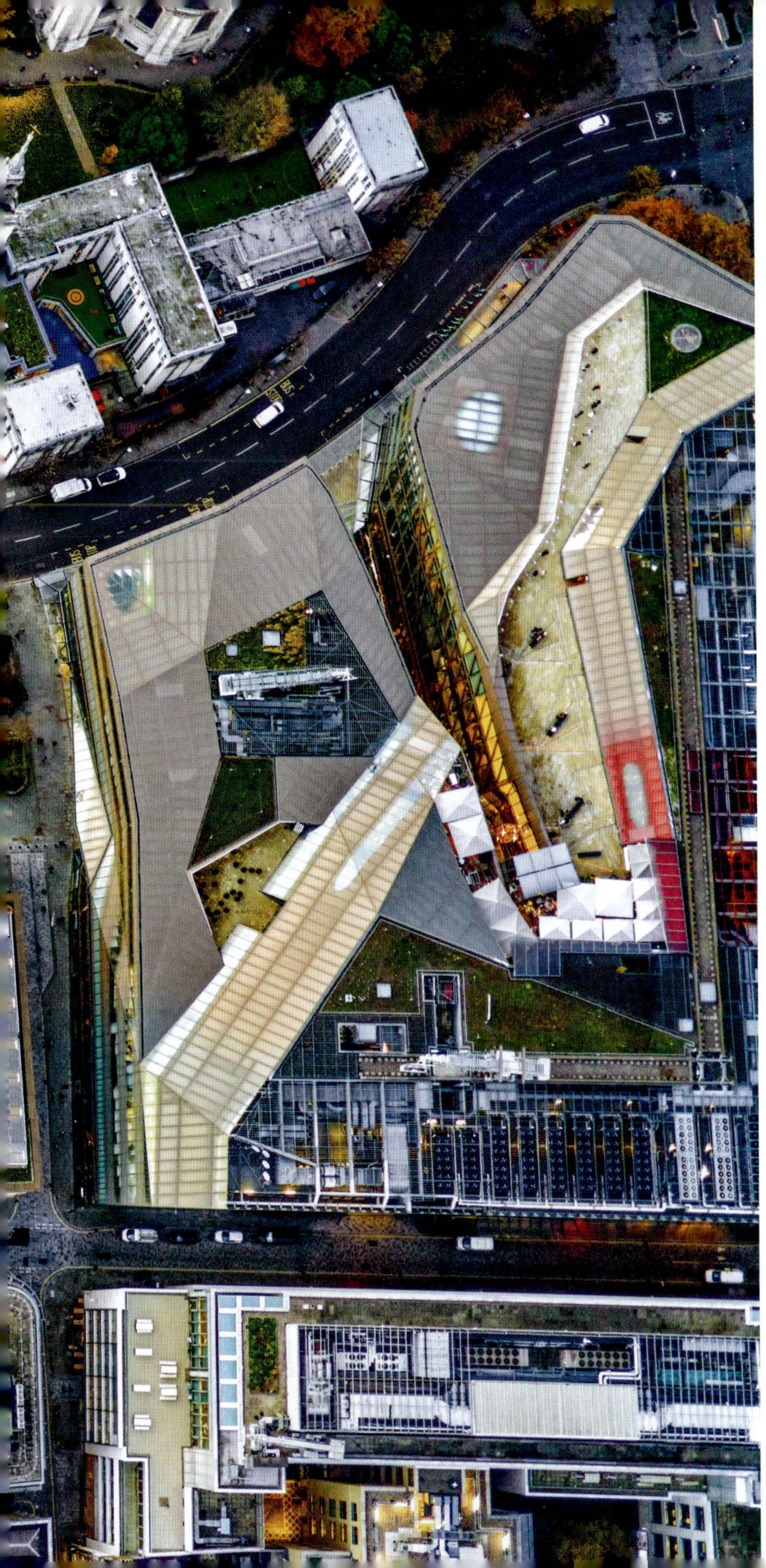

Looking down on the City of London, with the Reflection Garden and Festival Gardens of St. Paul's Cathedral churchyard at top, Bracken House (home of the *Financial Times* newspaper) at left, and the huge office and shopping complex One New Change at right

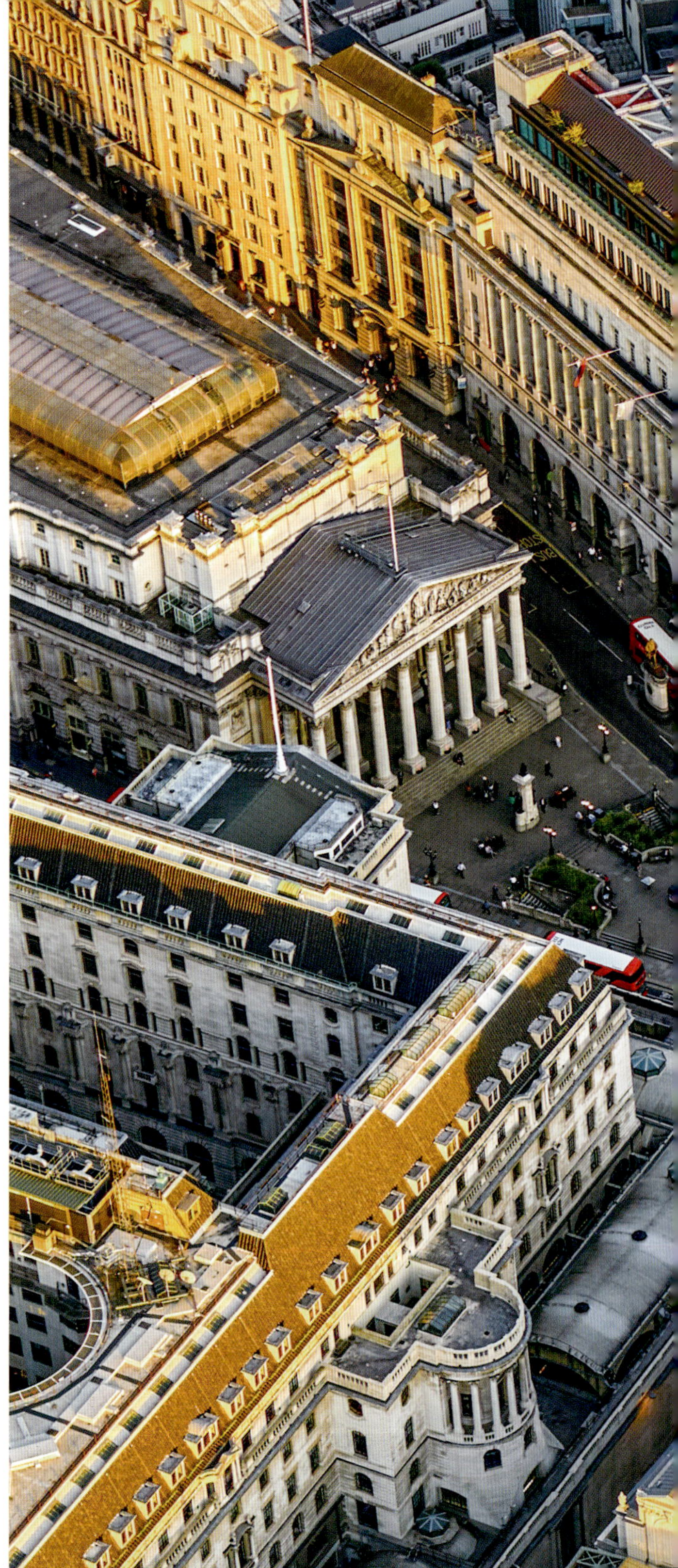

The dome-topped Argyll office building, which sits at an ancient crossing of the old city where Cornhill, Poultry, Threadneedle, Lombard, and King William Streets meet, with the Royal Exchange at left and St. Mary Woolnoth church at right

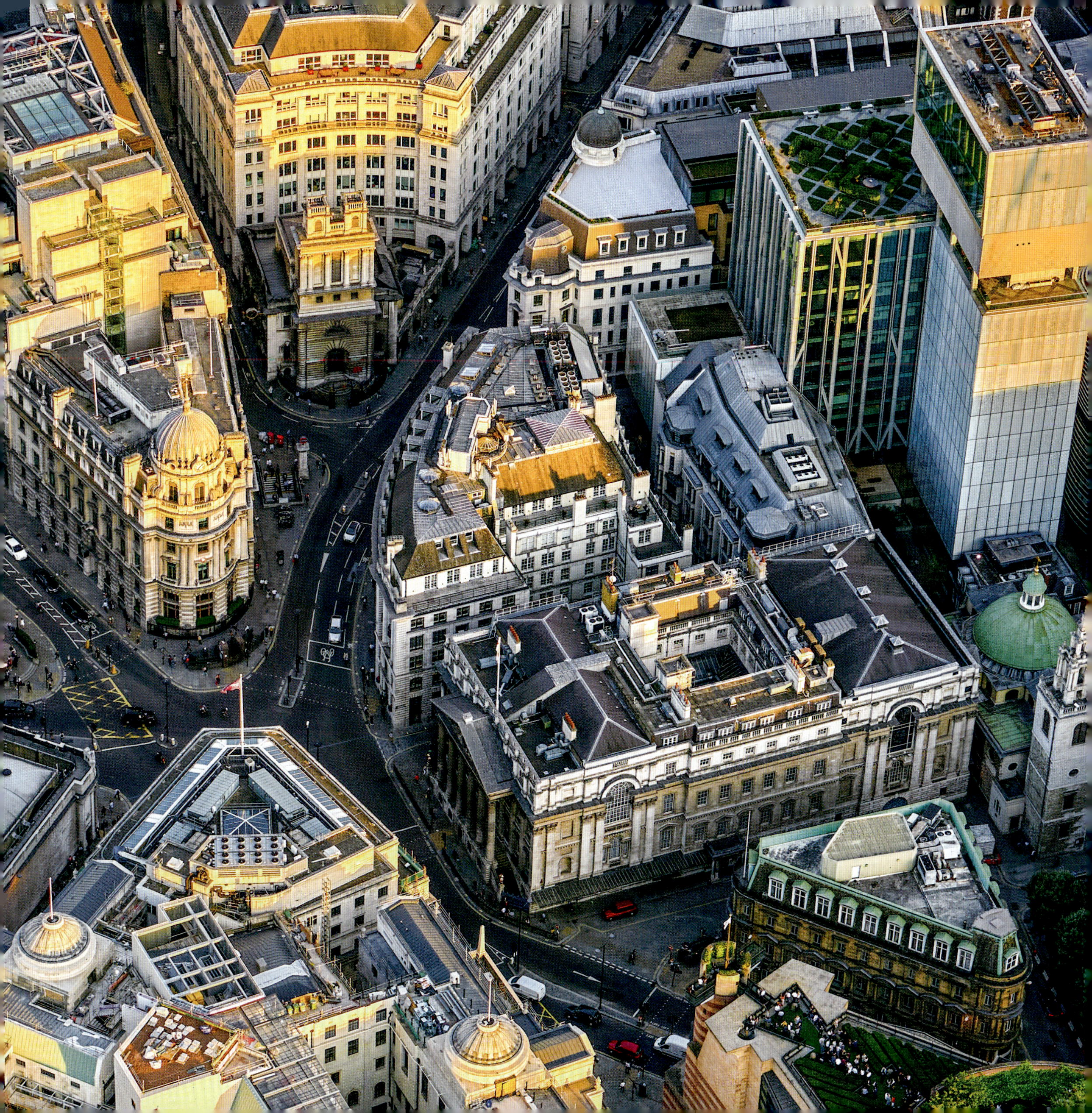

Opposite: The classical facade of the Royal Exchange in the heart of the City of London

Page 78: Bank of England

Page 79: The three-chevron shape of NatWest Tower, the fifth-tallest tower in the city

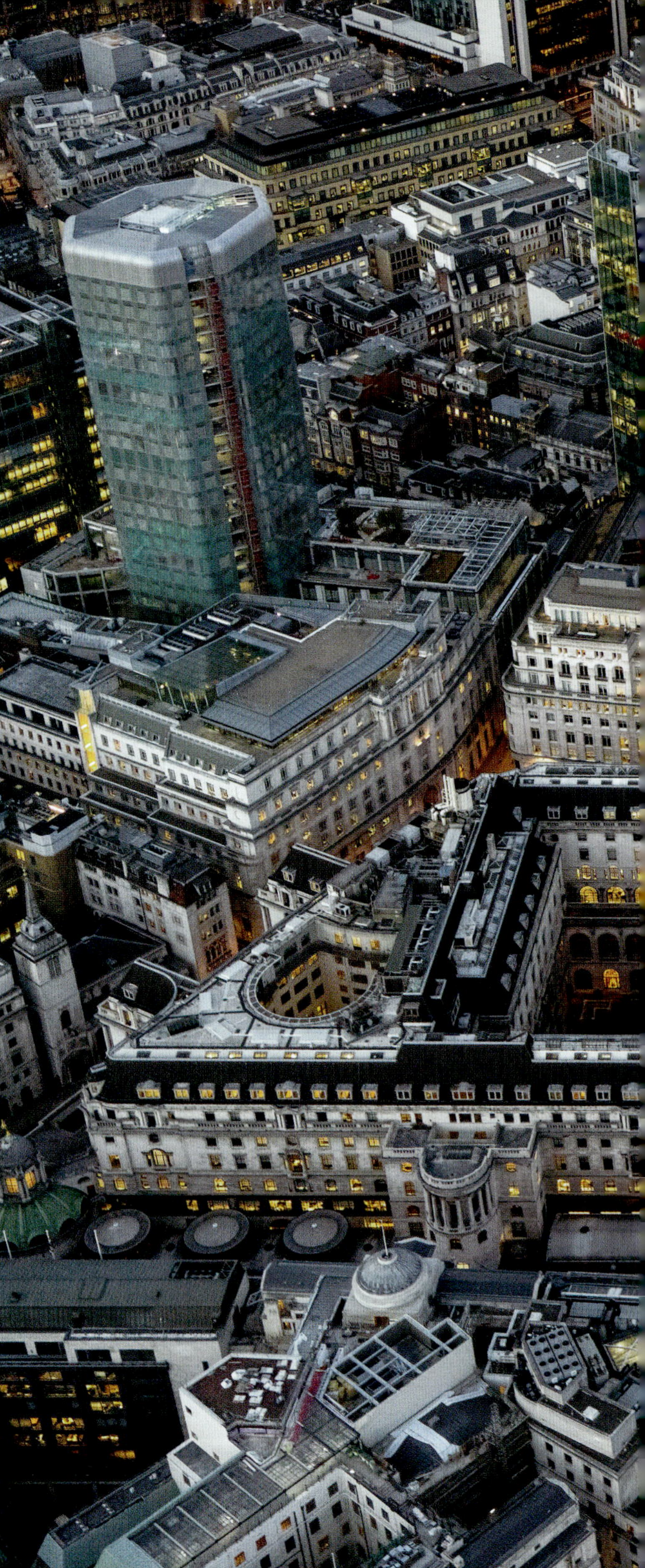

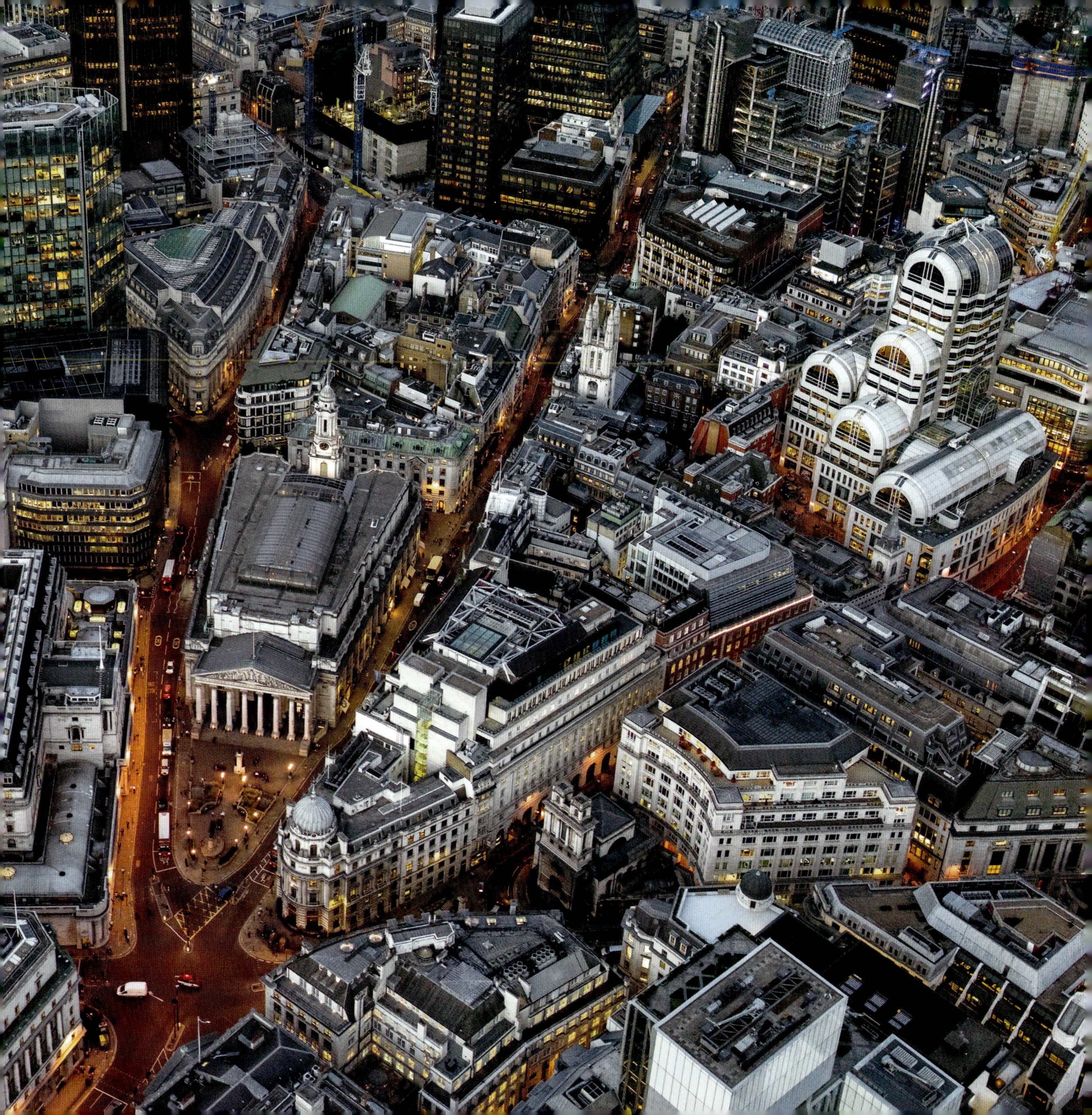

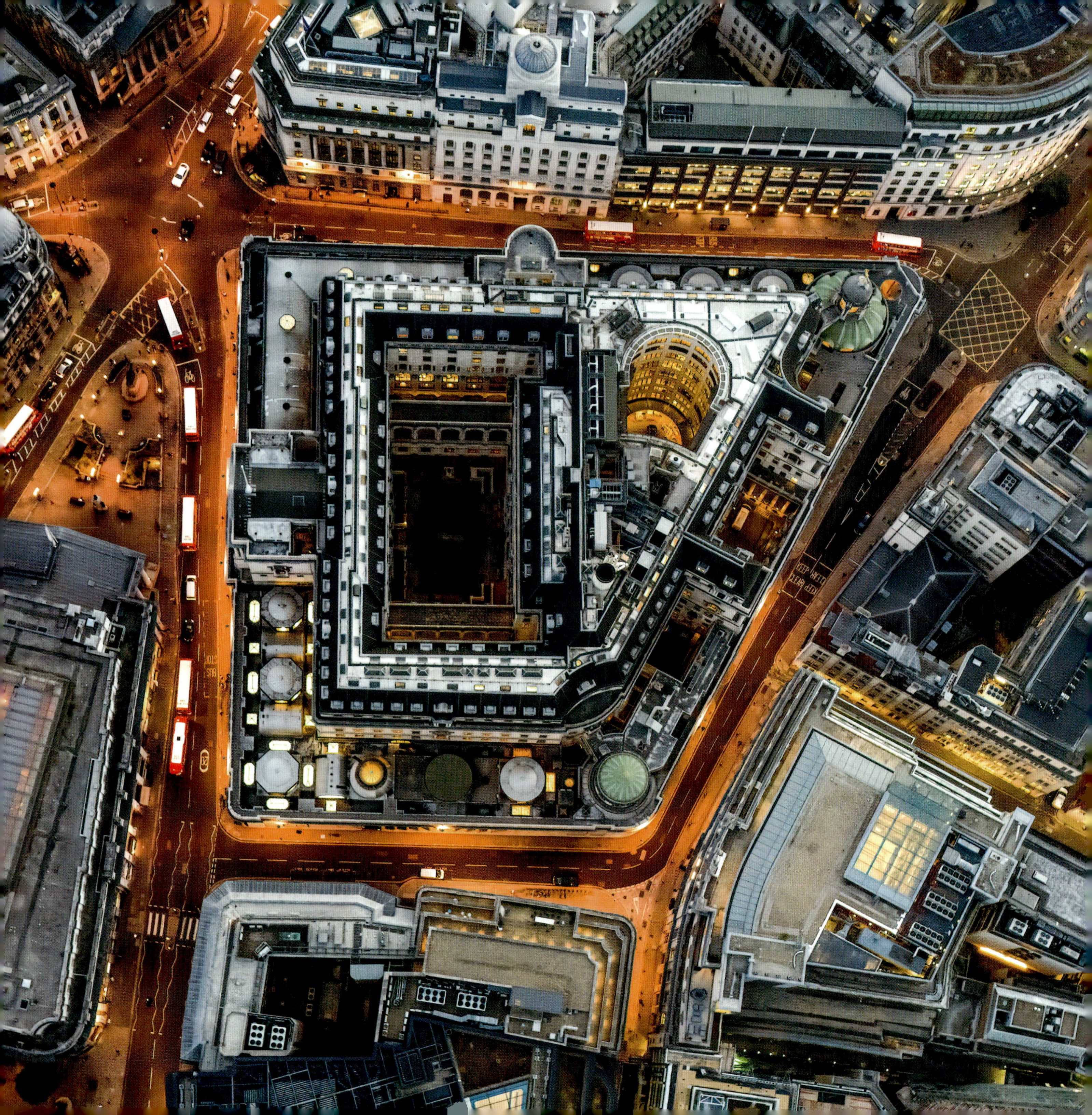

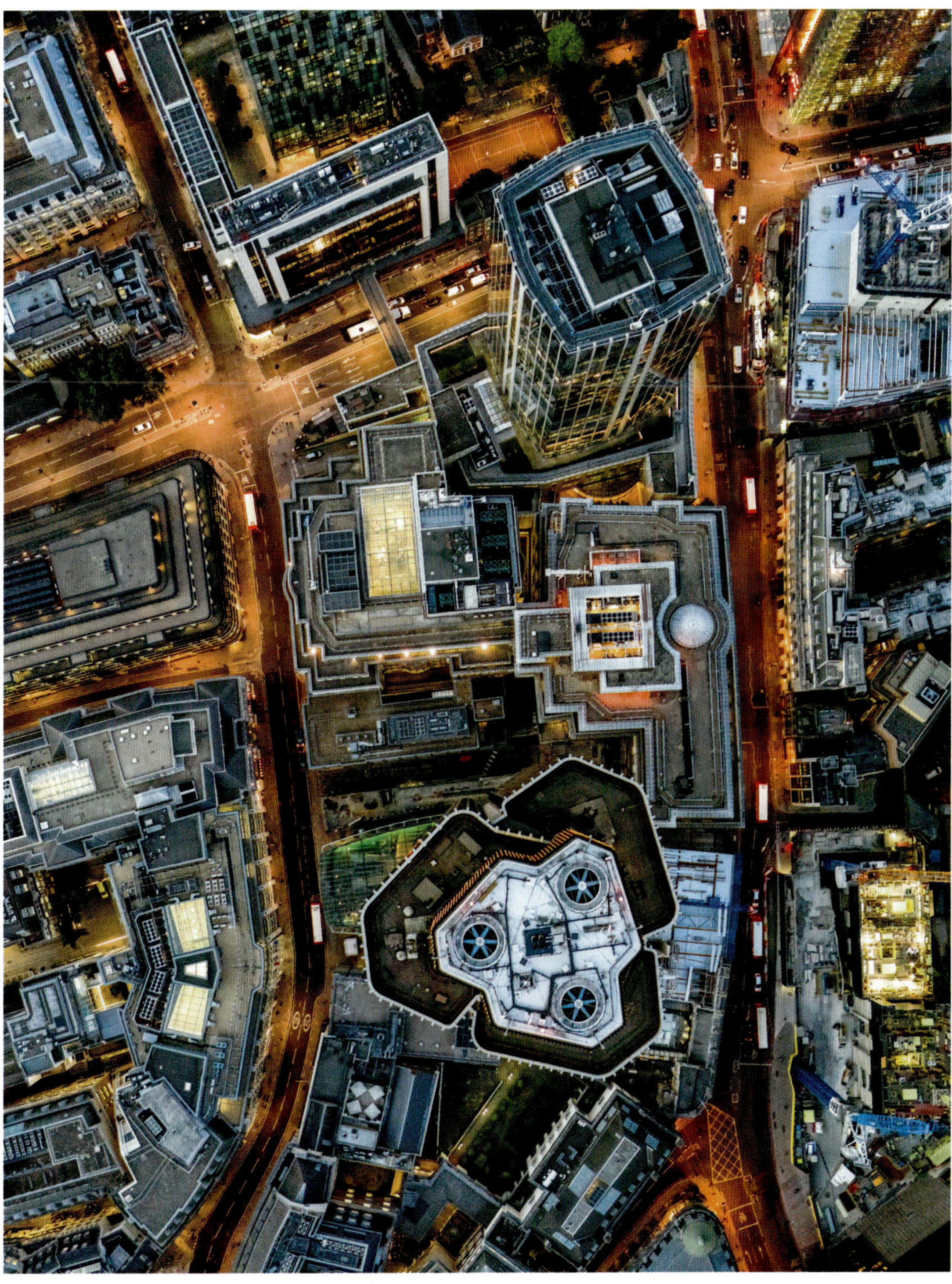

Guildhall, the center of services for the City of London and the oldest surviving secular medieval building in the city; its Great Hall dates from 1411

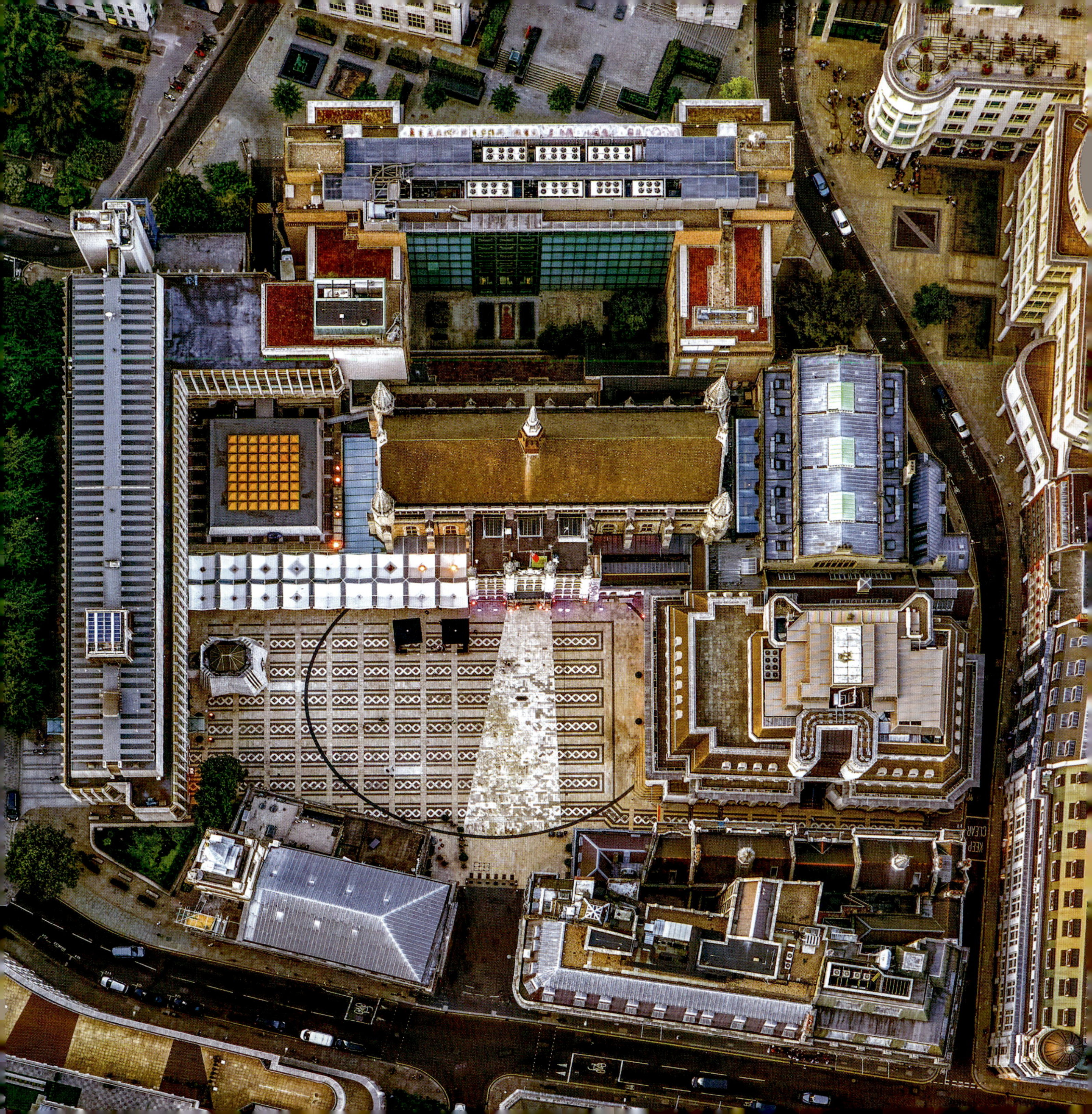
KEEP CLEAR

Smithfield Market, with the pocket park Smithfield Rotunda Garden, established in 1872, at lower left

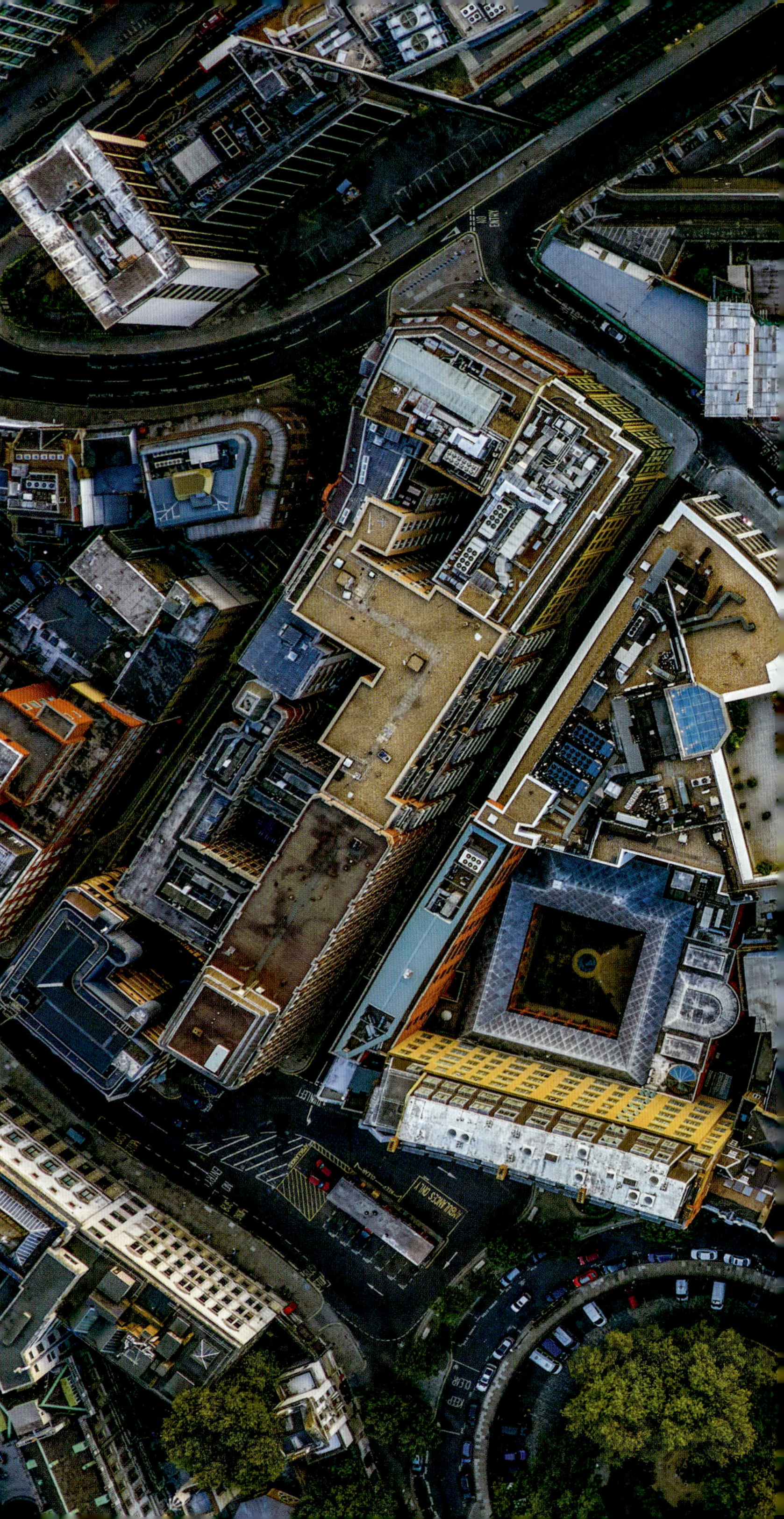

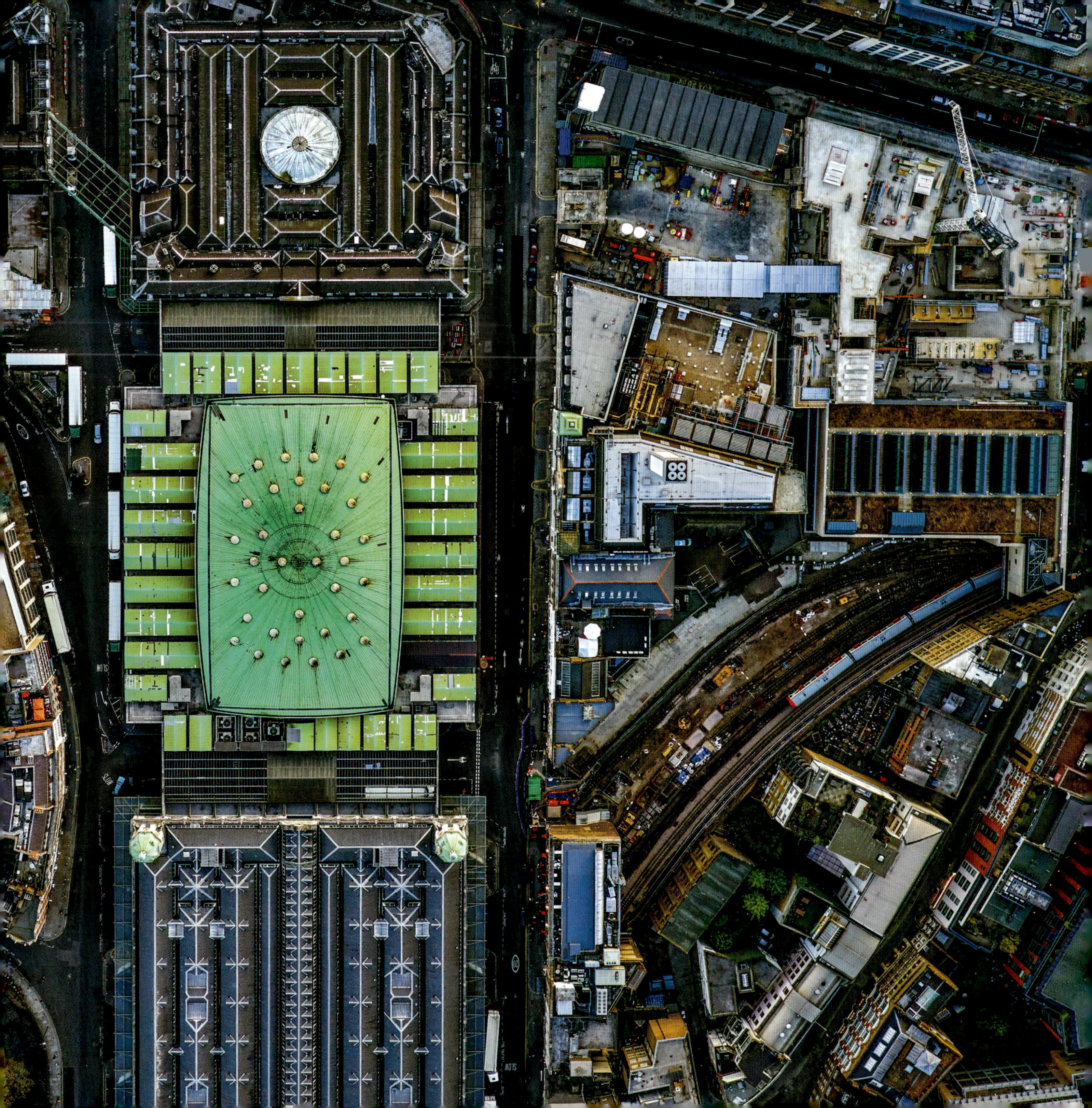

The semicircular shape of the residential Frobisher Crescent faces the Barbican Art Gallery and various art and music schools, cinemas, and other buildings of the Barbican Centre

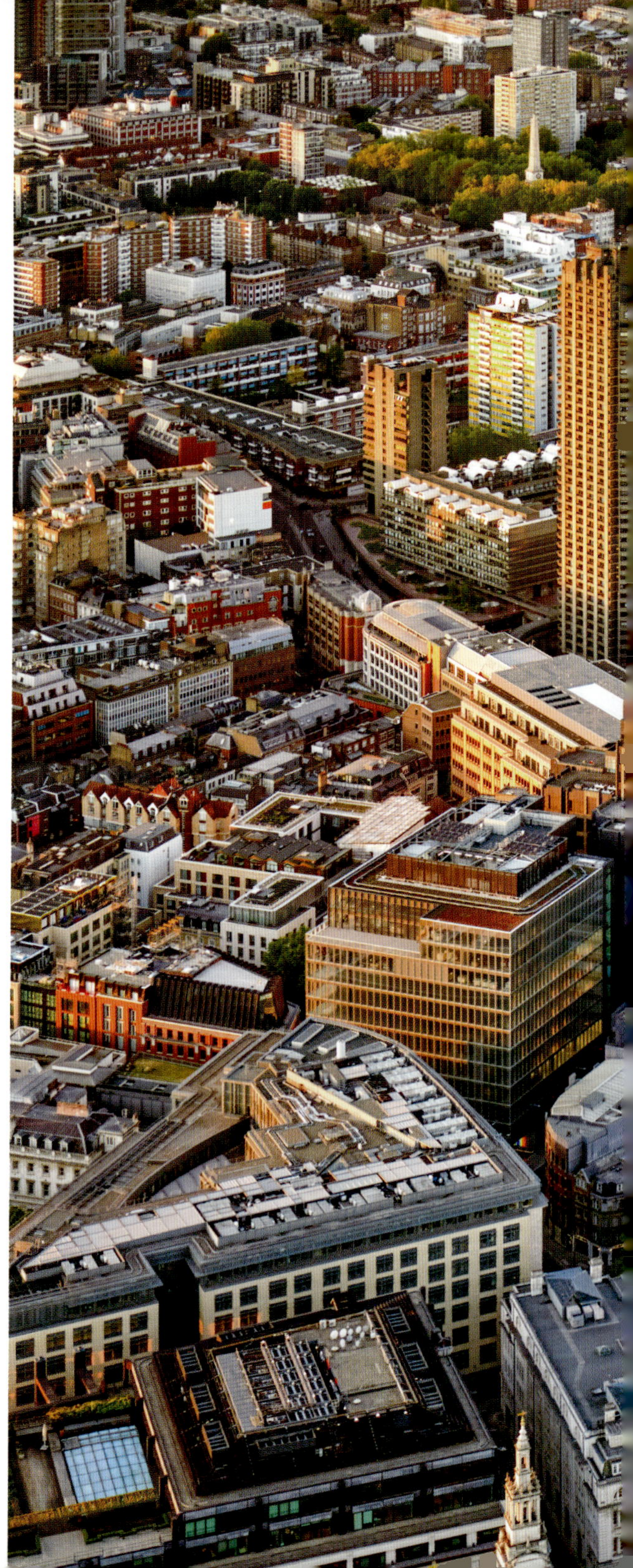

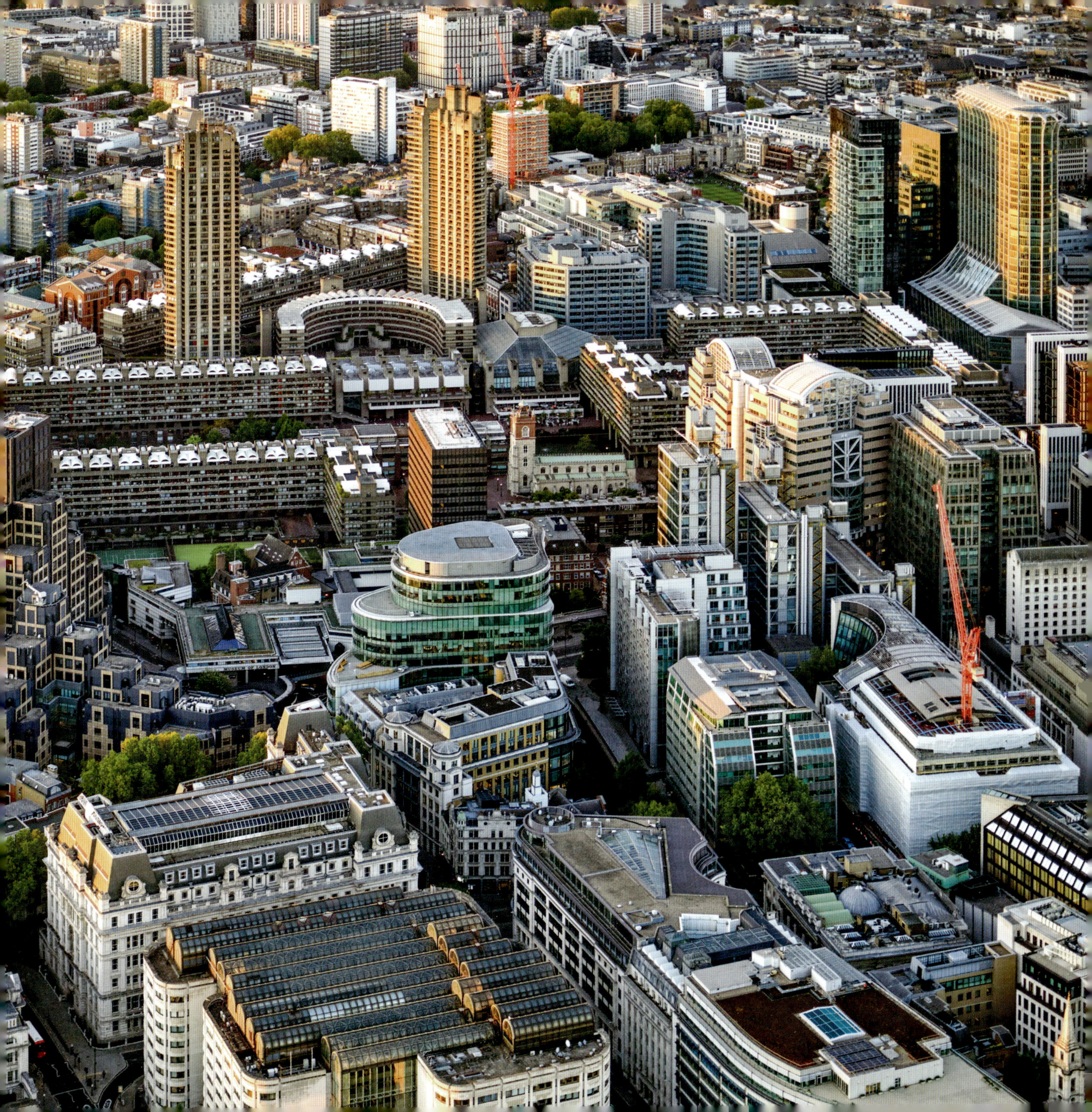

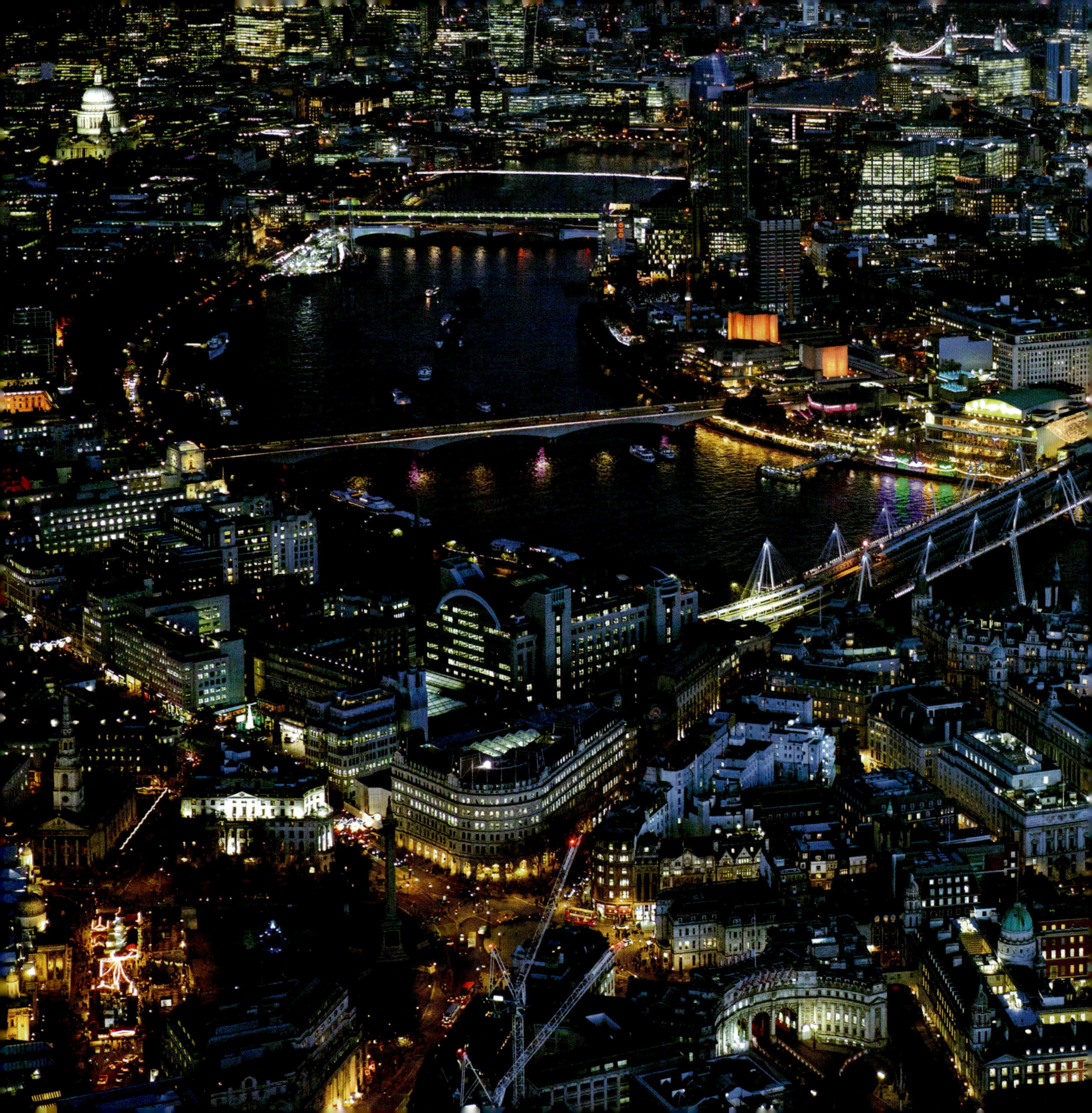

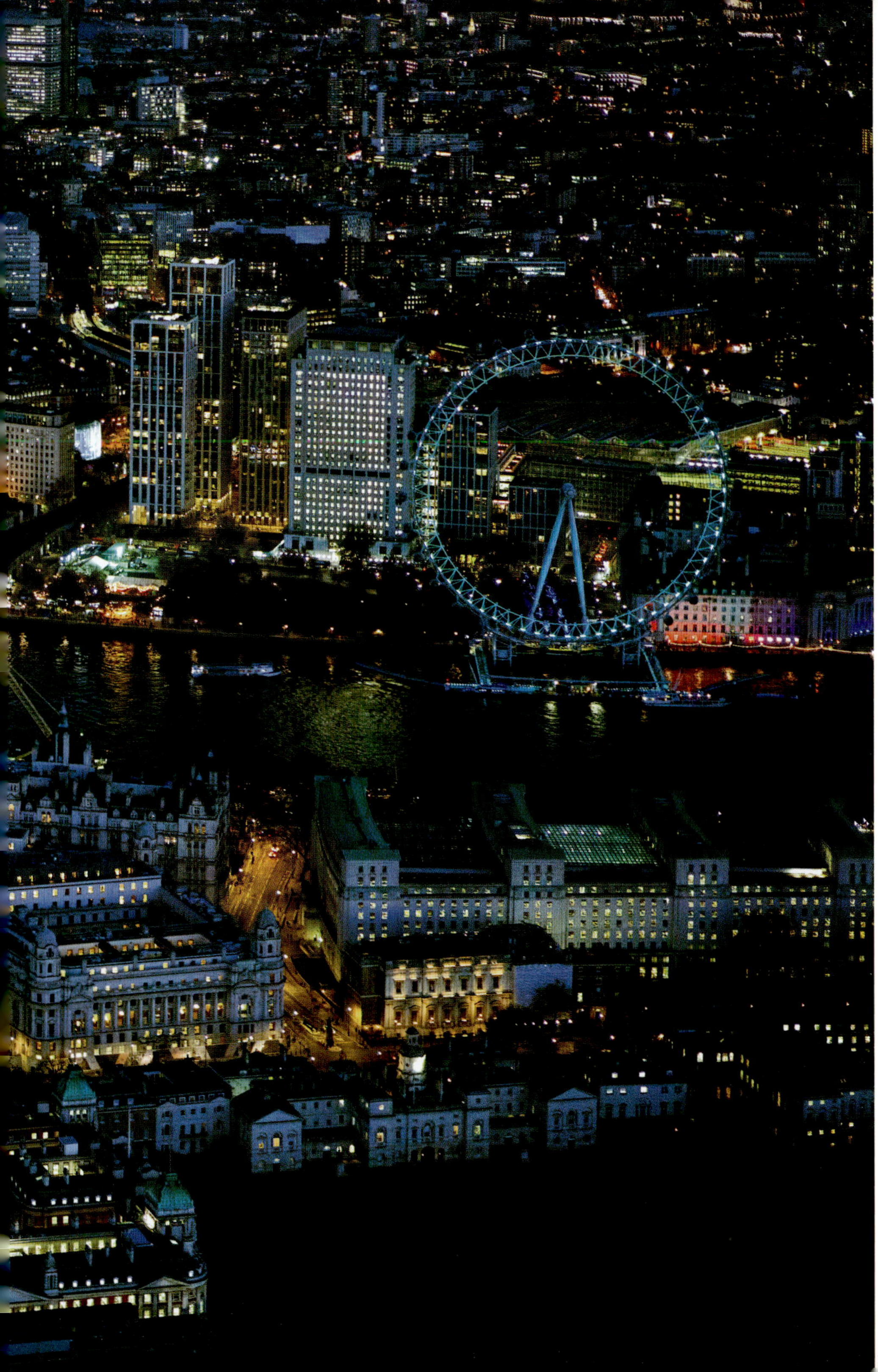

River Thames, with the Charing Cross railway bridge at center

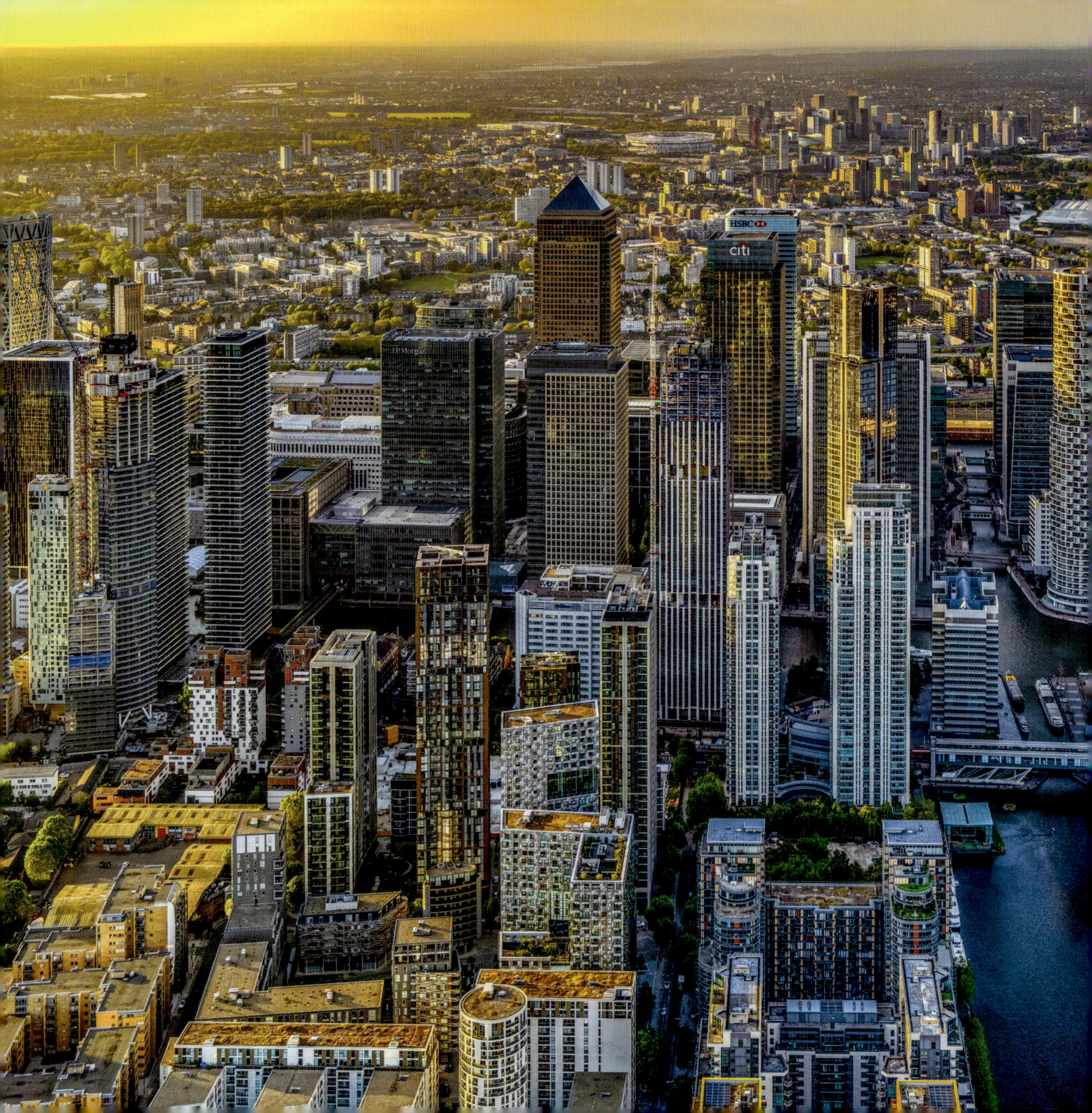
HSBC
citi

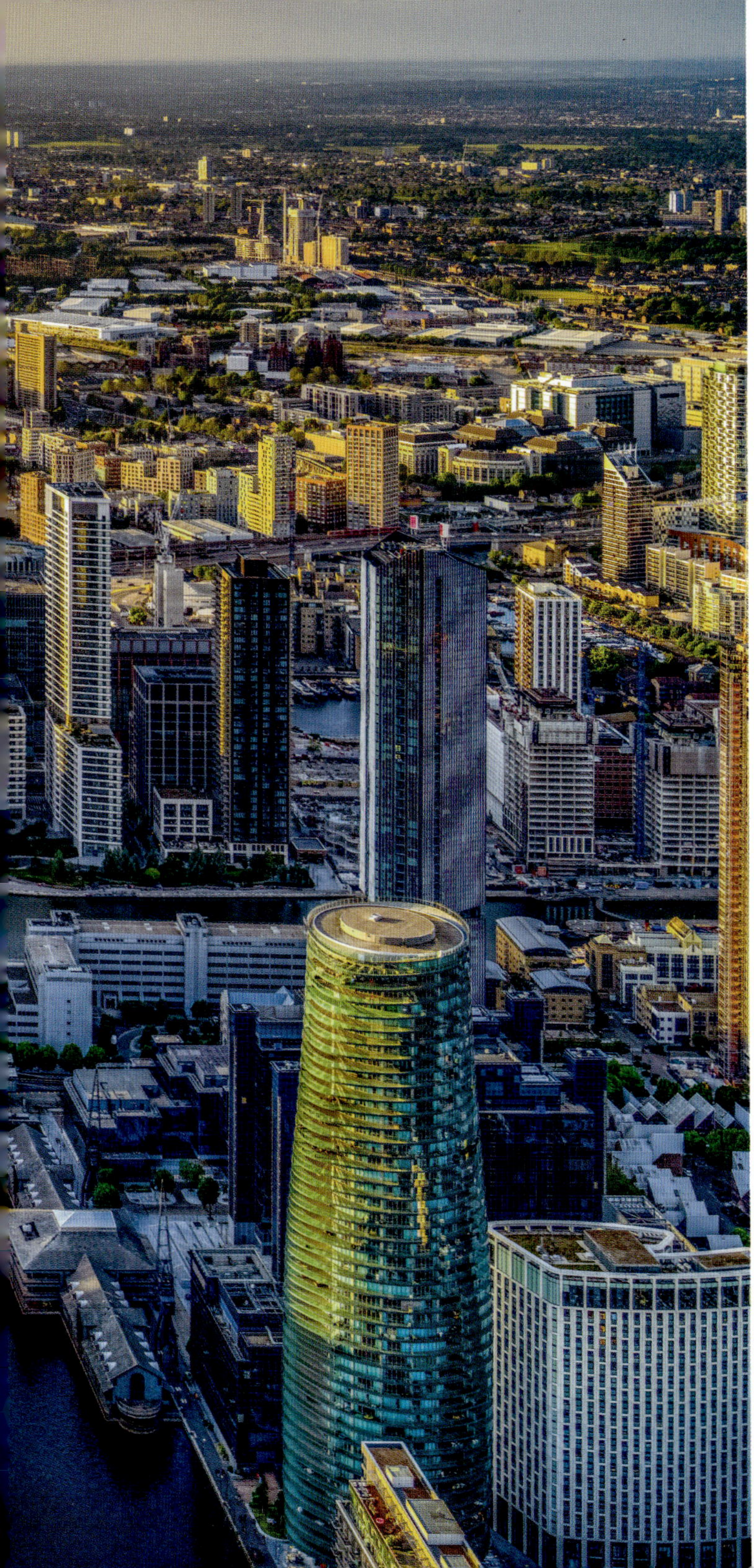

Canary Wharf, a large residential and office area reclaimed from former docklands, just east of the City of London

90 Canary Wharf at night

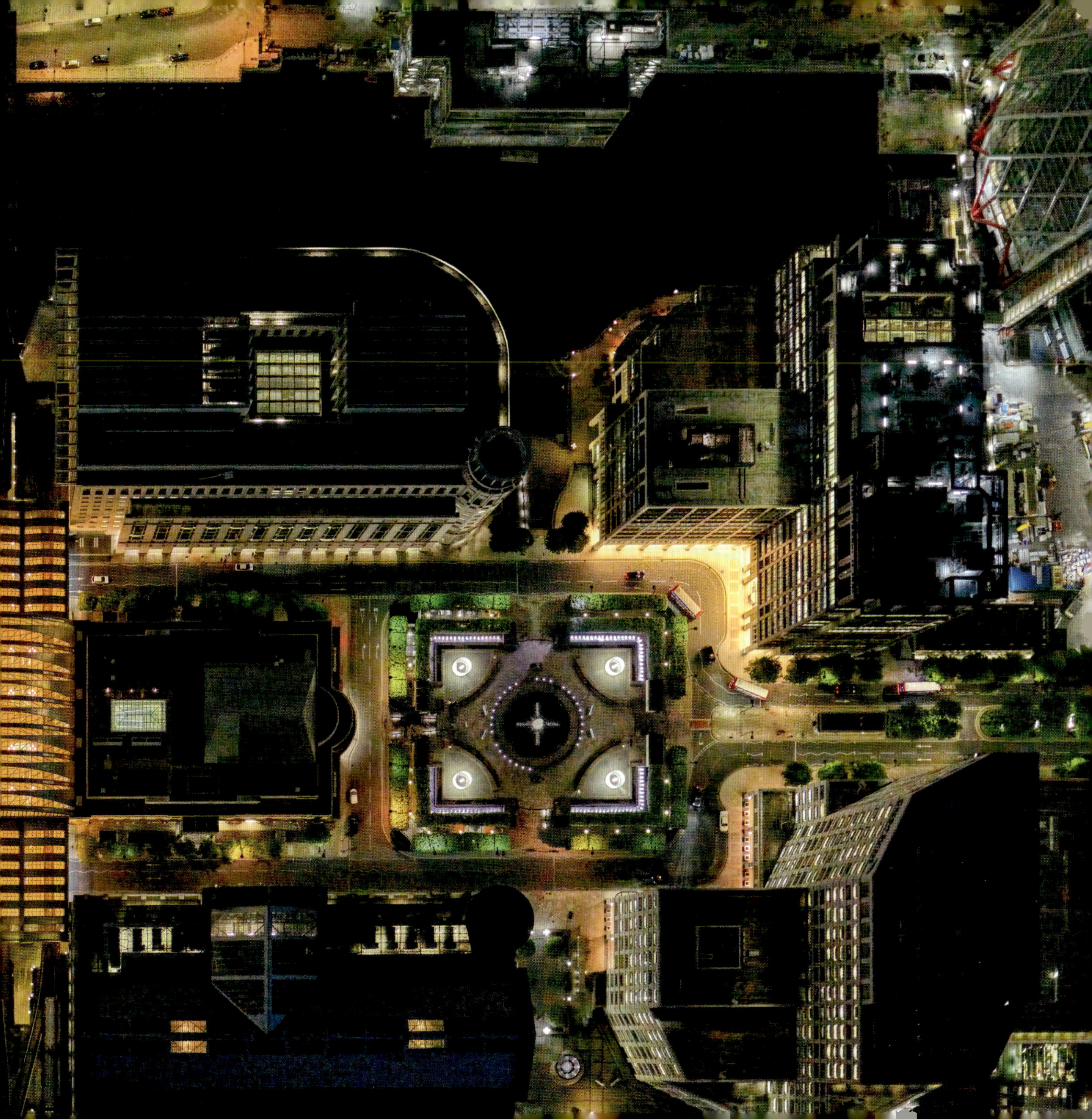

92 PICCADILLY PLUS

PICCADILLY PLUS

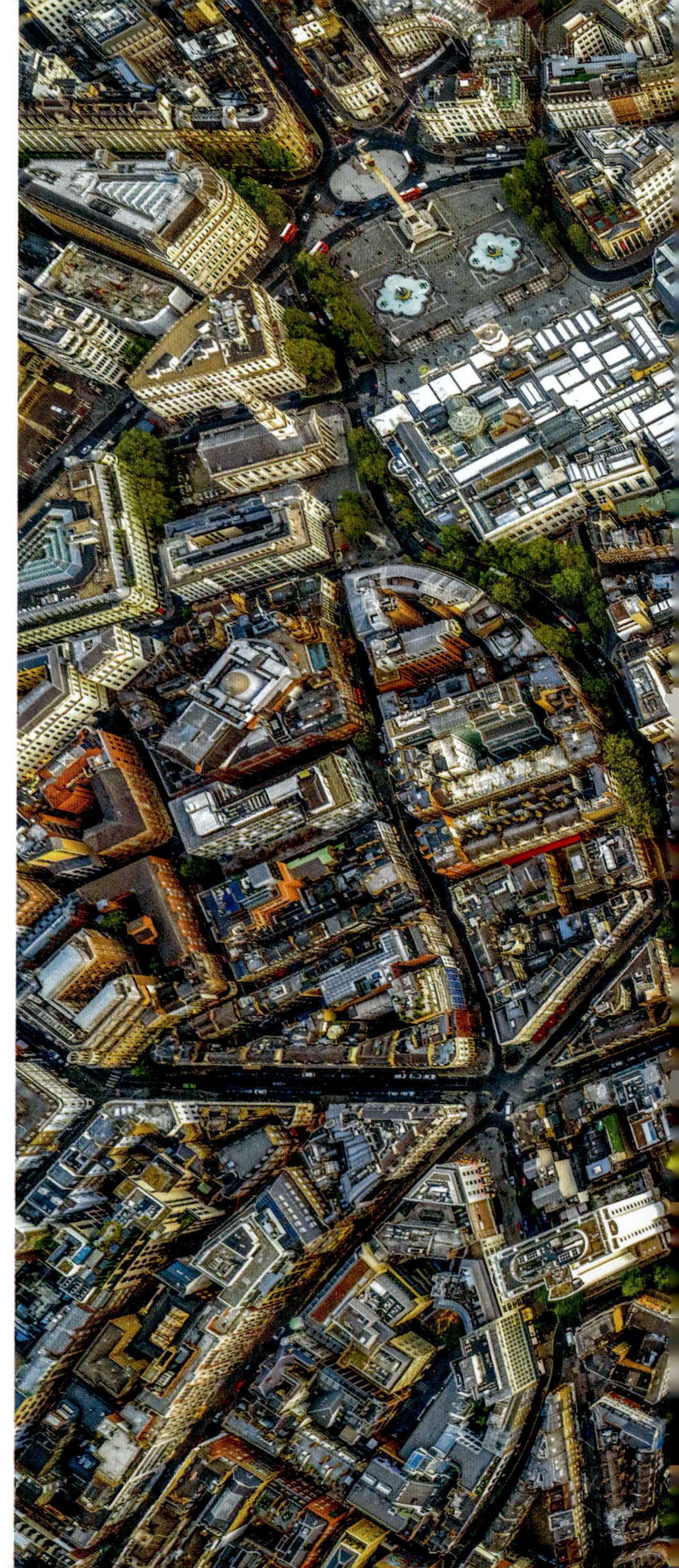

The Piccadilly area, including Soho, with Trafalgar Square at upper left, Leicester Square below it to the right, and Piccadilly Circus and Regent Street at upper right

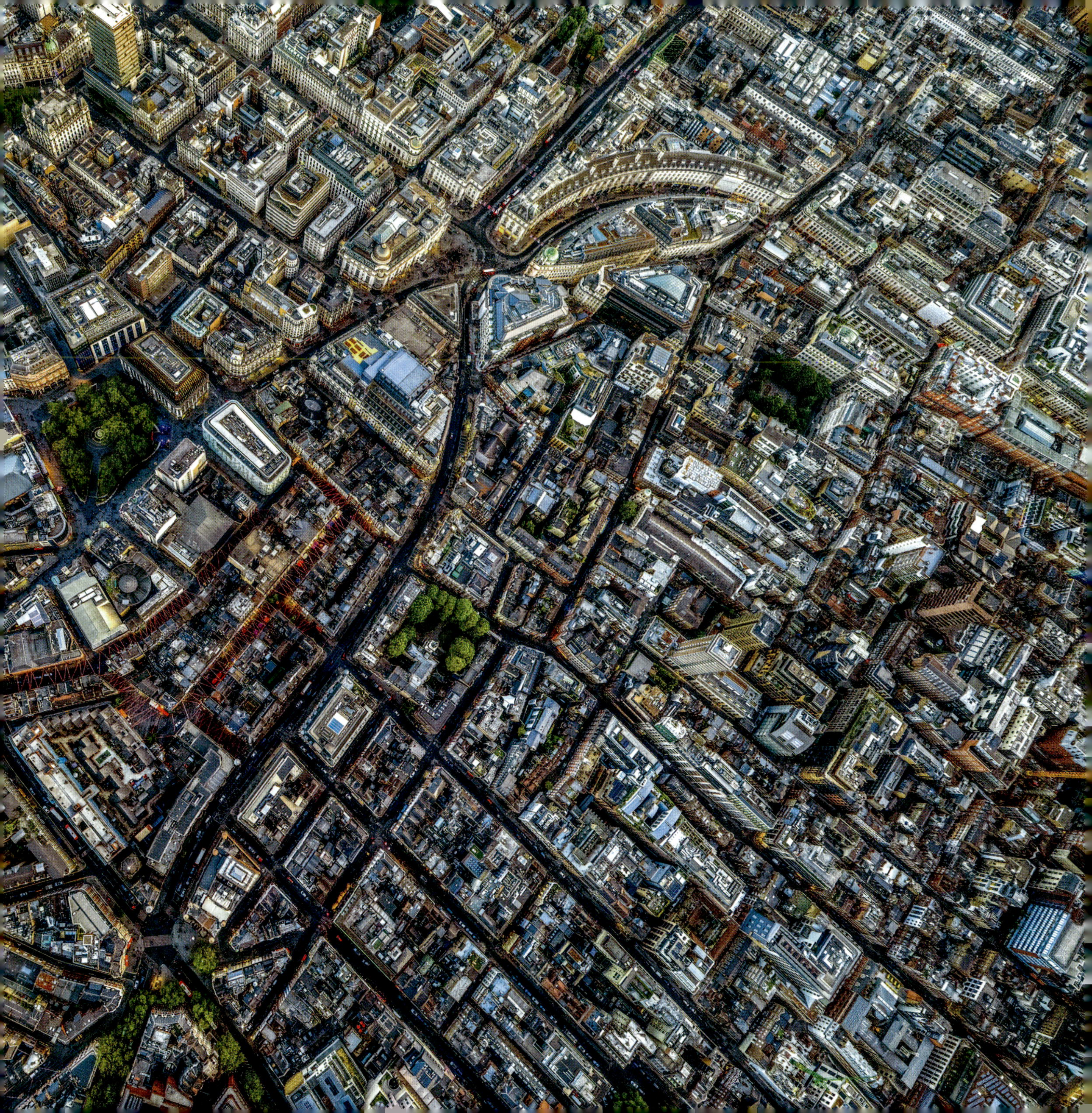

Opposite: Looking west on the Strand, with St. Mary le Strand at center, below the curvaceous, tree-lined Aldwych

Pages 96–97: The Embankment, centered on Somerset House, with the Strand and Aldwych above

Page 98: Somerset House, with the plaza set up for ice-skating

Page 99: The Savoy Hotel at center

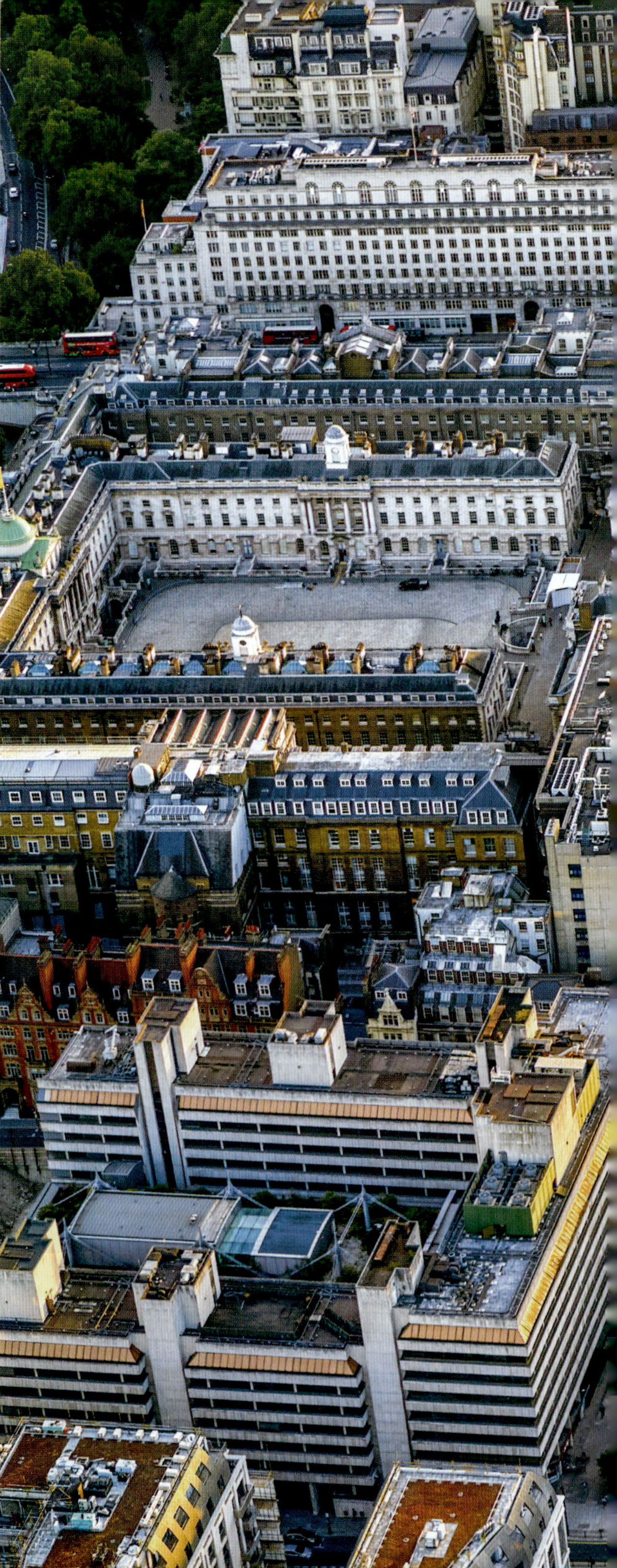

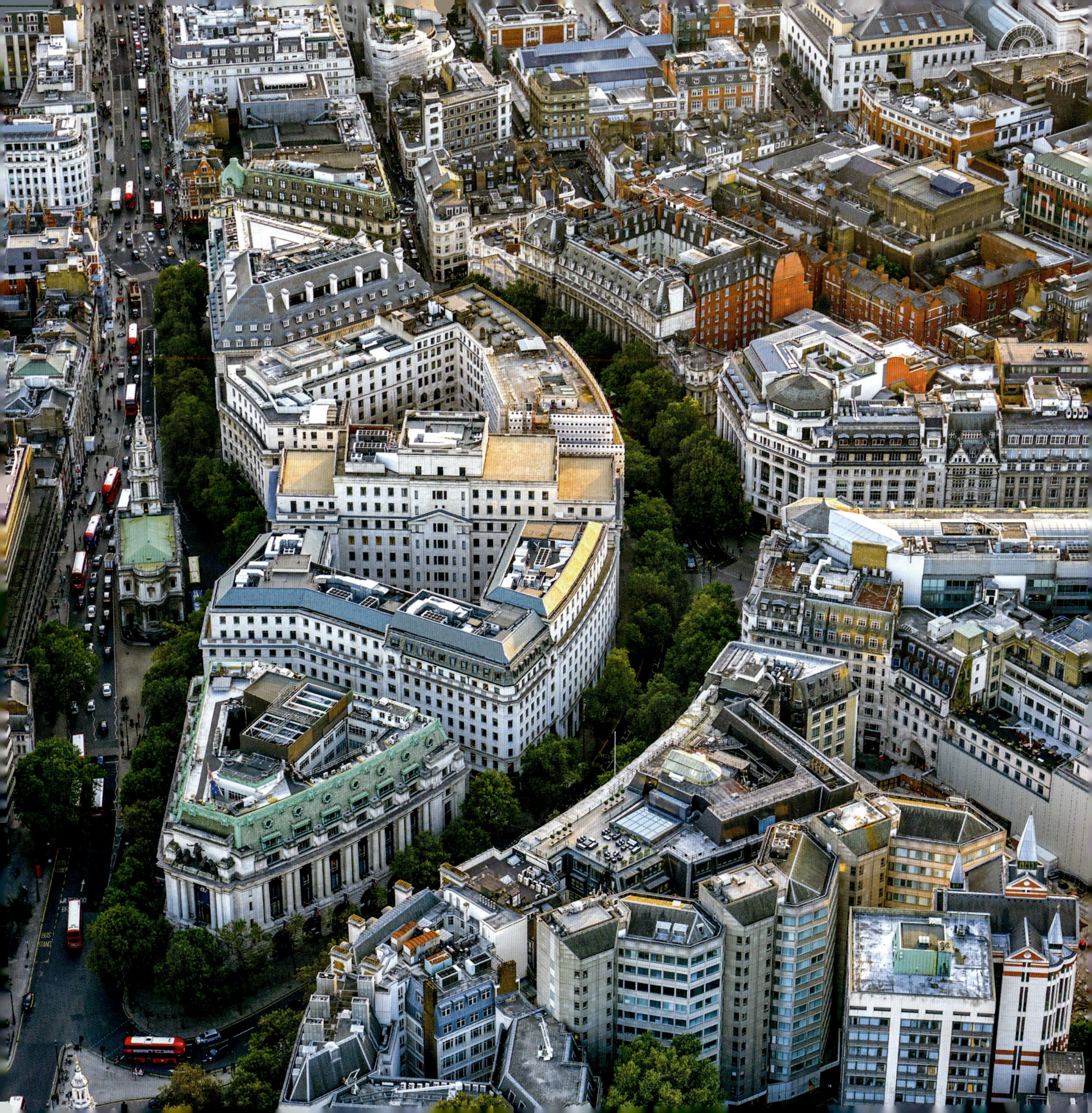

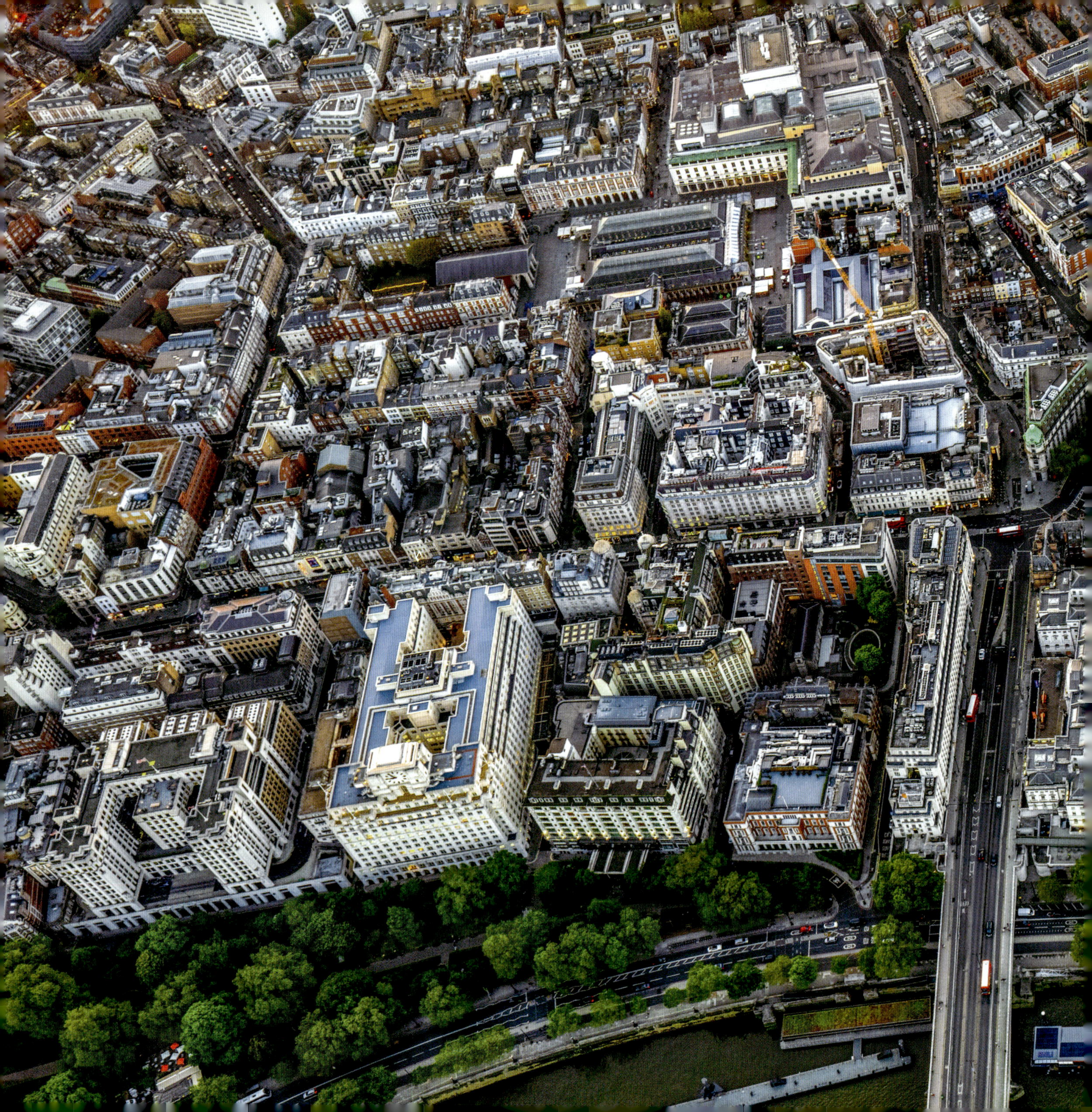

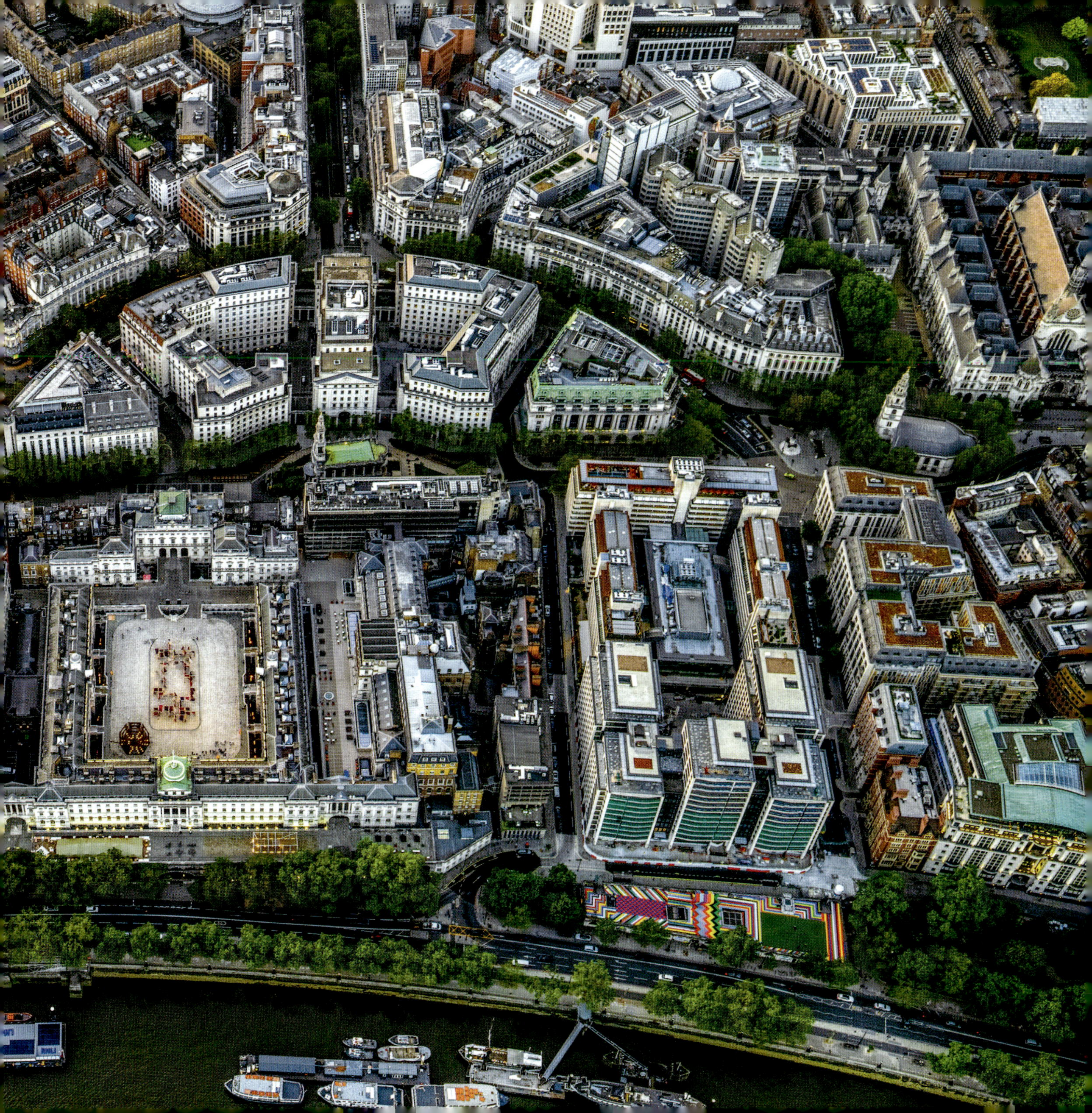

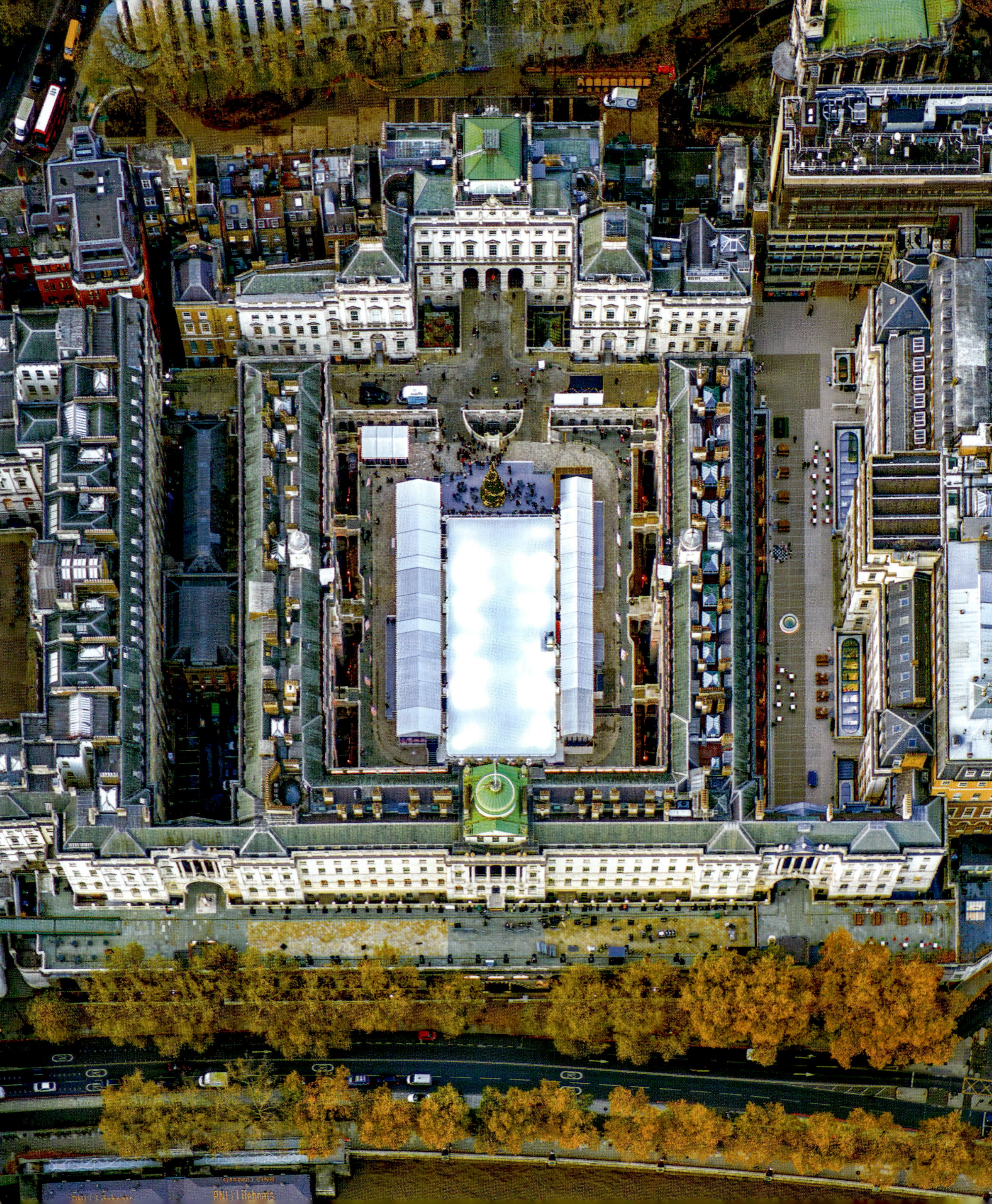

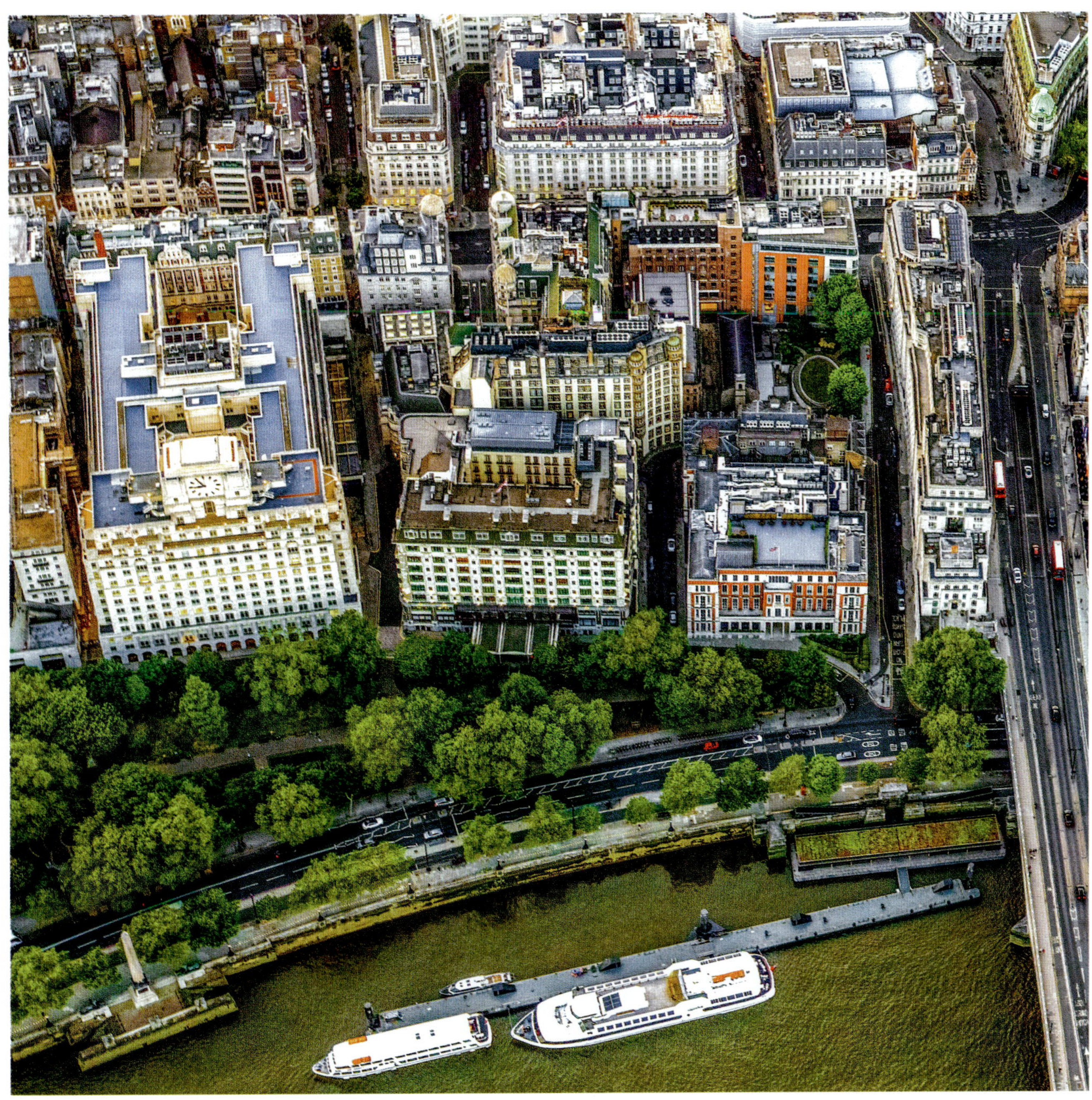

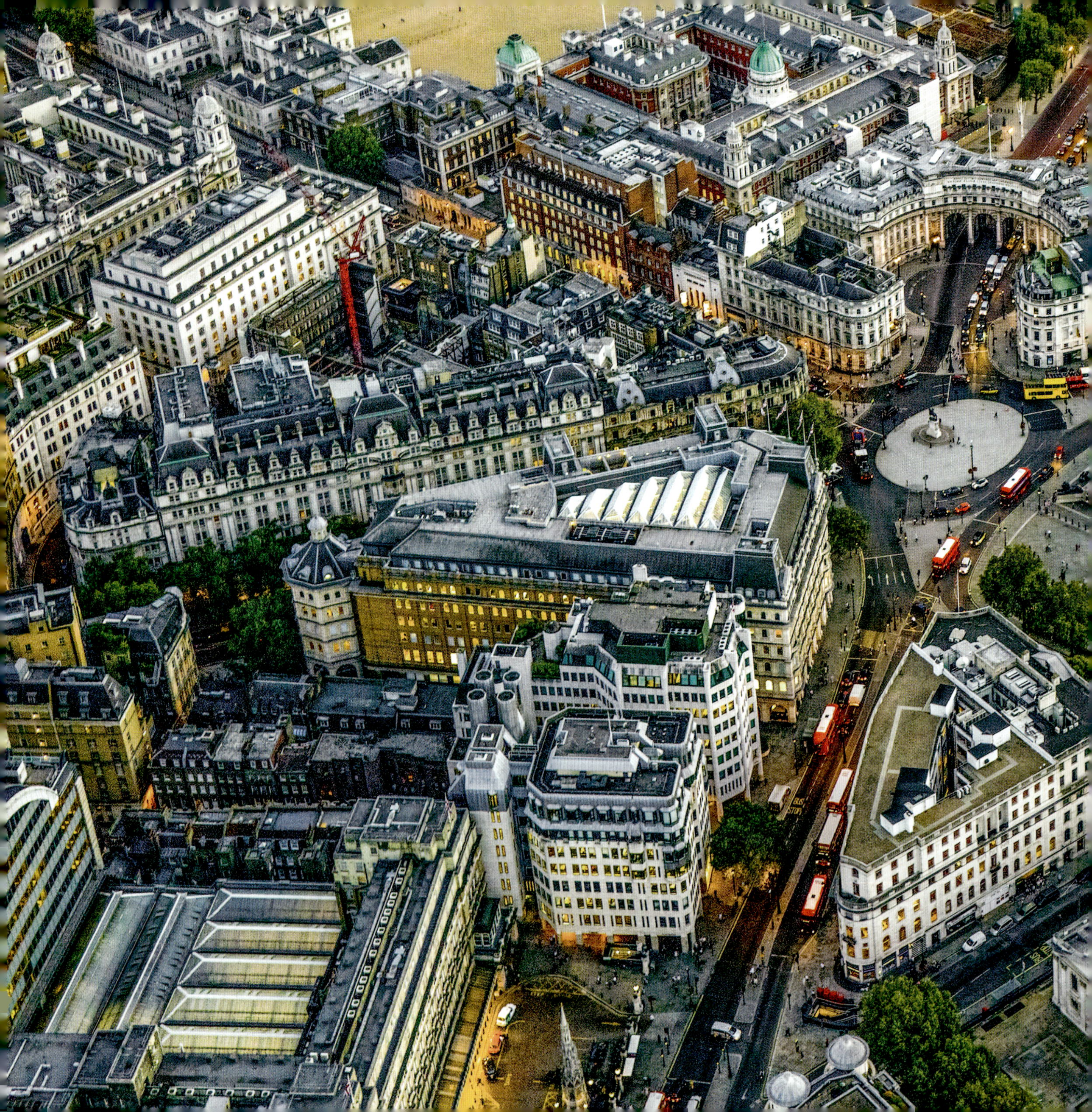

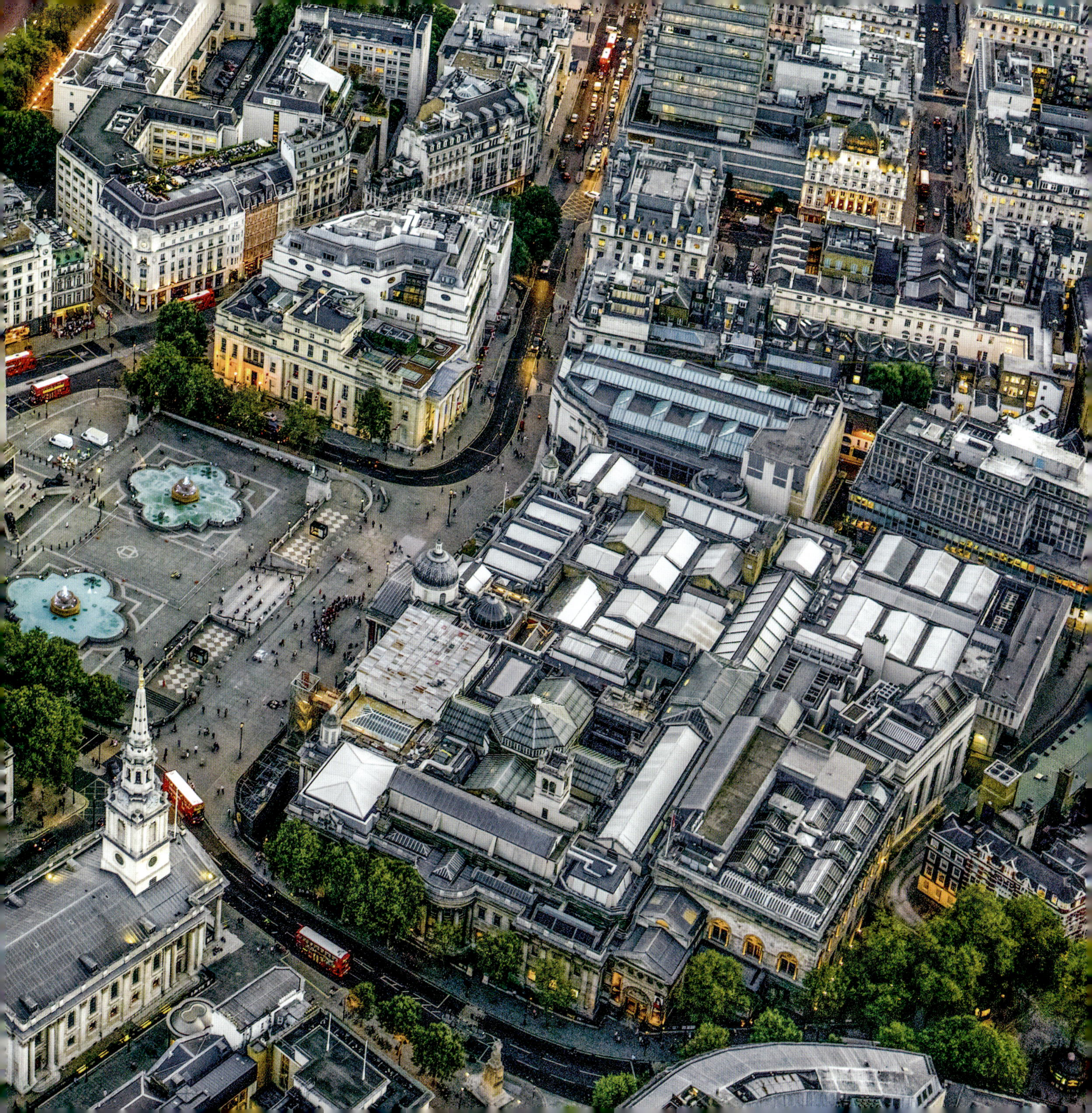

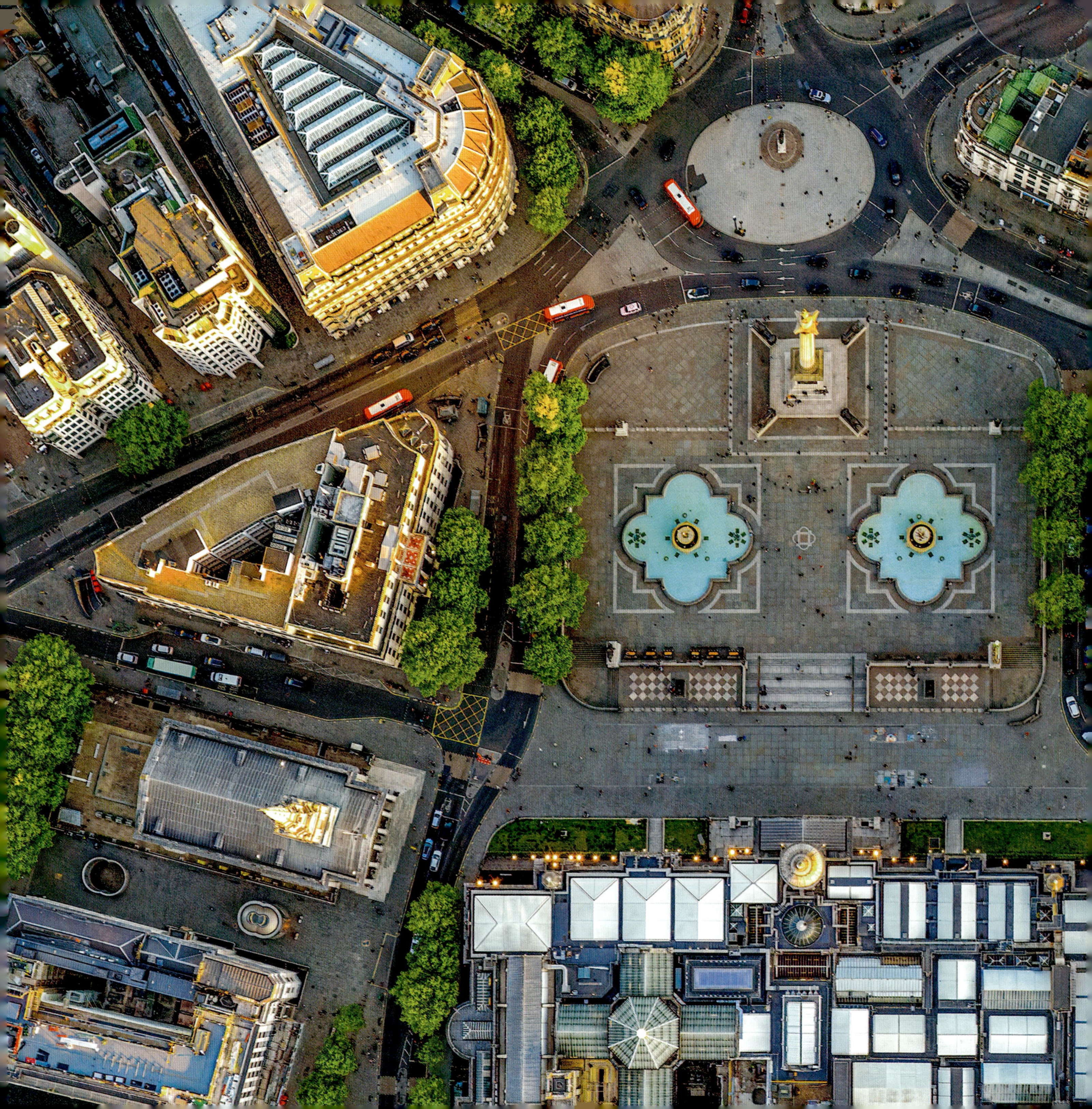

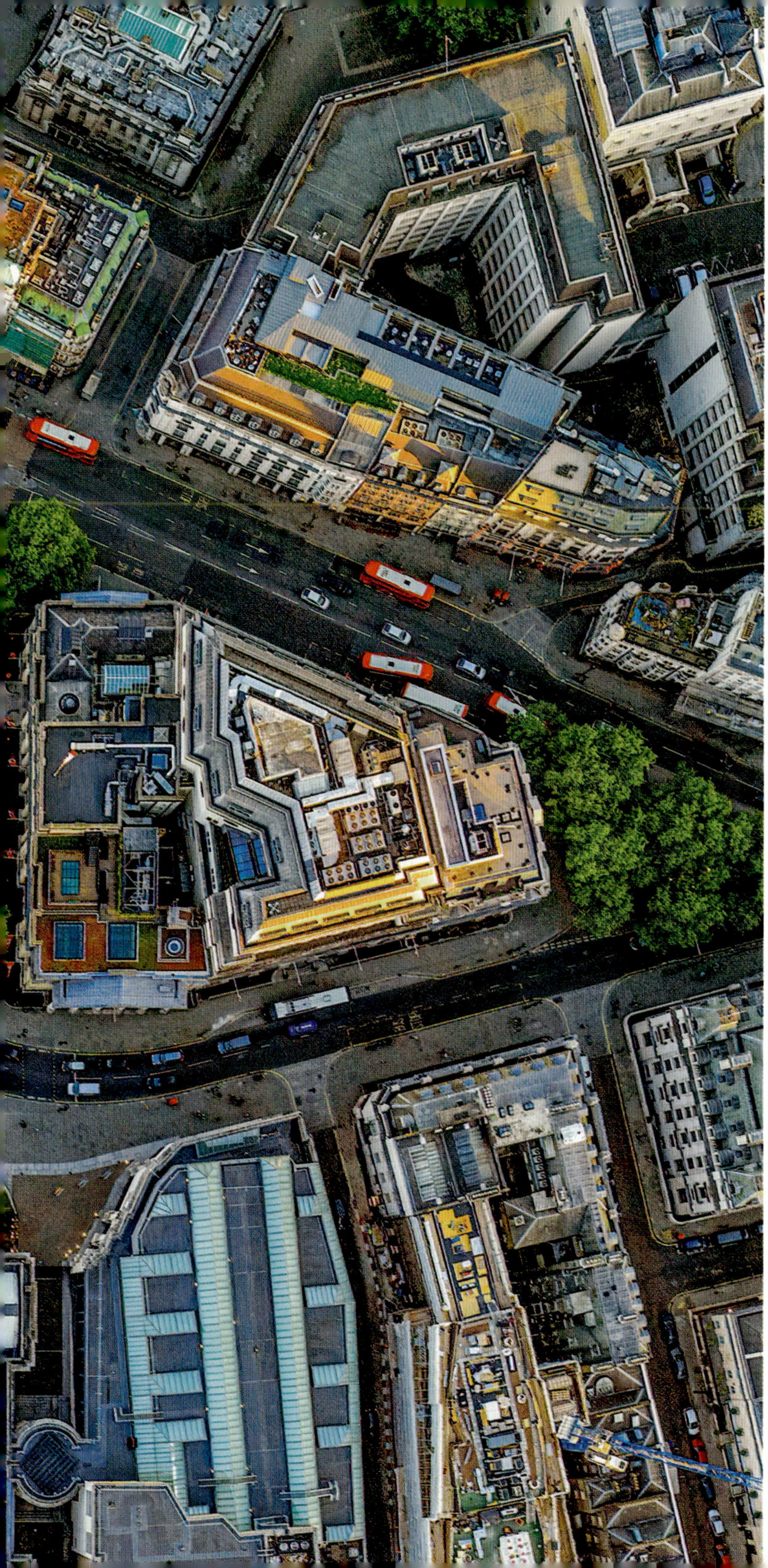

Pages 100–101: Trafalgar Square, with Admiralty Arch at top center, the National Gallery to the right, and St. Martin-in-the Fields at bottom center

Opposite: Looking down on Trafalgar Square from above the National Gallery

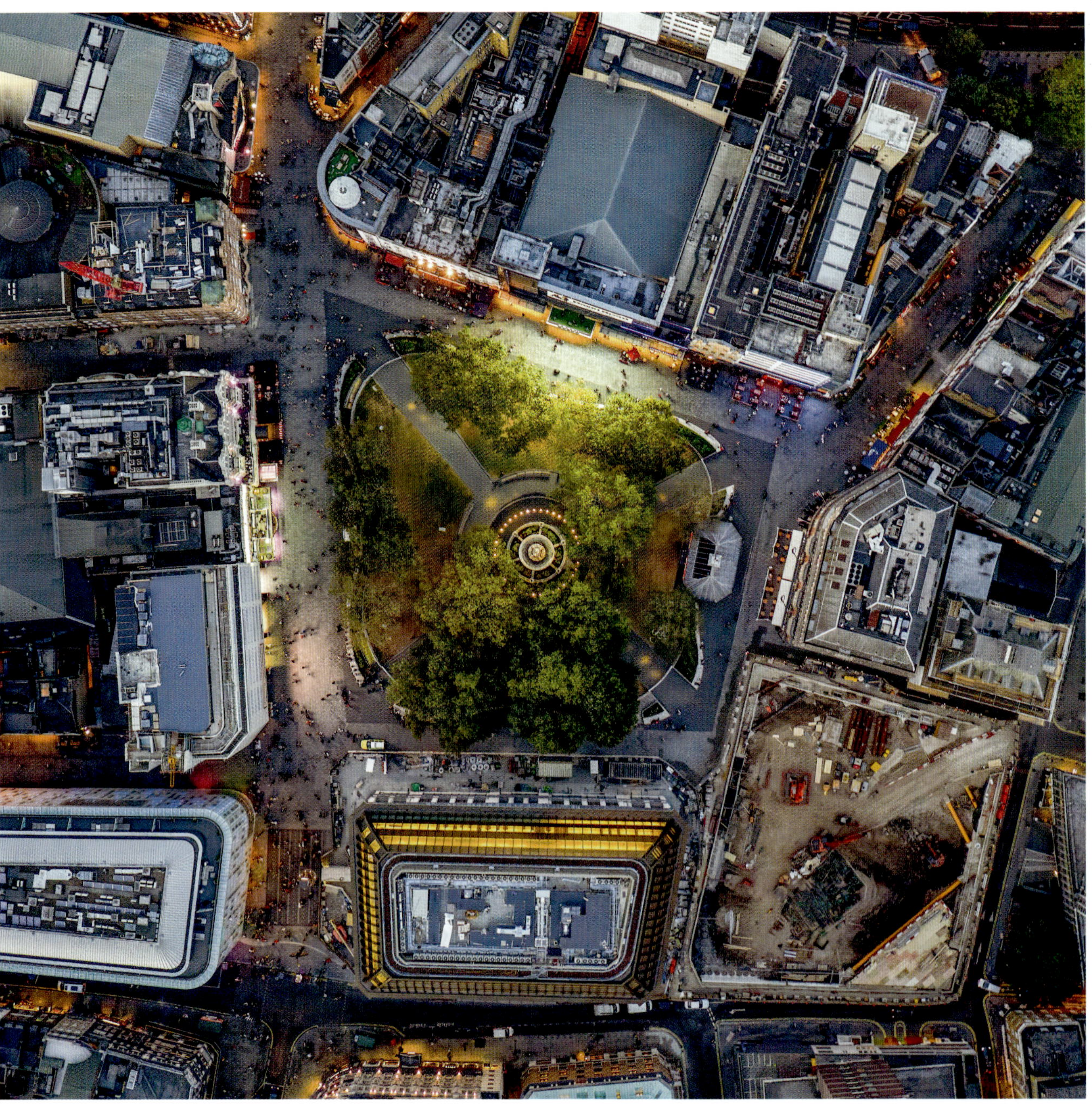

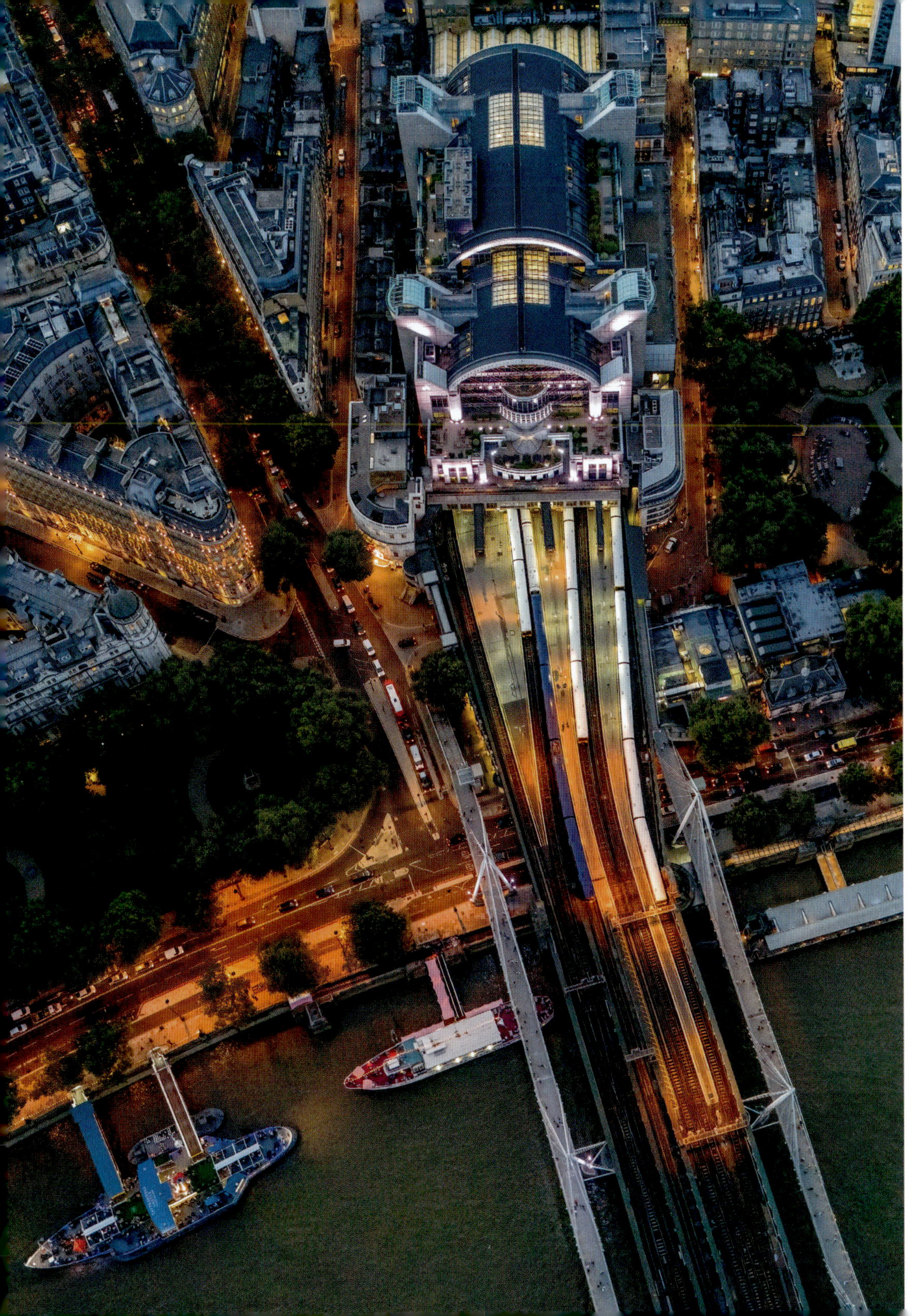

Opposite: Leicester Square

Left: Charing Cross railway station

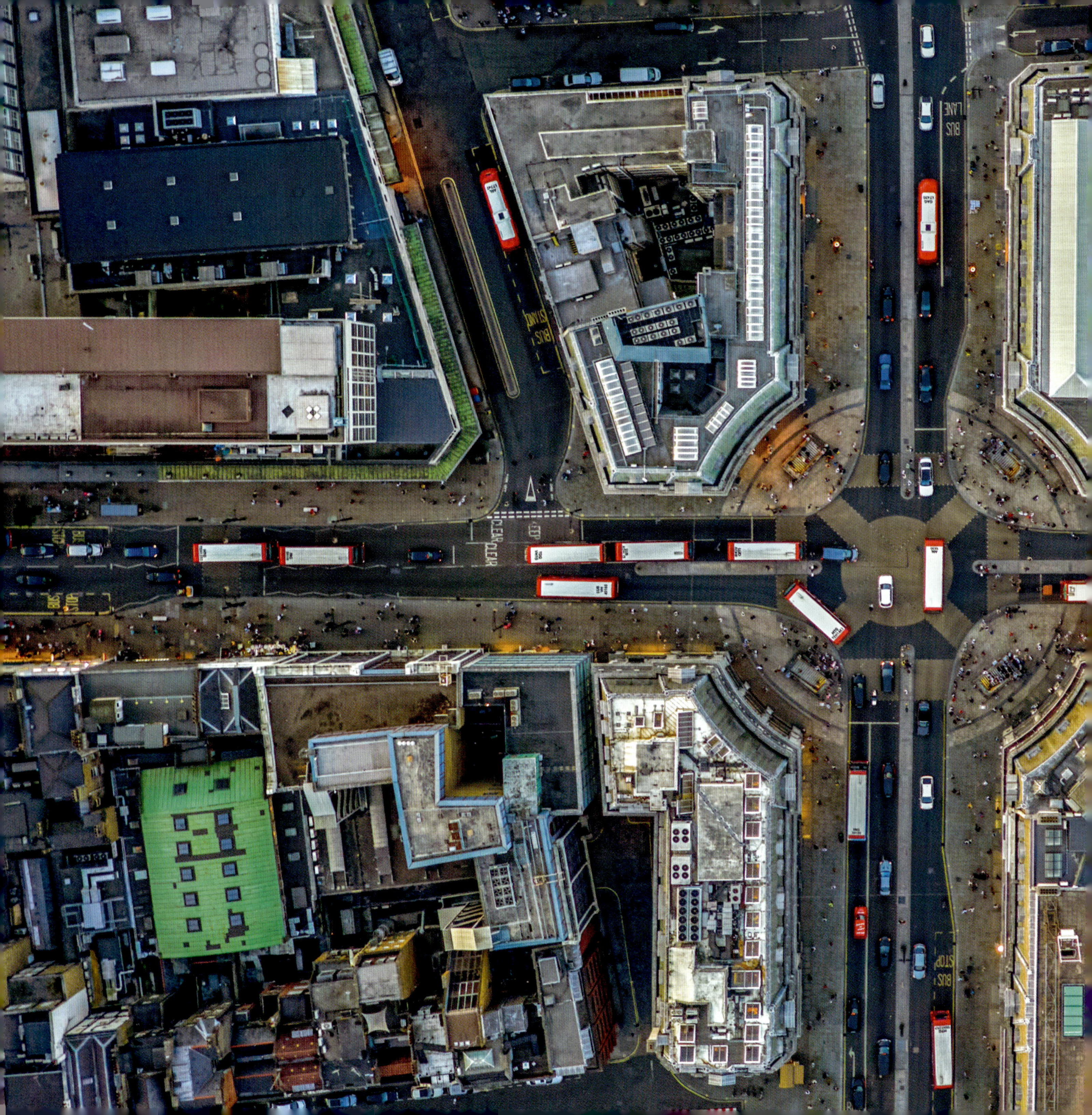

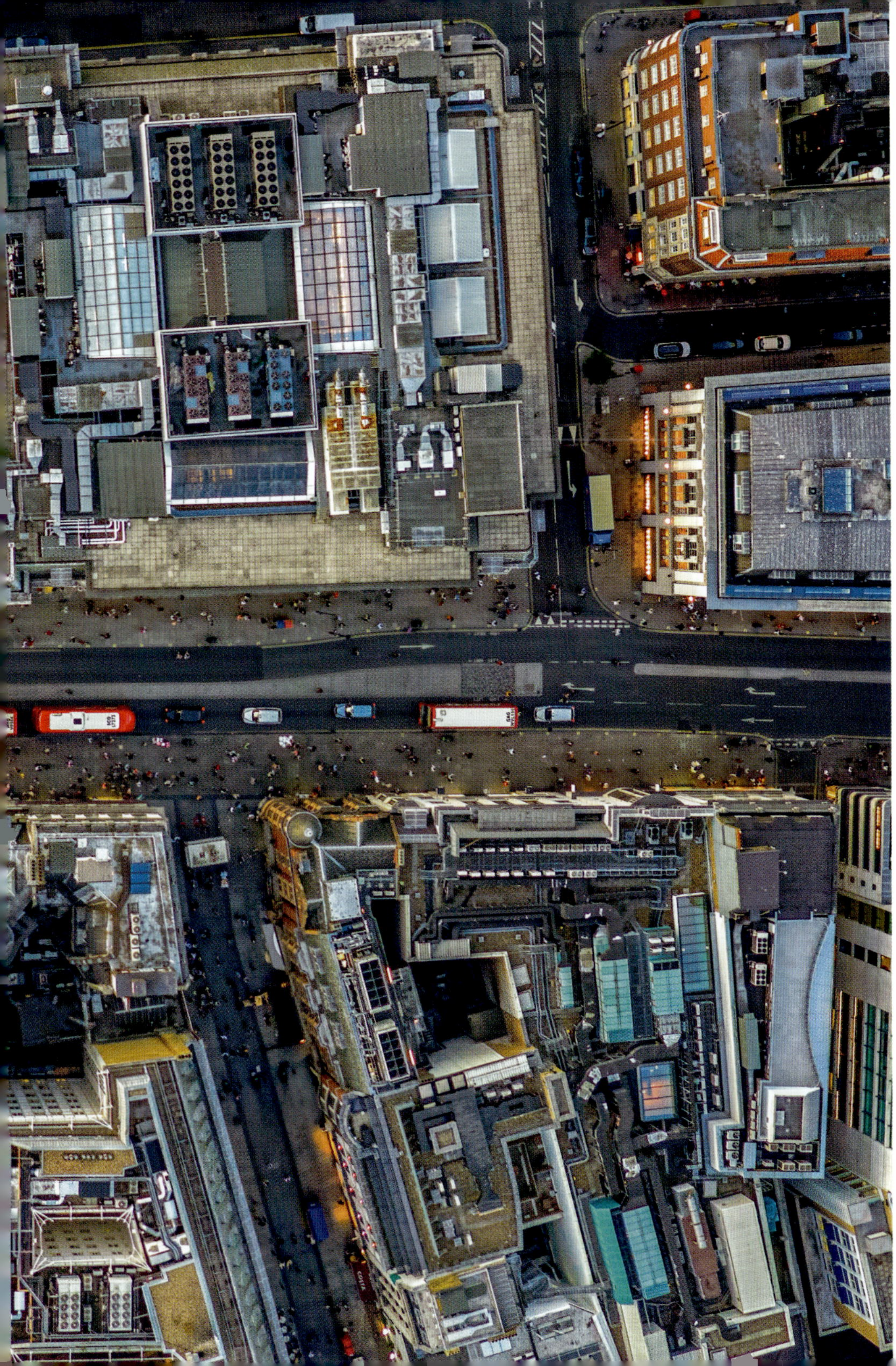

Opposite: Oxford Circus, with Oxford Street running east–west, bisected by Regent Street

Page 108: Berkeley Square

Page 109: Covent Garden

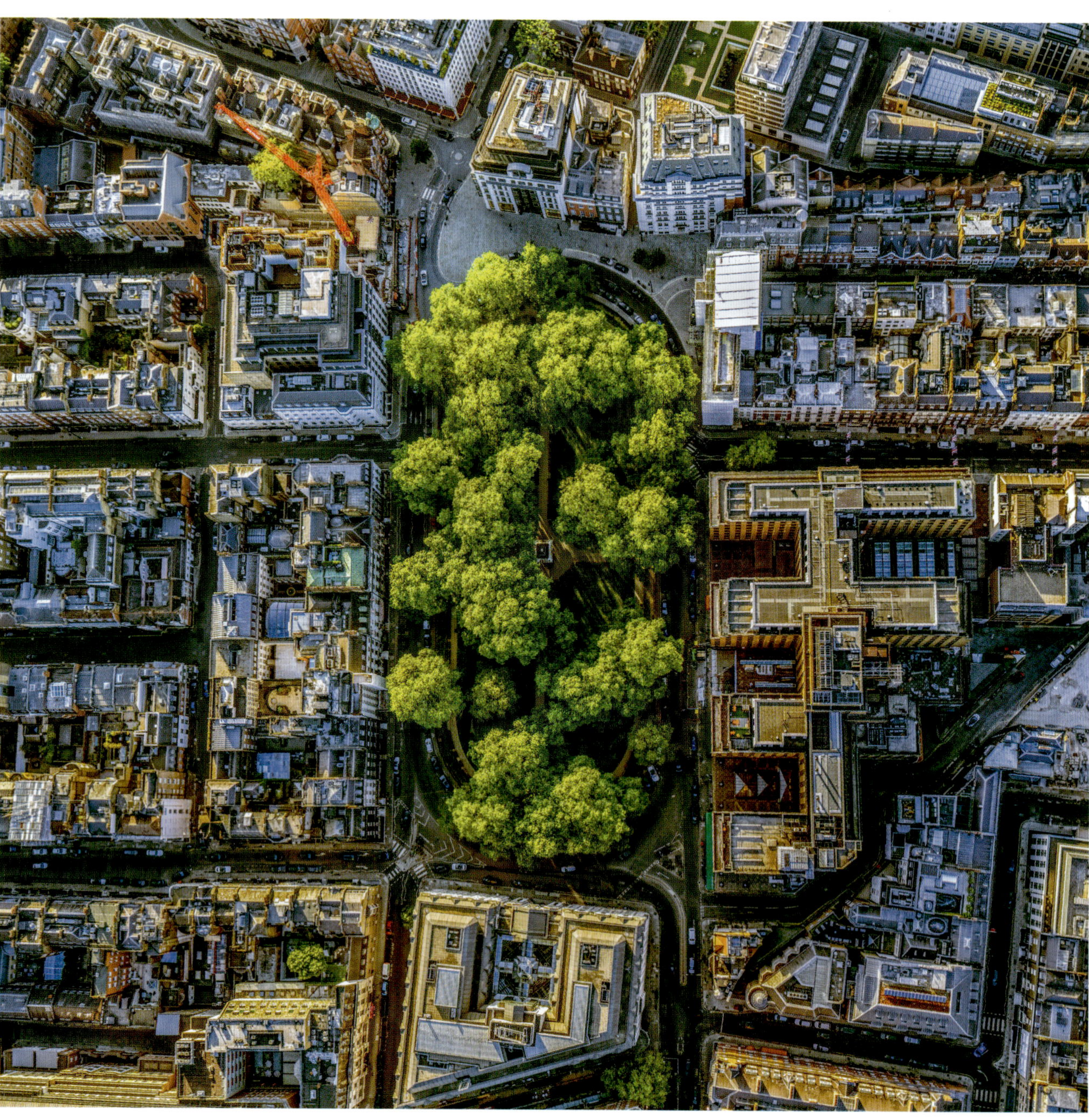

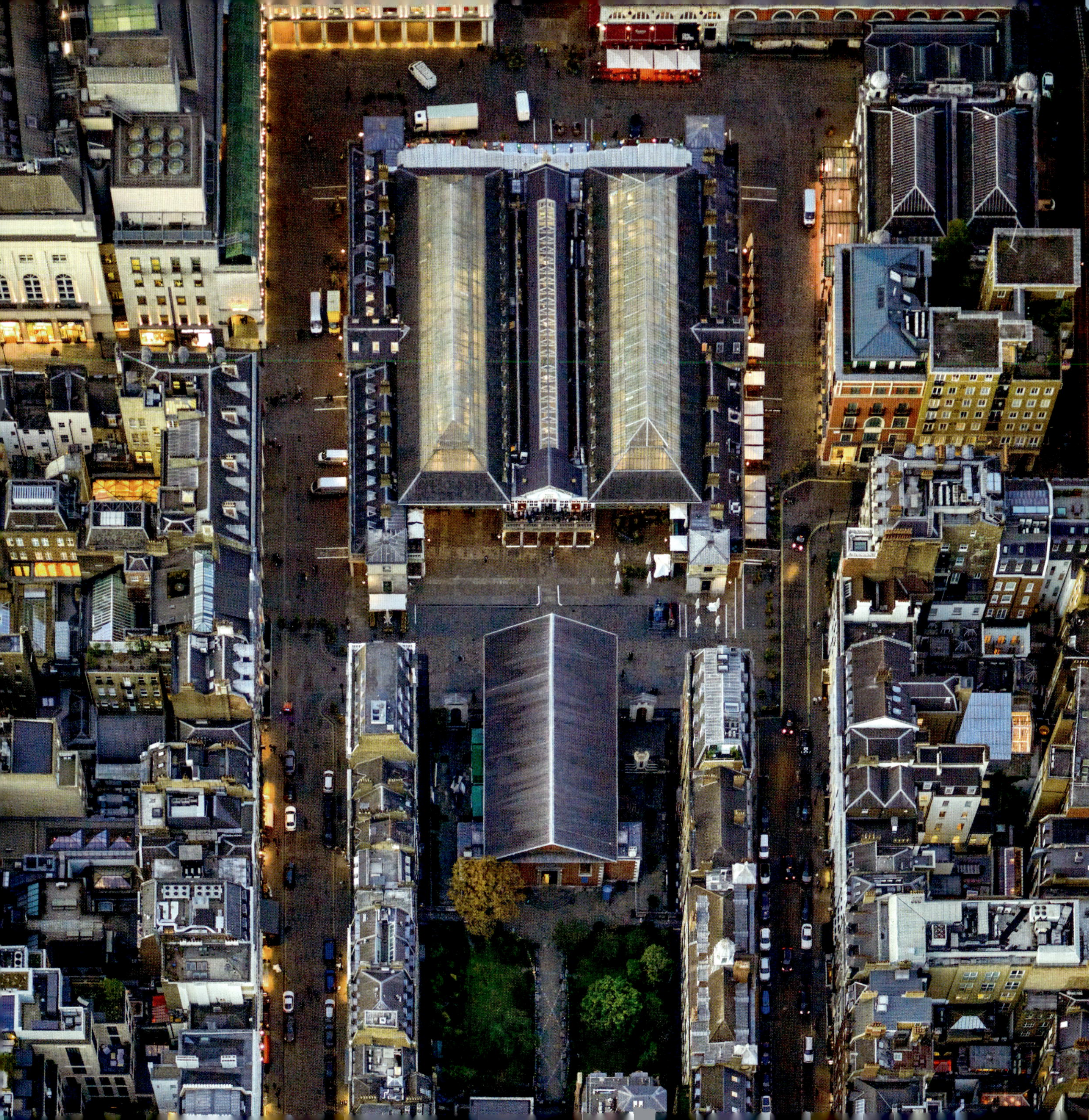

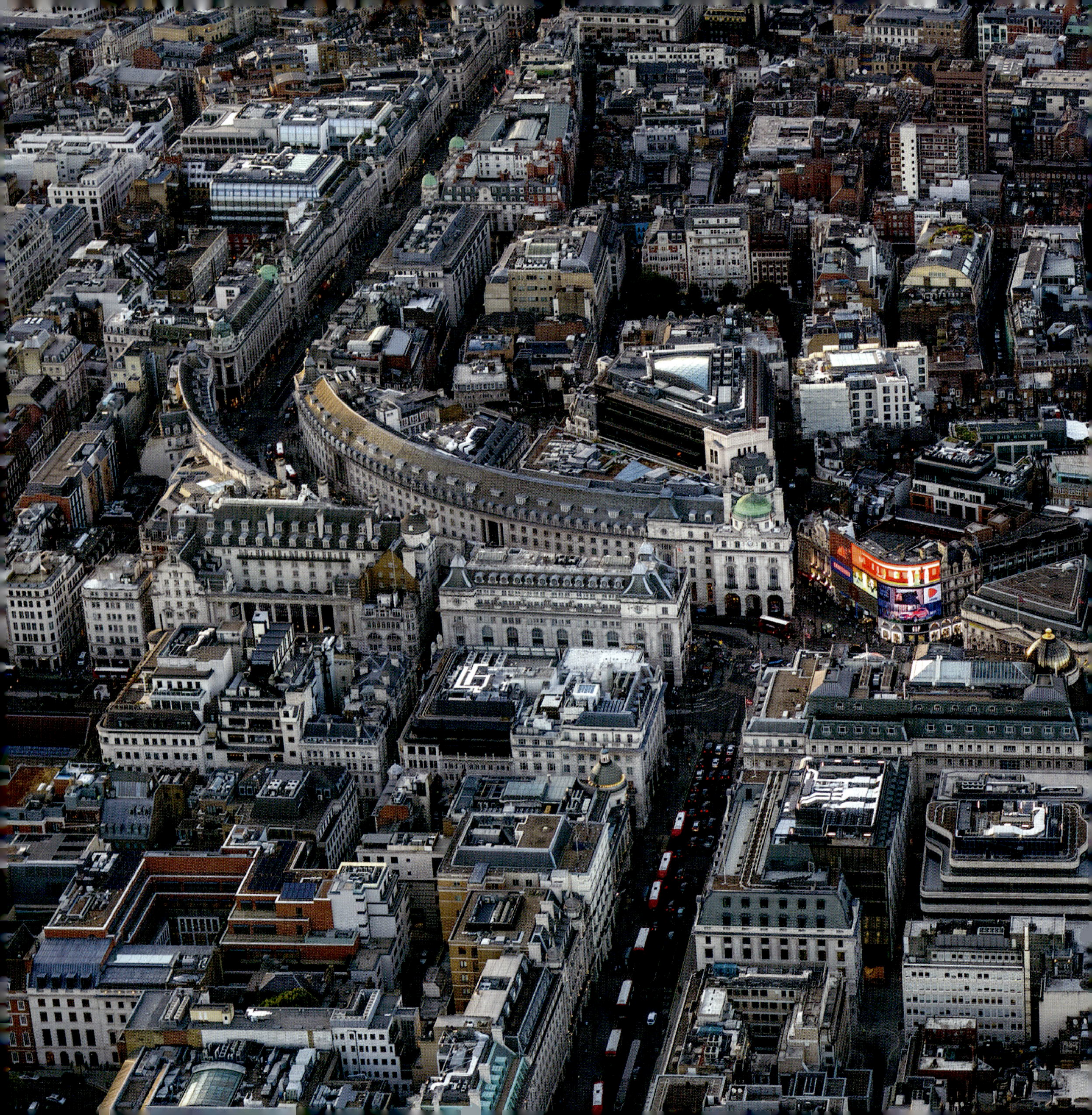

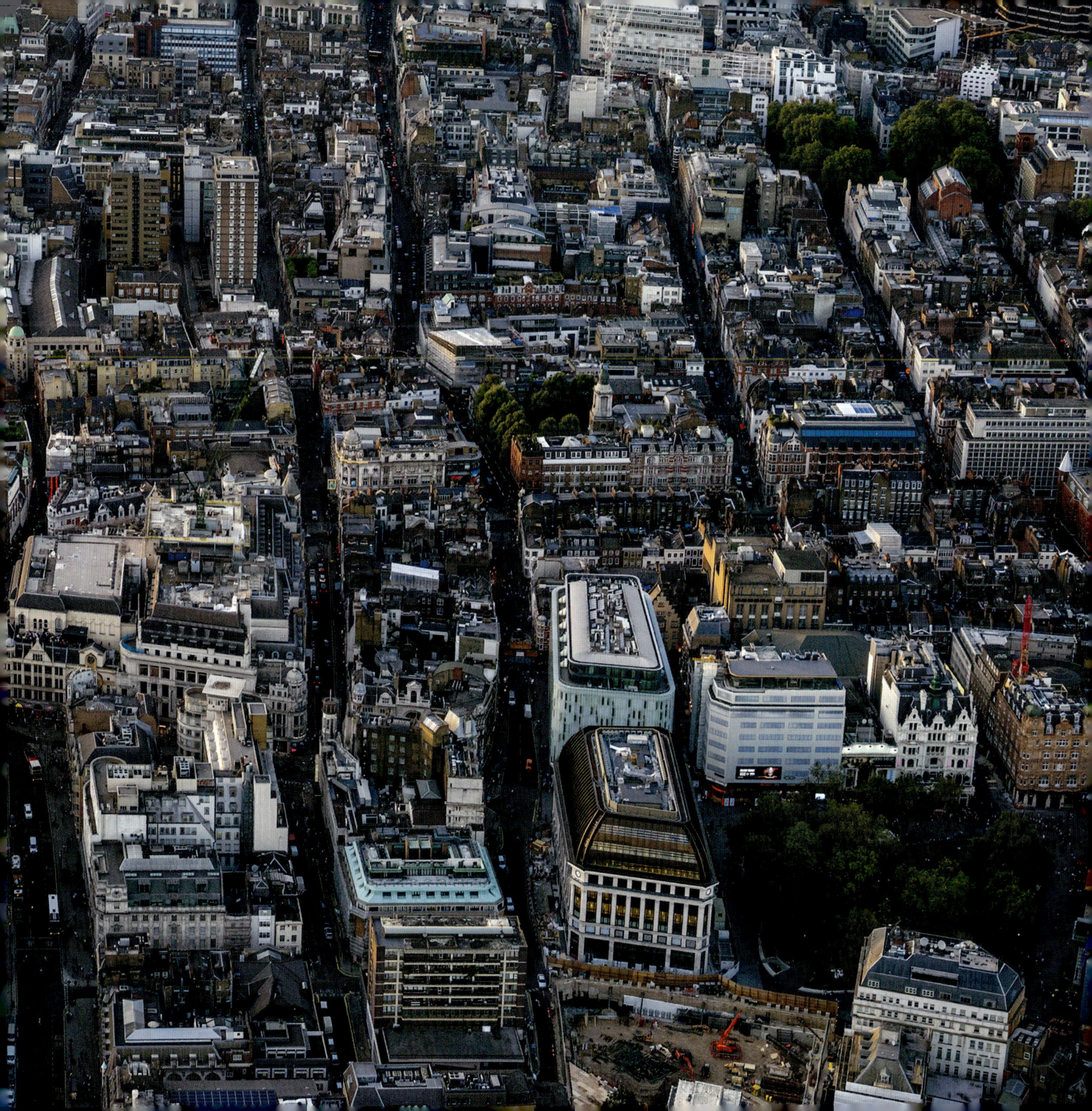

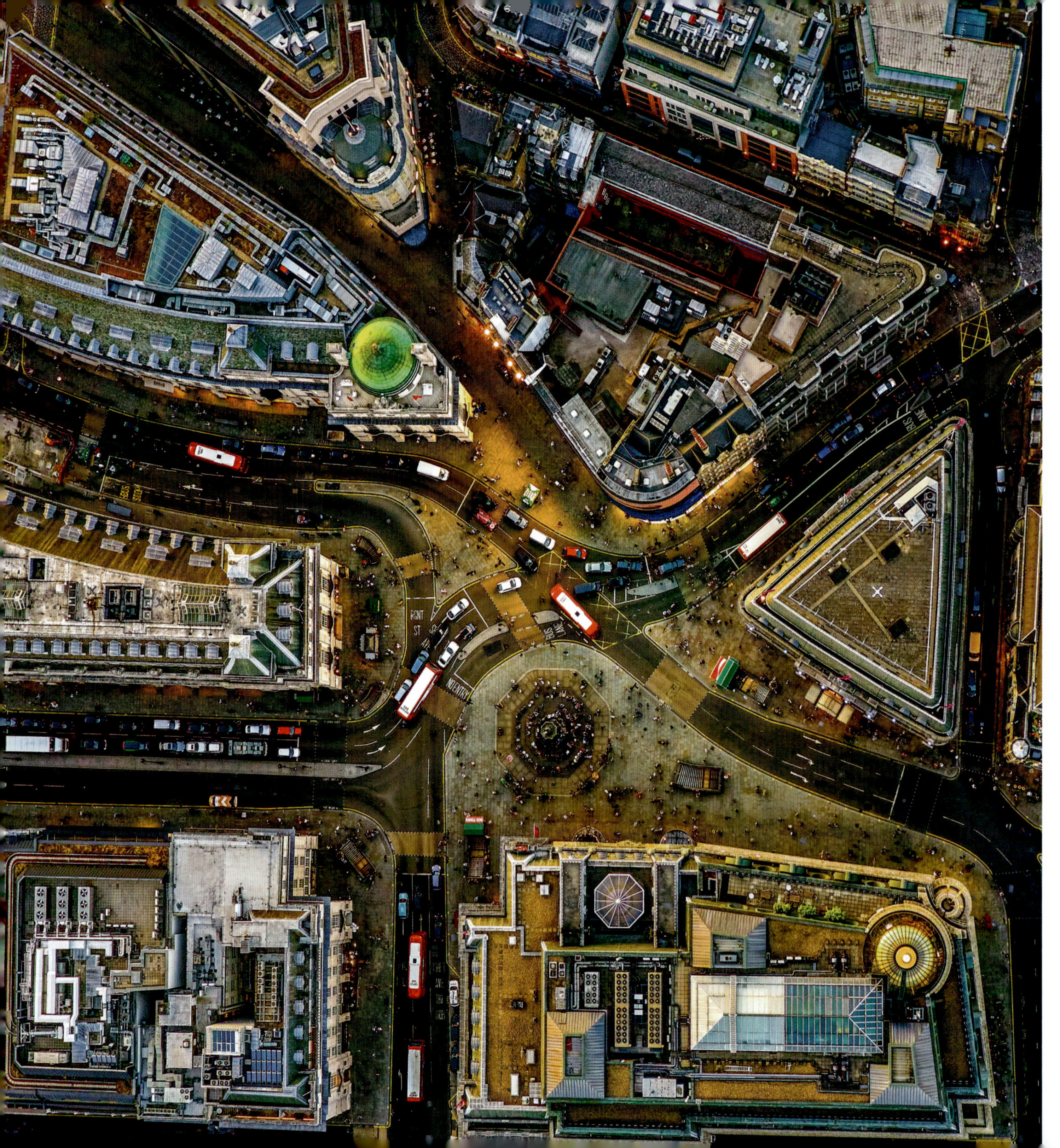

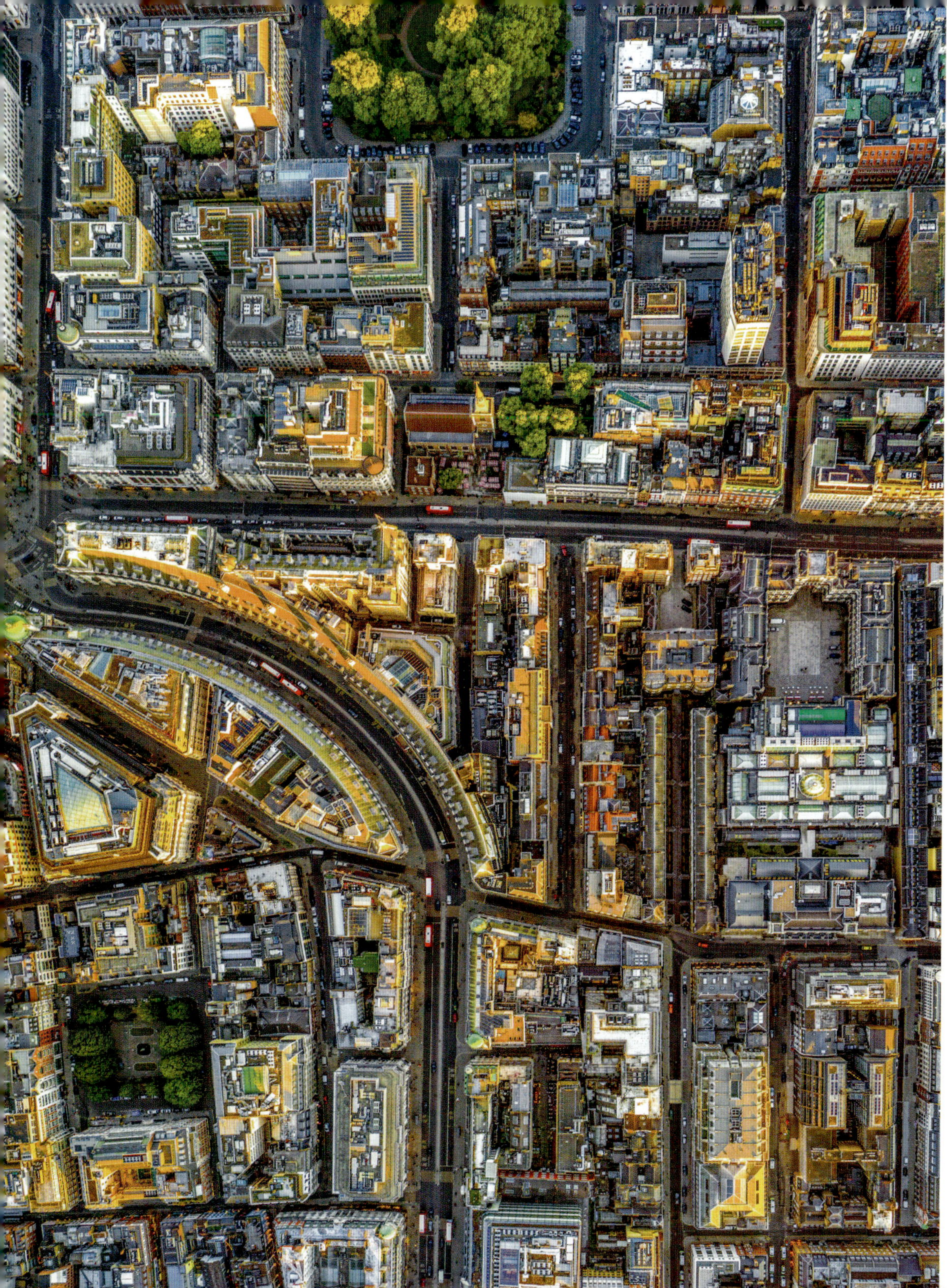

Pages 110–111 and Opposite: Piccadilly Circus

Left: Regent Street

Opposite: Victoria and Albert Museum

Page 116: The front entrance of the Natural History Museum

Page 117: Looking down on the Natural History Museum

Page 118: Tate Britain, which houses 500 years of British art, facing the Thames in the Millbank section of Westminster

Page 119: A view of the British Museum at night showing the remarkable glass roof over the Great Court

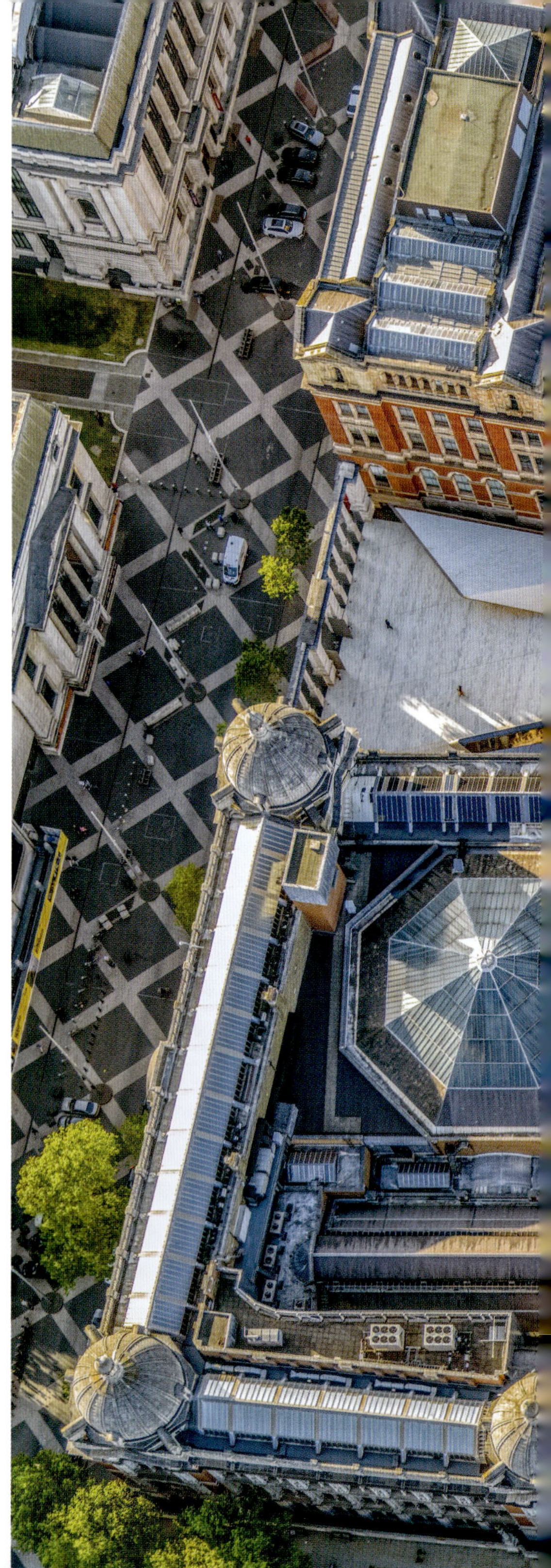

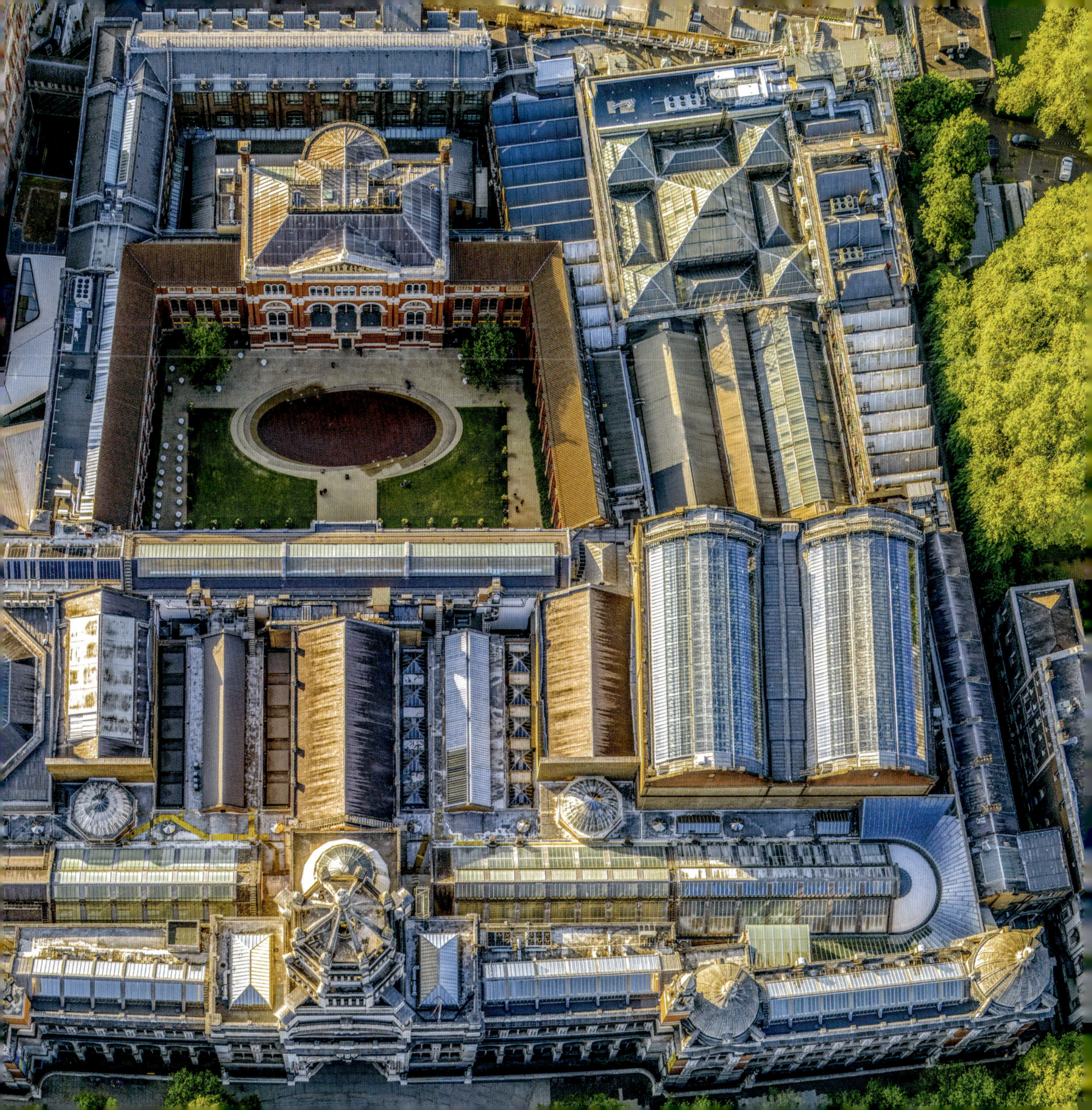

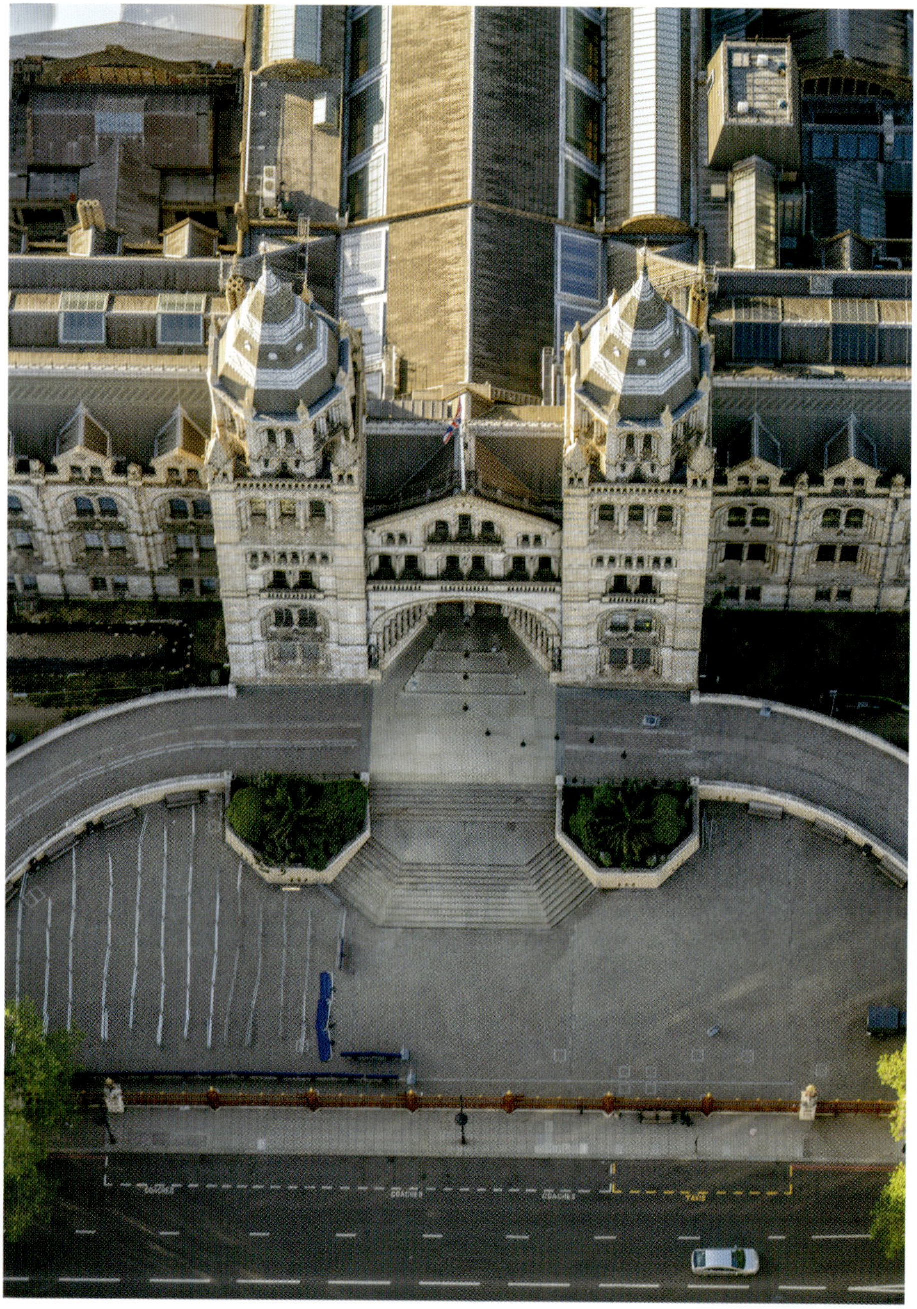

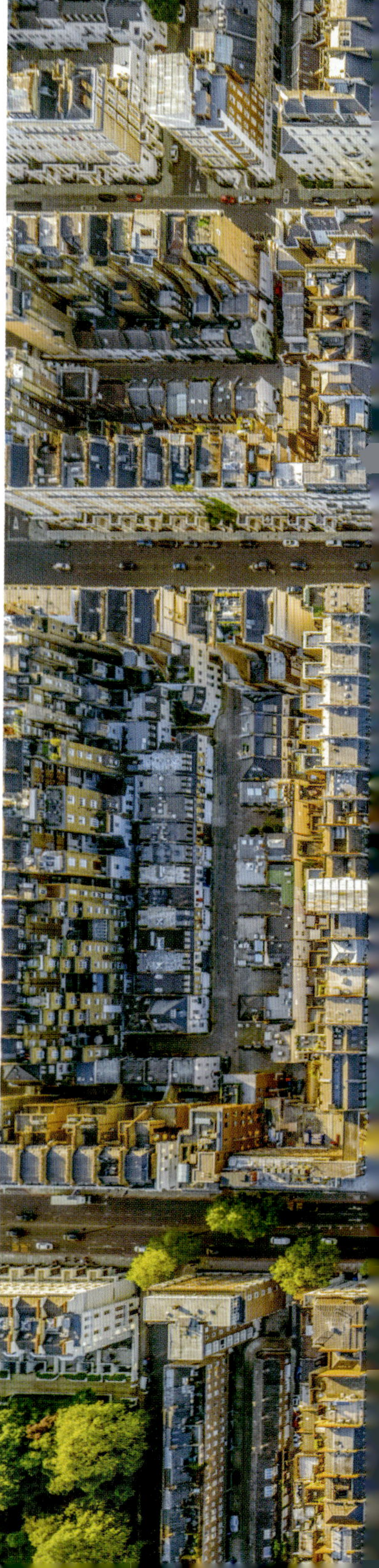

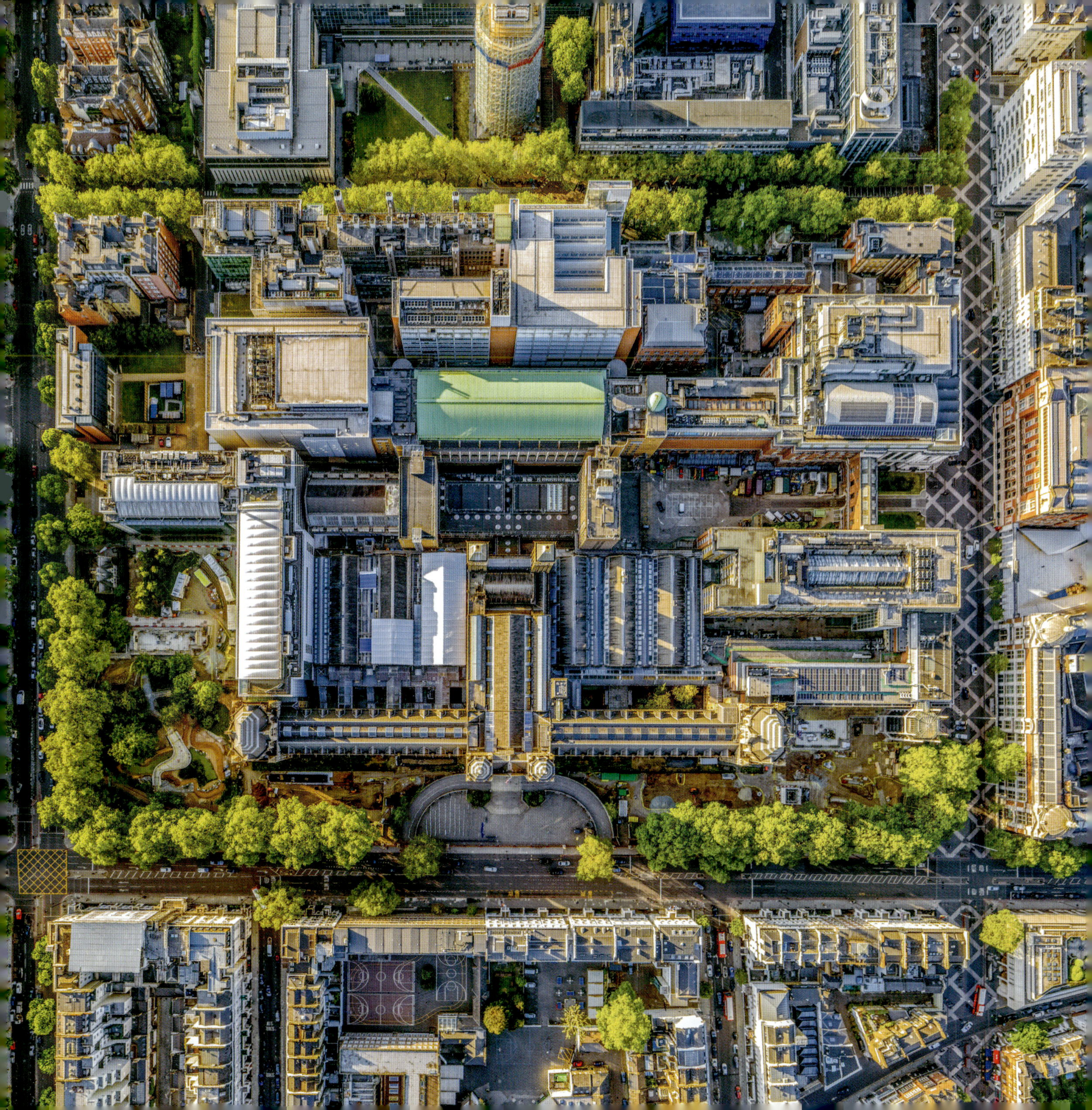

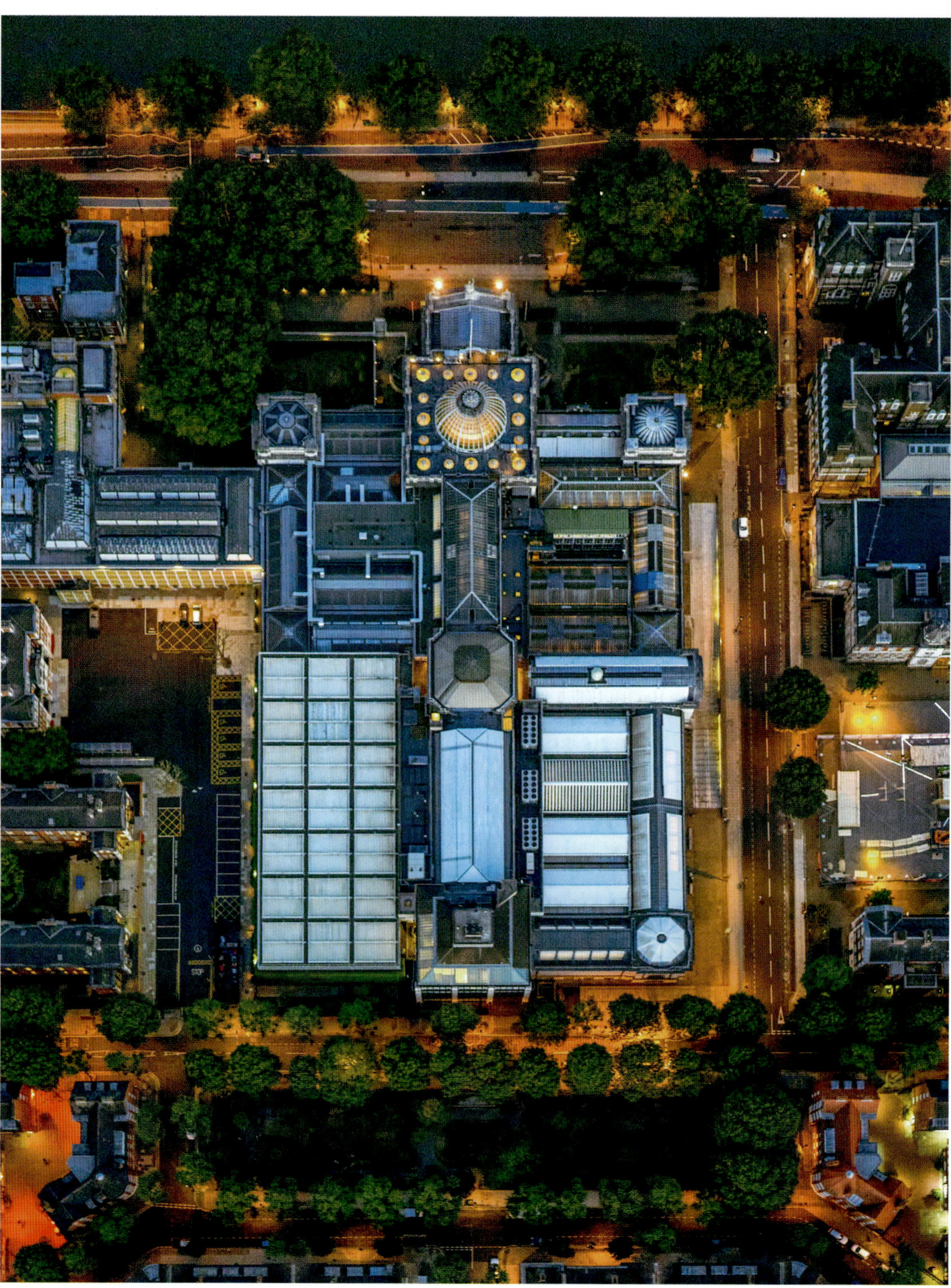

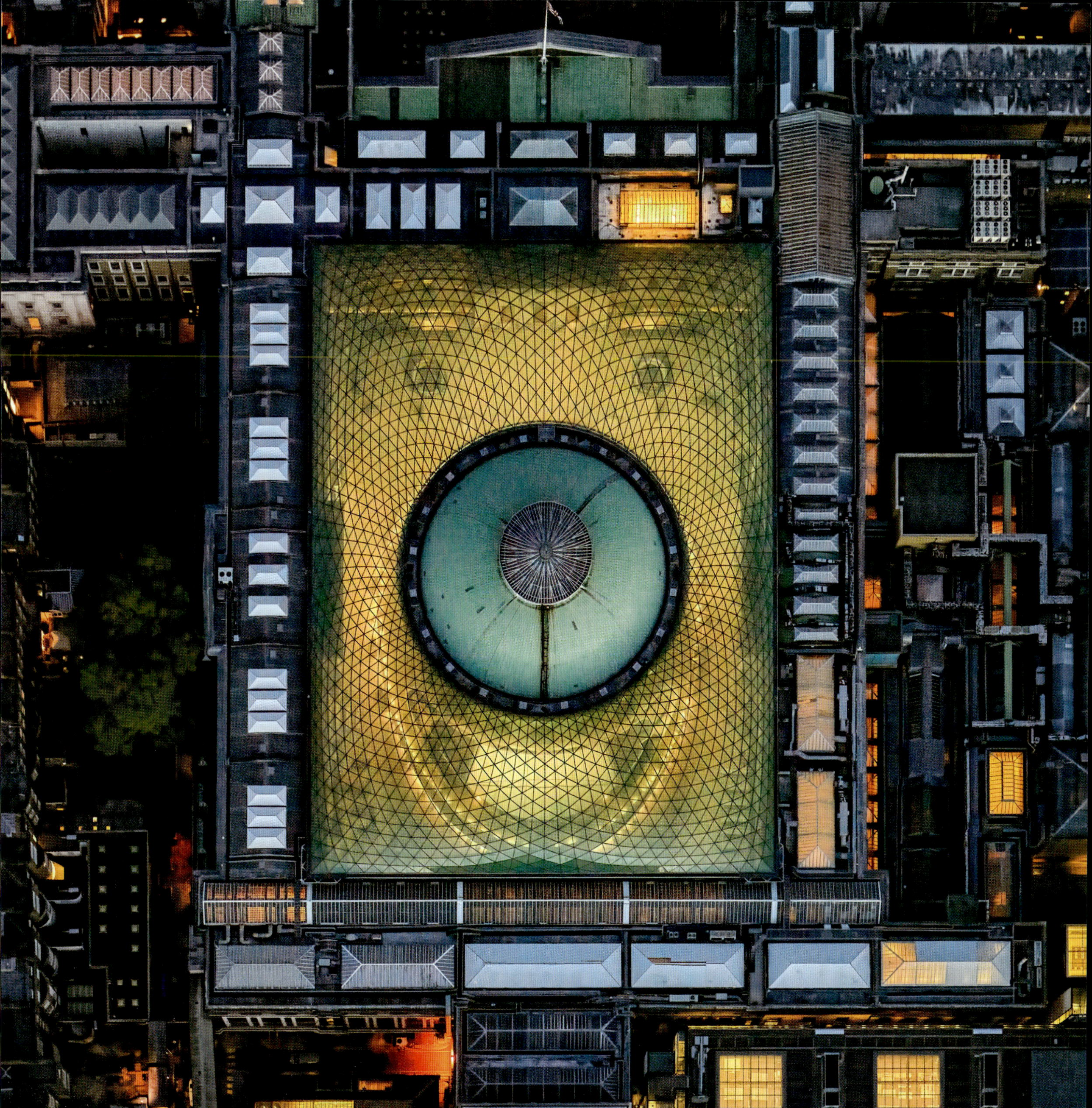

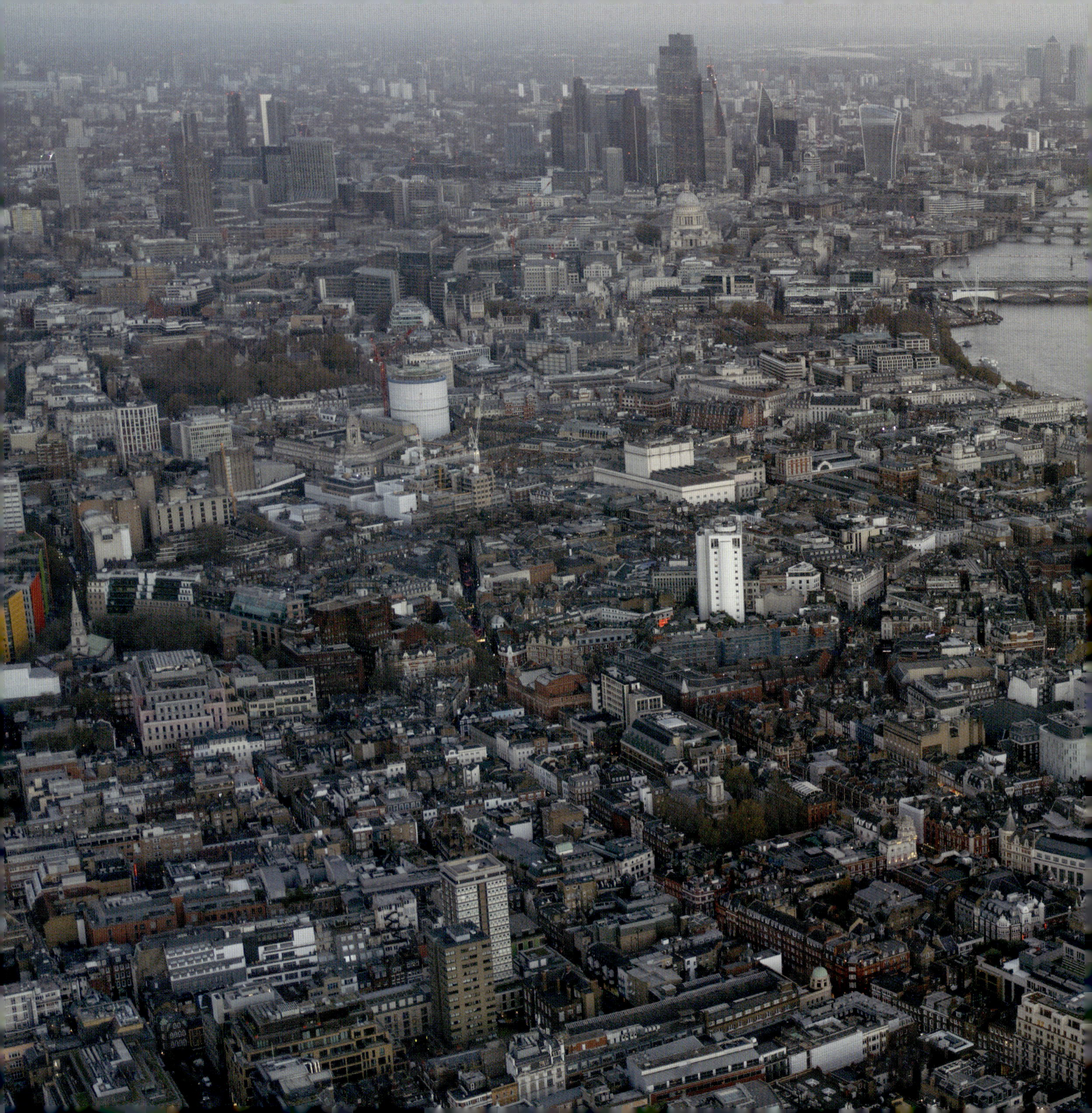

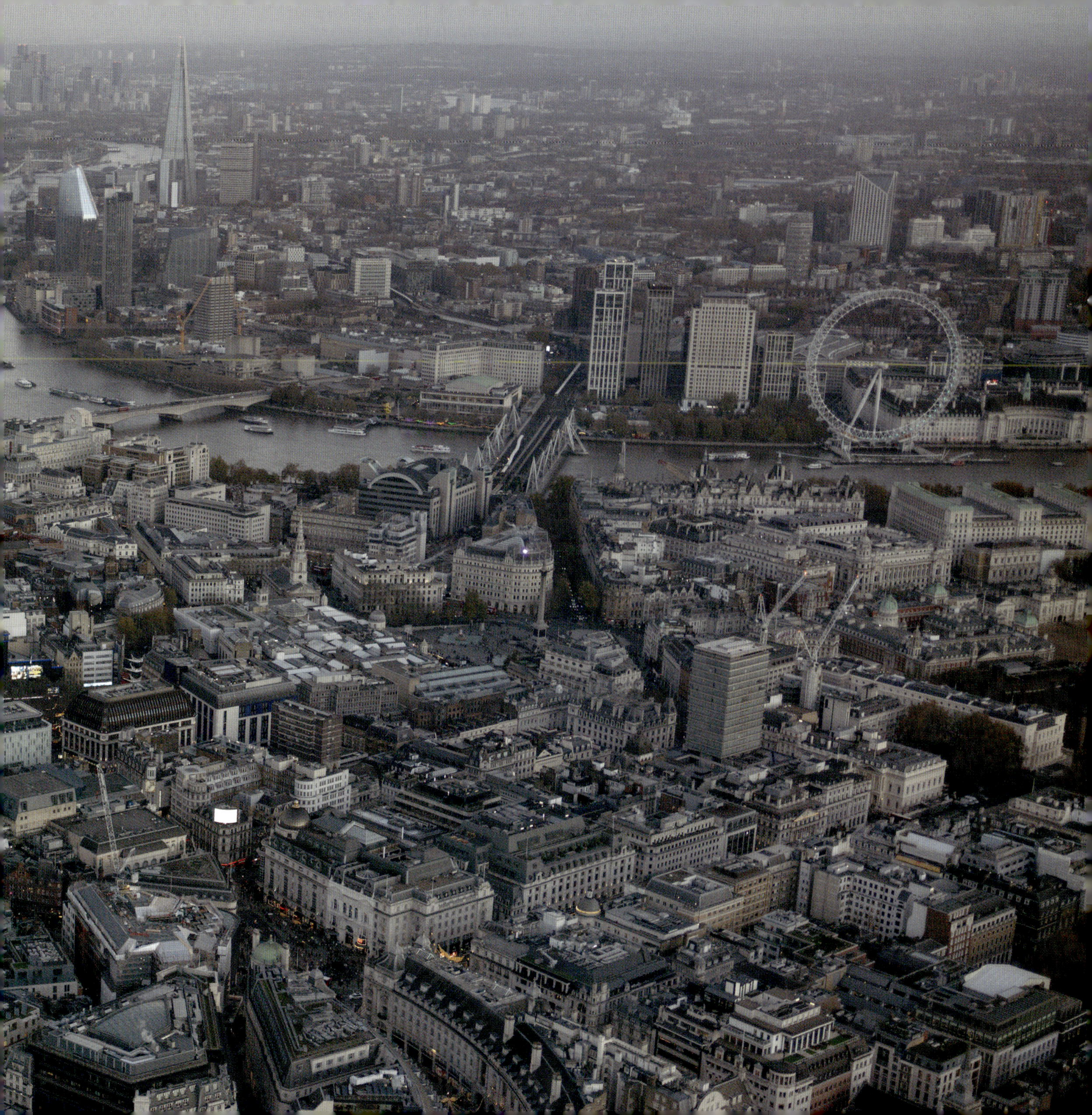

Pages 120–121: Looking toward the South Bank over the Piccadilly Circus area

Right: BT Tower, also known as the GPO Tower, Post Office Tower, and Telecom Tower

Opposite: Lord's Cricket Ground

Page 124: Wembley Stadium

Page 125: Emirates Stadium, home of Arsenal Football Club

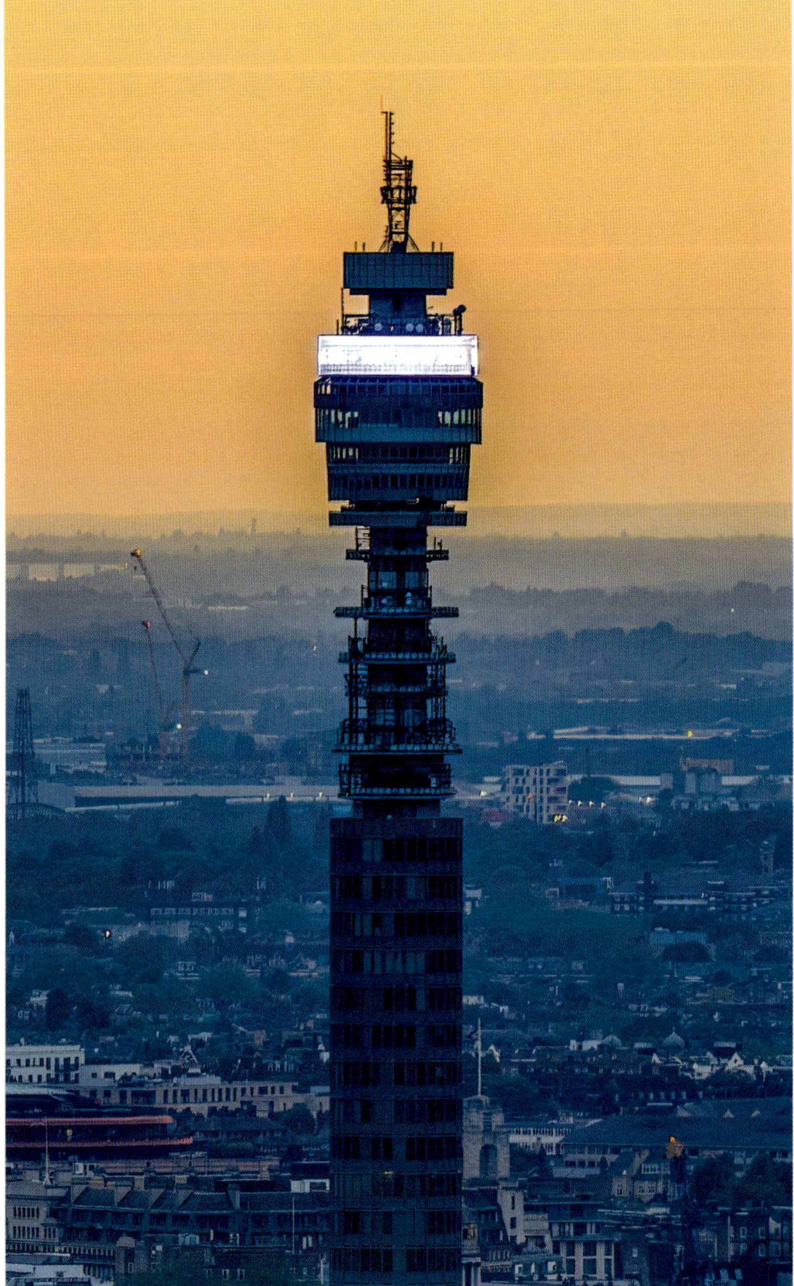

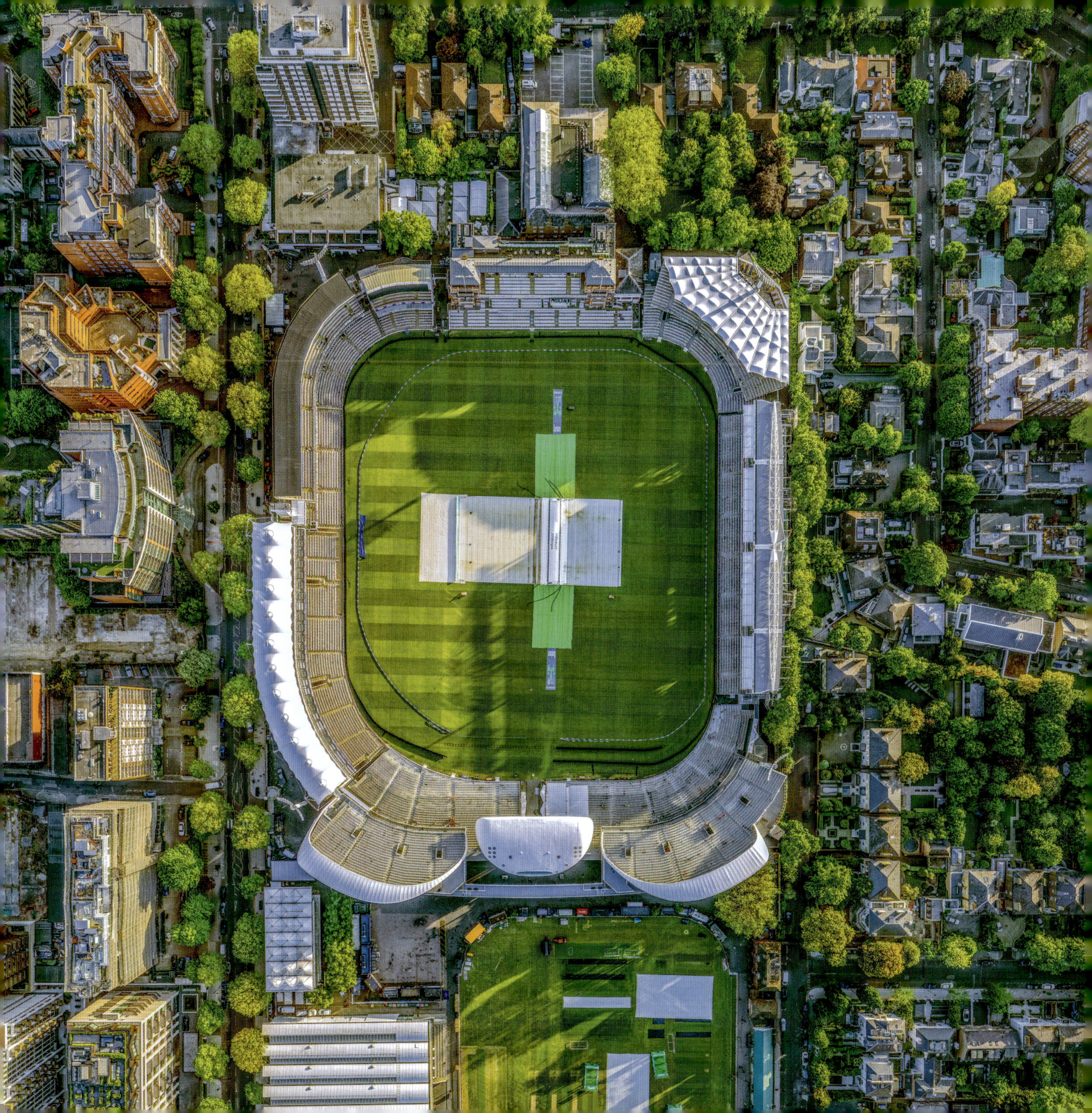

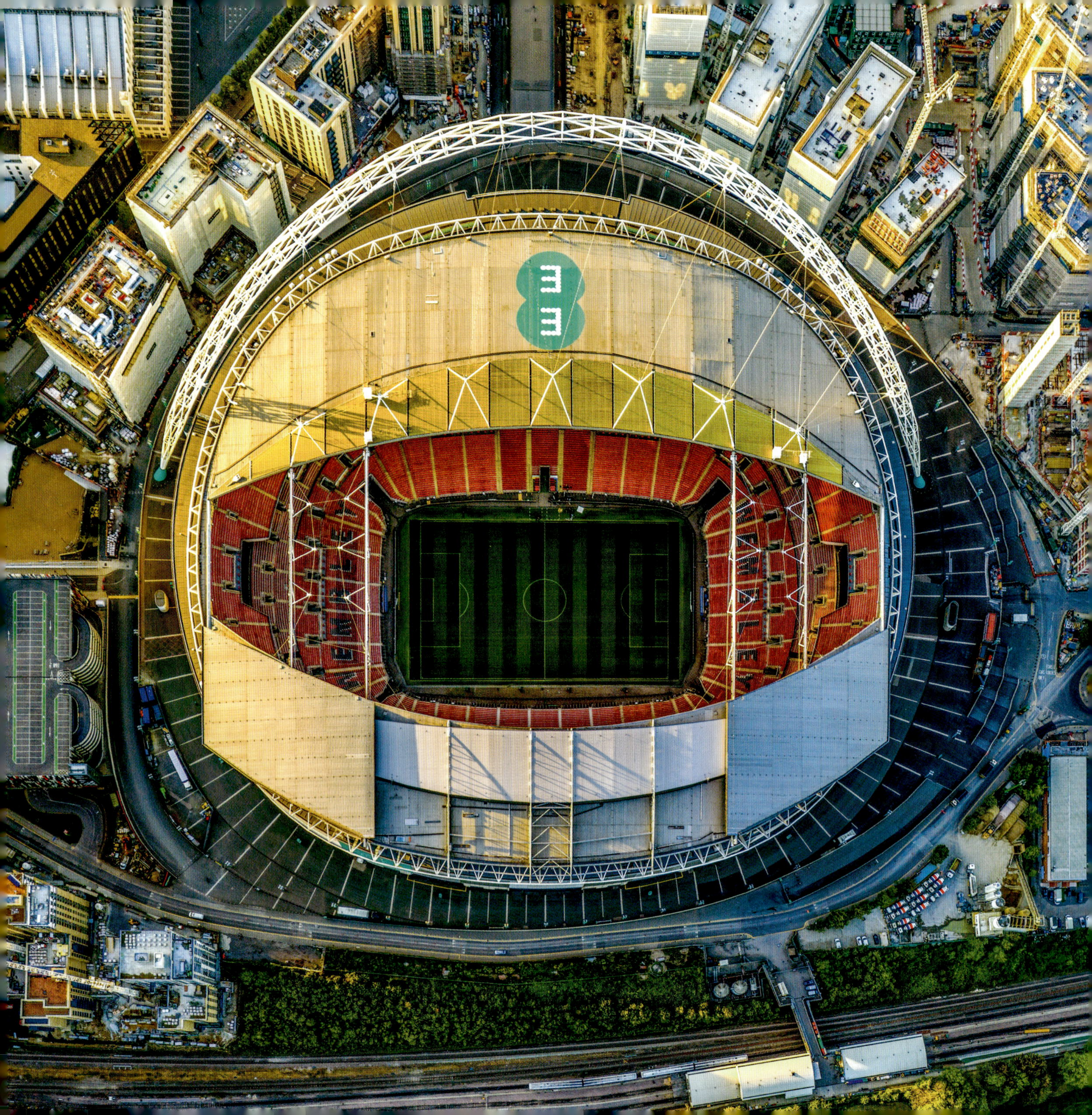
WEMBLEY
WEMBLEY

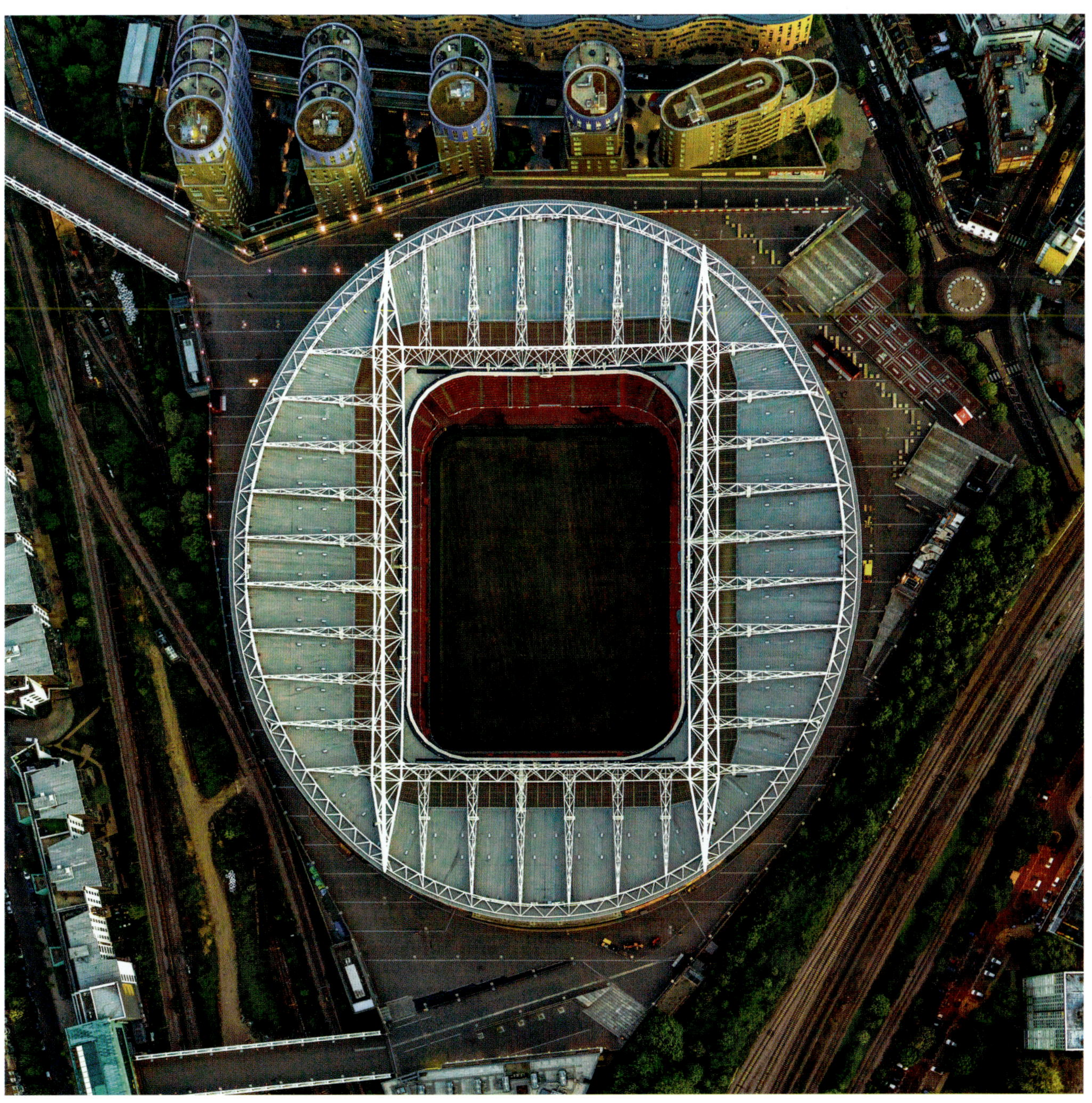

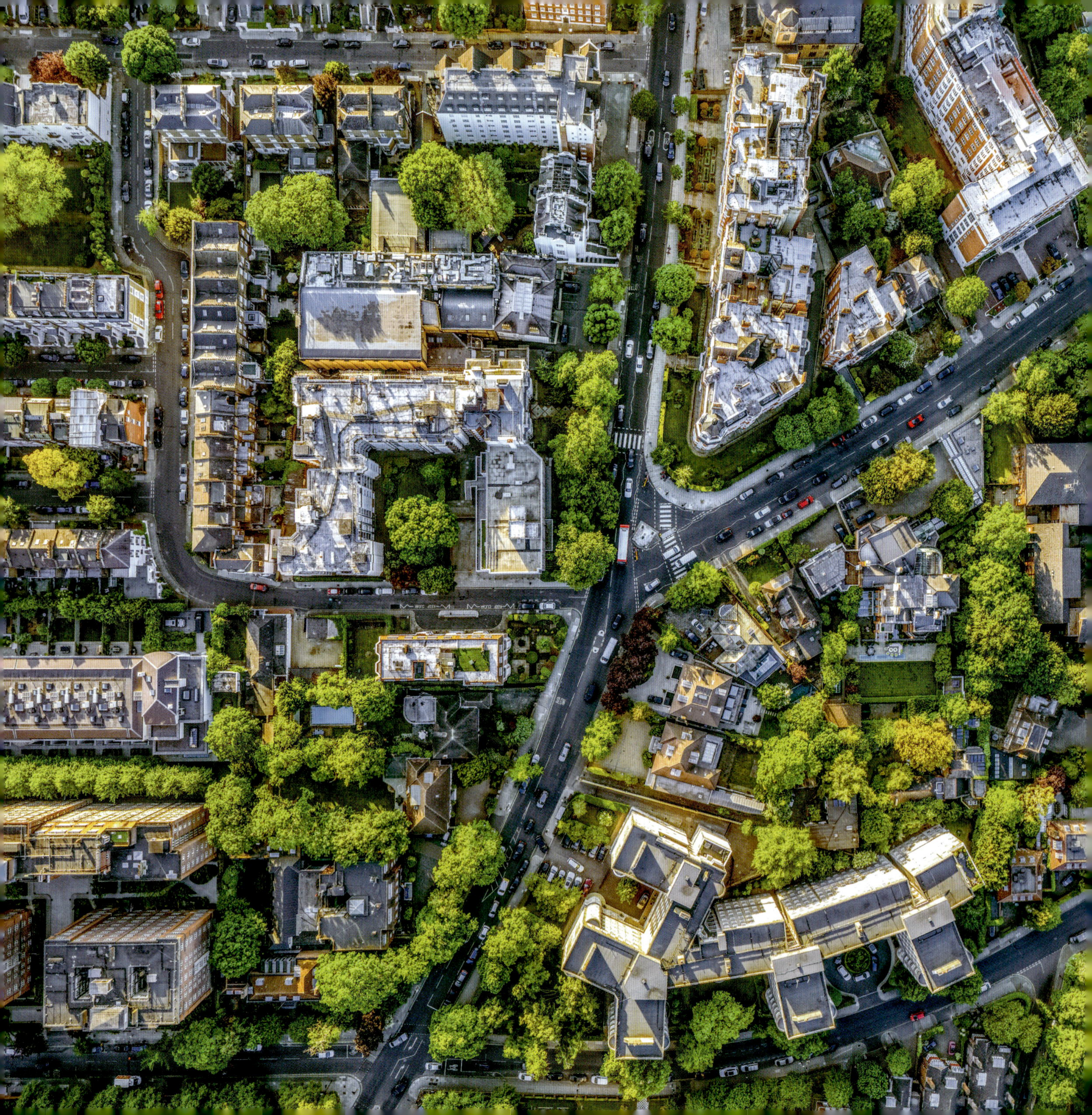

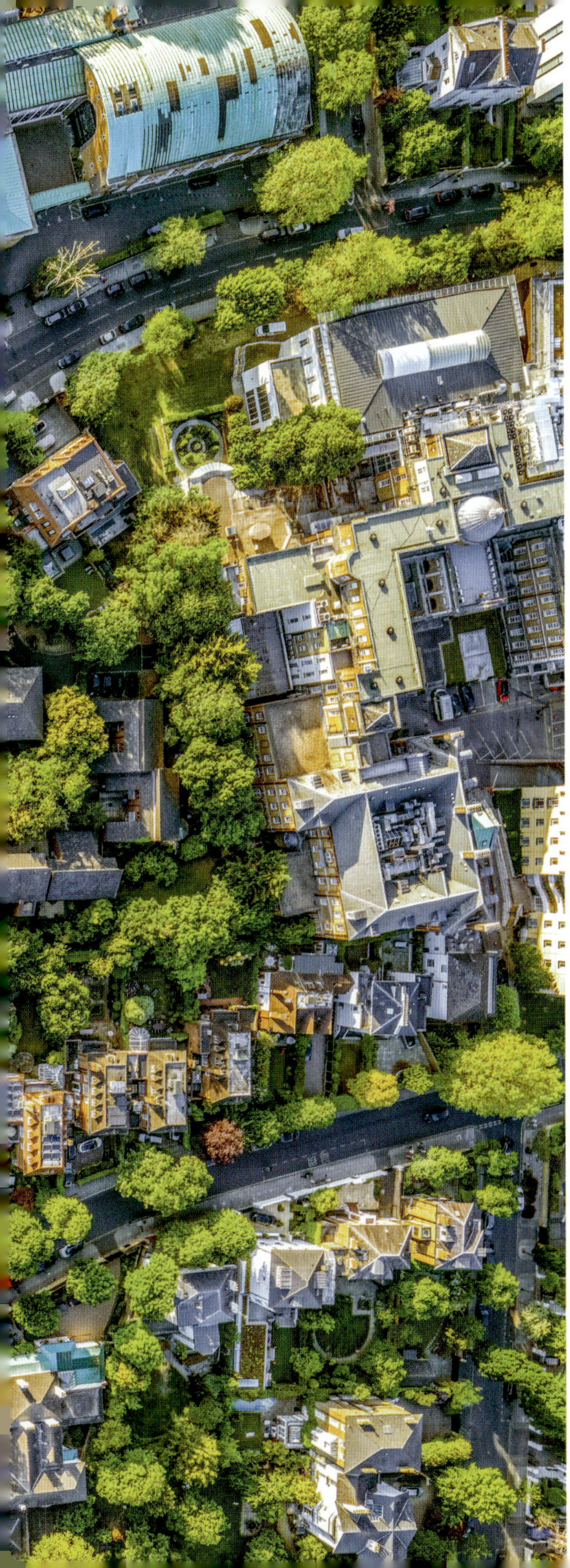

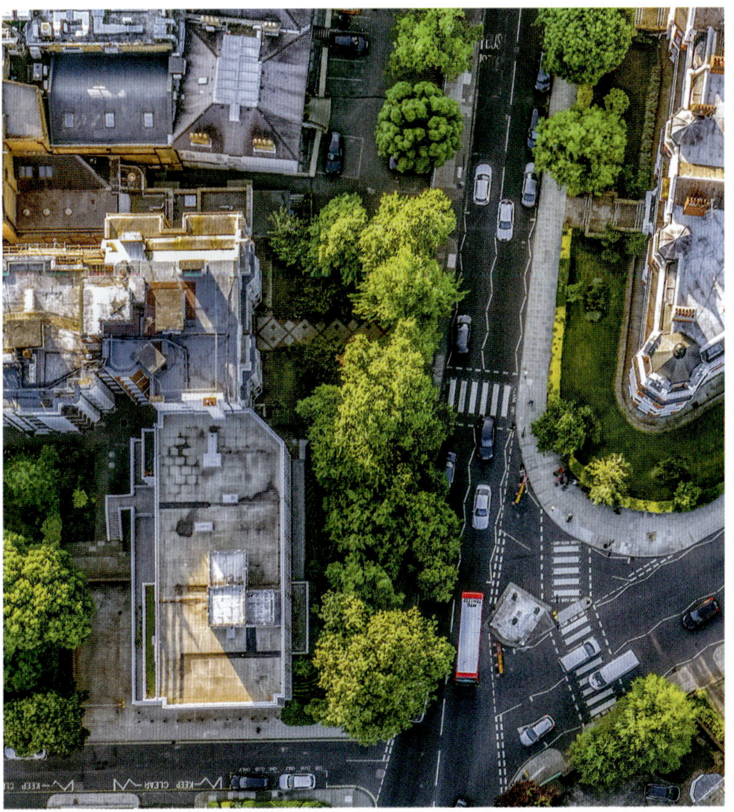

Opposite and Above: Abbey Road Studios—where the Beatles recorded some of their most memorable songs and shot their famous album cover in the nearby crosswalk—at upper left, near the confluence of Abbey Road (running north–south), Grove End Road (coming down from the right), and Hall Road (at bottom) in St. John's Wood

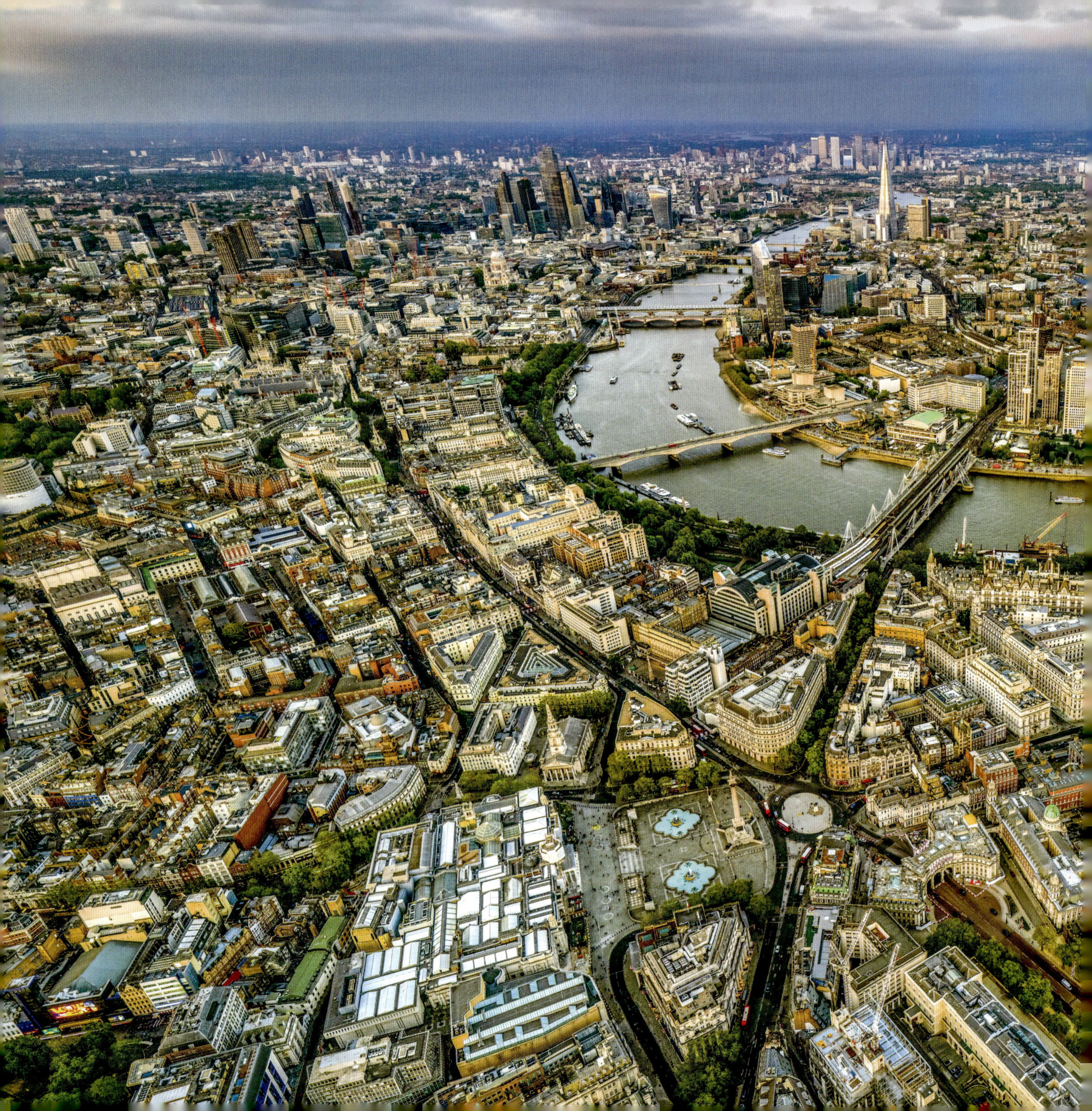

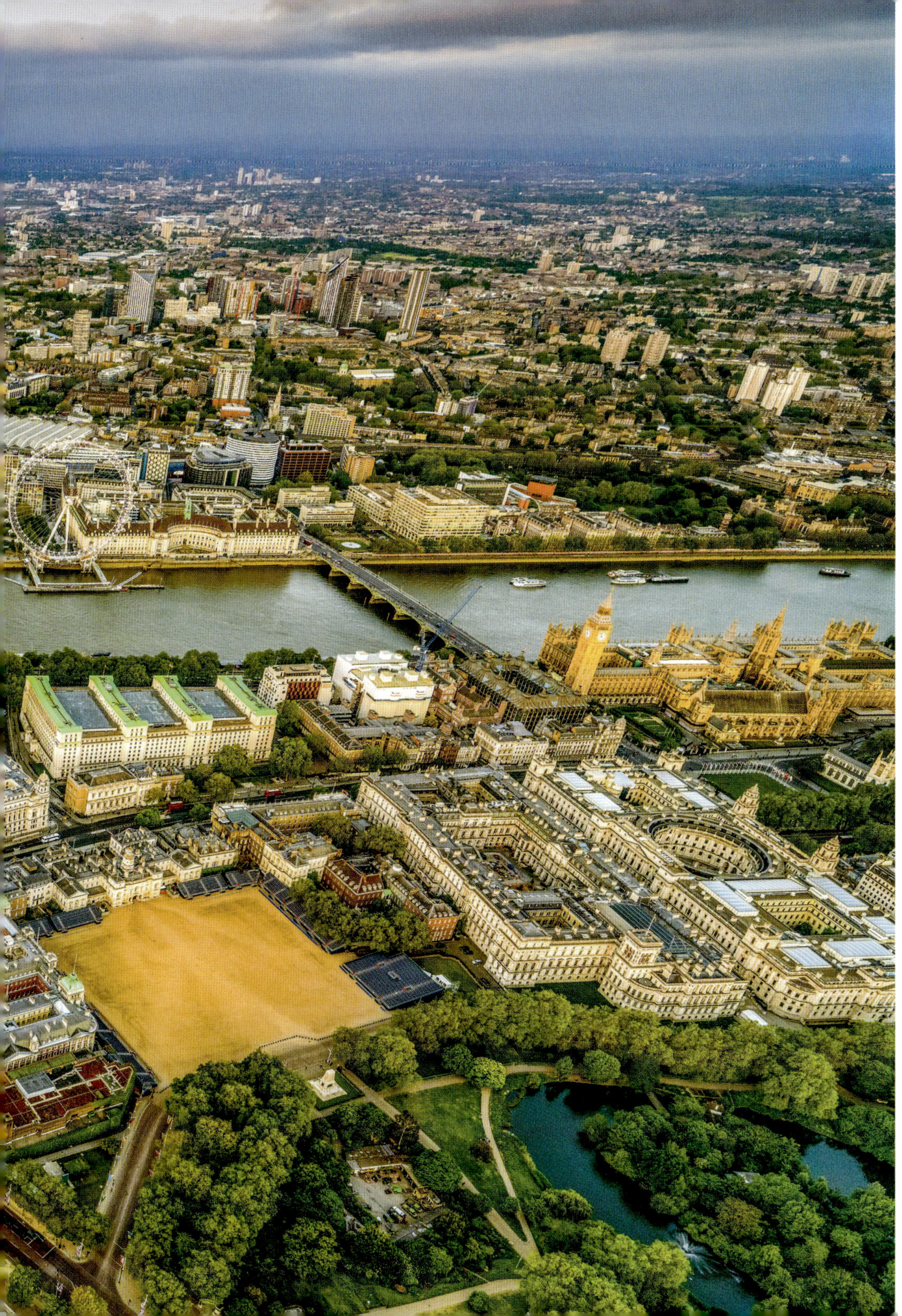

Looking east over the city

130

SOUTH BANK

Opposite: The Shard at sunset, with the London Bridge railway station at its base

Pages 132–133: Looking across Waterloo railway station and the London Eye toward Westminster

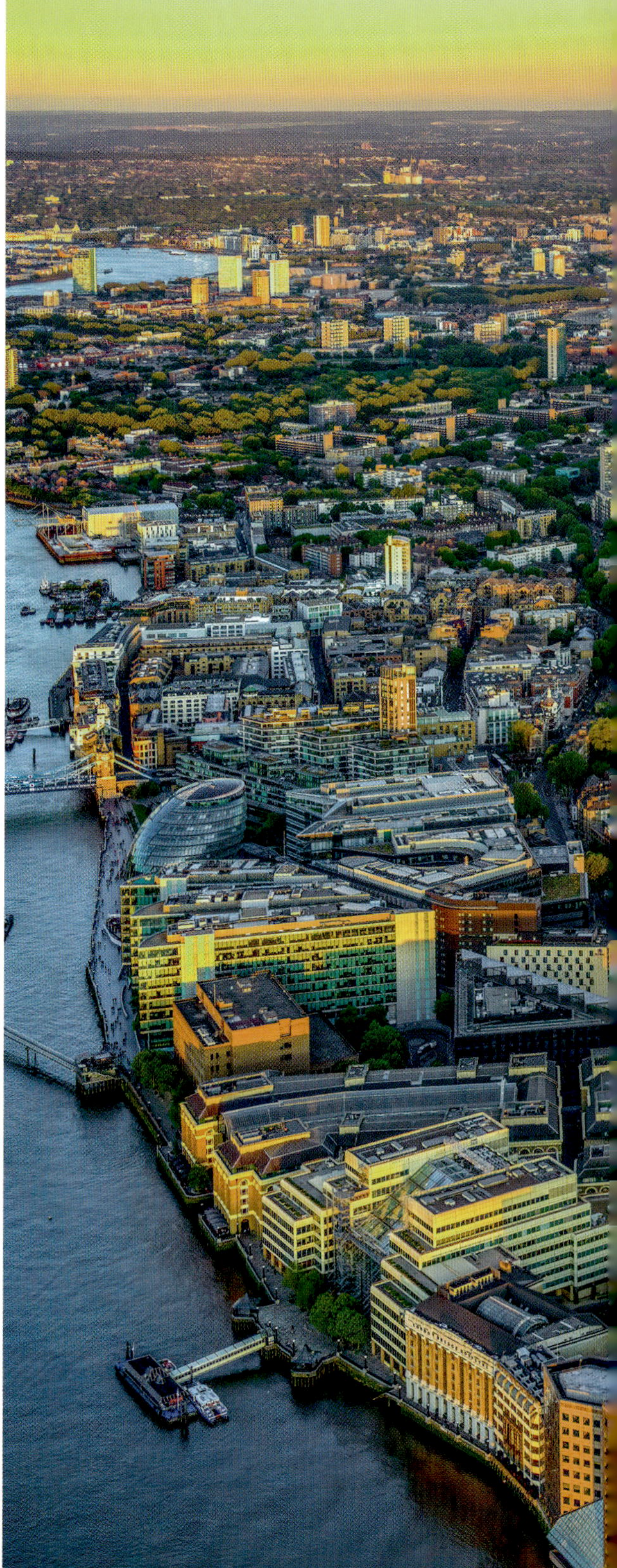

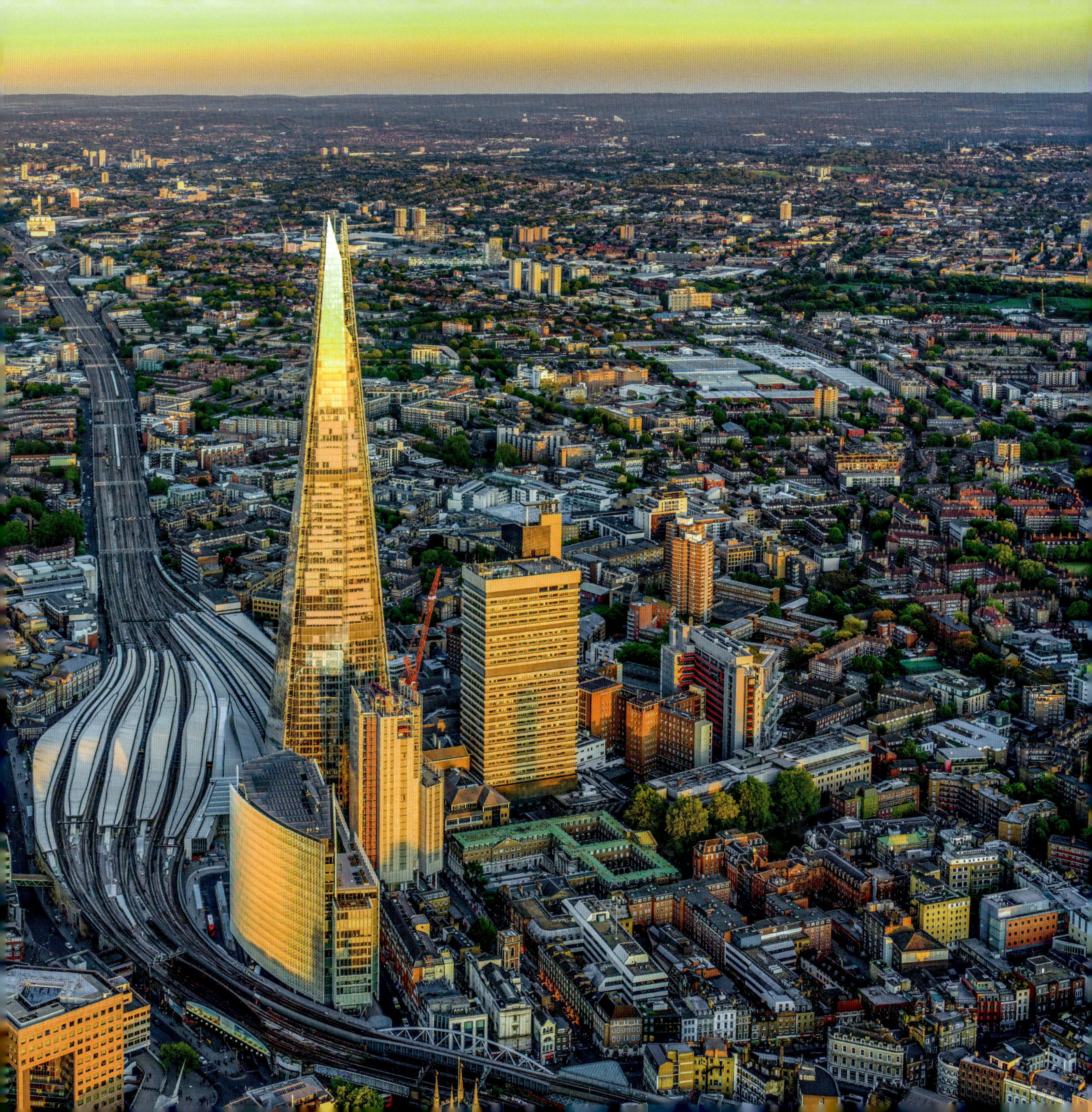

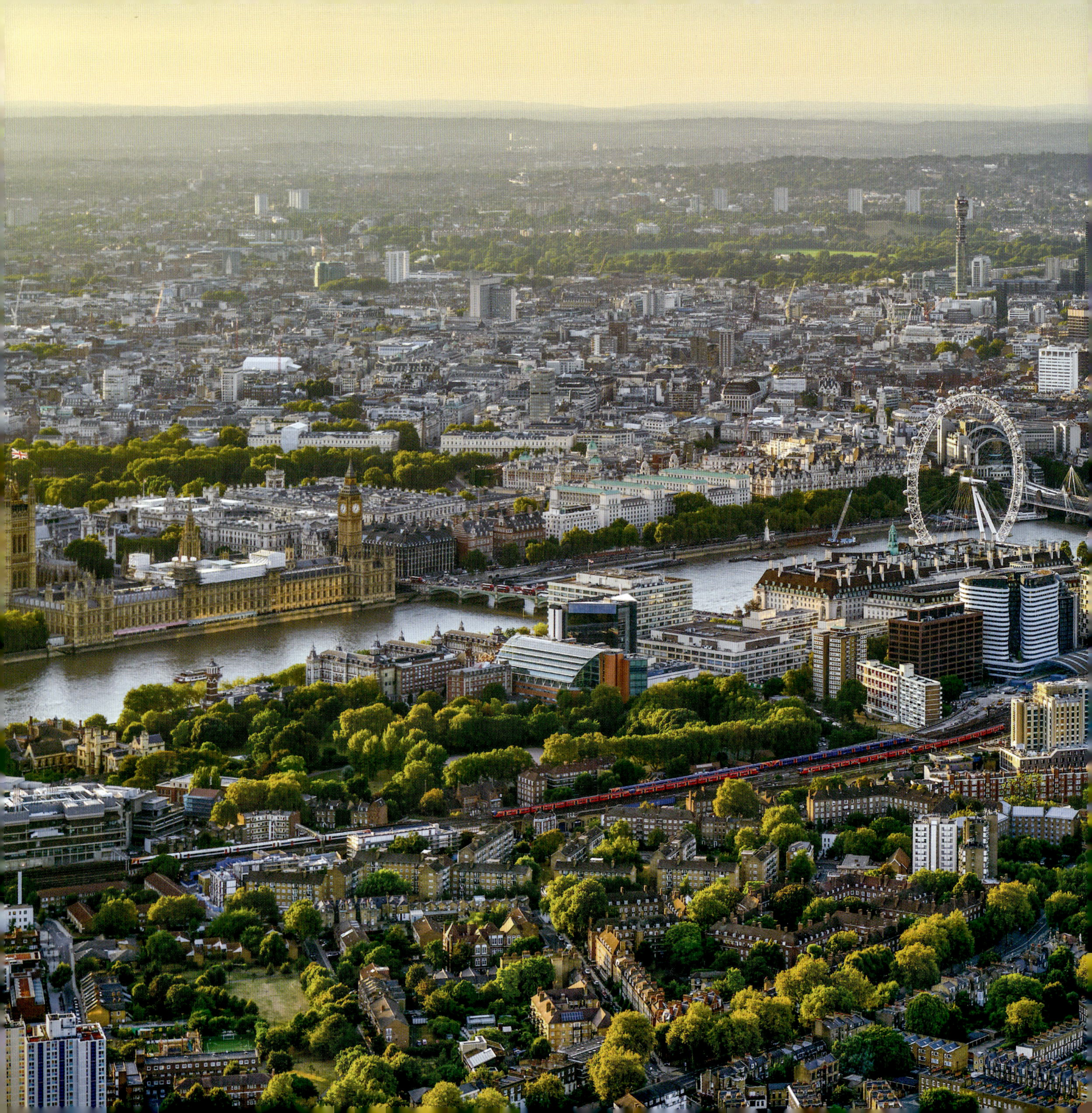

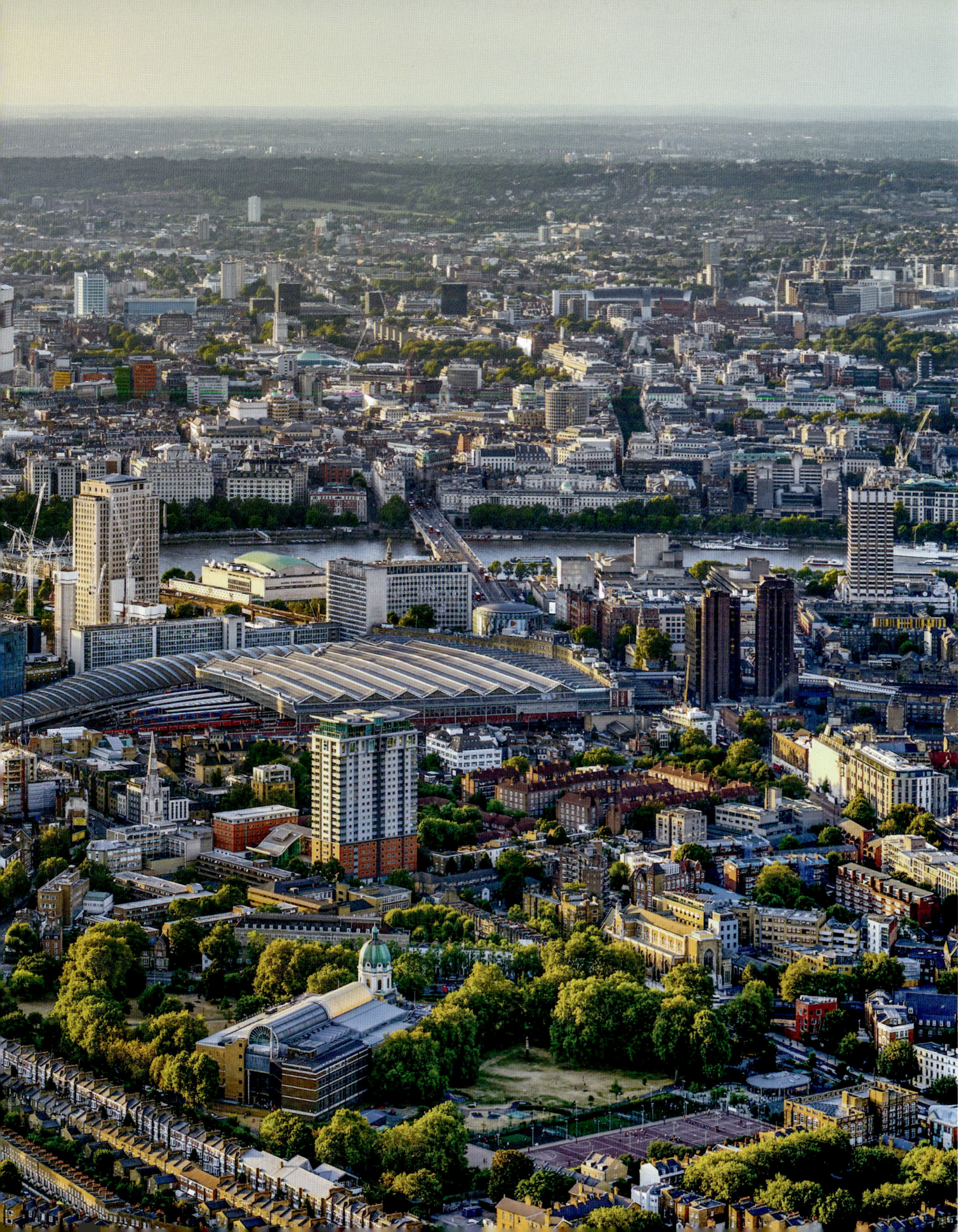

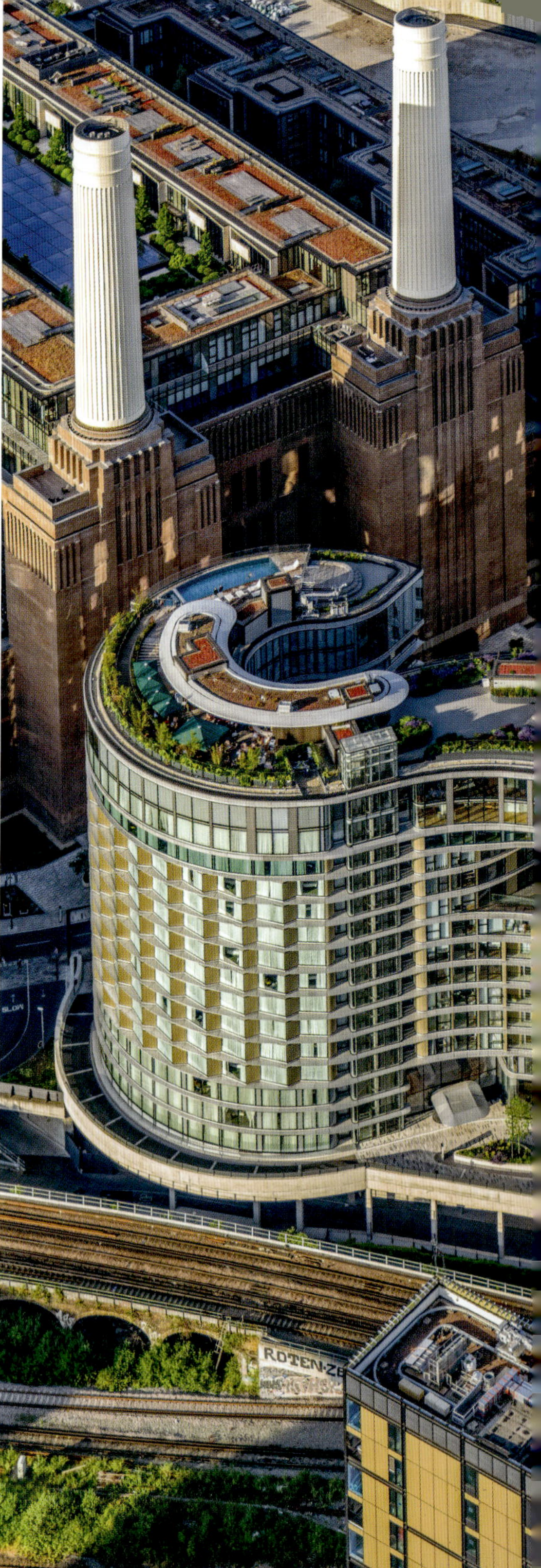

Opposite: Foster + Partners–designed apartment complex with roof gardens near the Battersea Power Station

Pages 136 & 137: Two views of the Shard at night

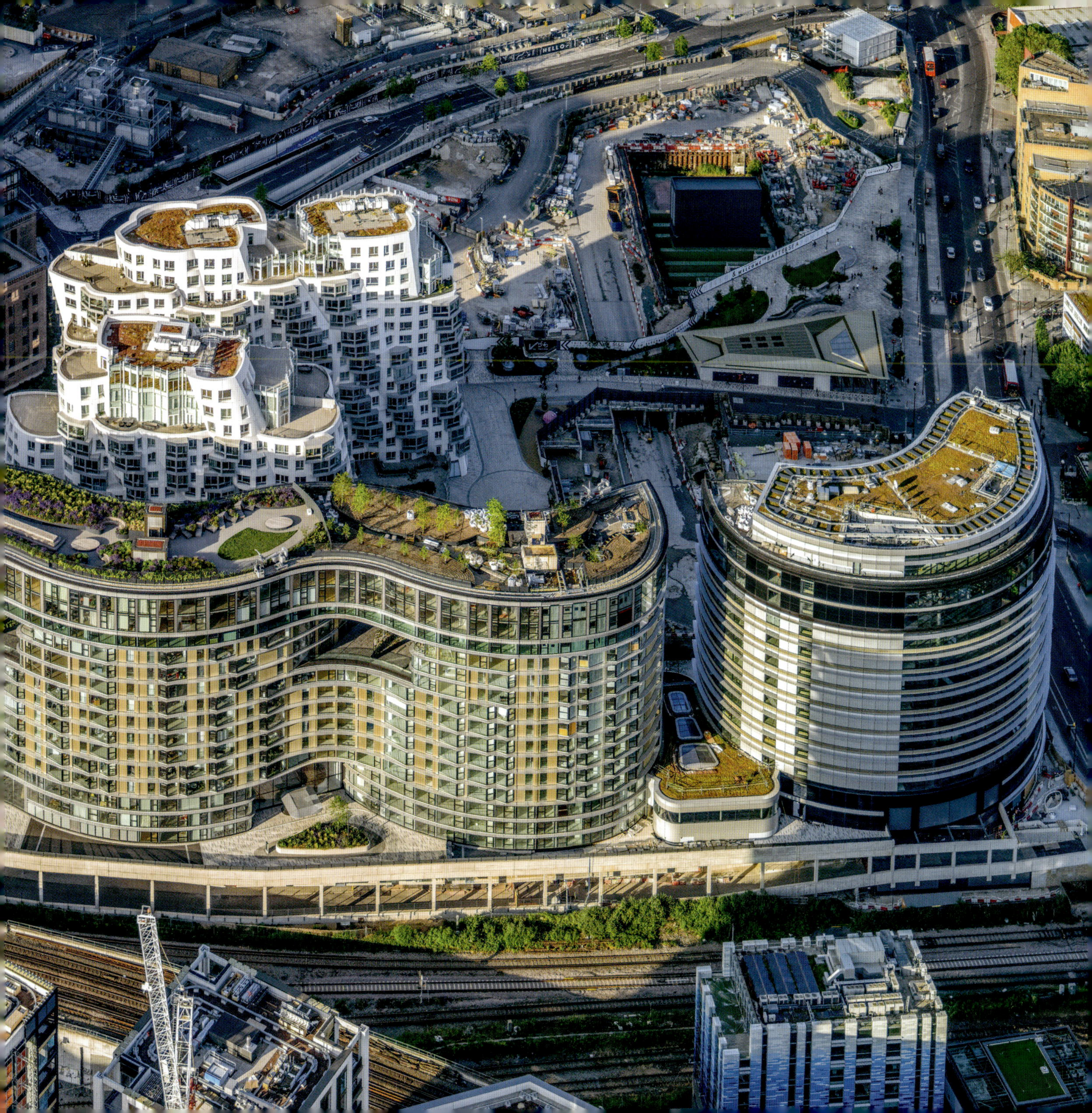

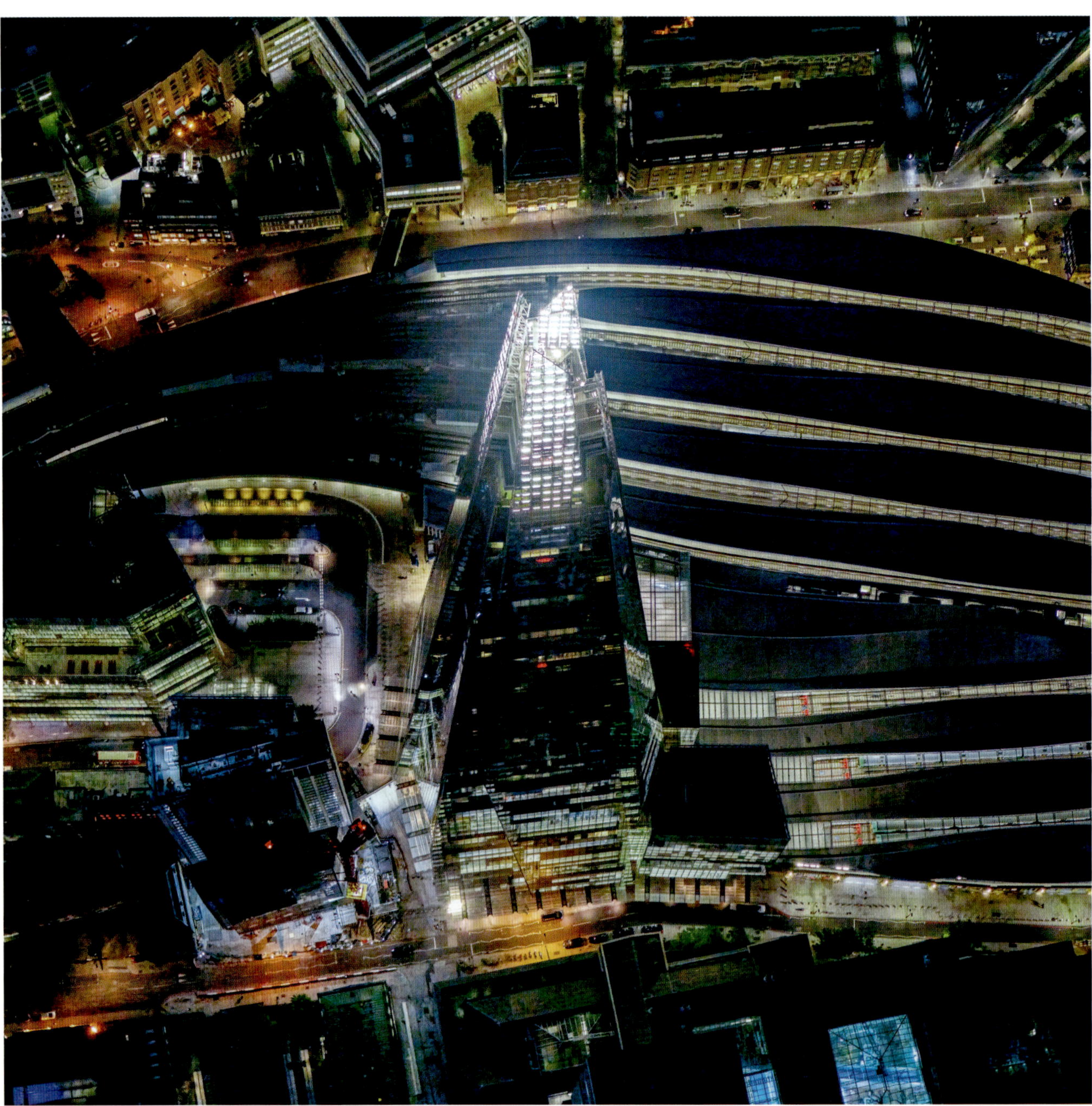

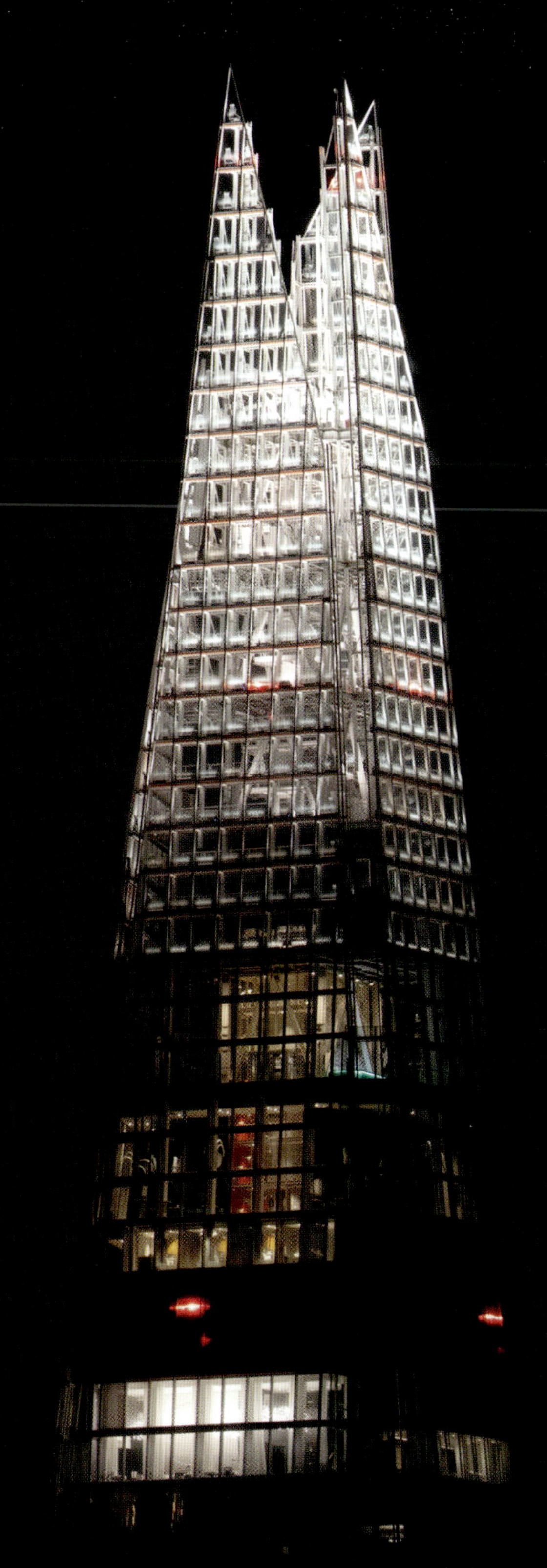

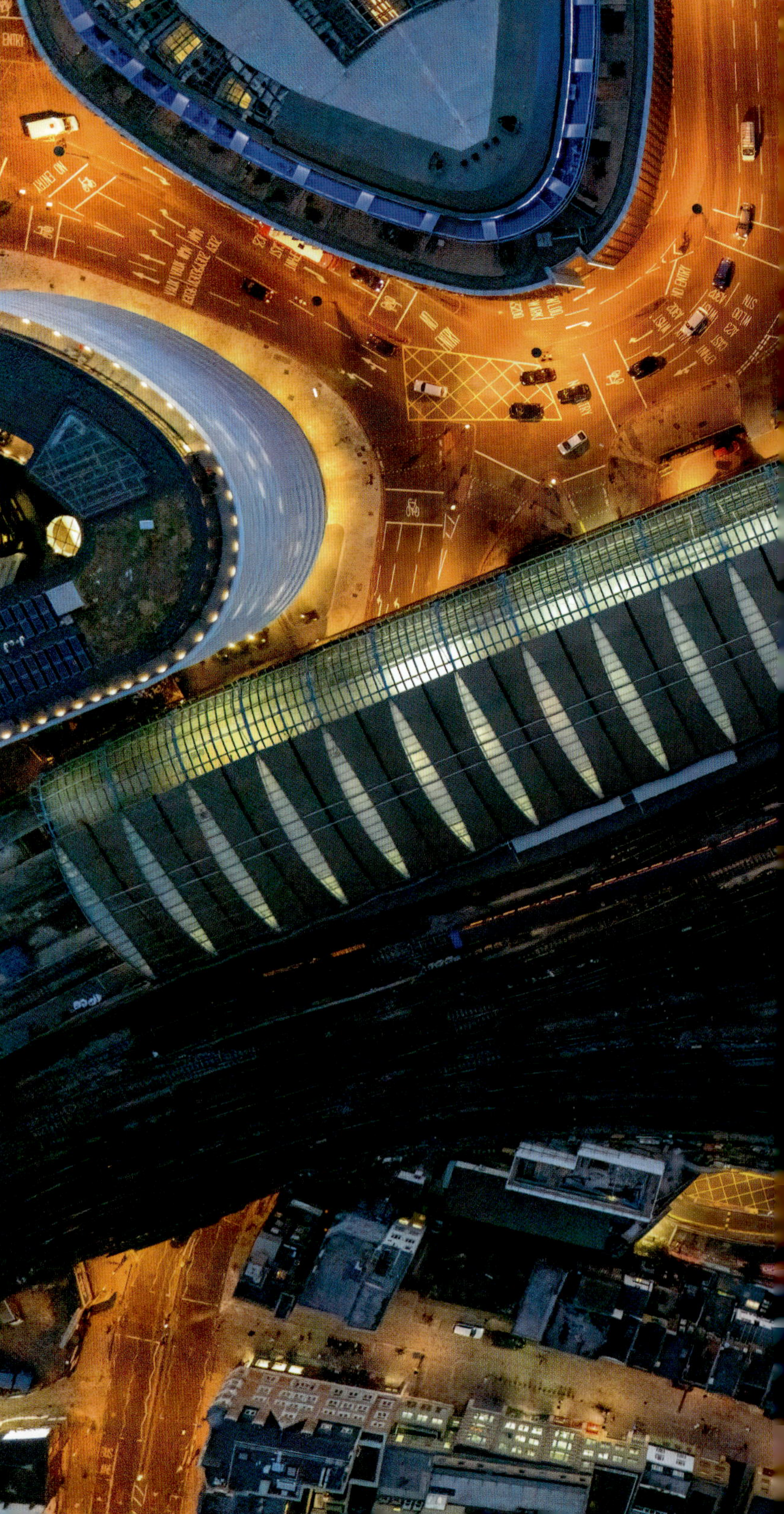

Opposite: The centipede-like international platforms of Waterloo railway station

Page 140: National Theatre, formally Royal National Theatre

Page 141: Shakespeare's Globe, with the Globe Theatre and the Sam Wanamaker Playhouse

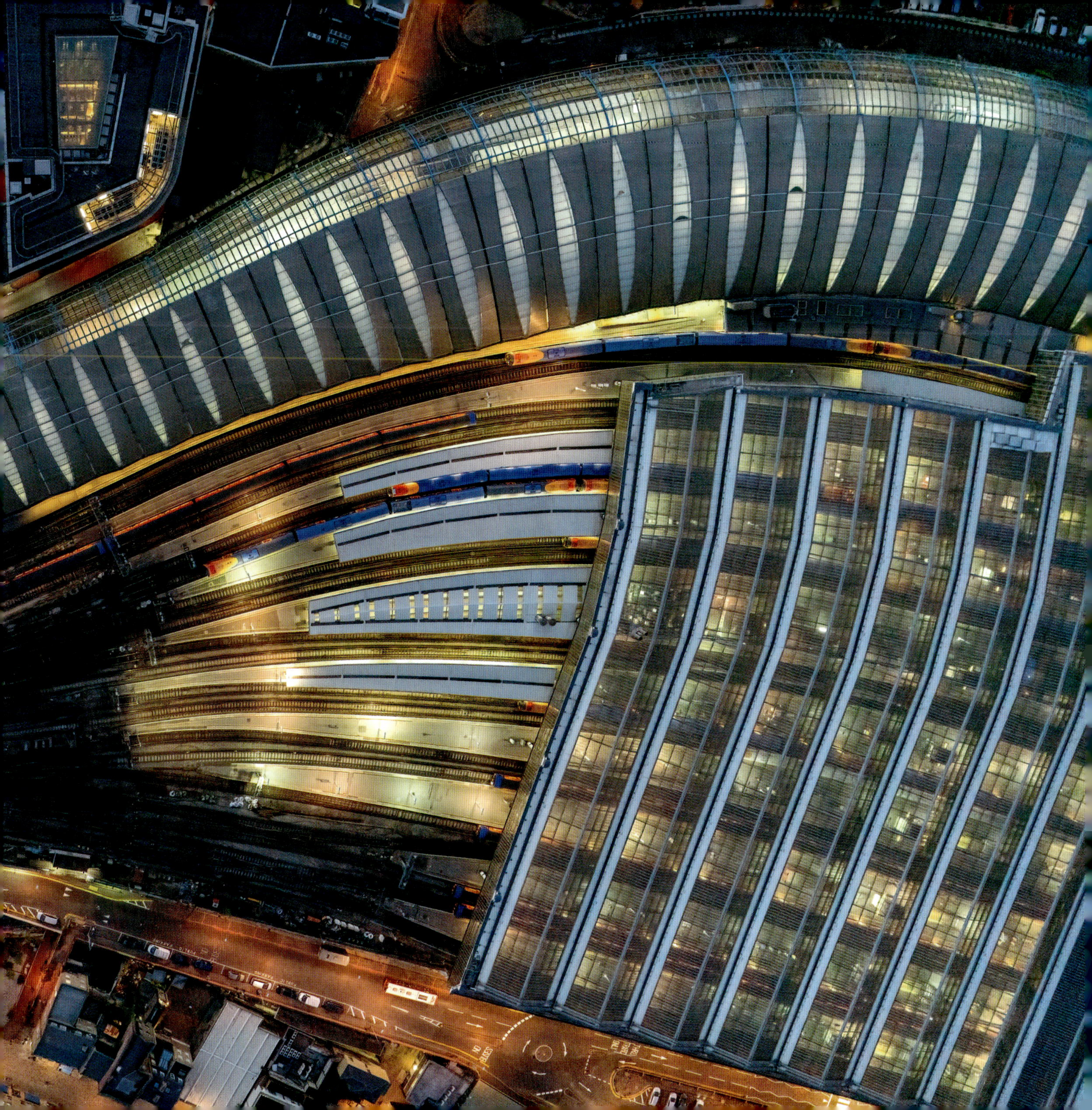

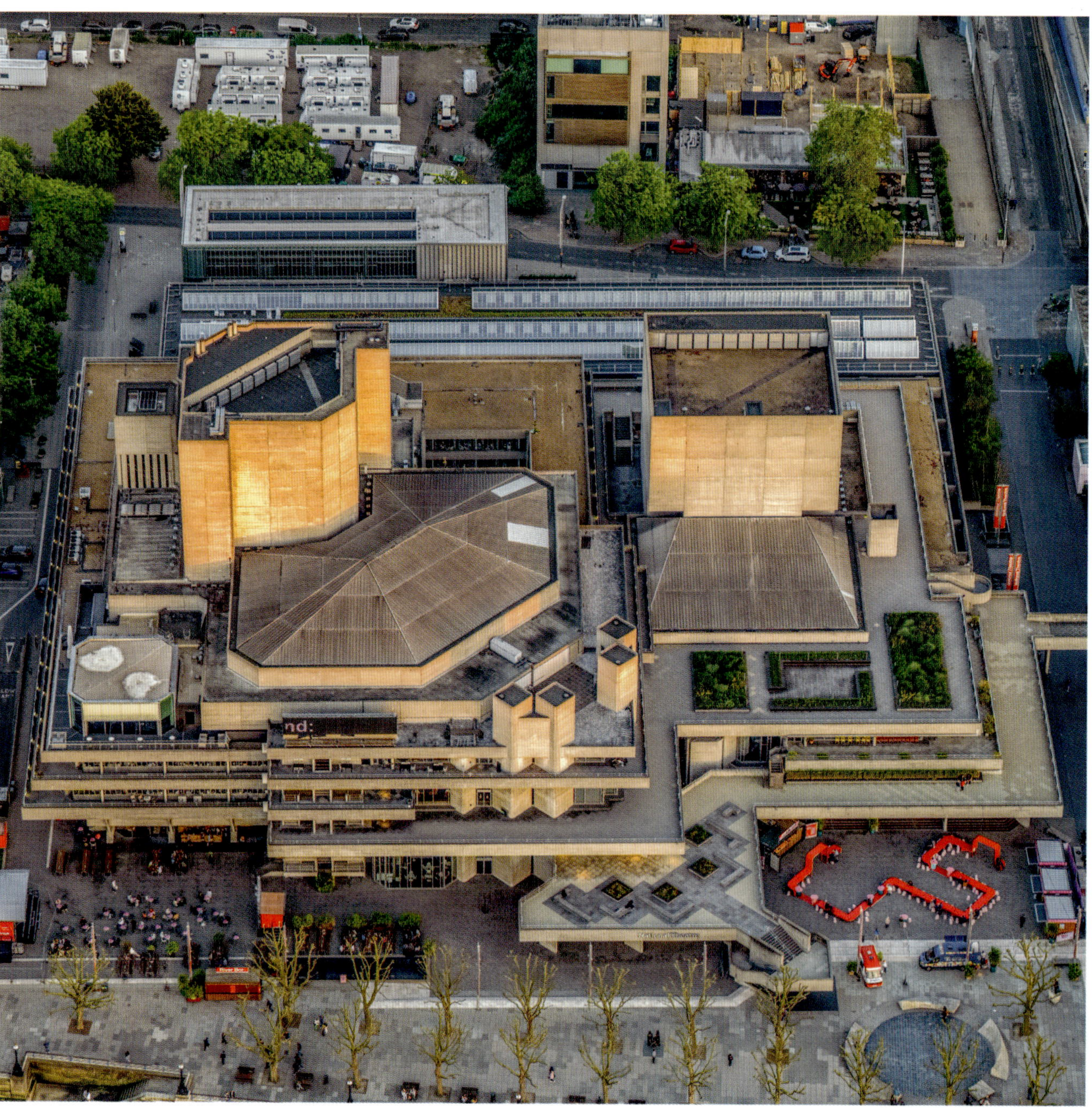

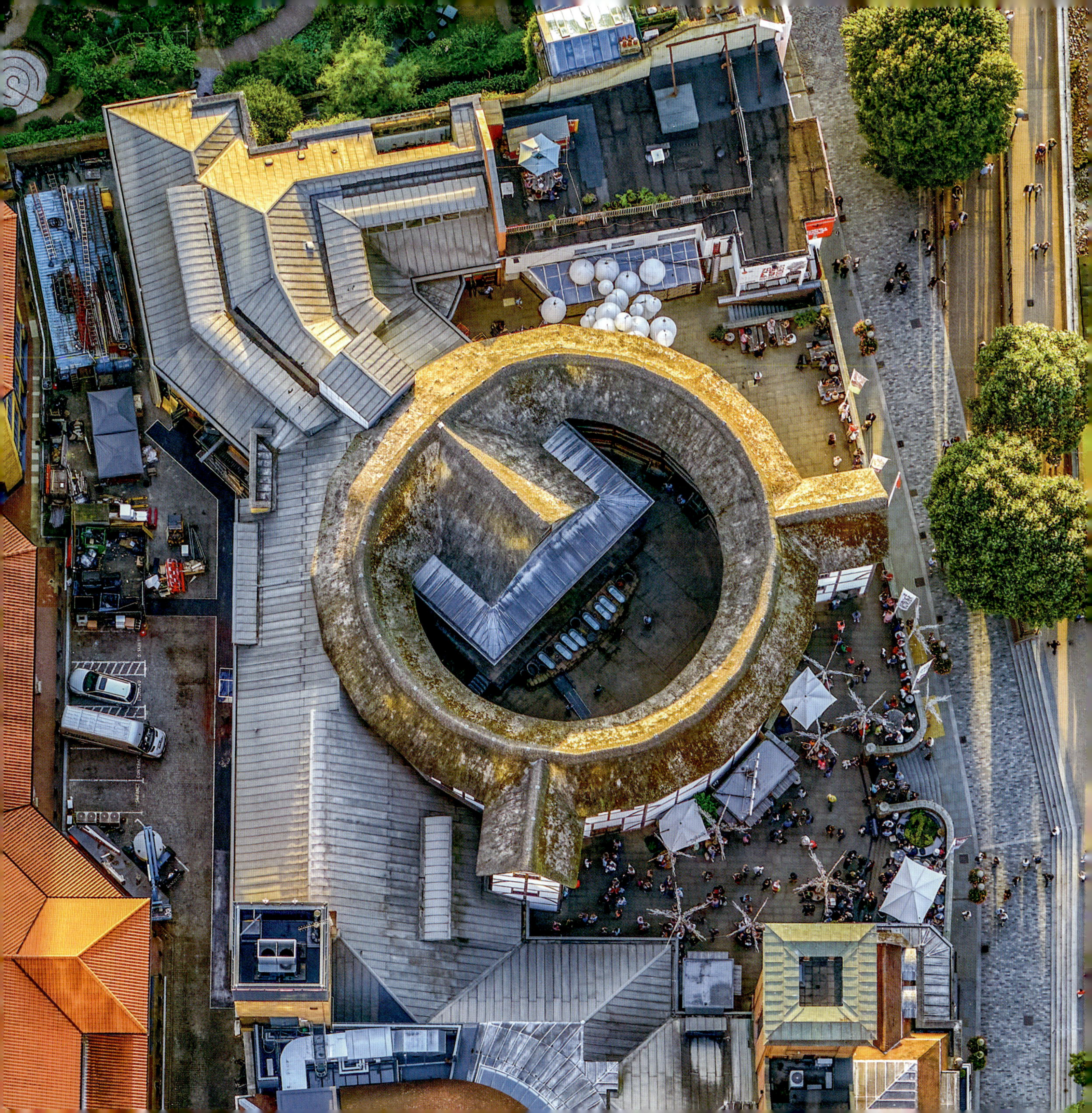

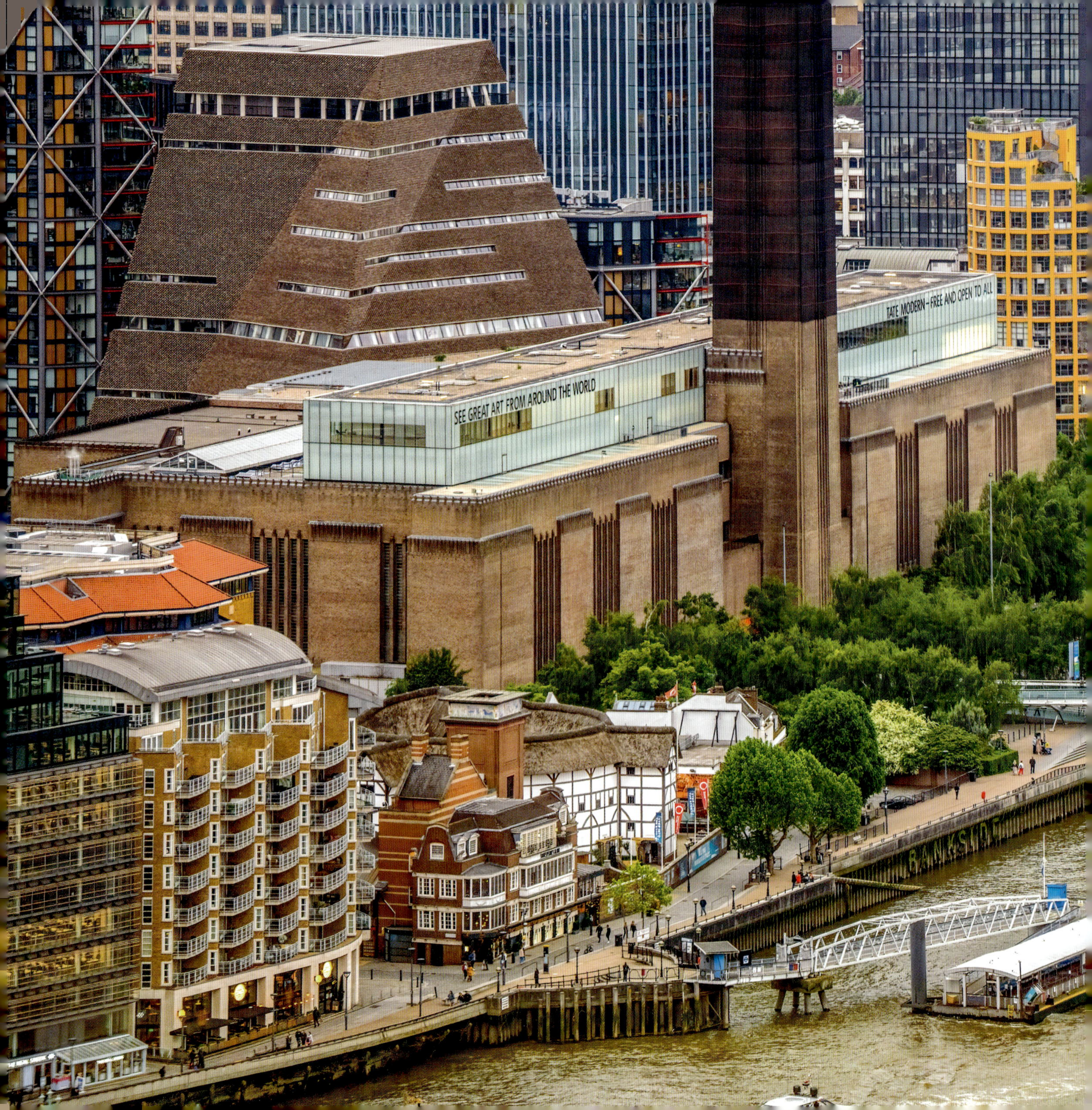
TATE MODERN—FREE AND OPEN TO ALL
SEE GREAT ART FROM AROUND THE WORLD
BANKSIDE

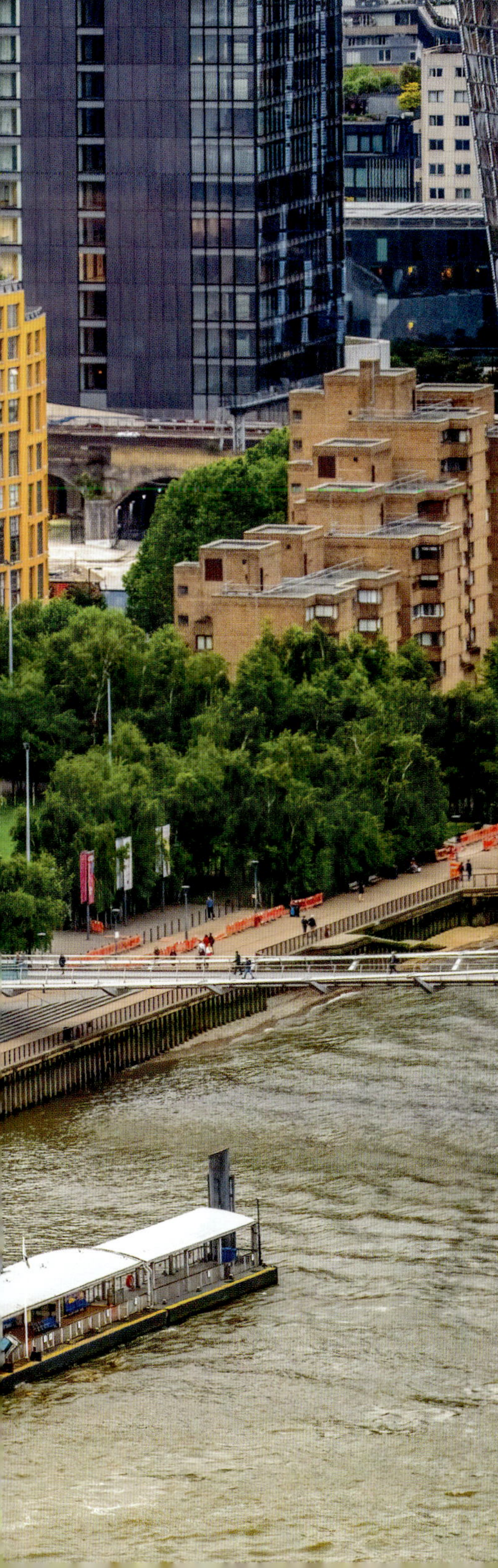

Tate Modern, with the Globe Theatre nearby

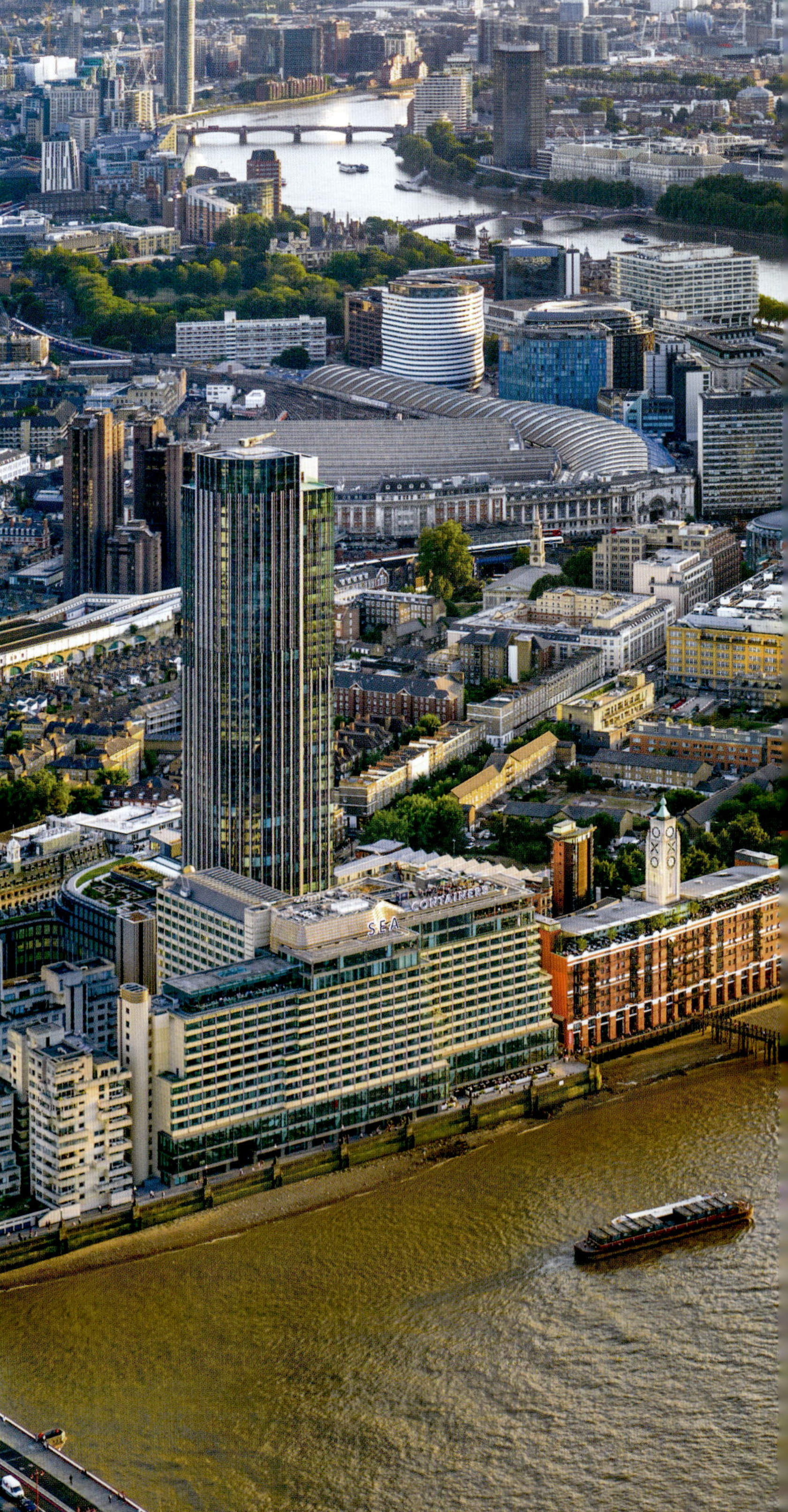

Opposite: A view of the South Bank, with the Sea Containers hotel at far left, the Oxo Tower at center, and the Queen's Walk and Gabriel's Wharf along the shore

Pages 146 & 147: Two views of the London Eye

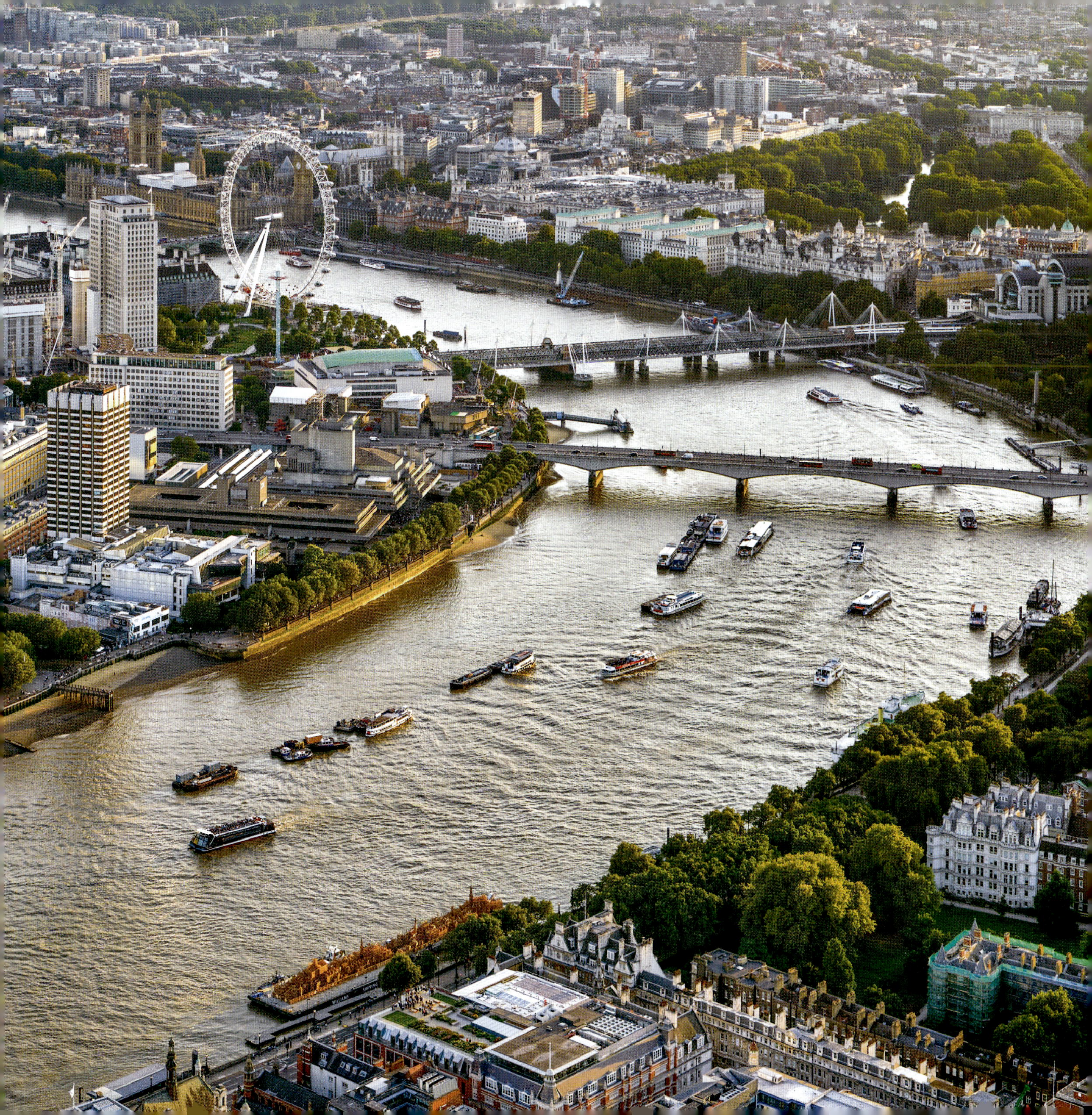

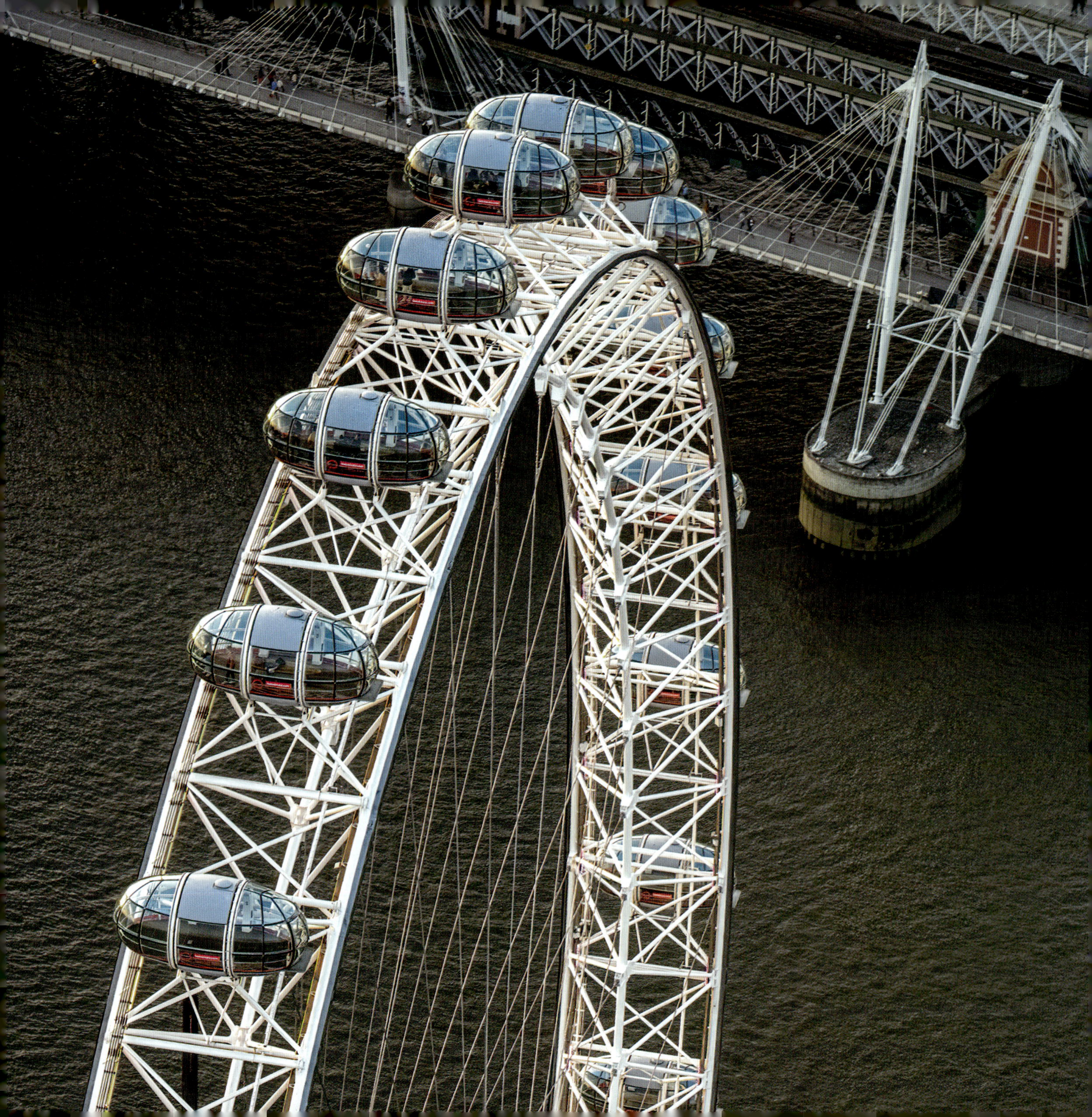

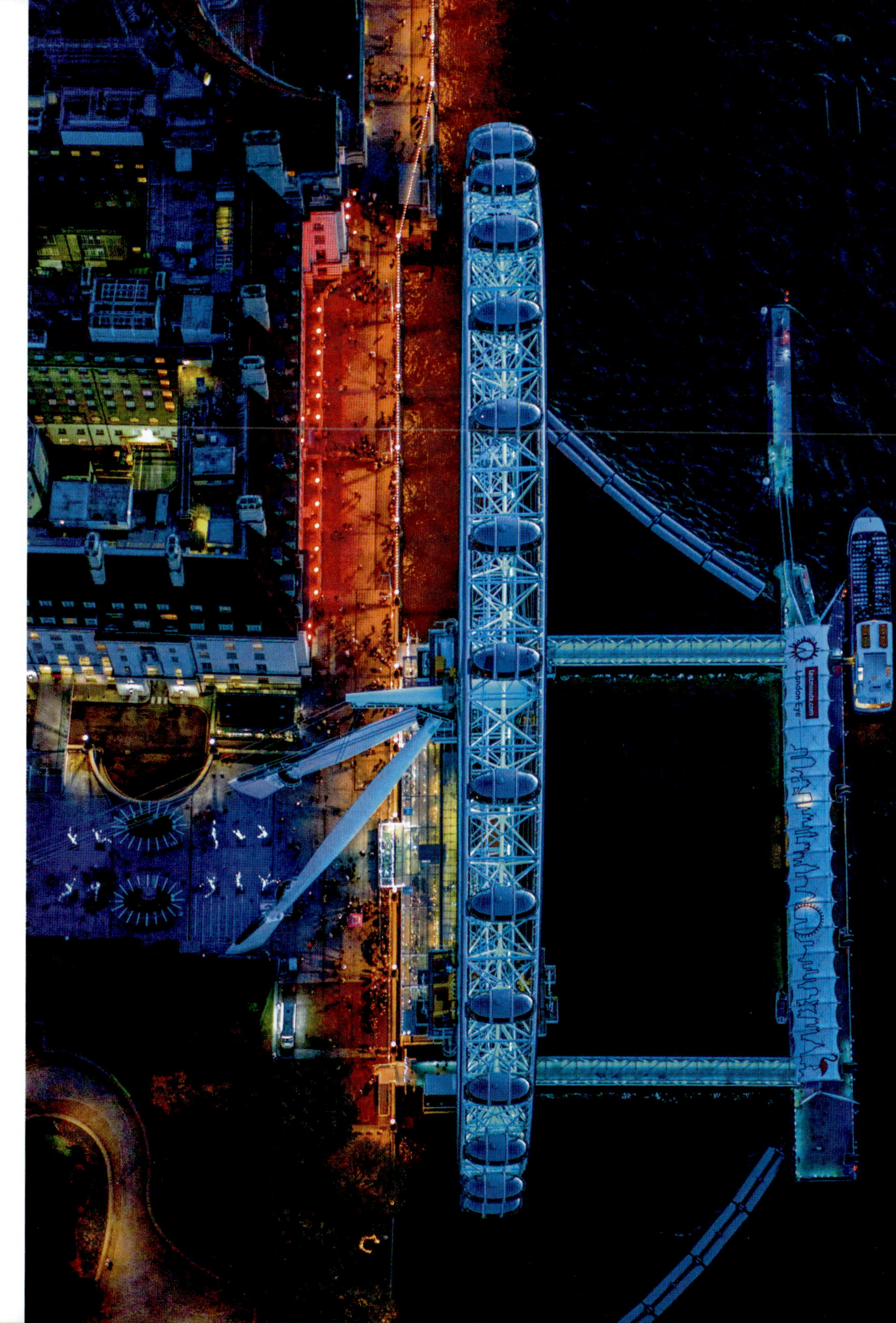
London Eye

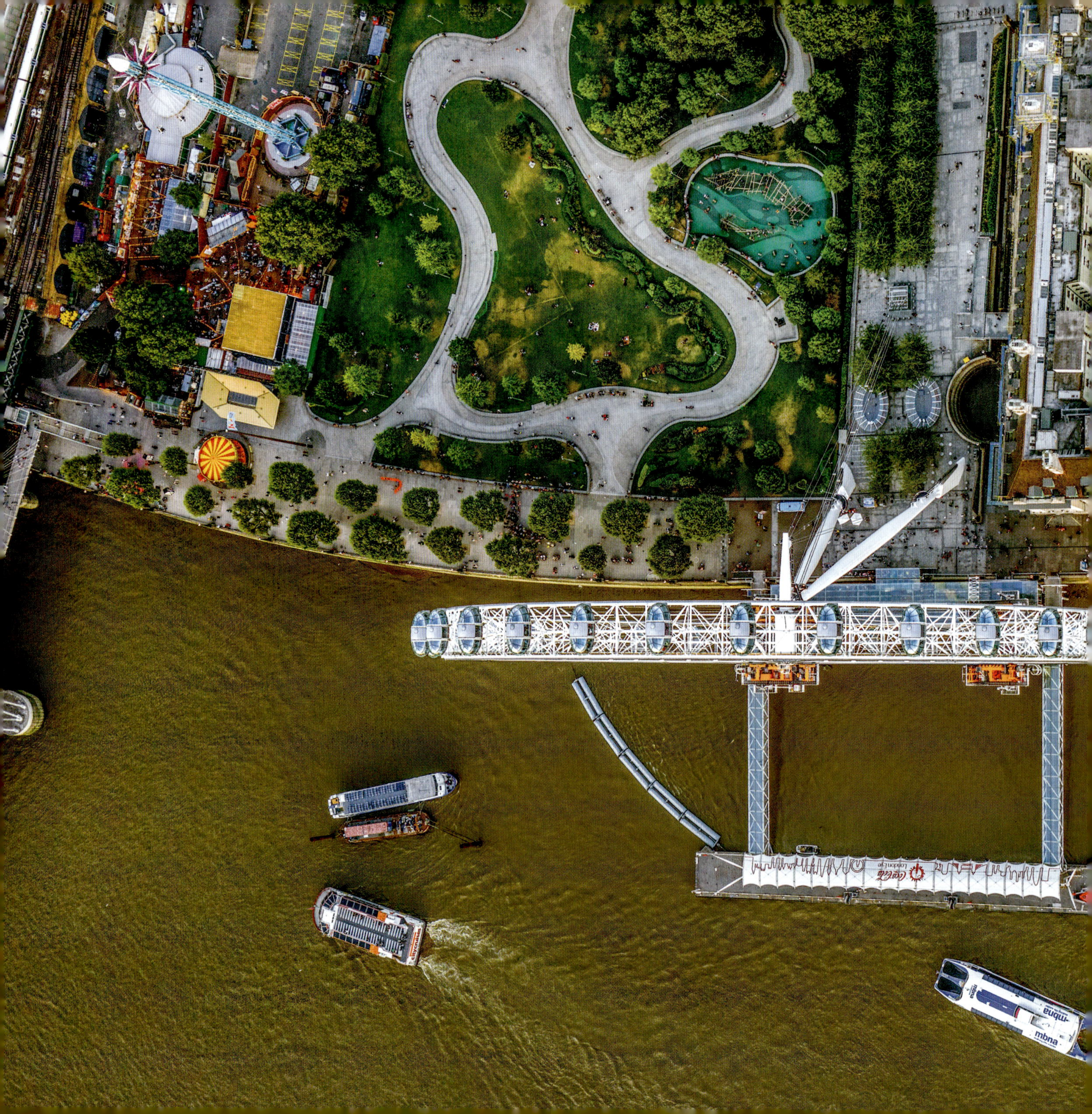
mbna

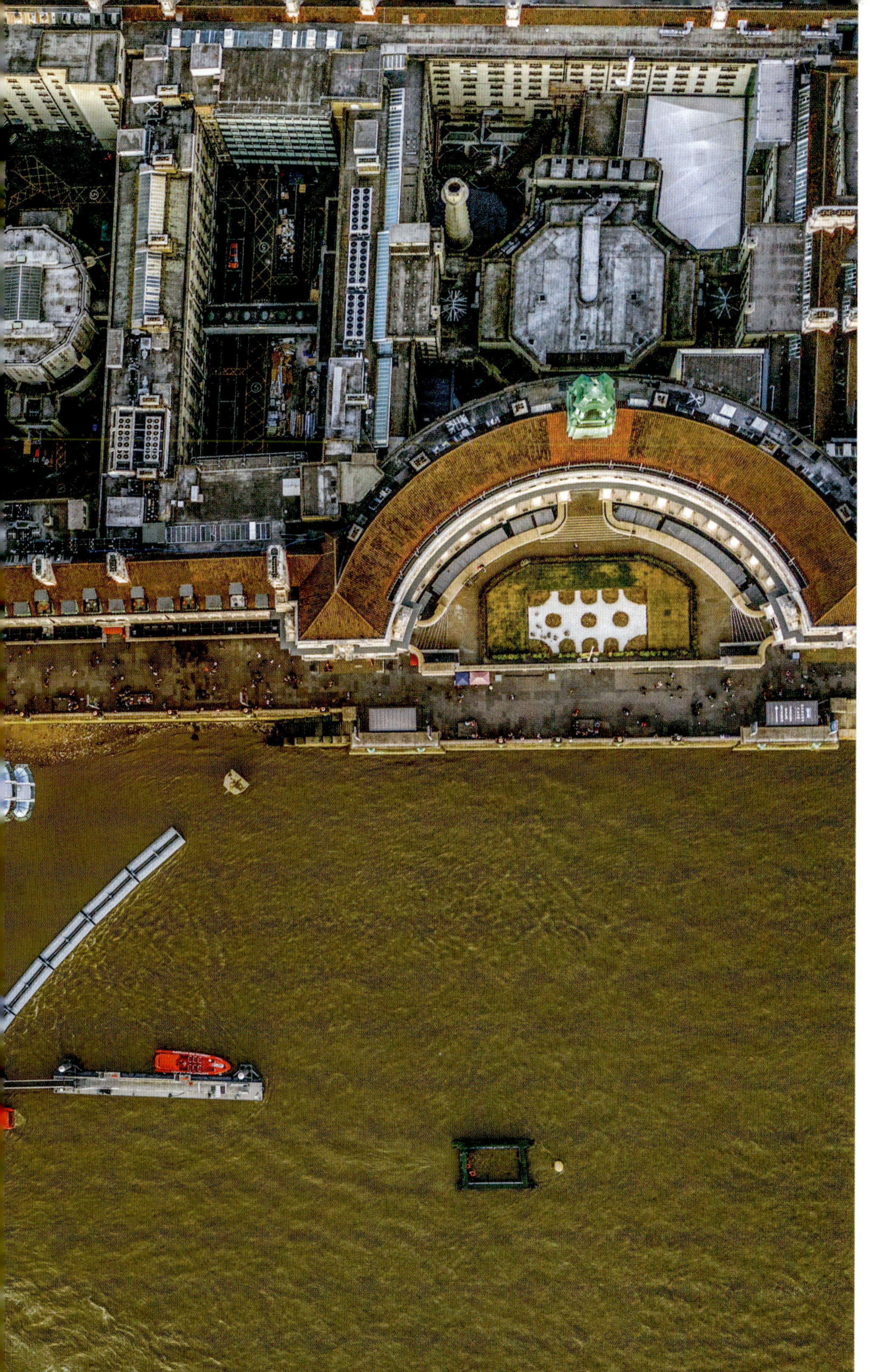

Looking down on the London Eye

Opposite: Old Royal Naval College, now the University of Greenwich

Page 152: Some of the buildings of the Old Royal Naval College

Page 153: *Cutty Sark* clipper ship, once used to bring tea from Asia, now preserved as a maritime museum near the Old Royal Naval College

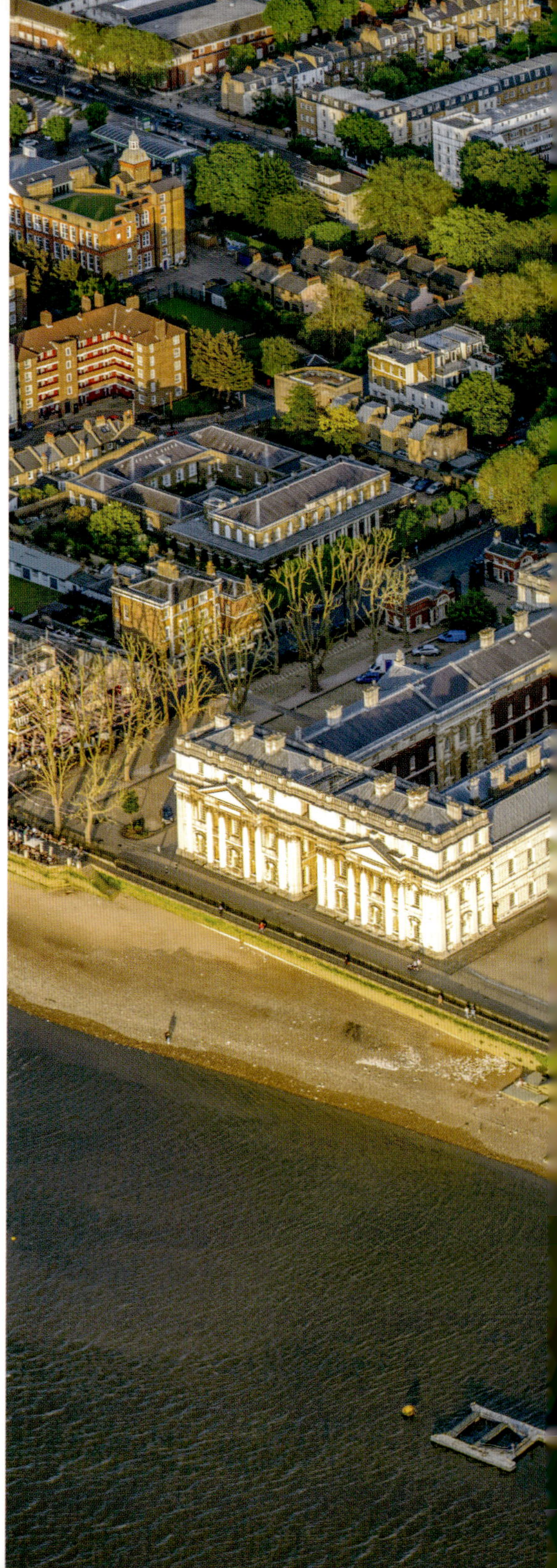

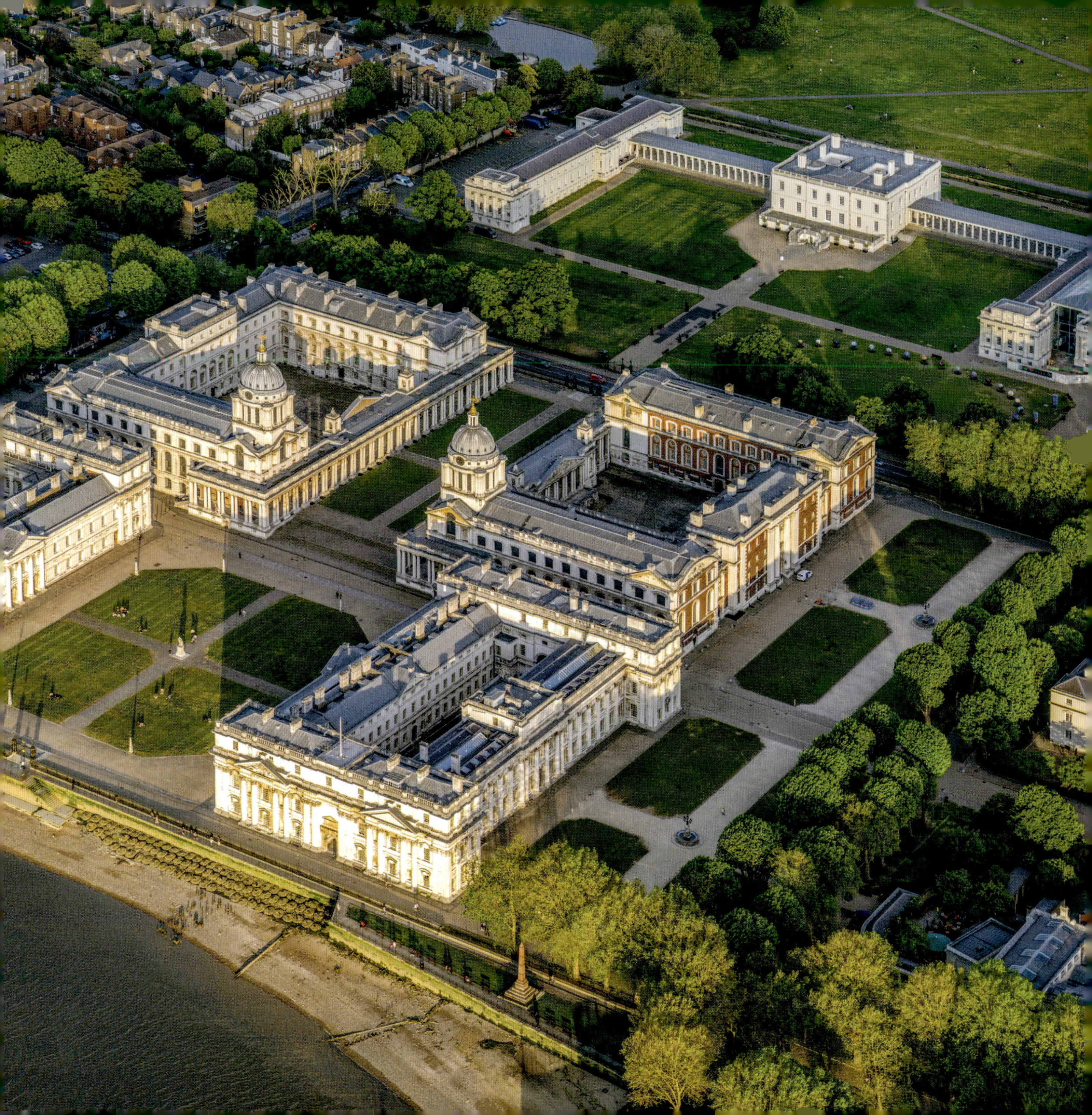

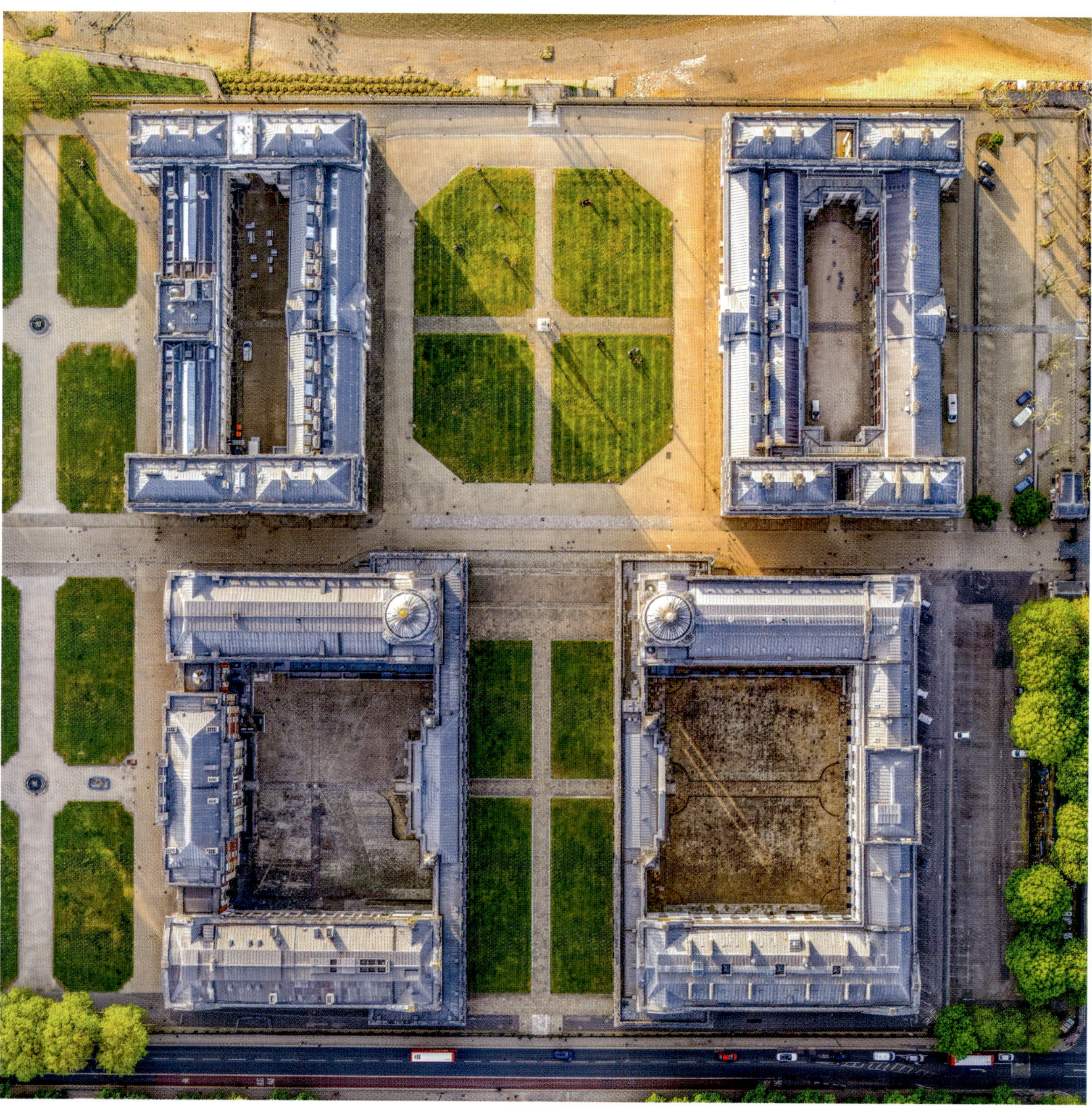

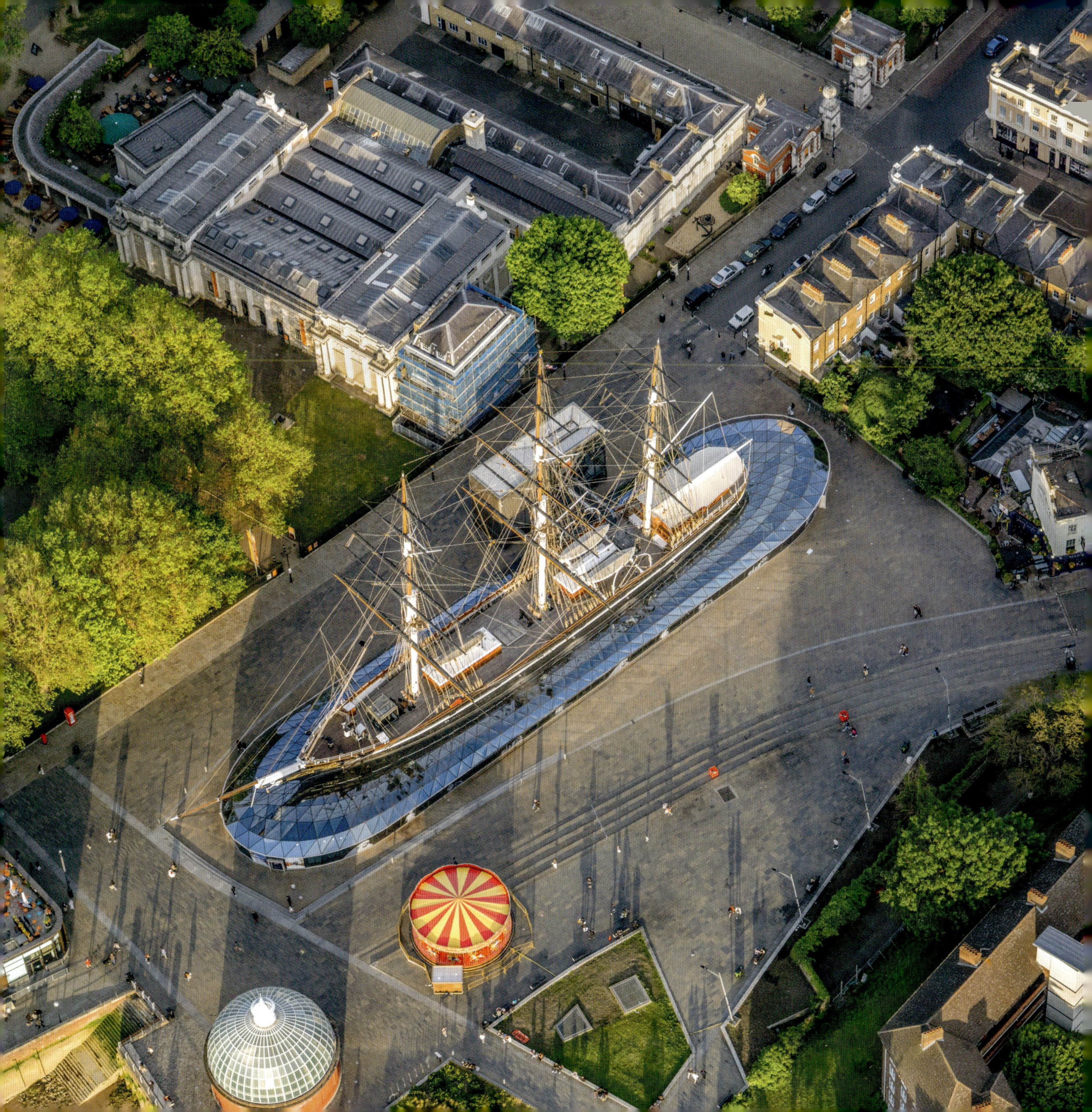

ROYAL PALACES

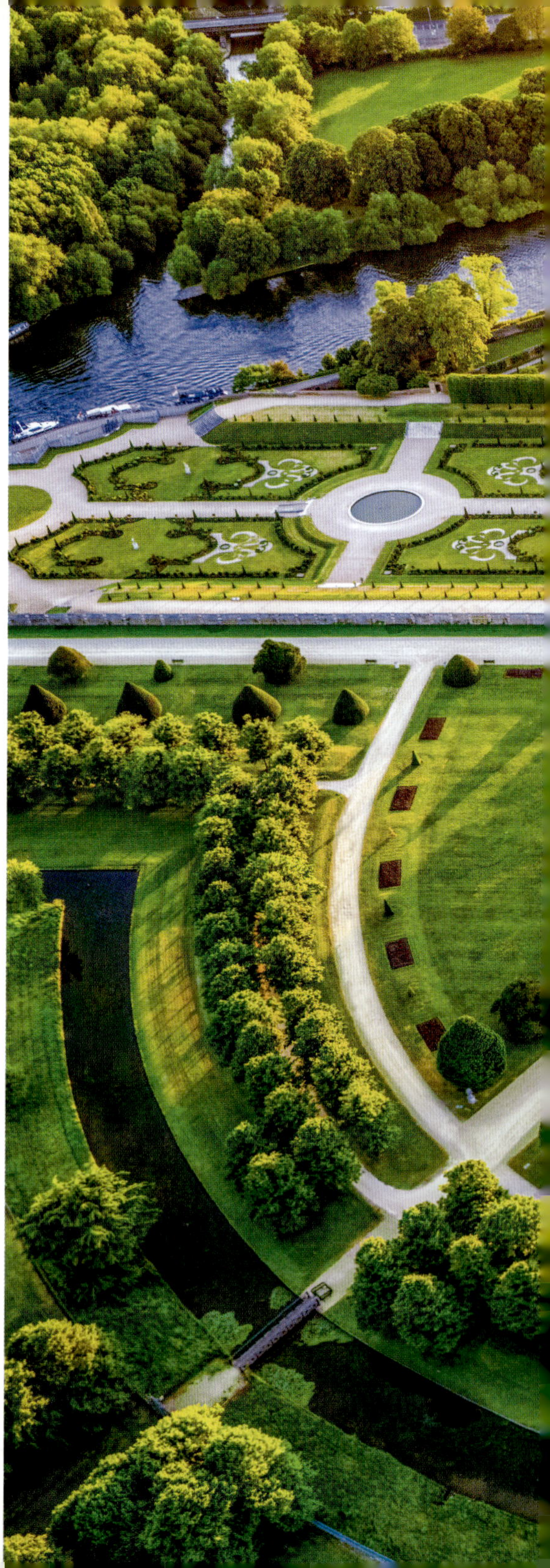

Opposite and Pages 156–157: Hampton Court Palace

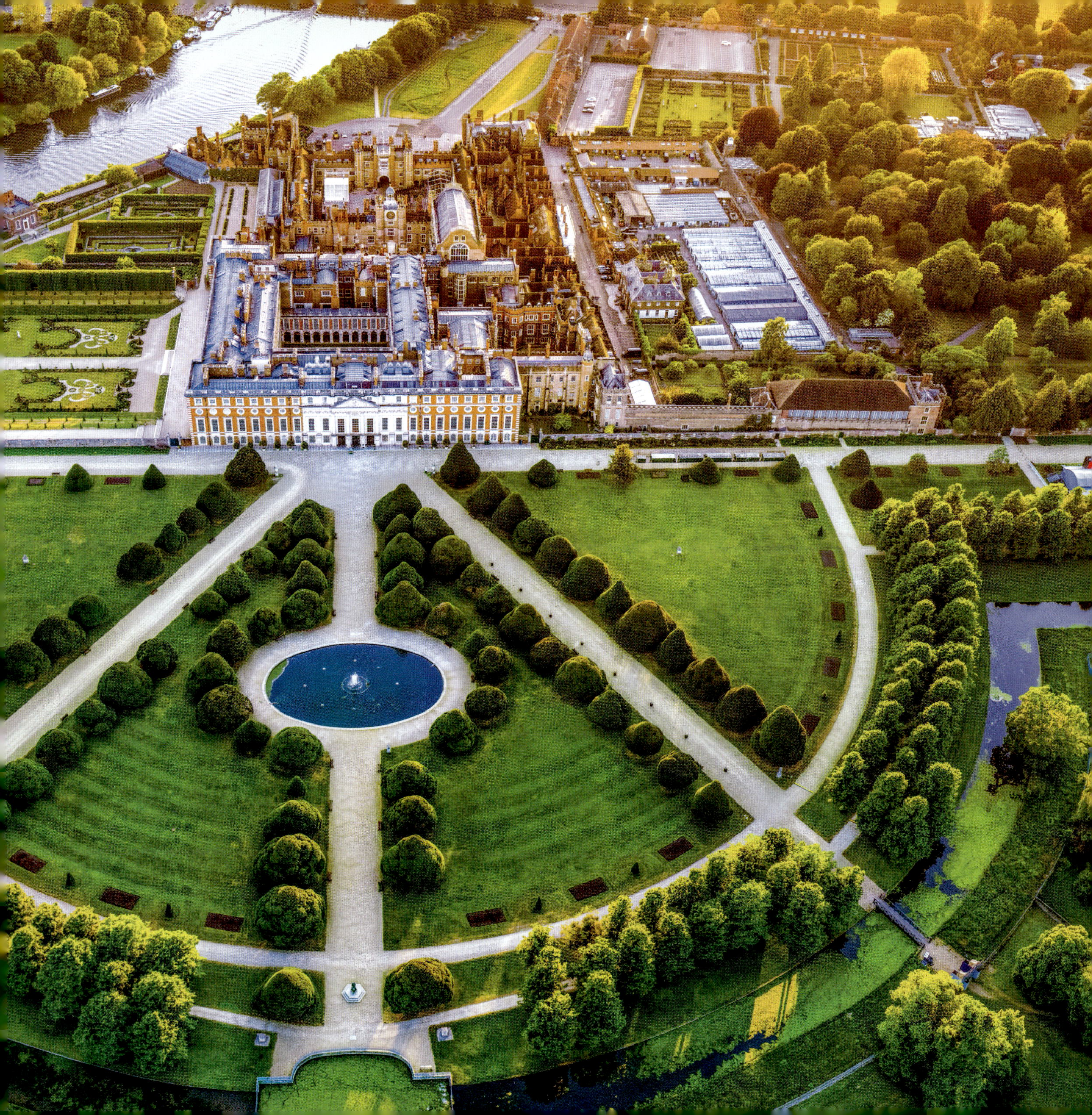

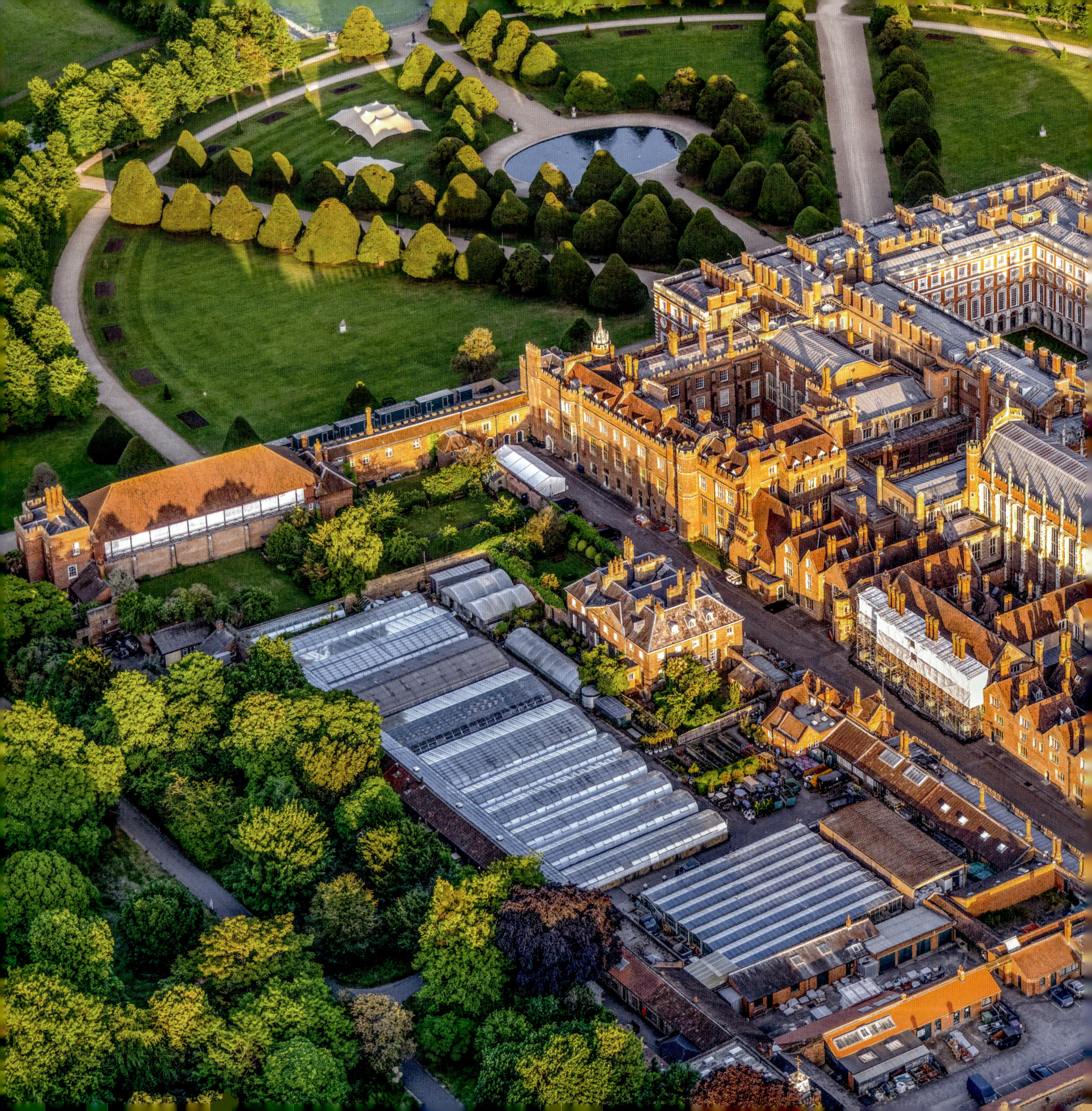

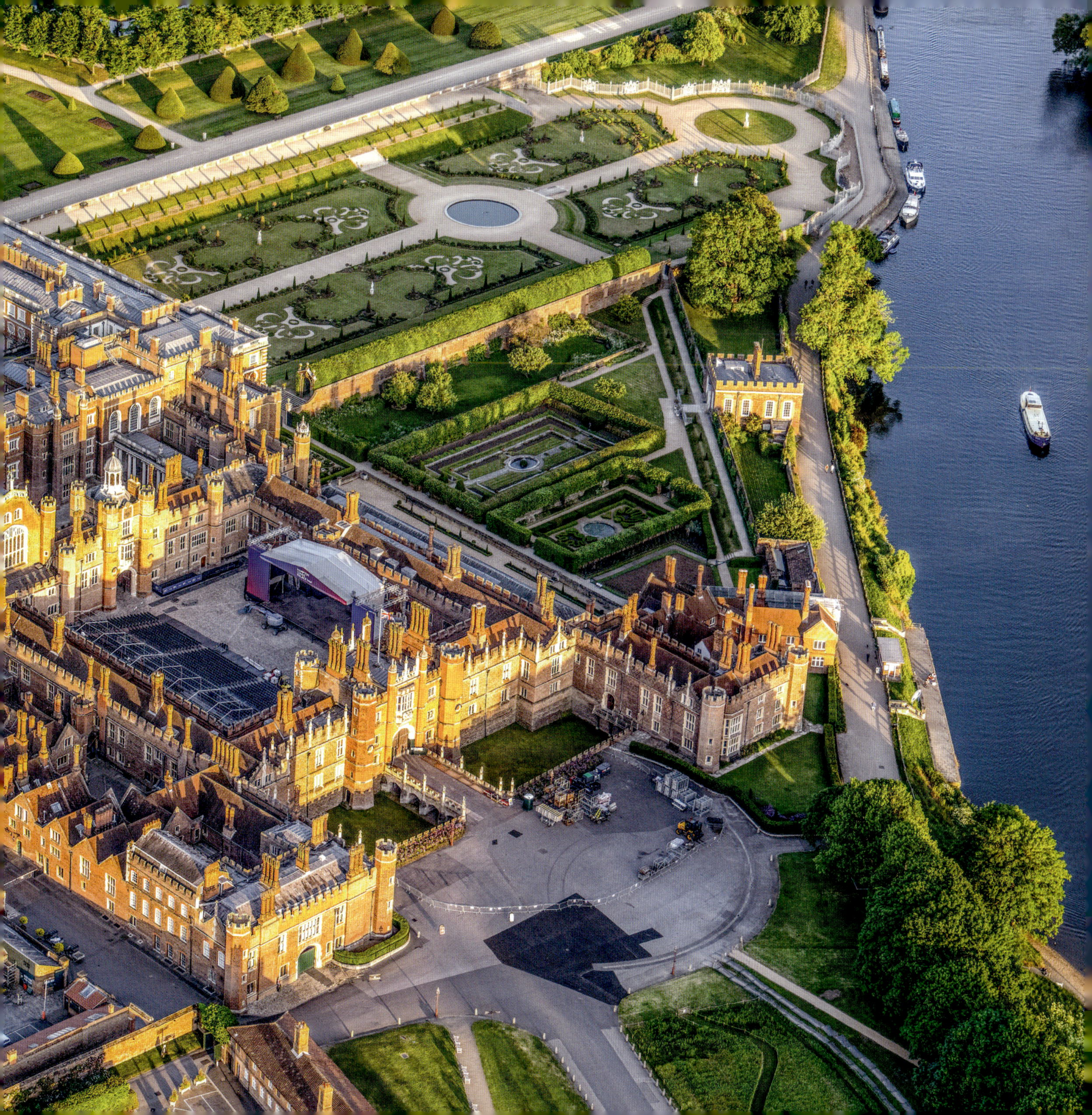

Privy Garden and Pond Gardens at Hampton Court Palace

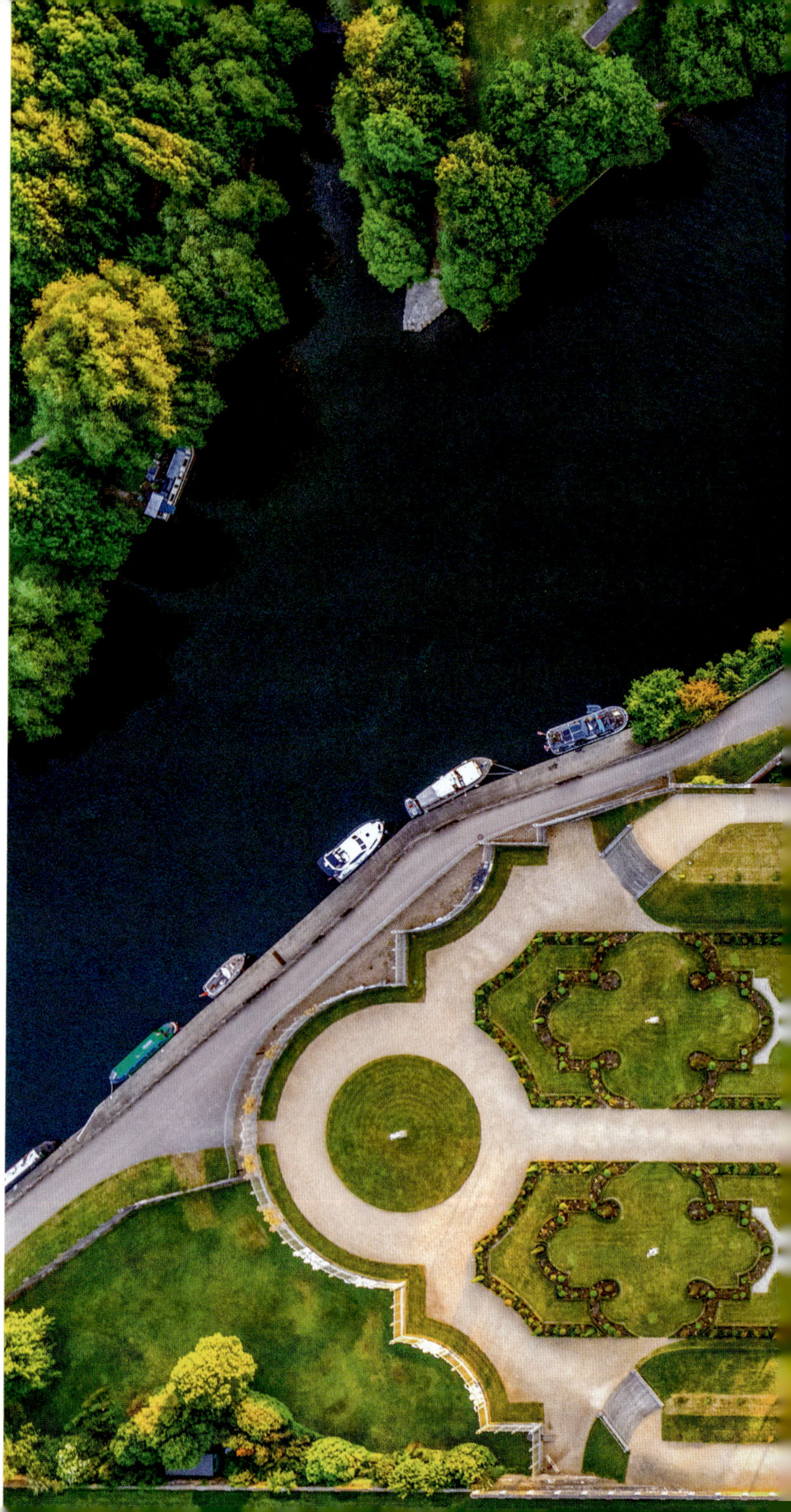

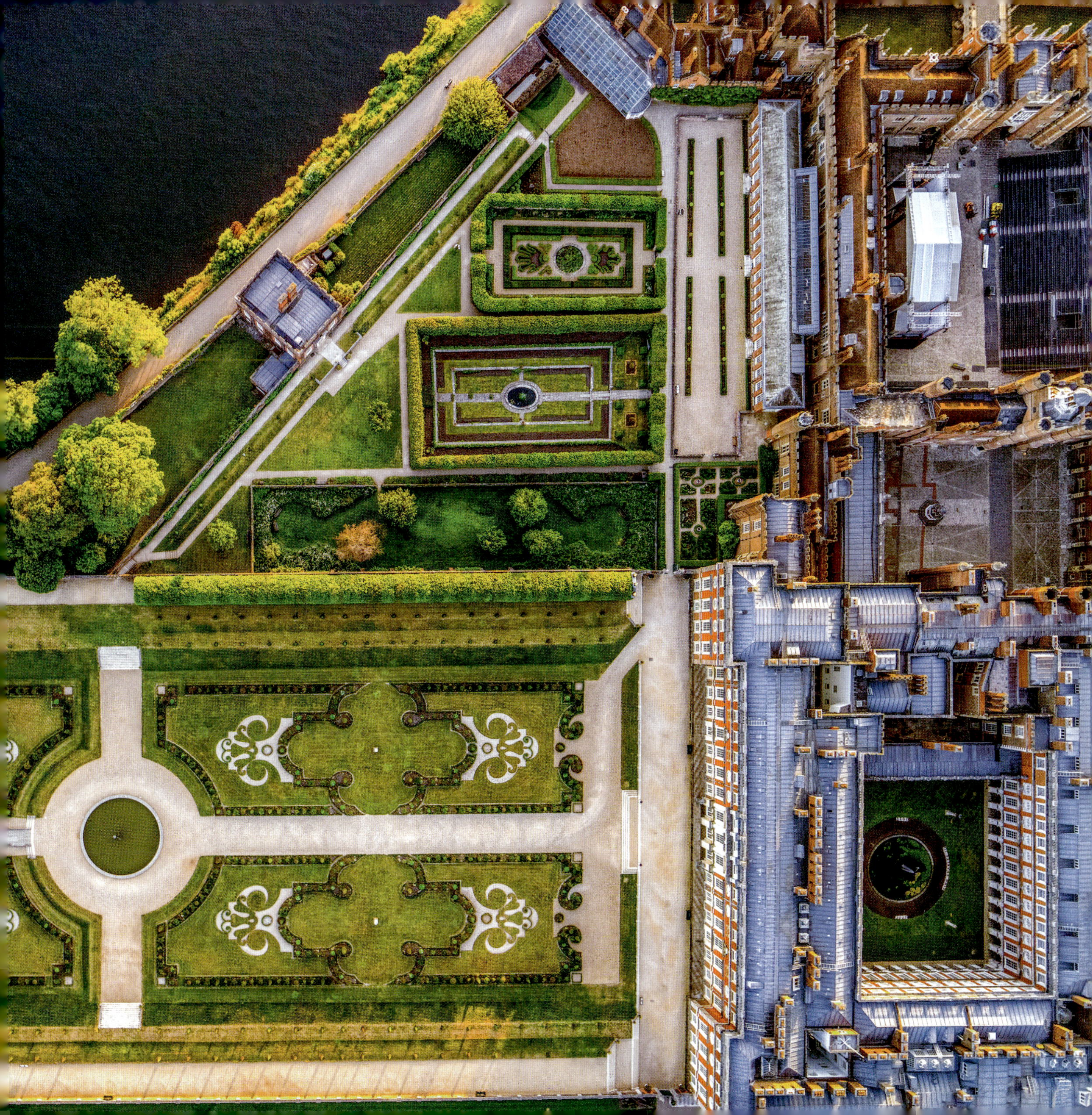

A floral tribute to the newly crowned King Charles III

in a small courtyard of Hampton Court Palace

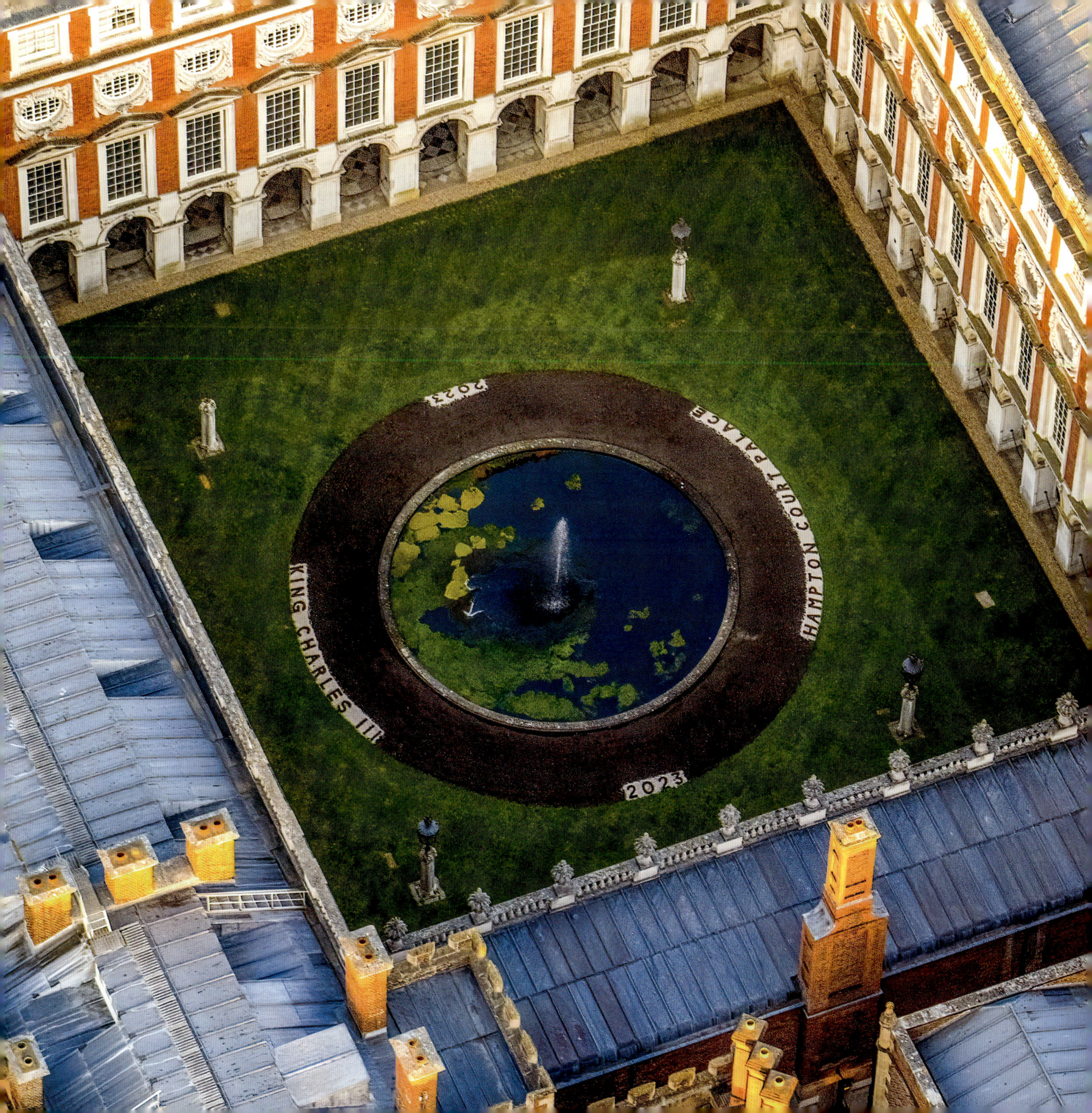
2023
HAMPTON COURT PALACE
KING CHARLES III
2023

Opposite and Page 164: Buckingham Palace

Page 165: Kensington Palace

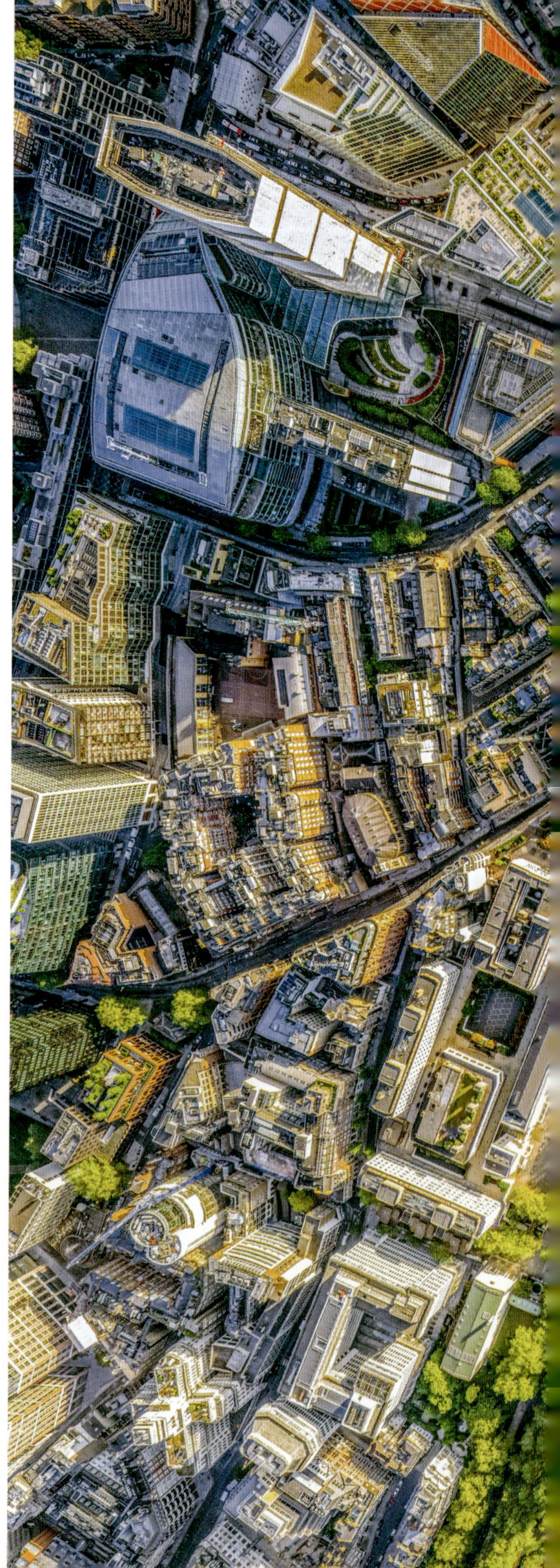

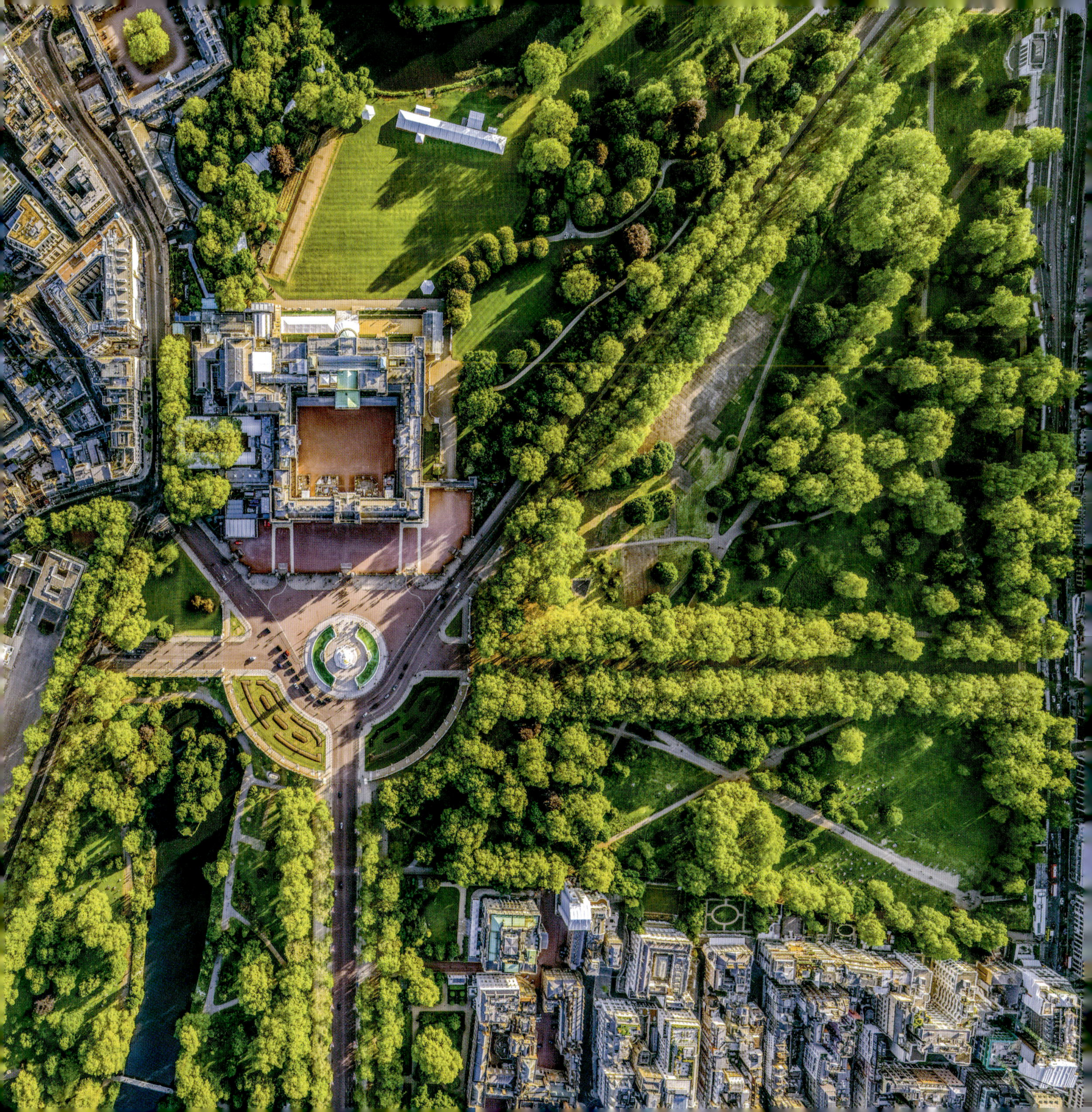

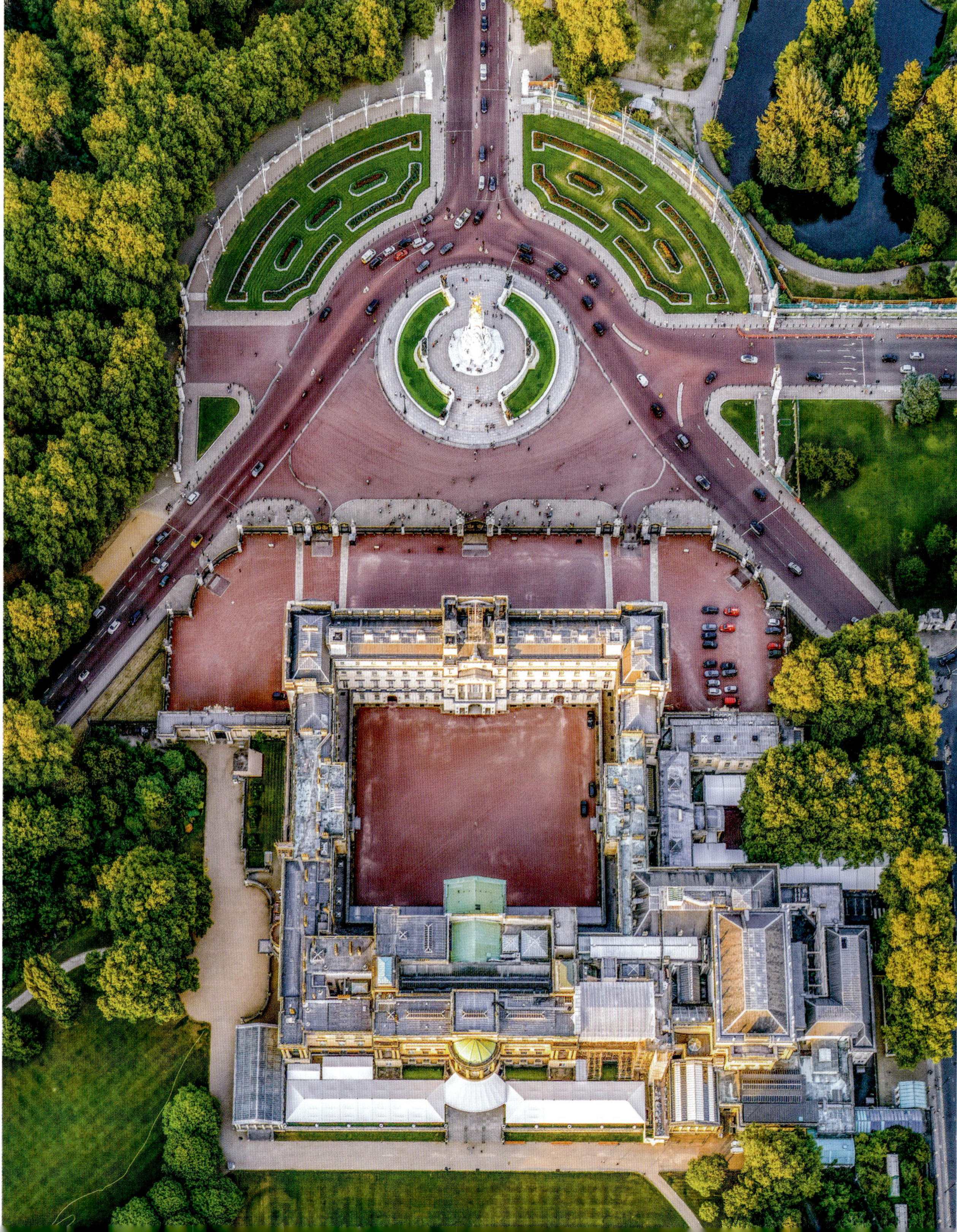

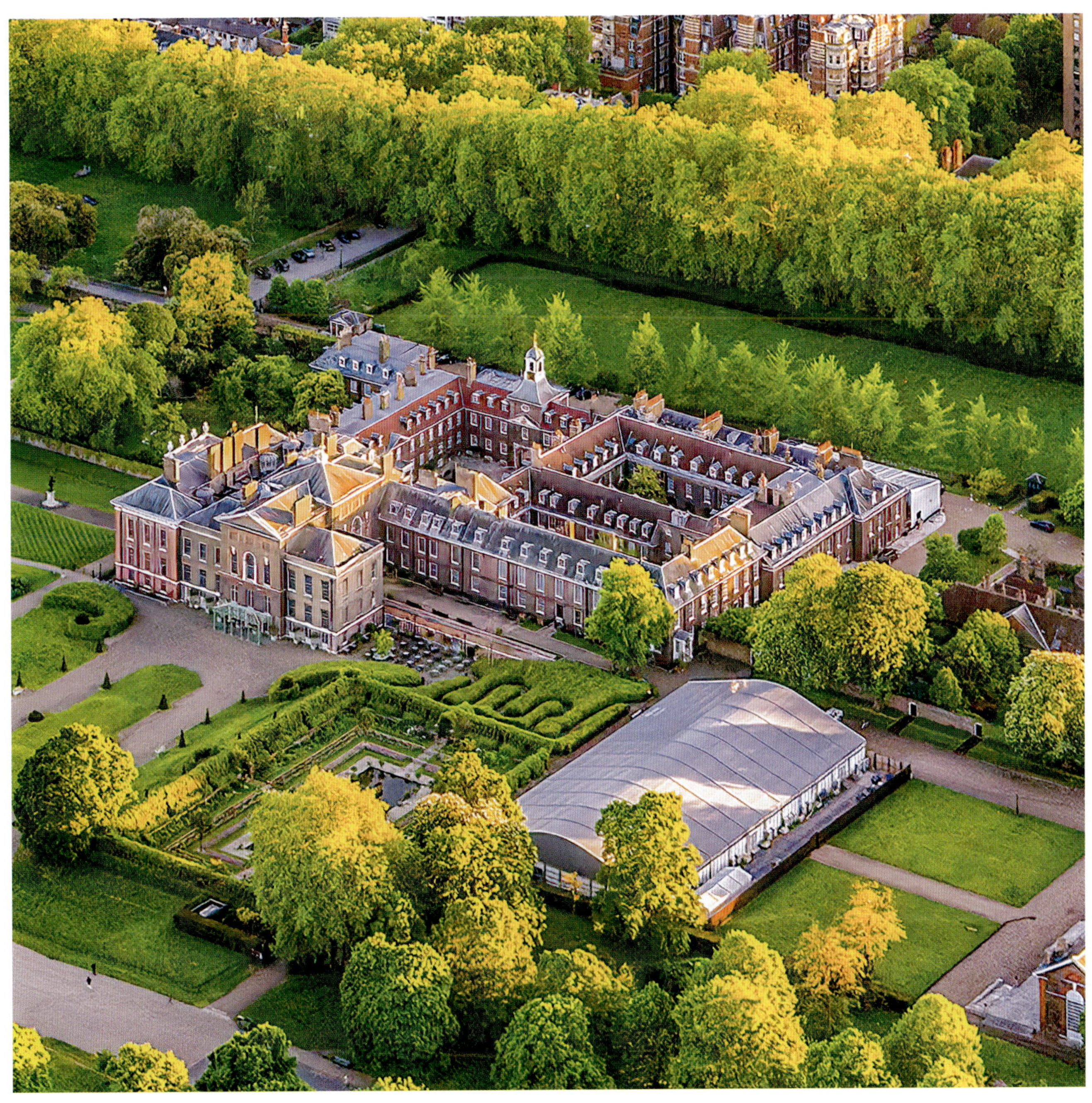

165

Kensington Palace and Kensington Palace Gardens

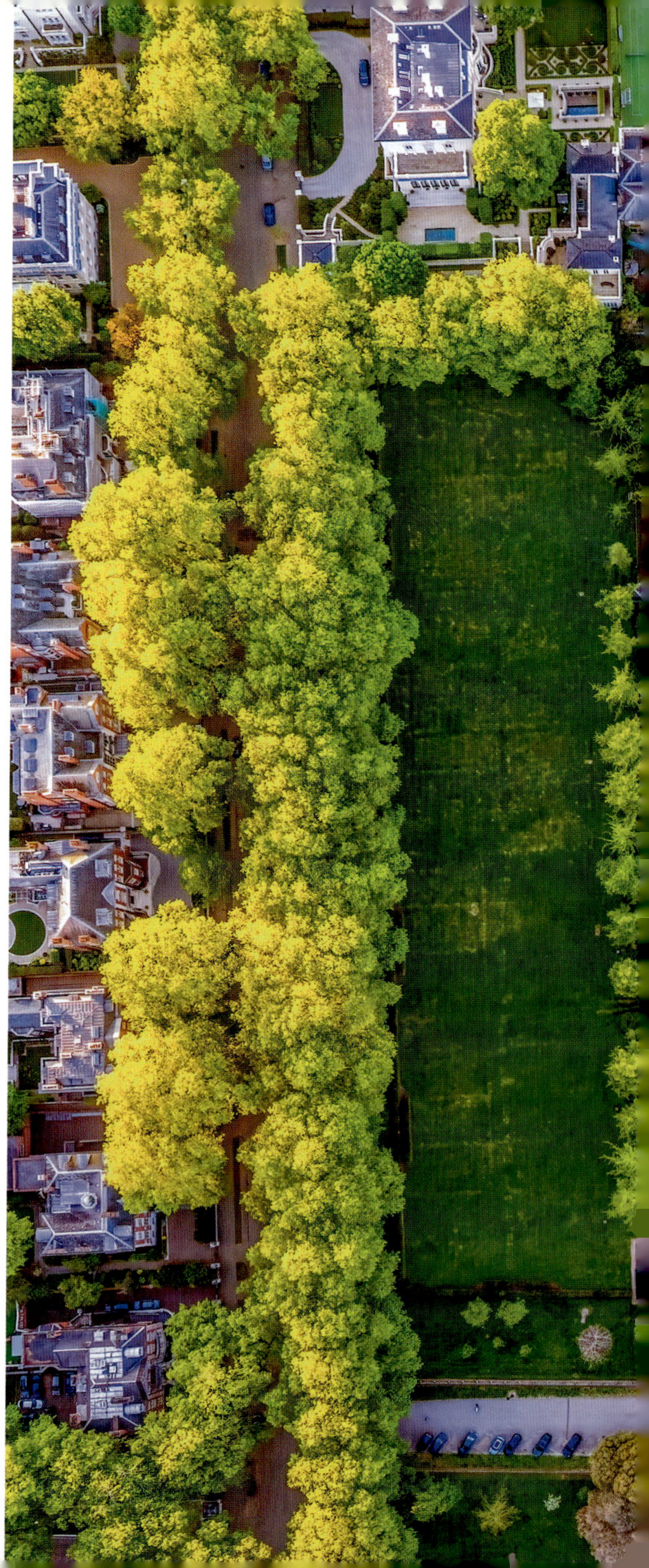

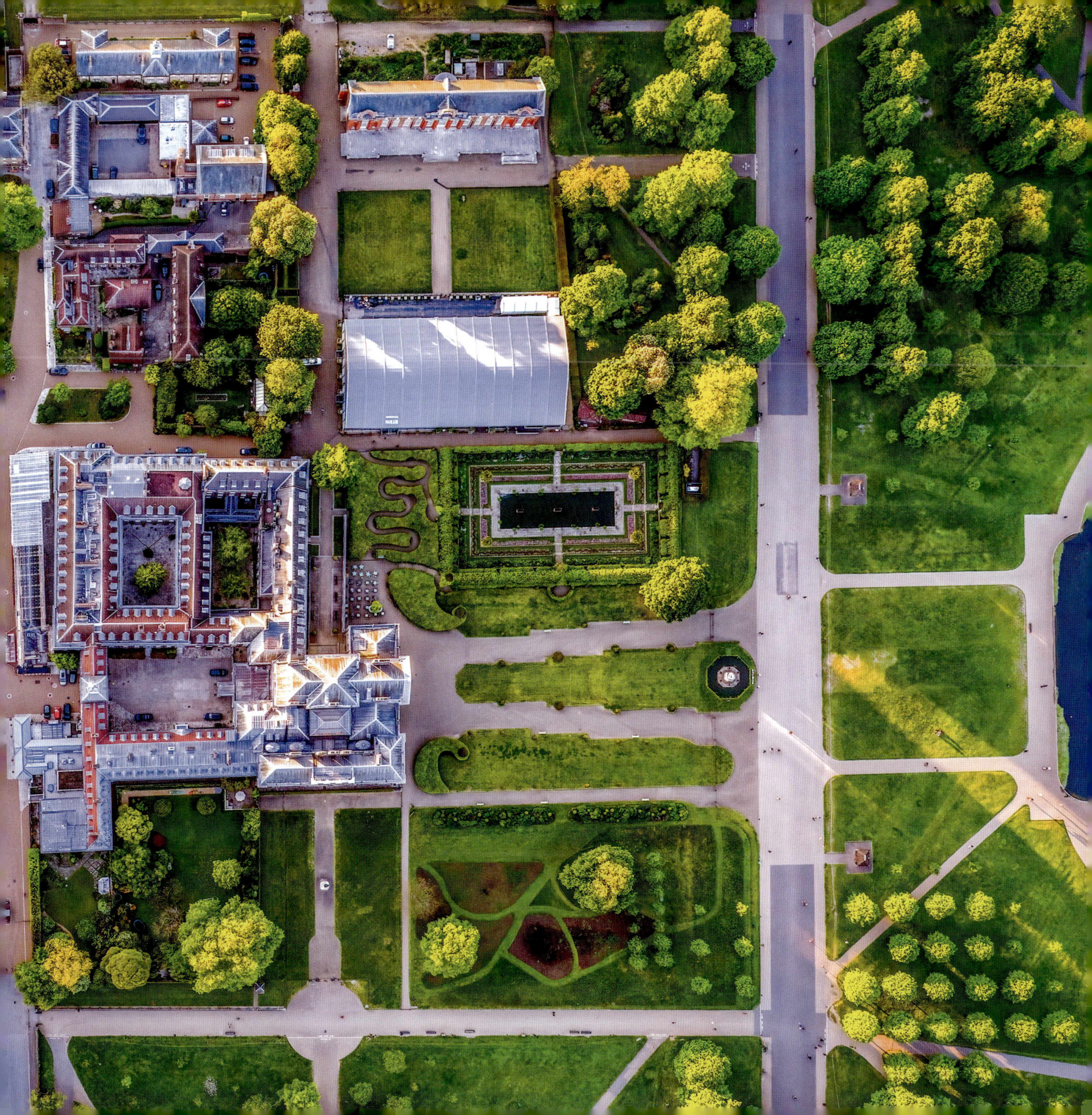

168

SEATS OF POWER

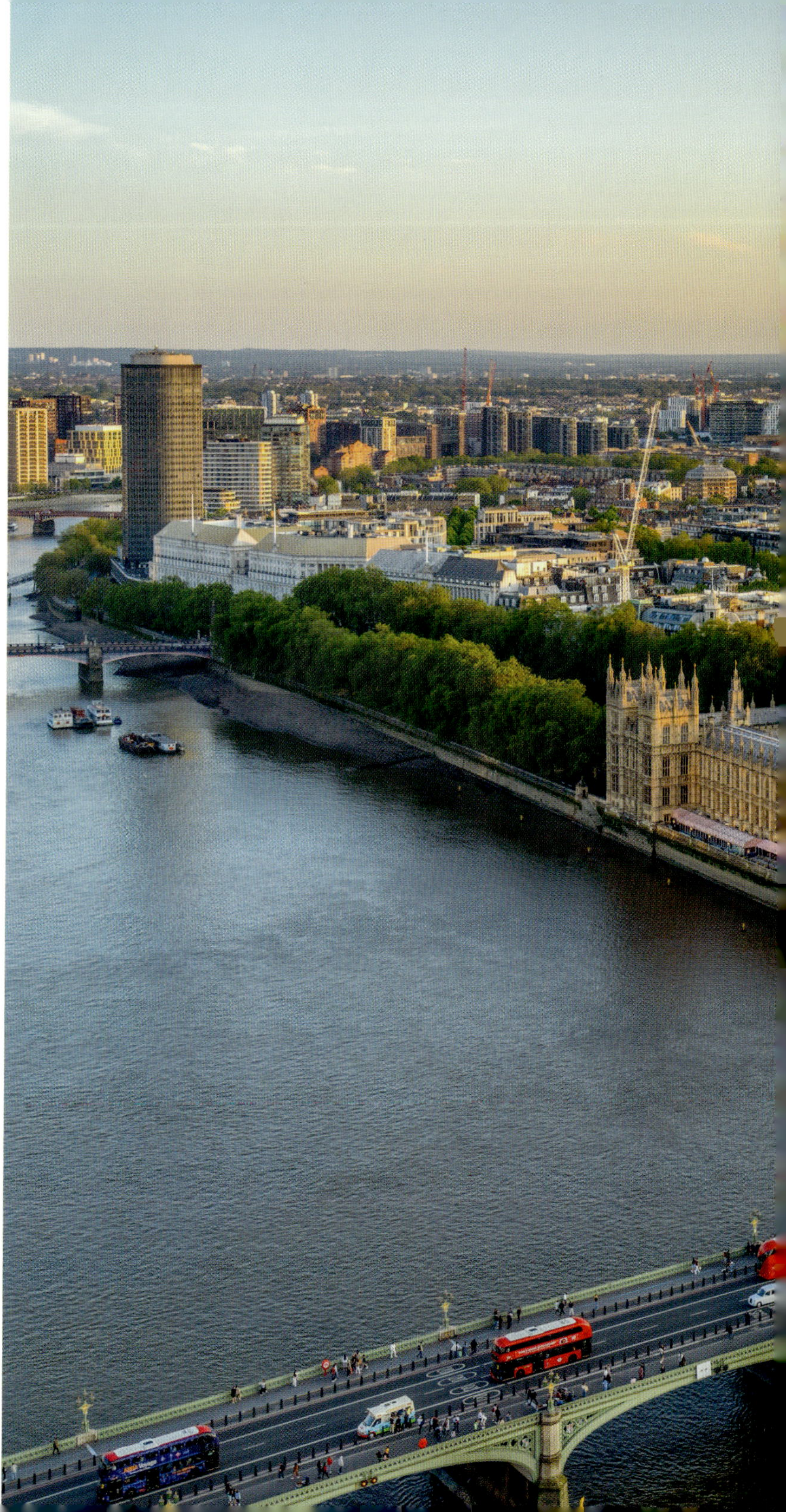

Westminster Bridge, Elizabeth Tower with Big Ben, and the Houses of Parliament

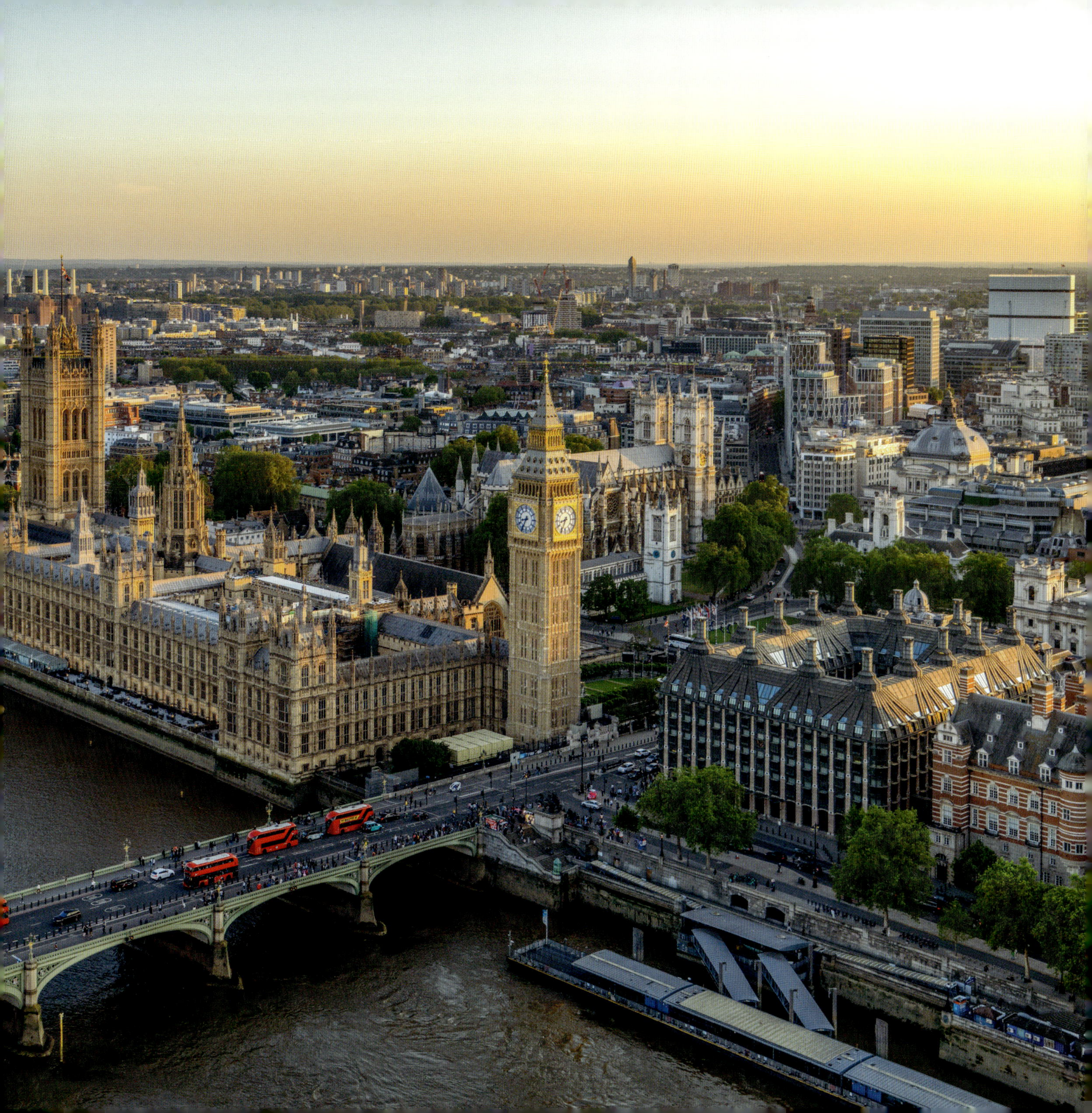

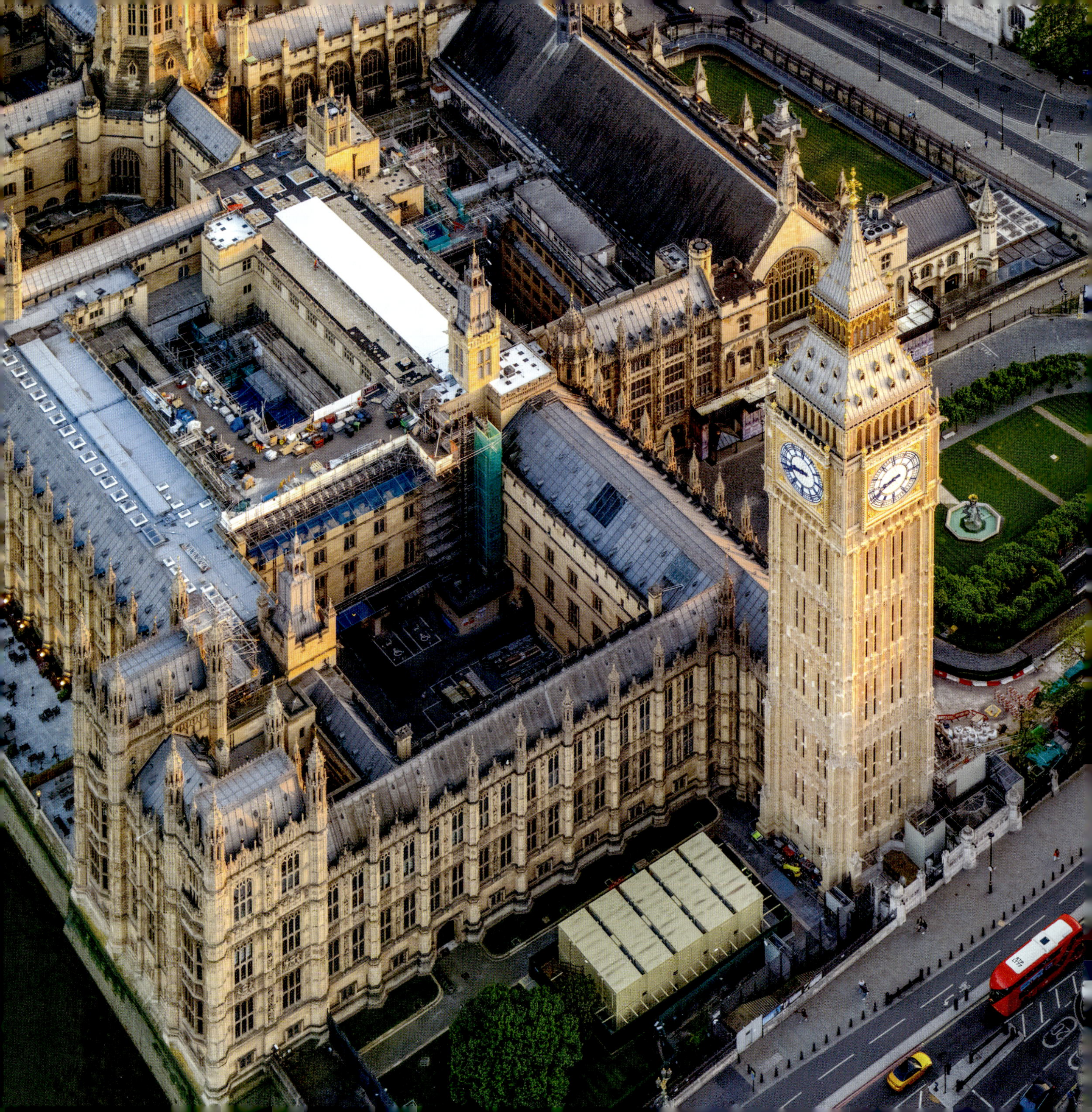

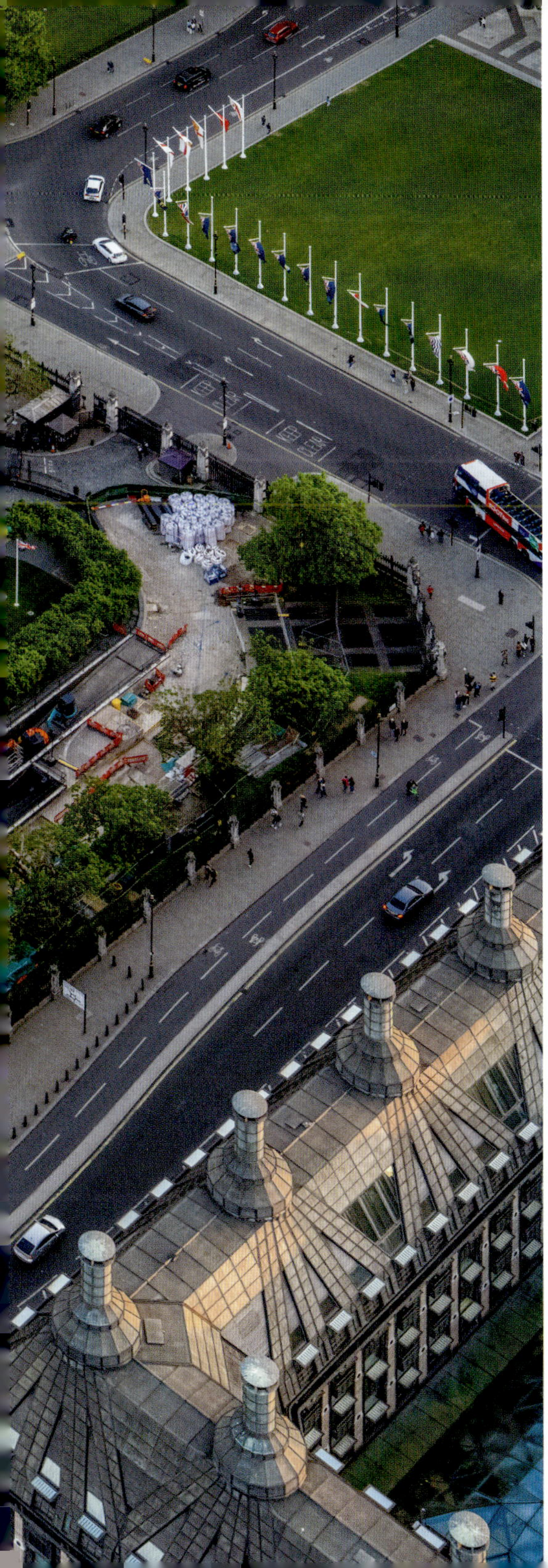

Elizabeth Tower and Big Ben, with the House of Lords and the House of Commons directly behind the tower and Westminster Hall with a dark slate roof at top

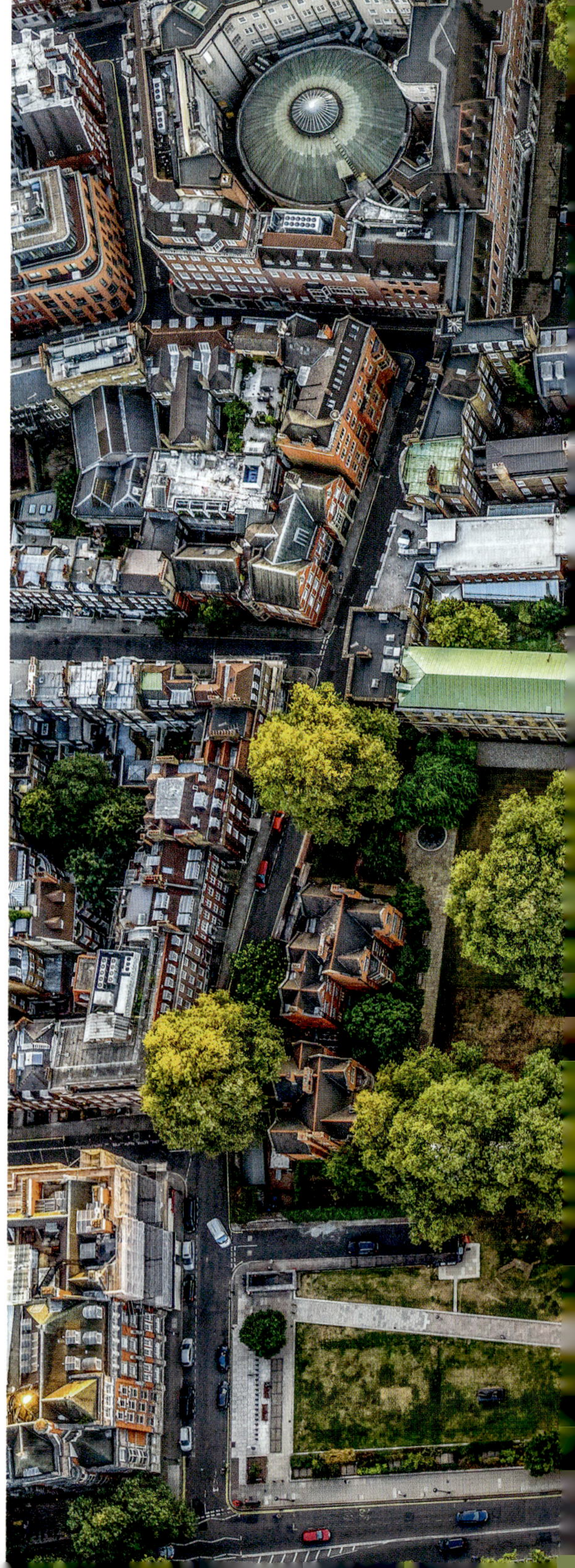

Westminster Abbey with attendant outbuildings, including the cloisters, Westminster School, the Dean's Yard, and the College Garden at right center

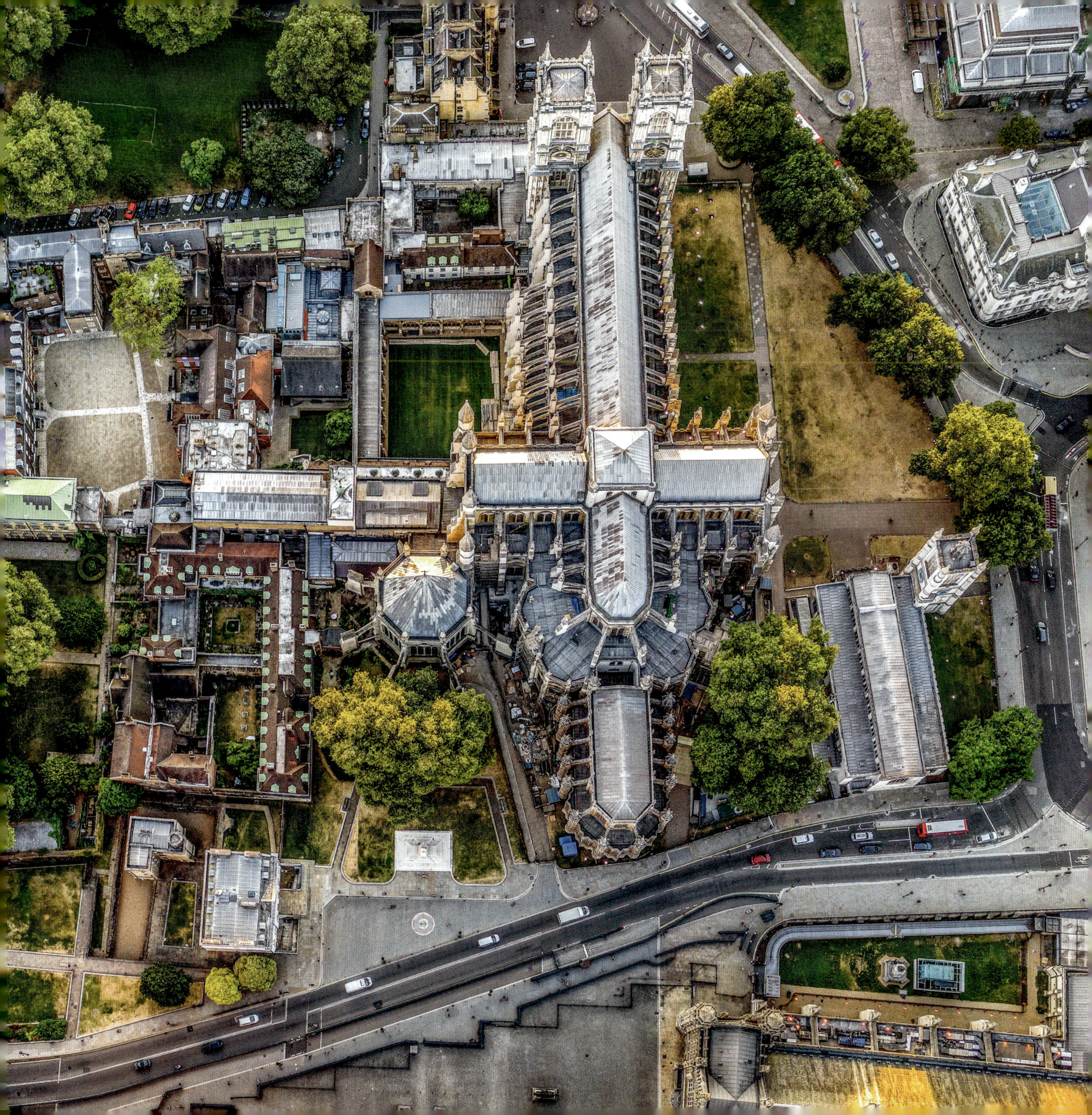

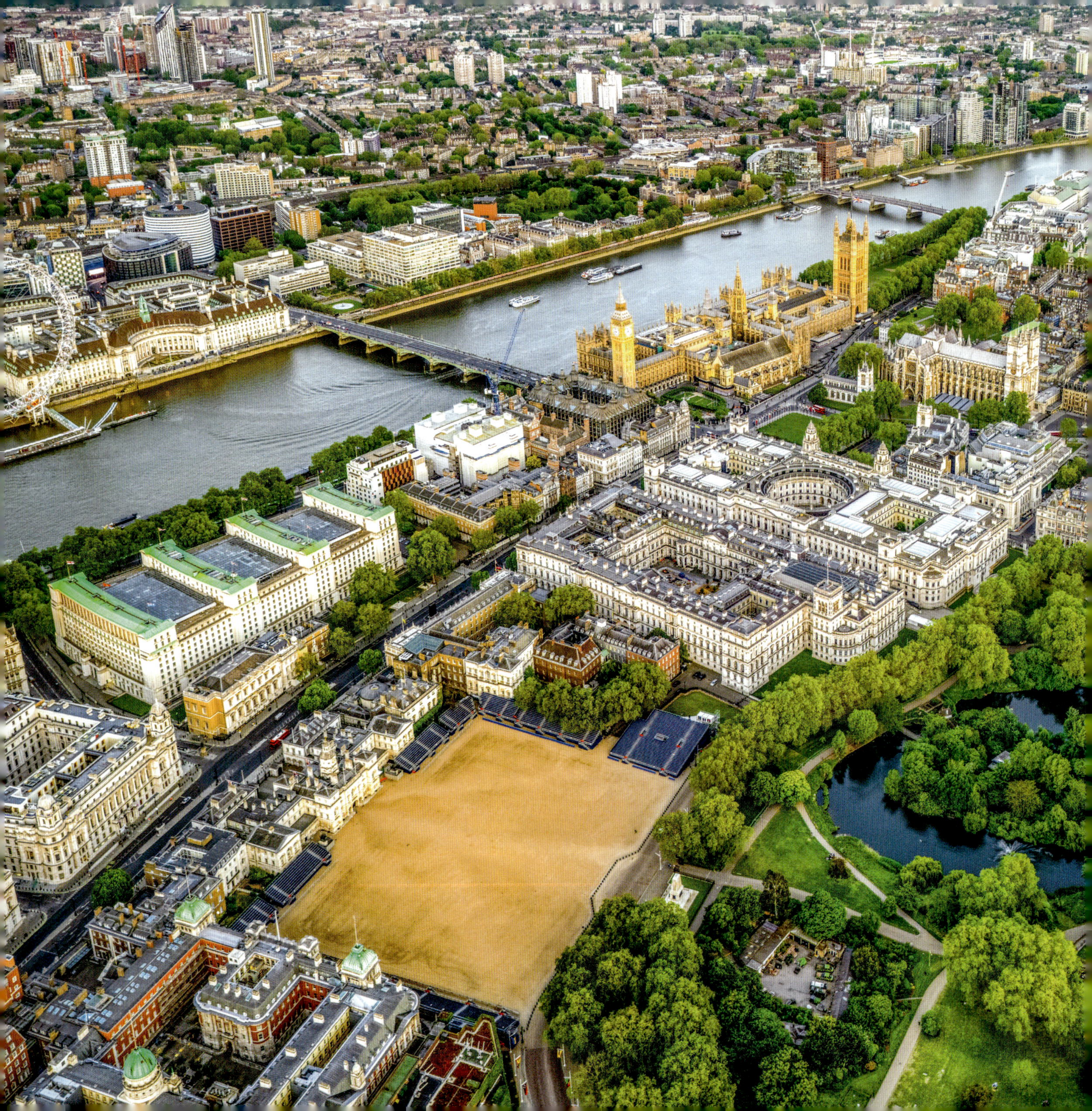

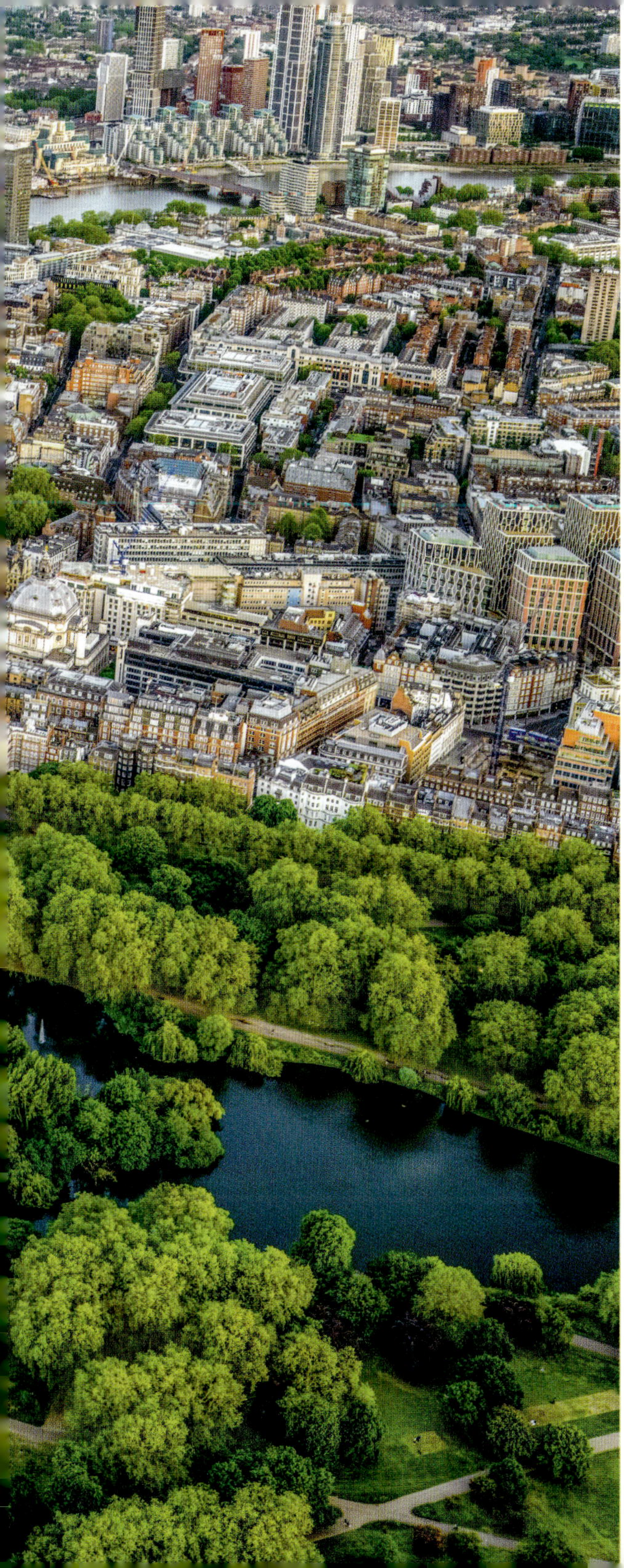

Opposite: Looking west across a corner of St. James's Park and the Horse Guards Parade at a sprawl of government buildings, Westminster Abbey, and the Houses of Parliament

Page 176: Big Ben and the Houses of Parliament at night

Page 177: His Majesty's Treasury offices (with the circular atrium), with the Imperial War Museum and Churchill War Rooms at the rear, and beside it the Foreign, Commonwealth, and Development Office; the red-brick buildings at lower left mark Downing Street, where No. 10 is the office of the prime minister

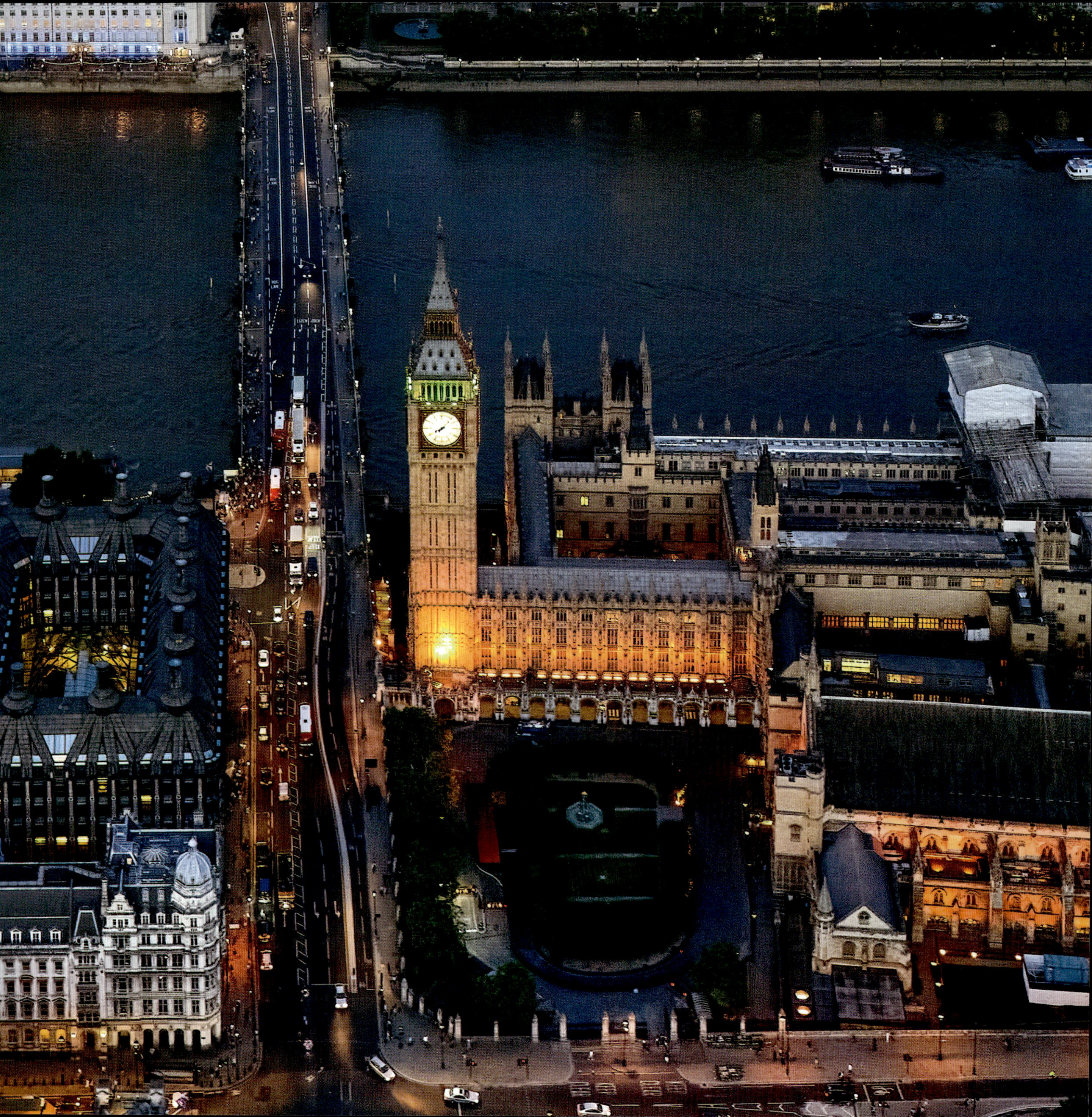

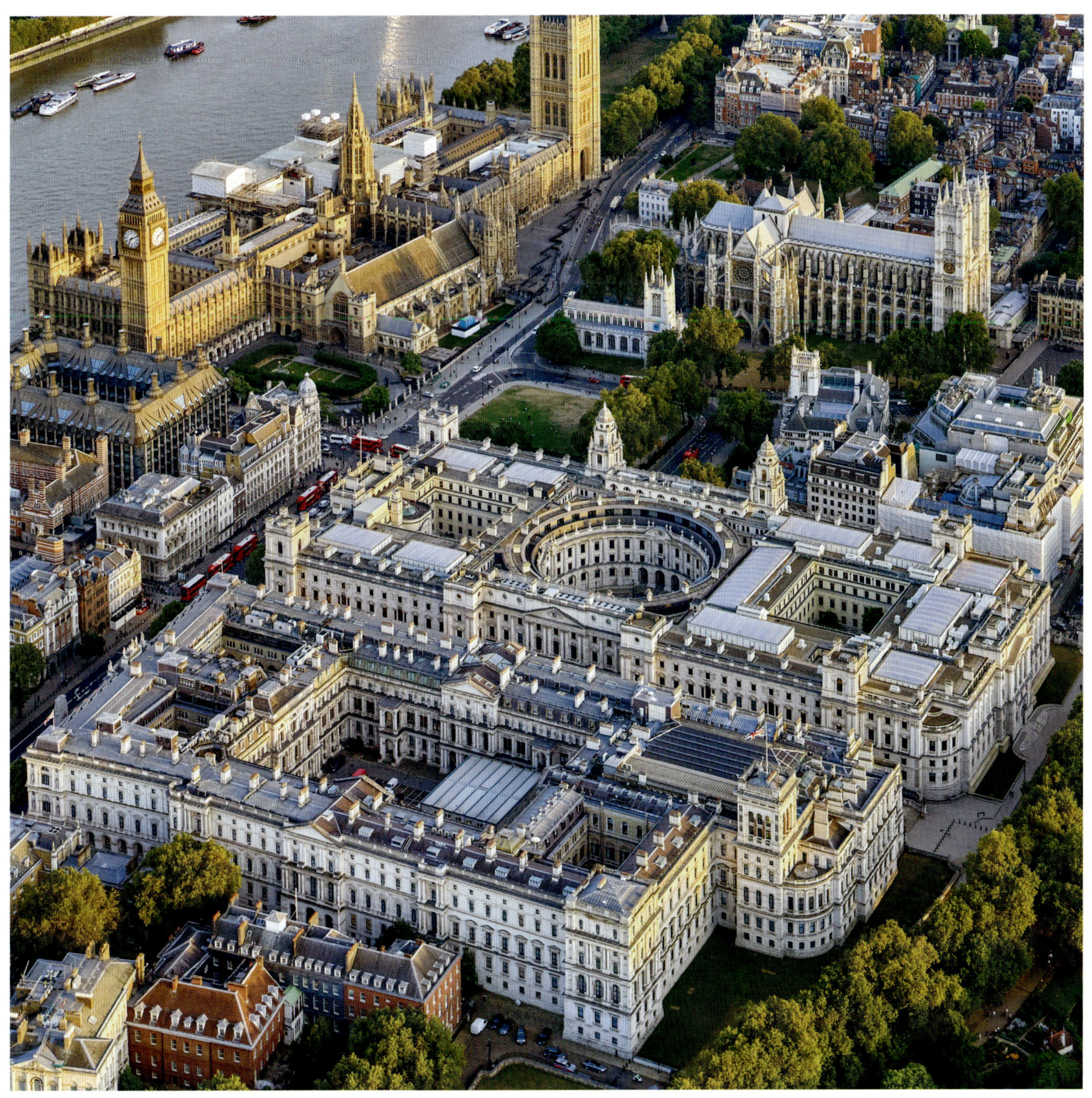

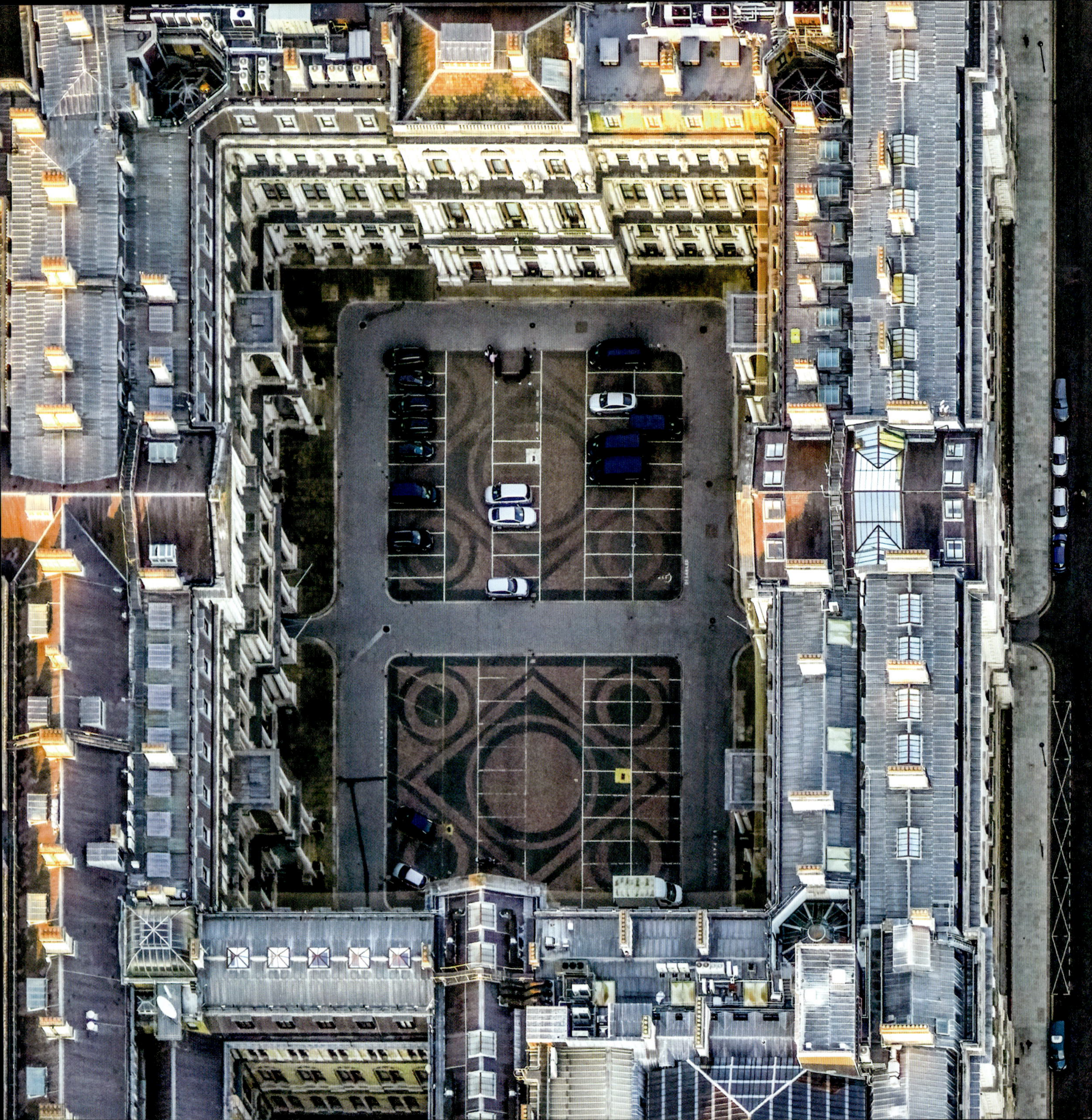

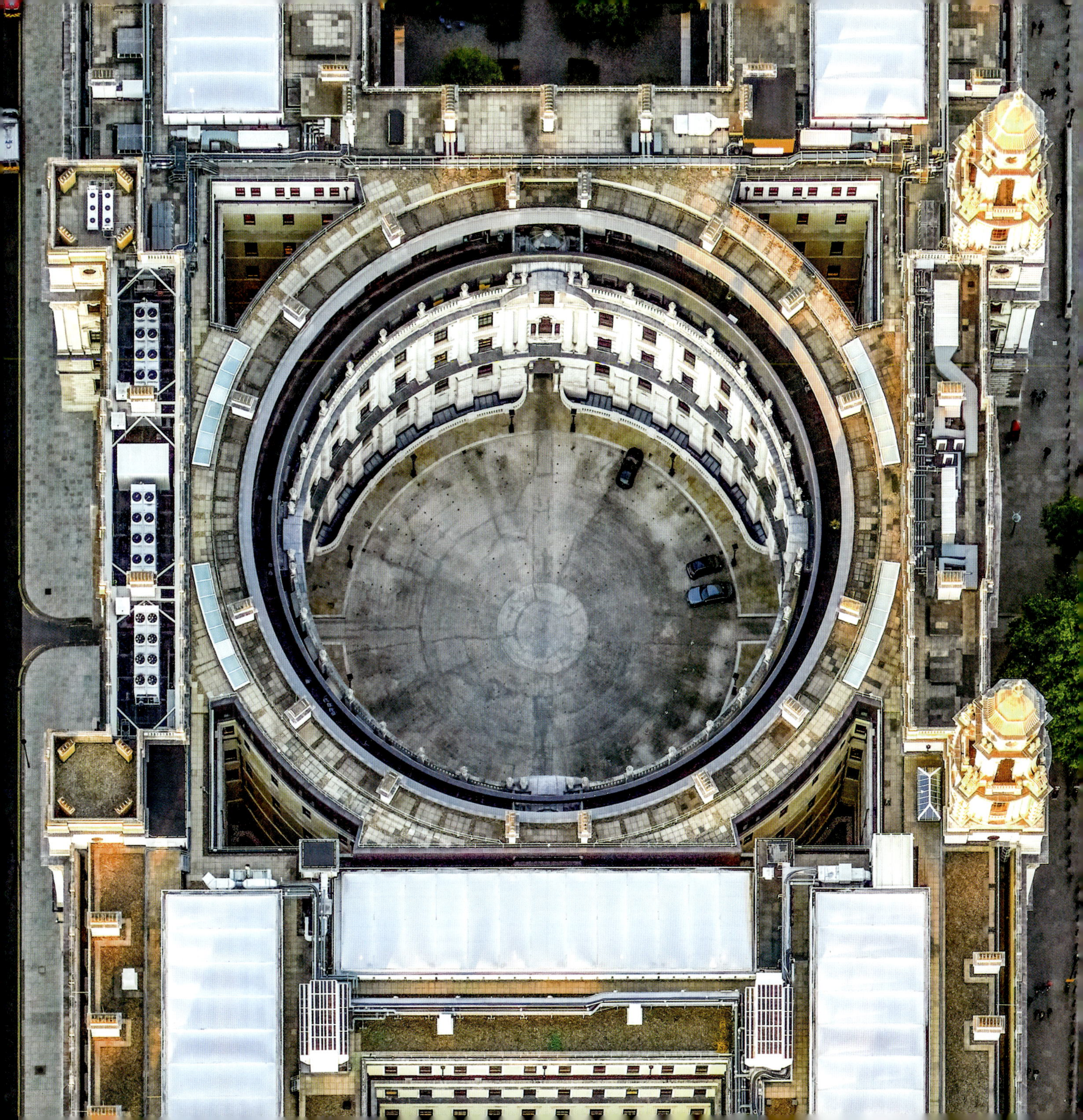

Pages 178–179: A close-up of the spectacular circular atrium of His Majesty's Treasury offices

Opposite: A parade of government office buildings along the Victoria Embankment, across Westminster Bridge Road from Big Ben, including Portcullis House (nearest to Elizabeth Tower), the House of Commons Library (at top), Richmond House, which houses the Department of Health (at center right), and headquarters of the Metropolitan Police at Scotland Yard (at lower right)

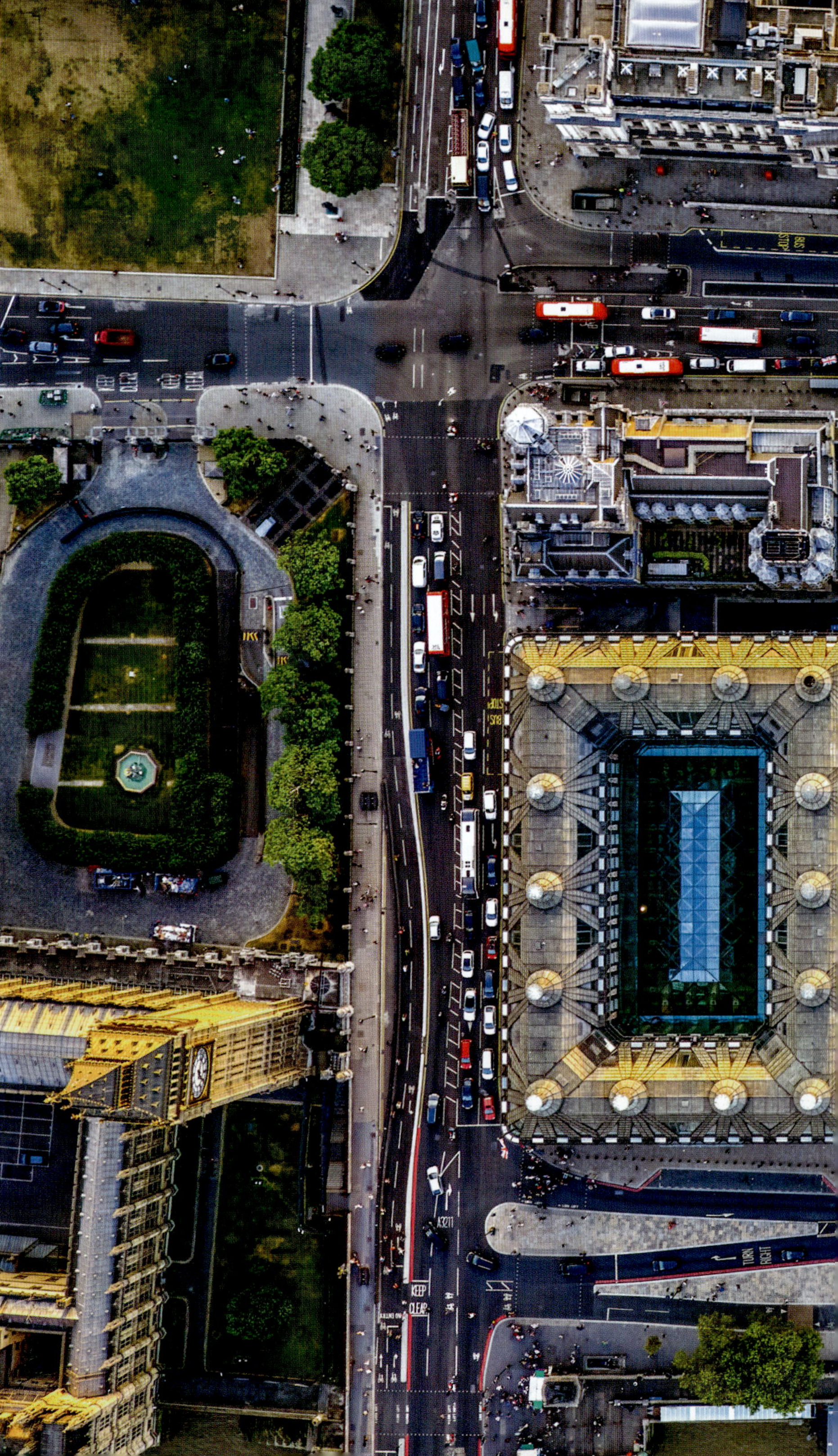

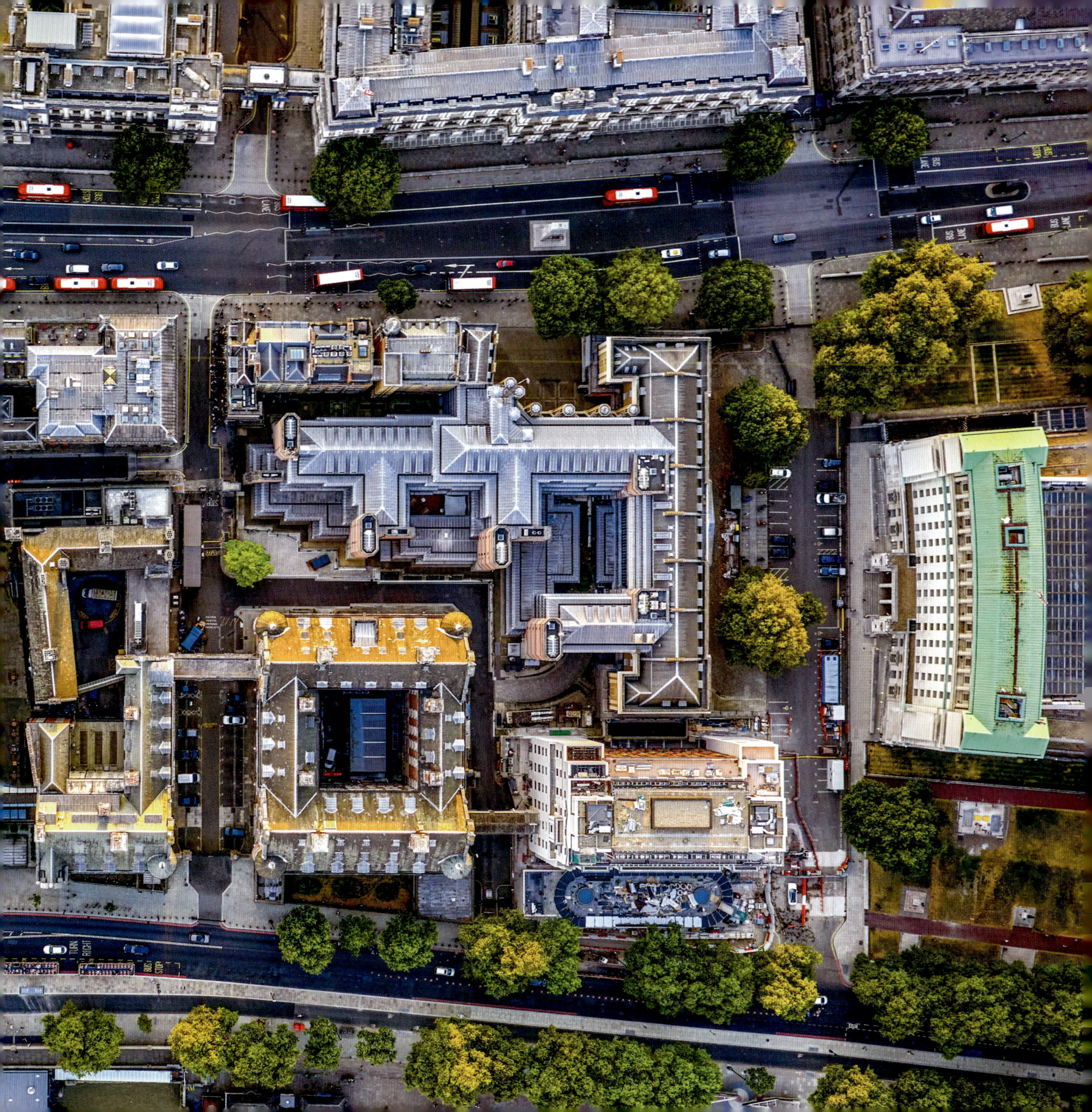

Right: City Hall in Southwark, formerly headquarters of the Greater London Authority

Opposite: Royal Courts of Justice, including the Central London County Court

Page 184: US Embassy in Nine Elms on the South Bank

Page 185: Winfield House, the private residence of the US ambassador, in Regent's Park

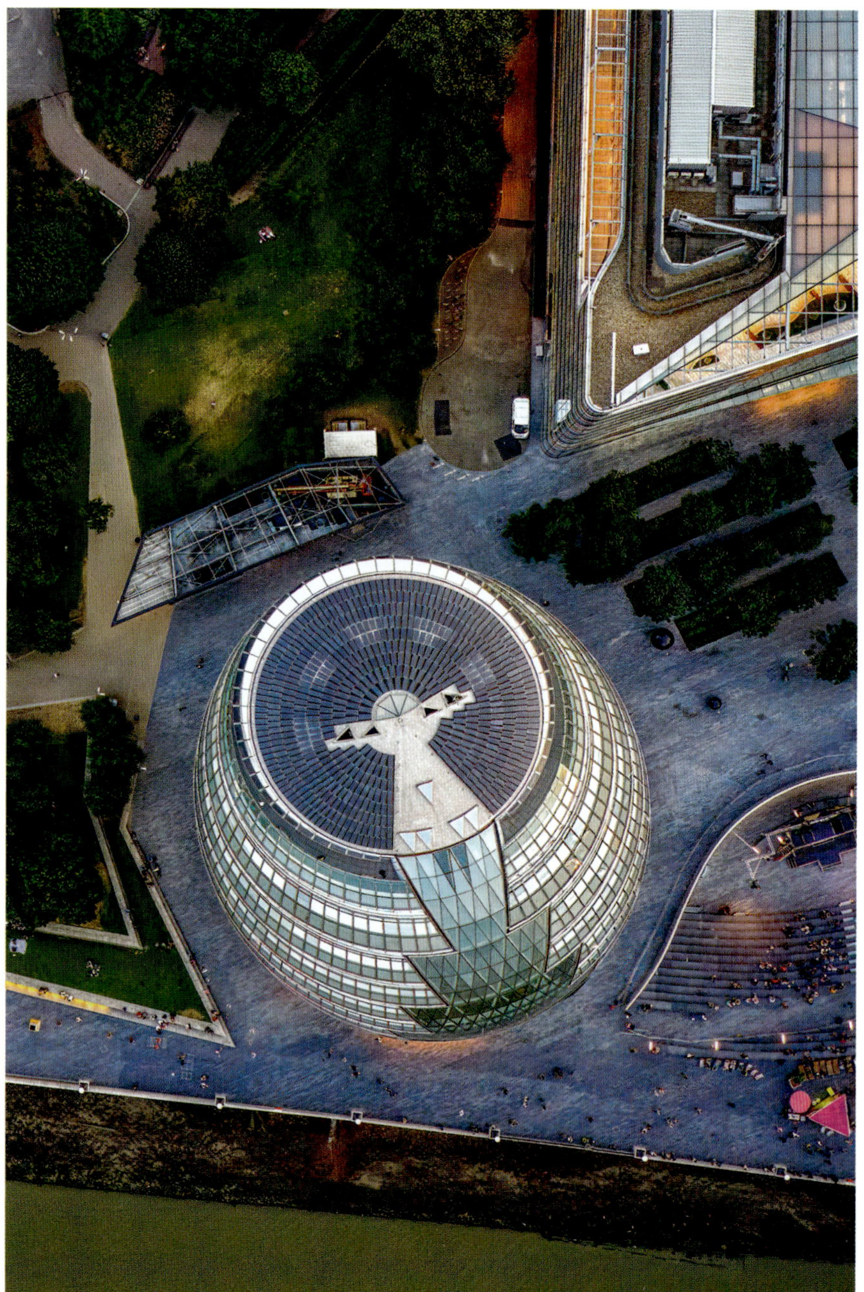

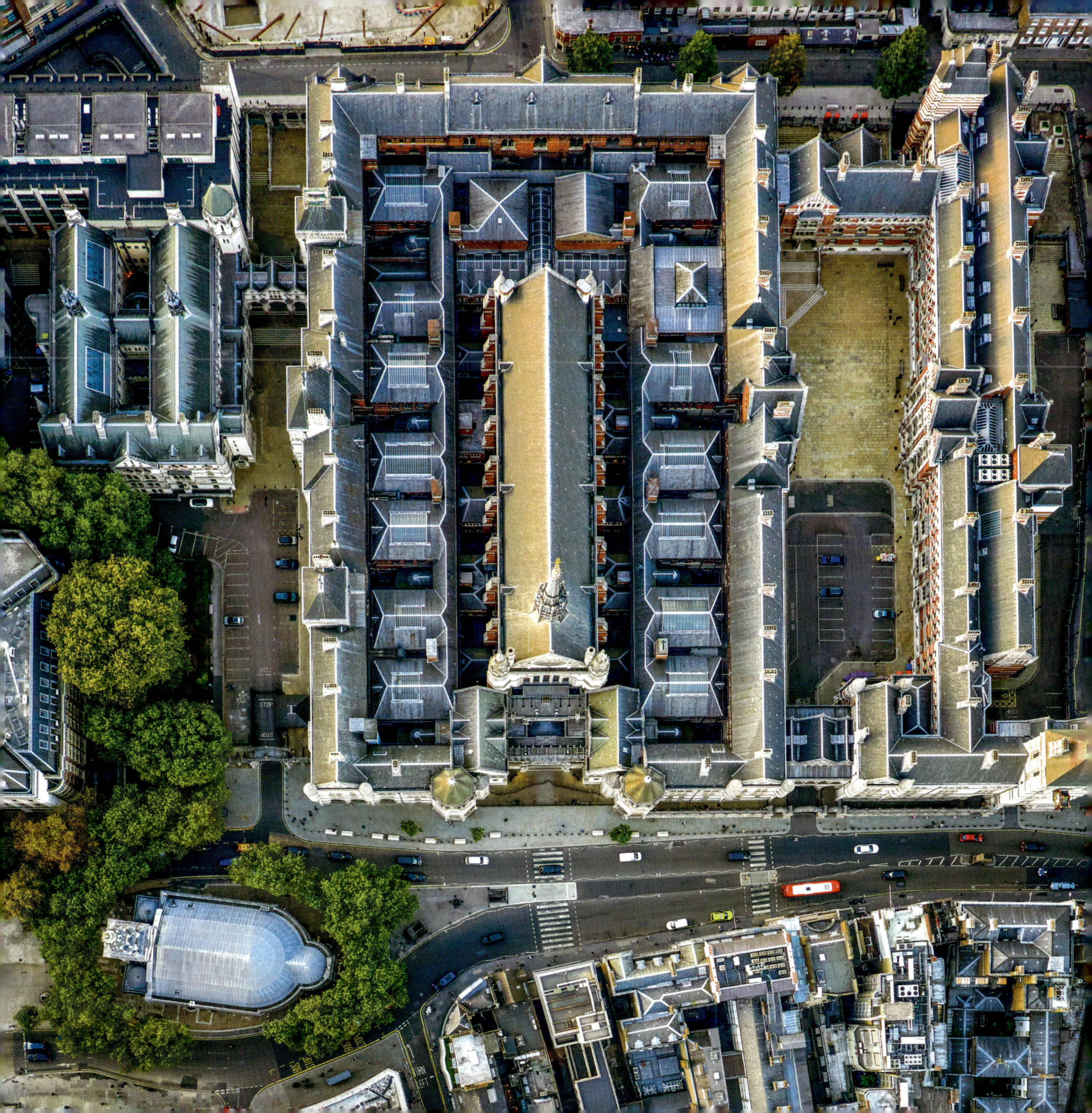

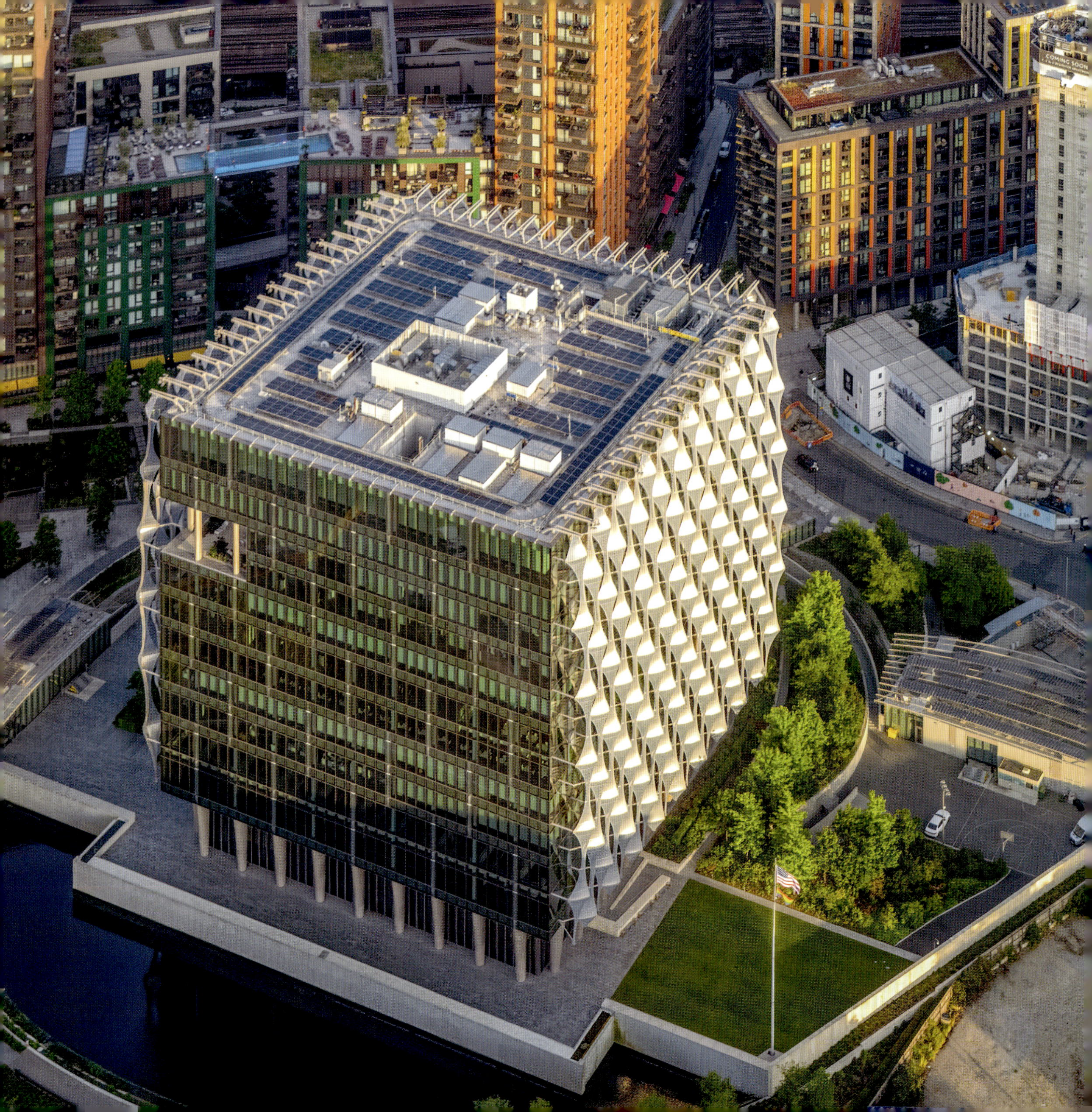
COMING SOON

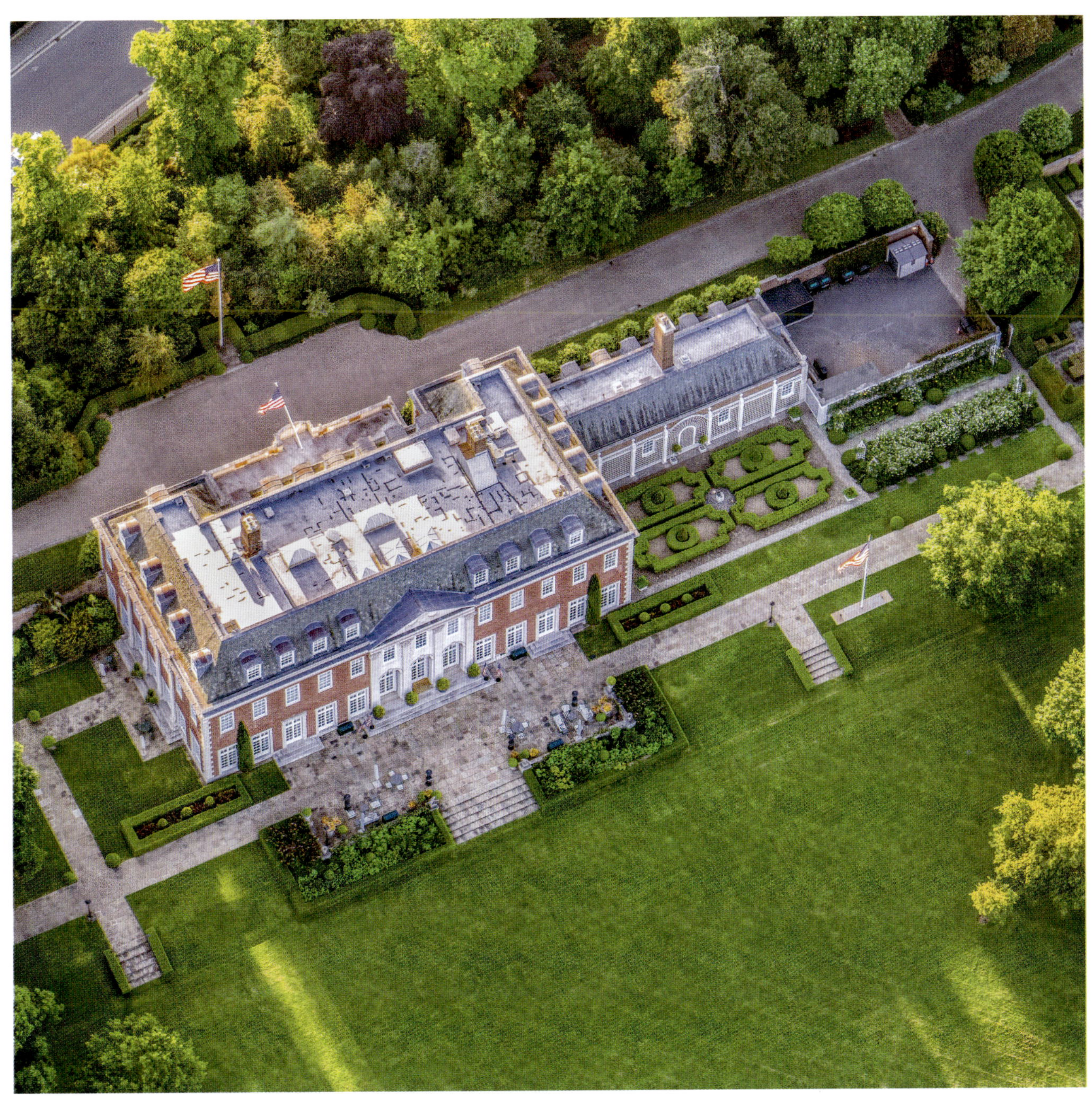

CHRISTMAS IN LONDON

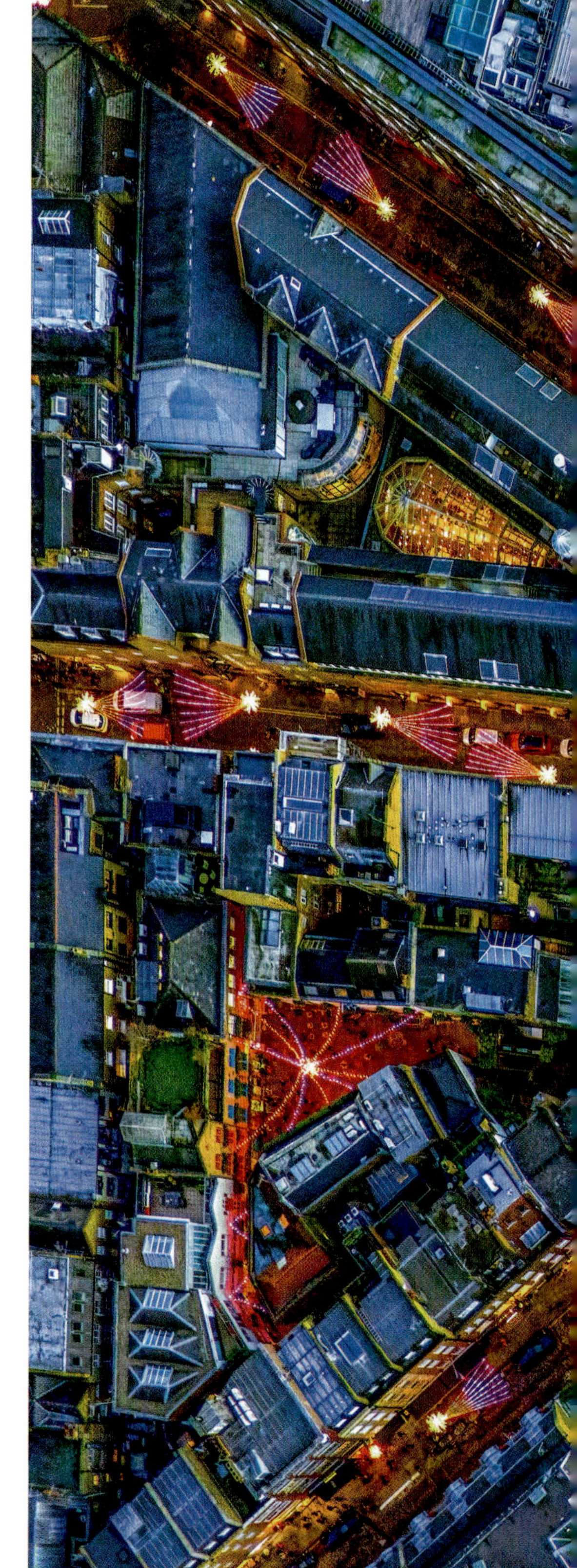

Opposite: Seven Dials during the holidays

Page 188: Black Friday shoppers along Oxford Circus

Page 189: Holiday lights on Coventry Street near Piccadilly Circus

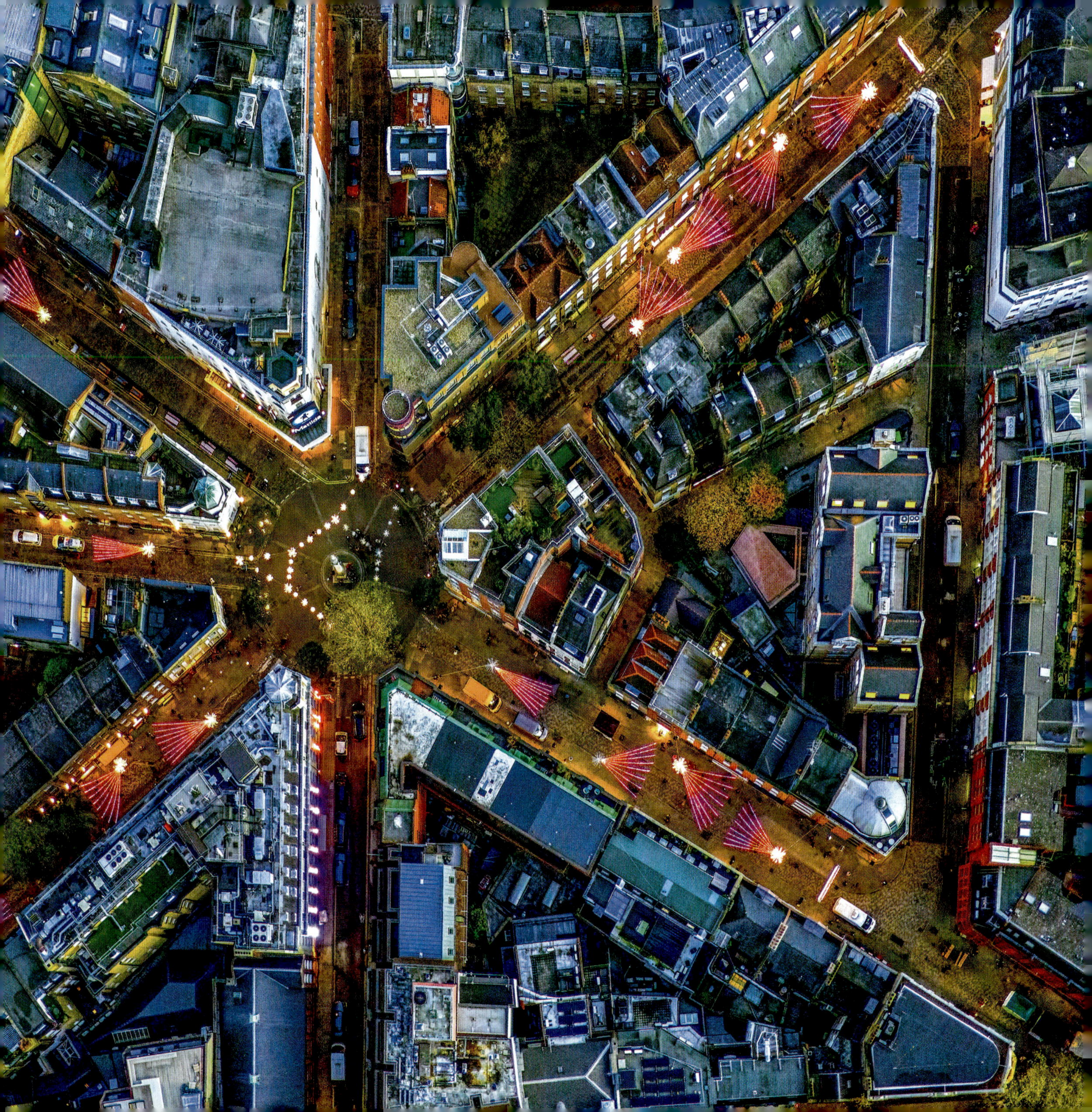

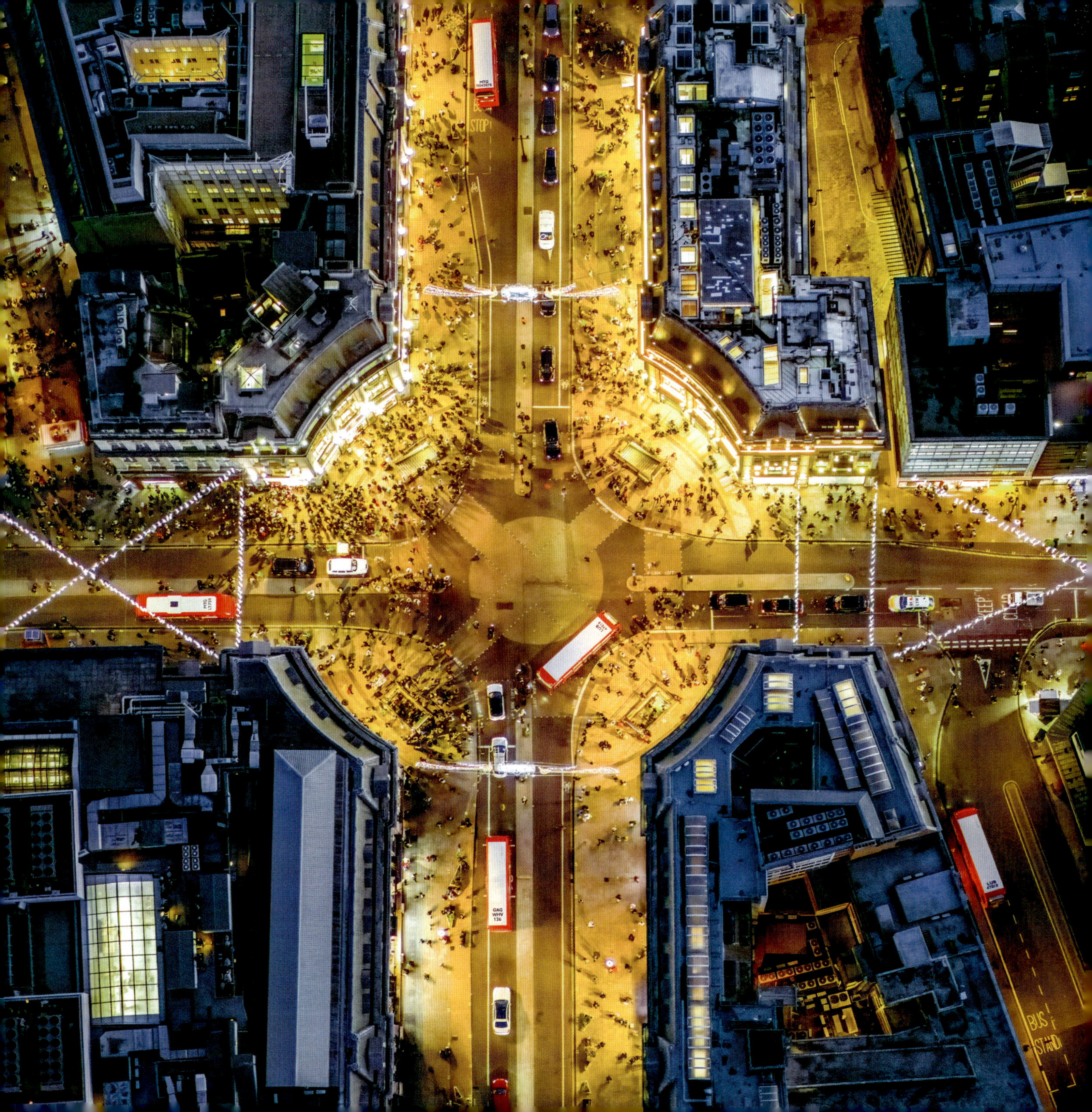
STOP

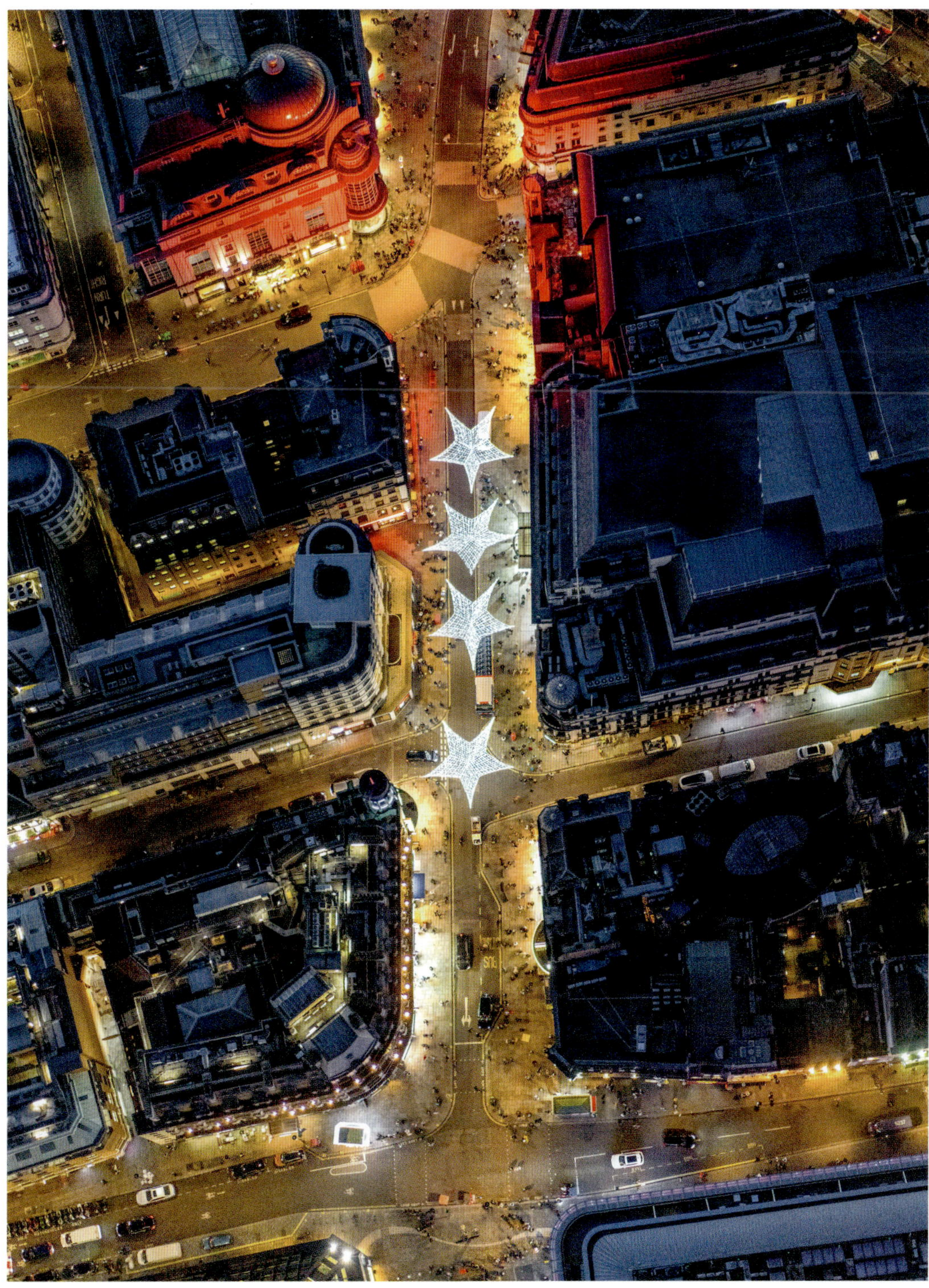

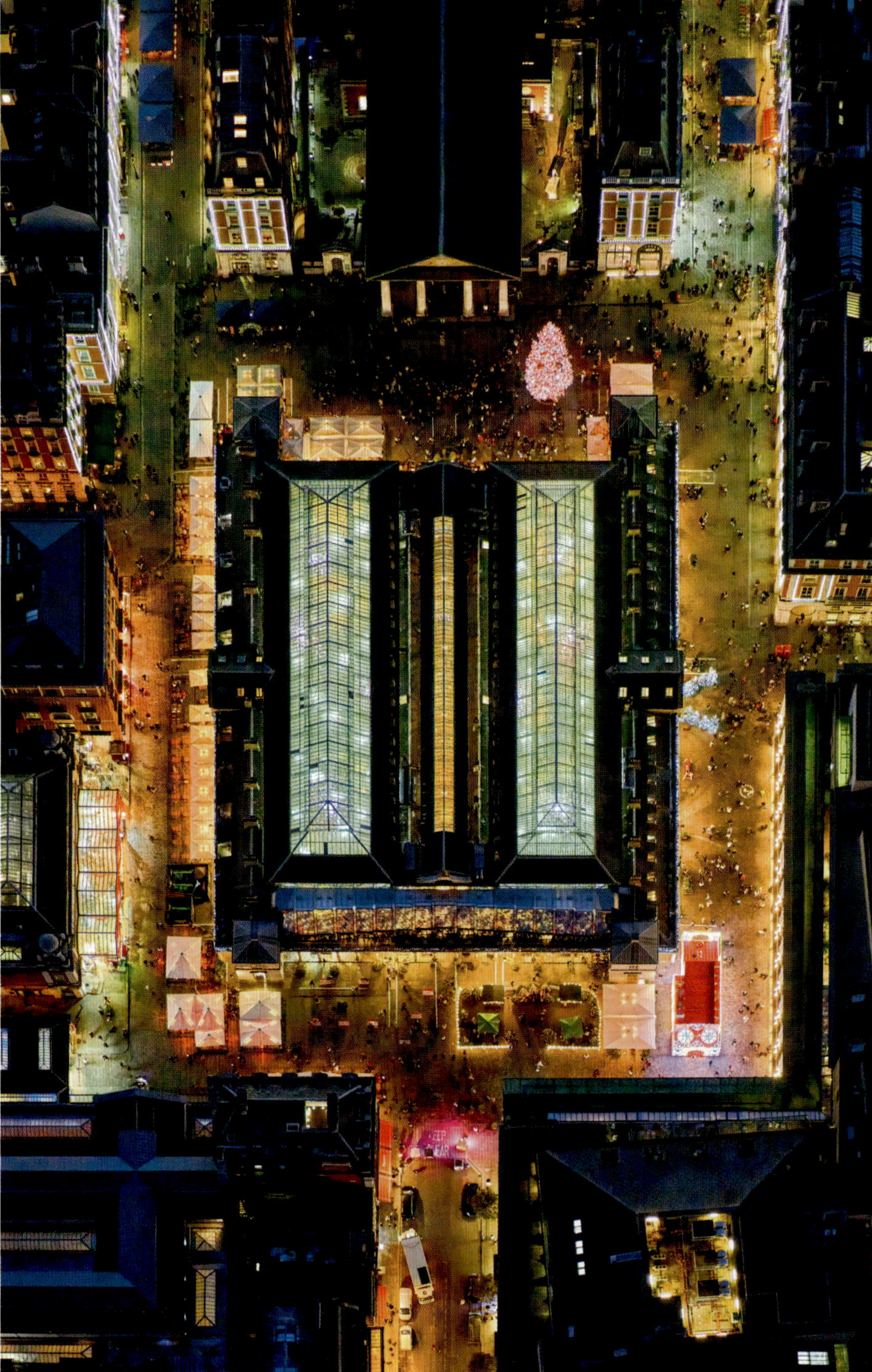

Right: Covent Garden at night

 Opposite: Angels on Regent Street

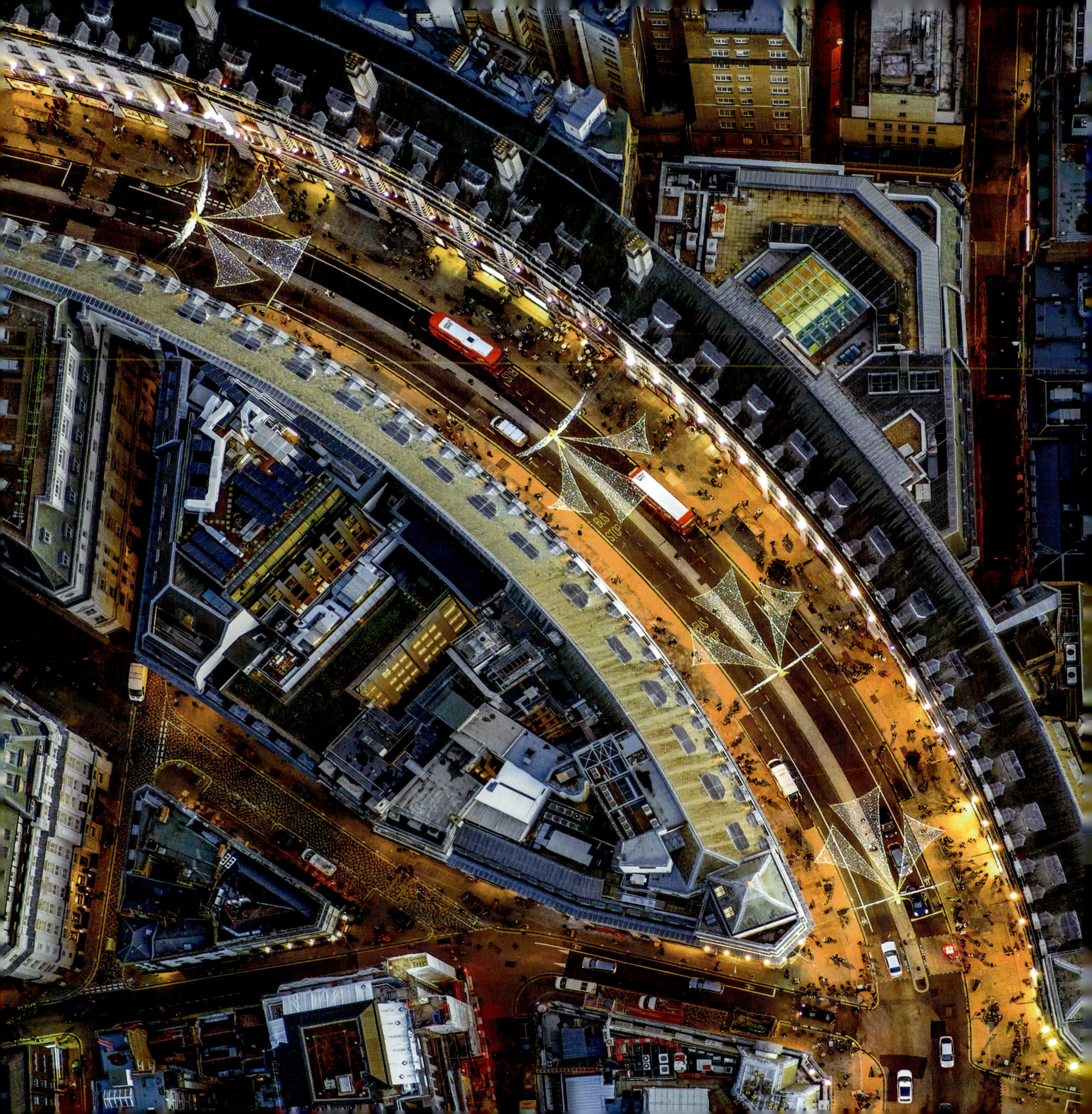

Opposite: A holiday fair in Leicester Square

Pages 194–195: Winter Wonderland fun fair in Hyde Park

Page 196: Close-up of Winter Wonderland

Page 197: Ice-skaters in the plaza of Somerset House

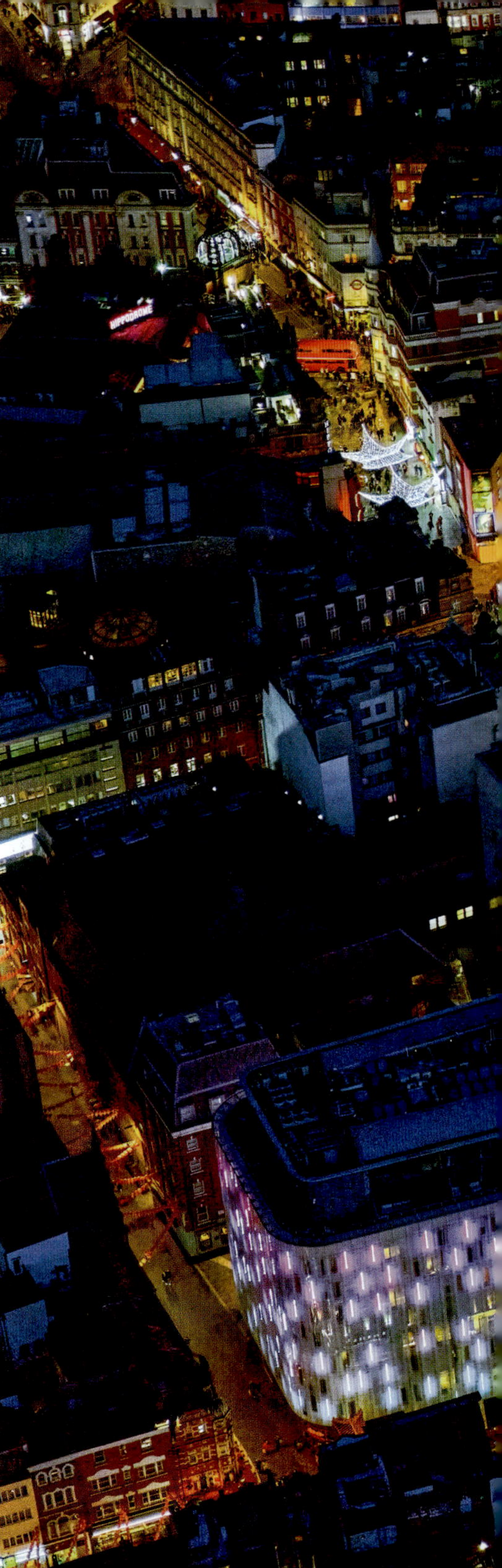

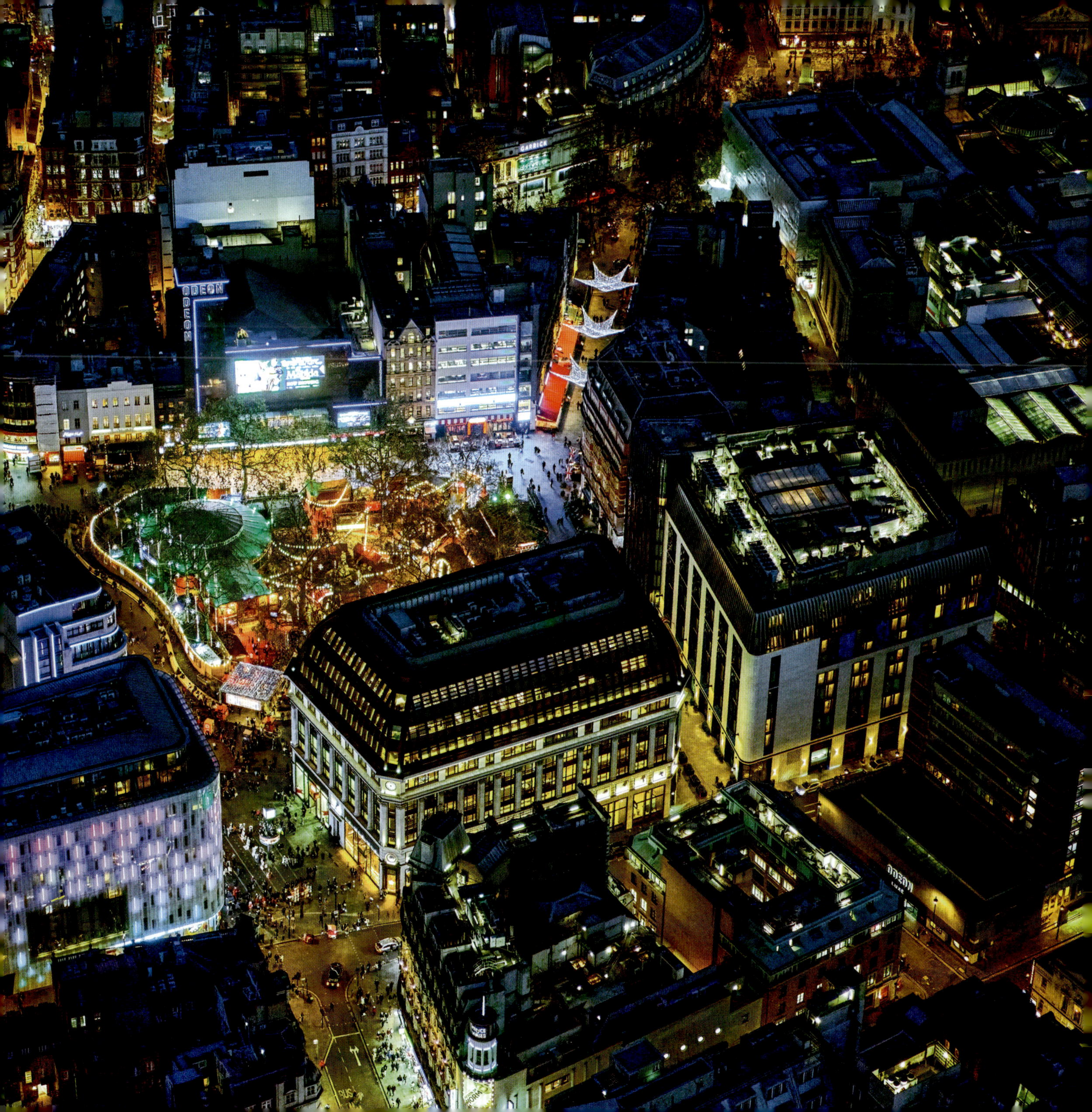
ODEON
ODEON
Matilda
GARRICK
ODEON

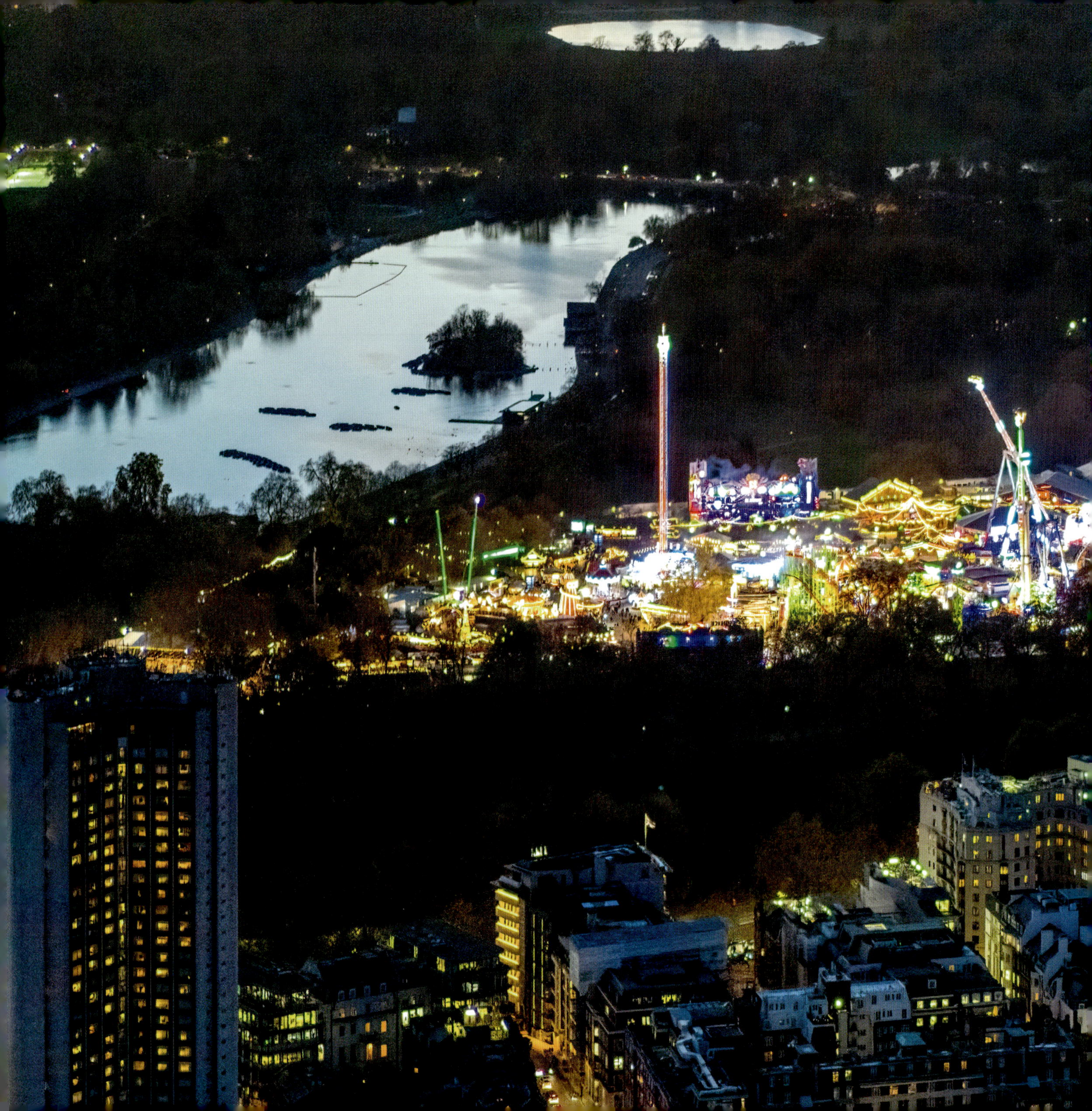

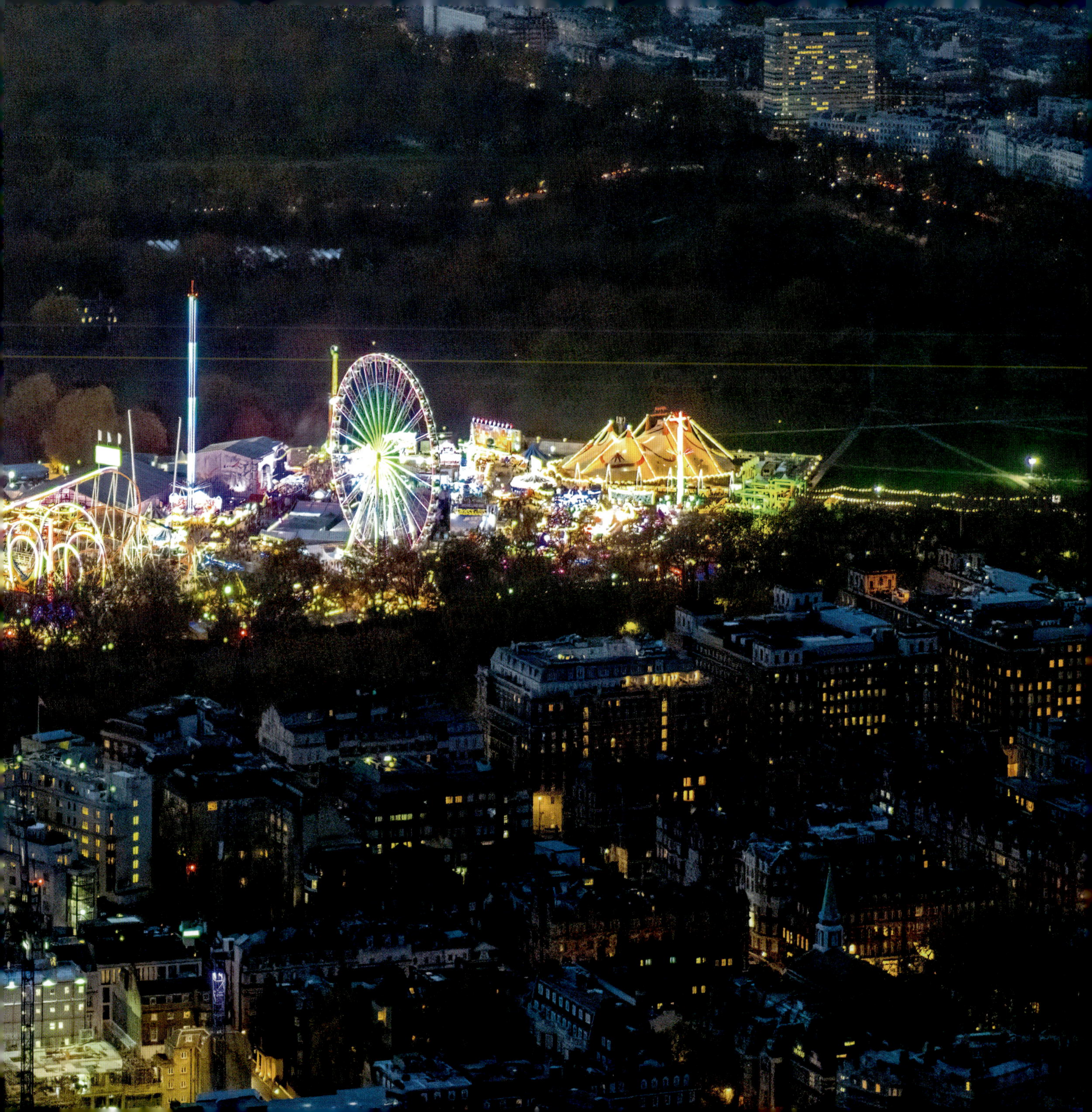

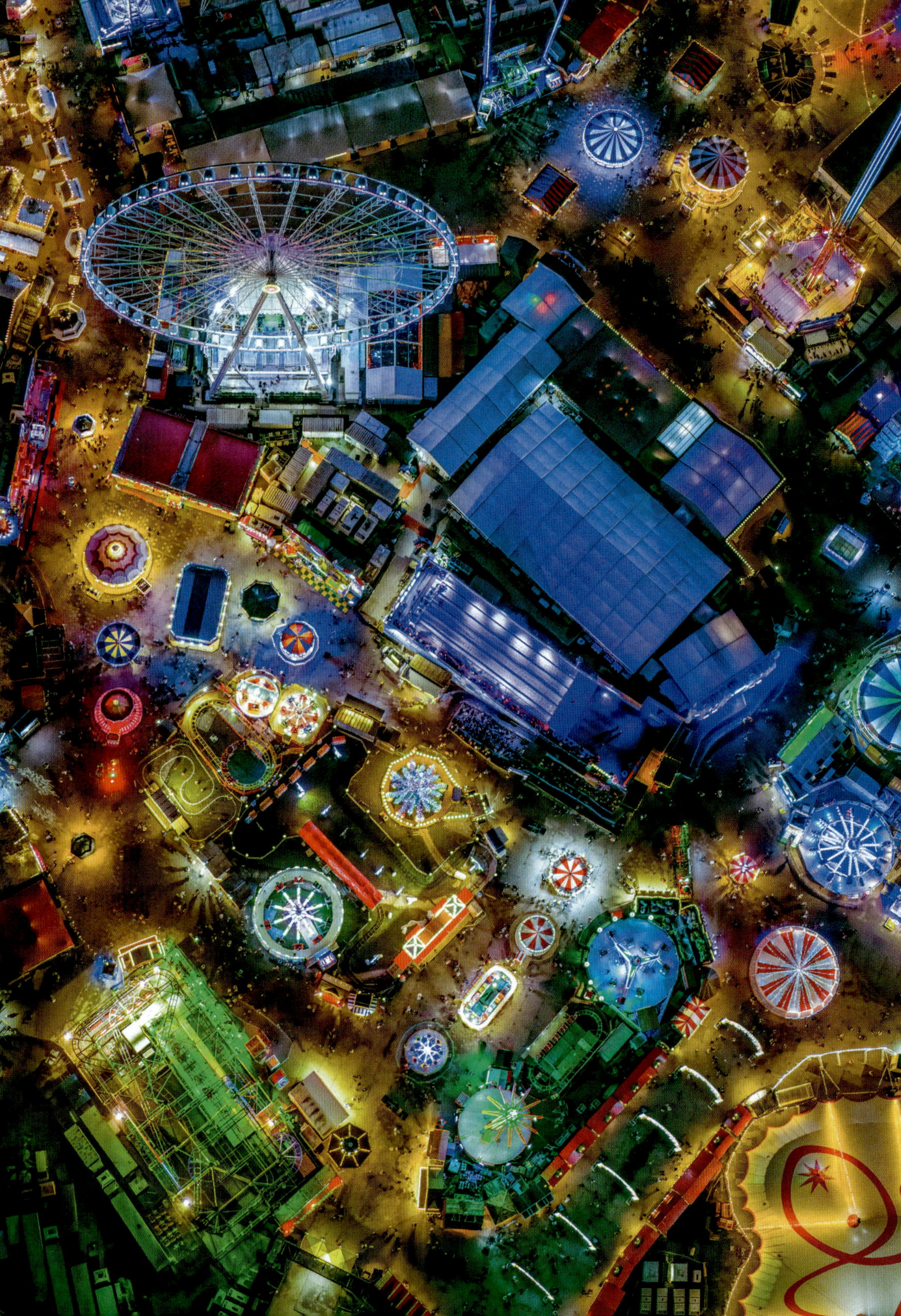

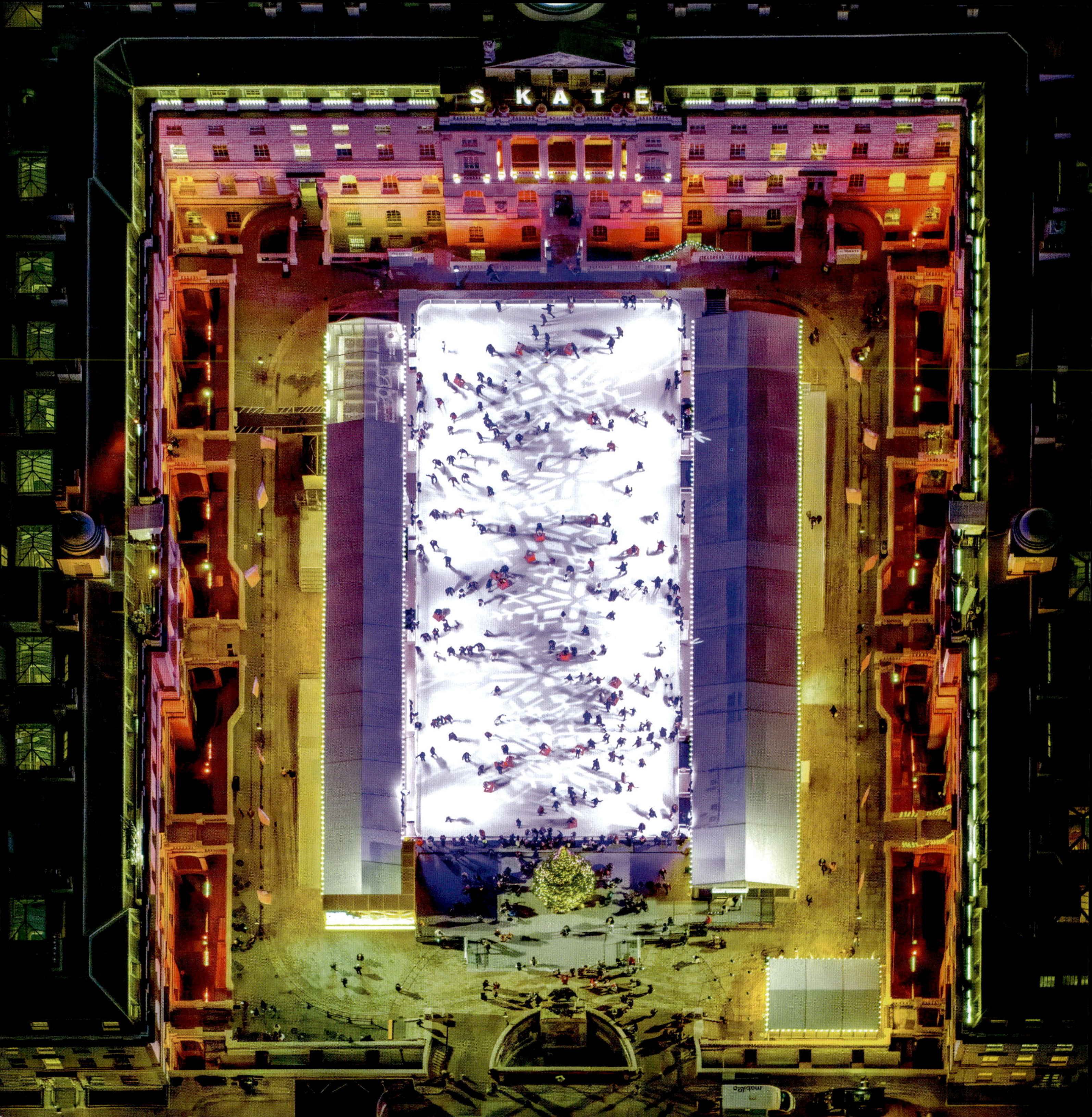
SKATE

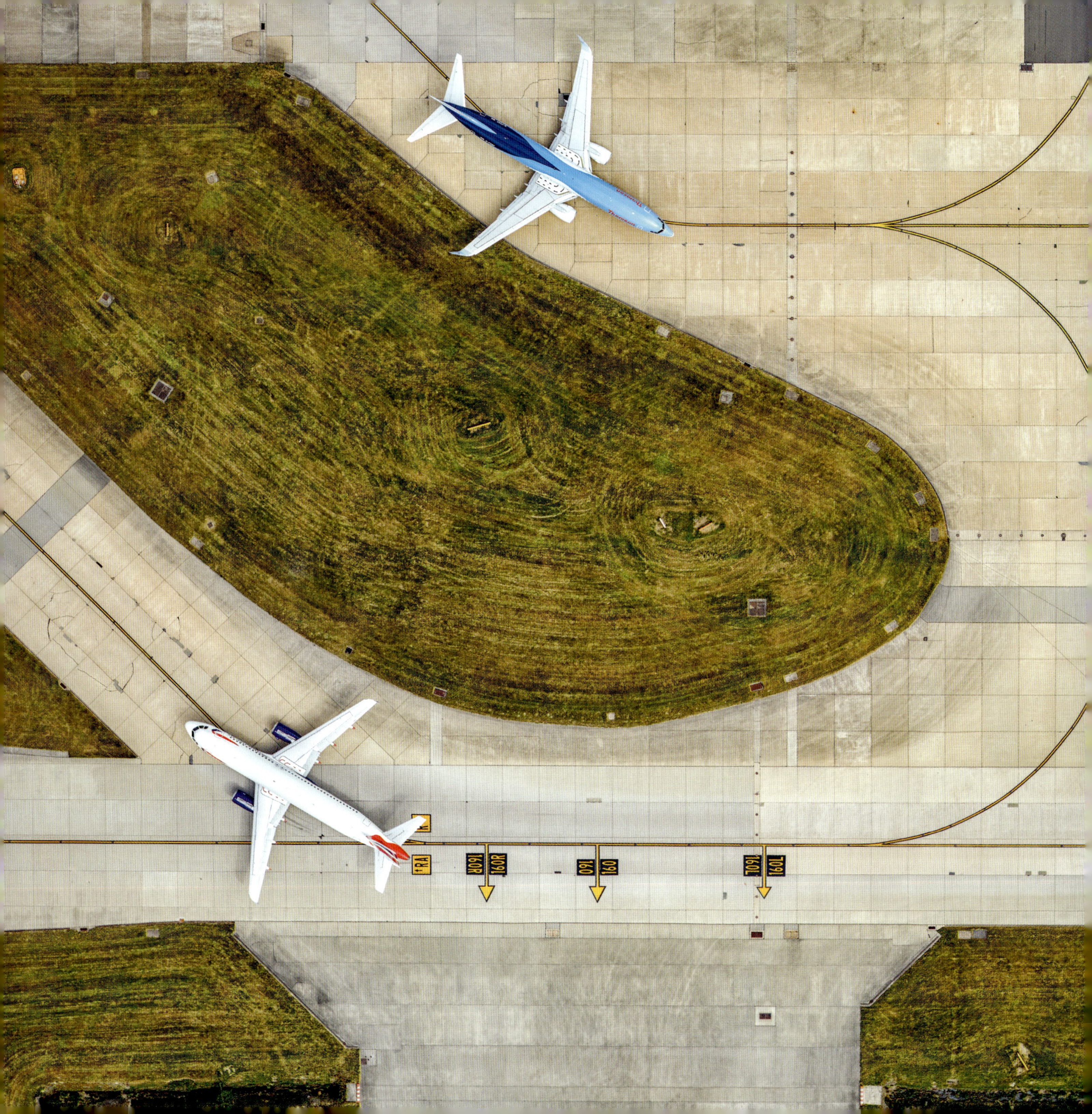

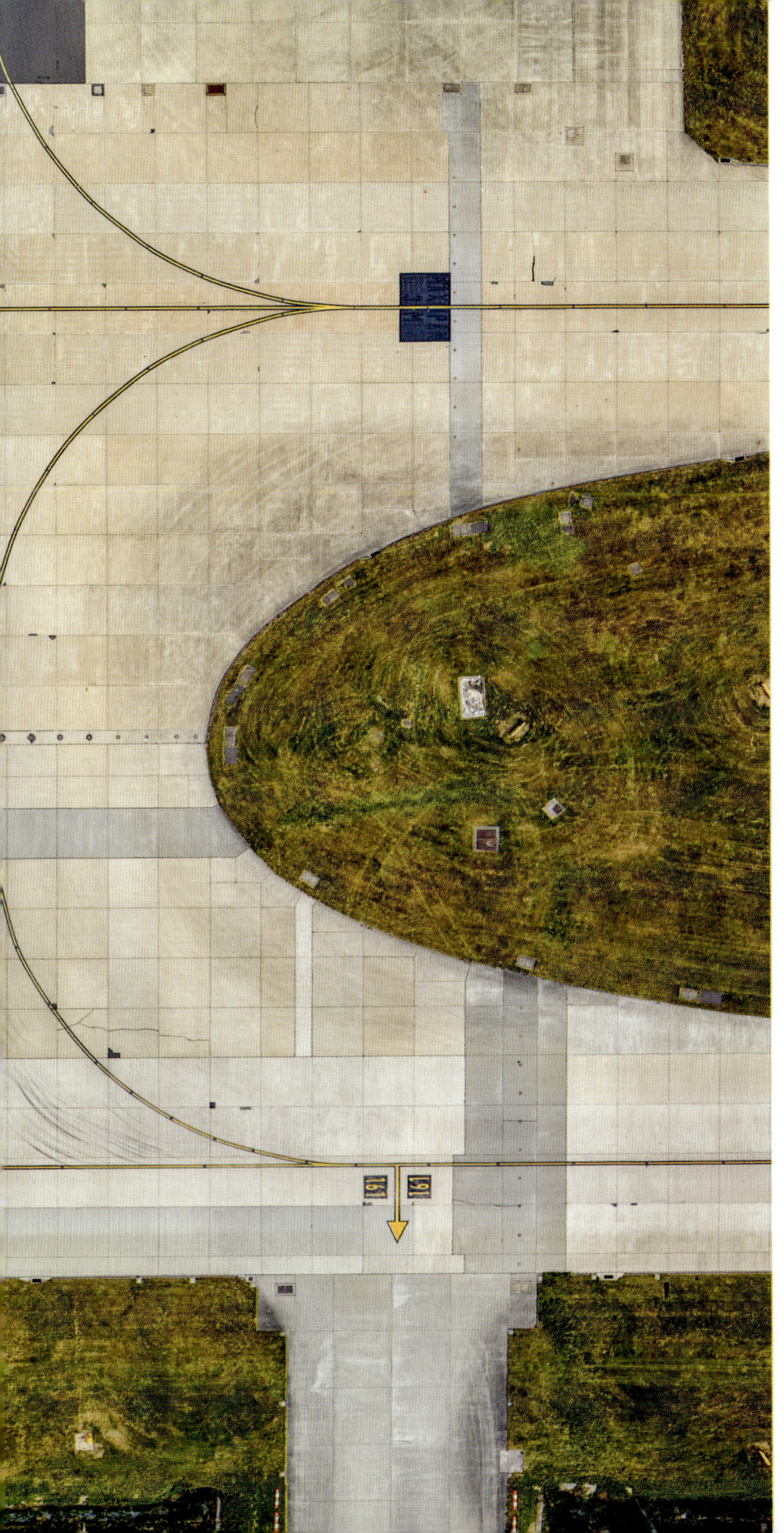

HEATHROW AND GATWICK

Opposite: Taxiways at Gatwick Airport

Page 200: A plane on taxiway at Gatwick Airport

Page 201: Gates of the South Terminal at Gatwick Airport

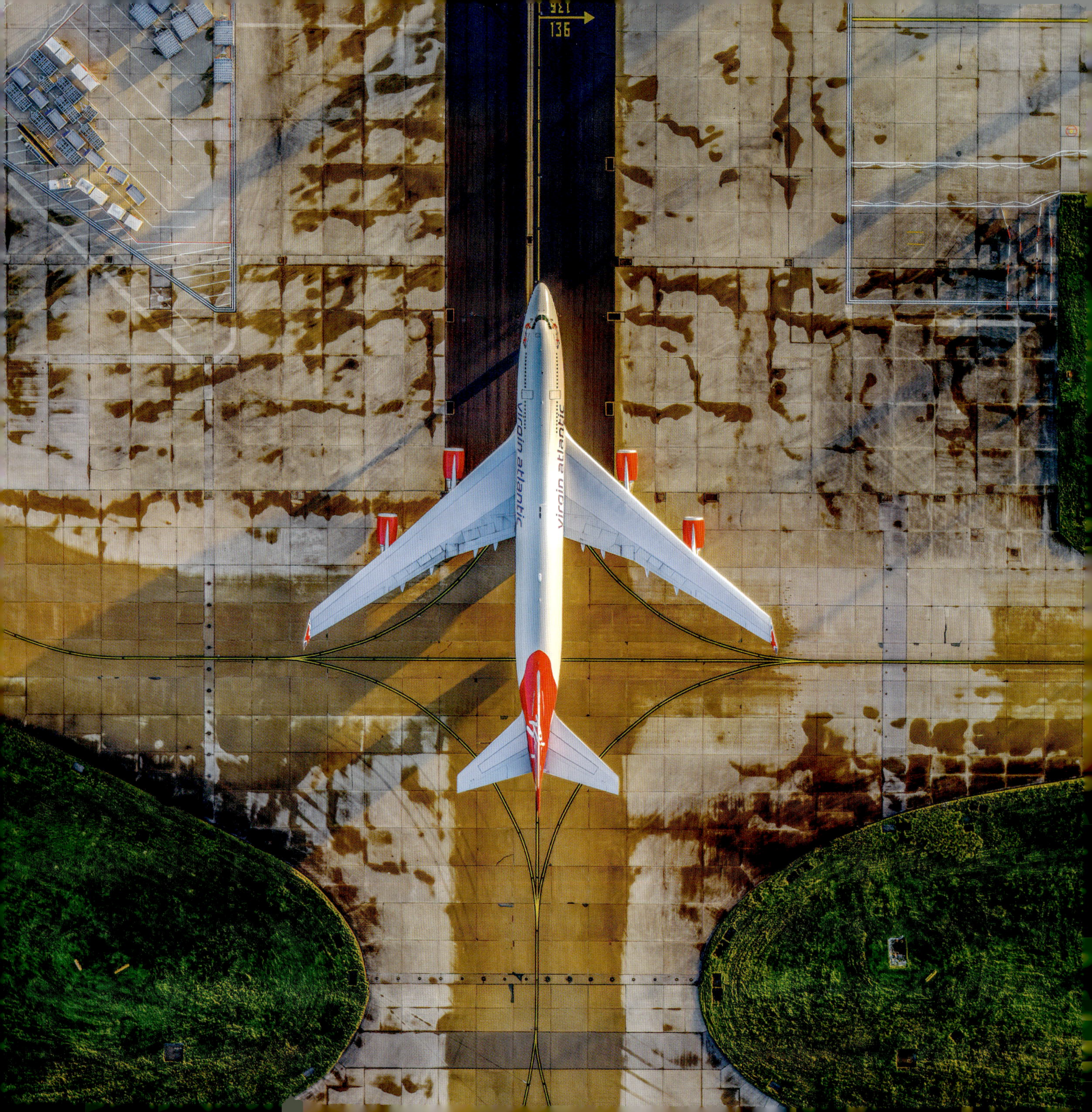
virgin atlantic
virgin atlantic
136

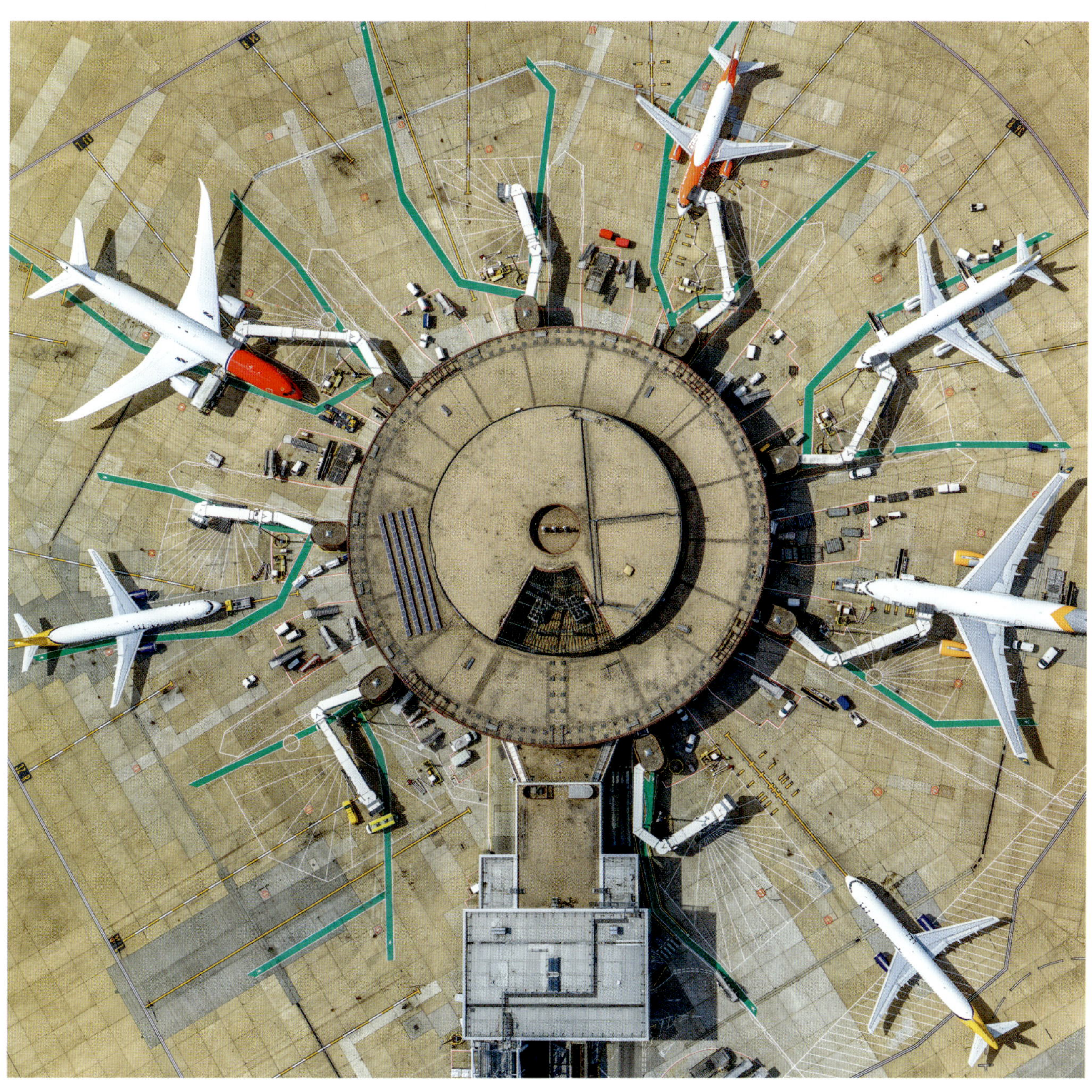

Opposite: Control tower at Gatwick Airport

Pages 204–205: Control tower and departure gates at Heathrow Airport

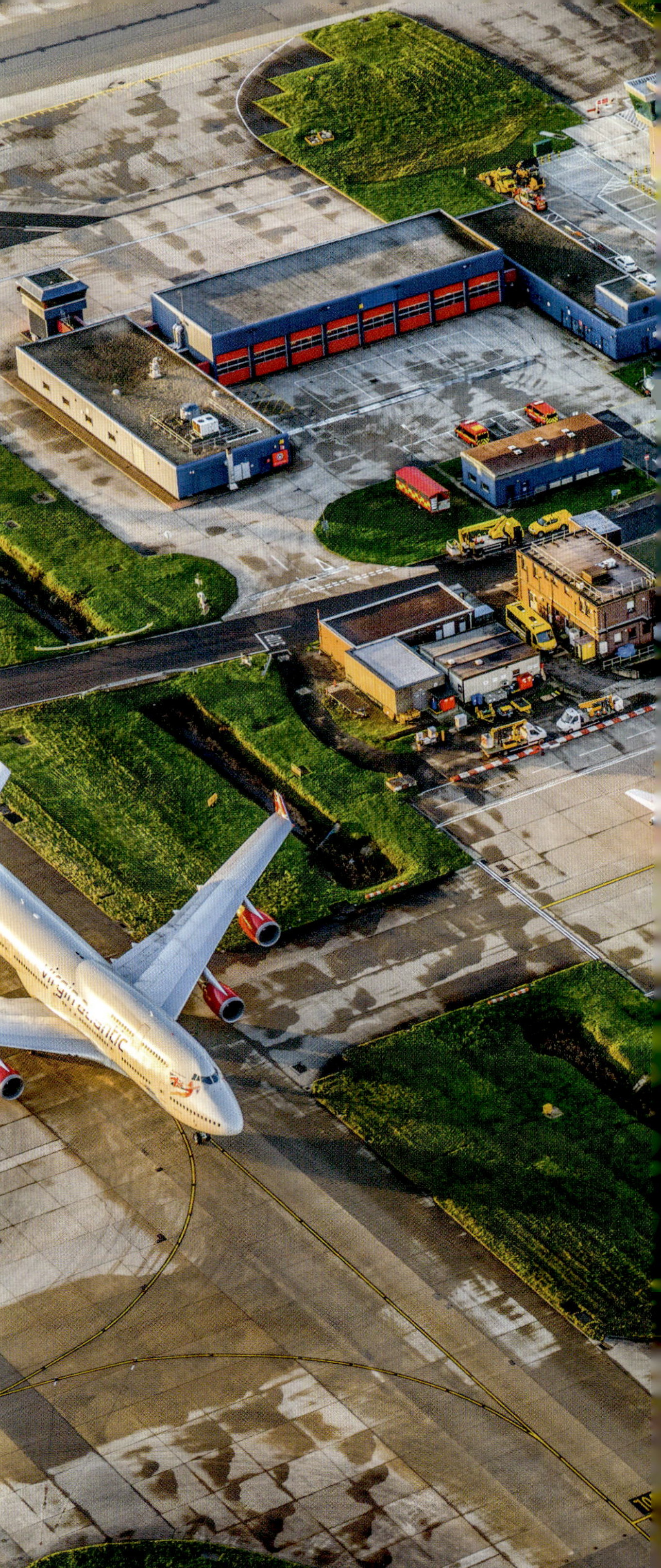

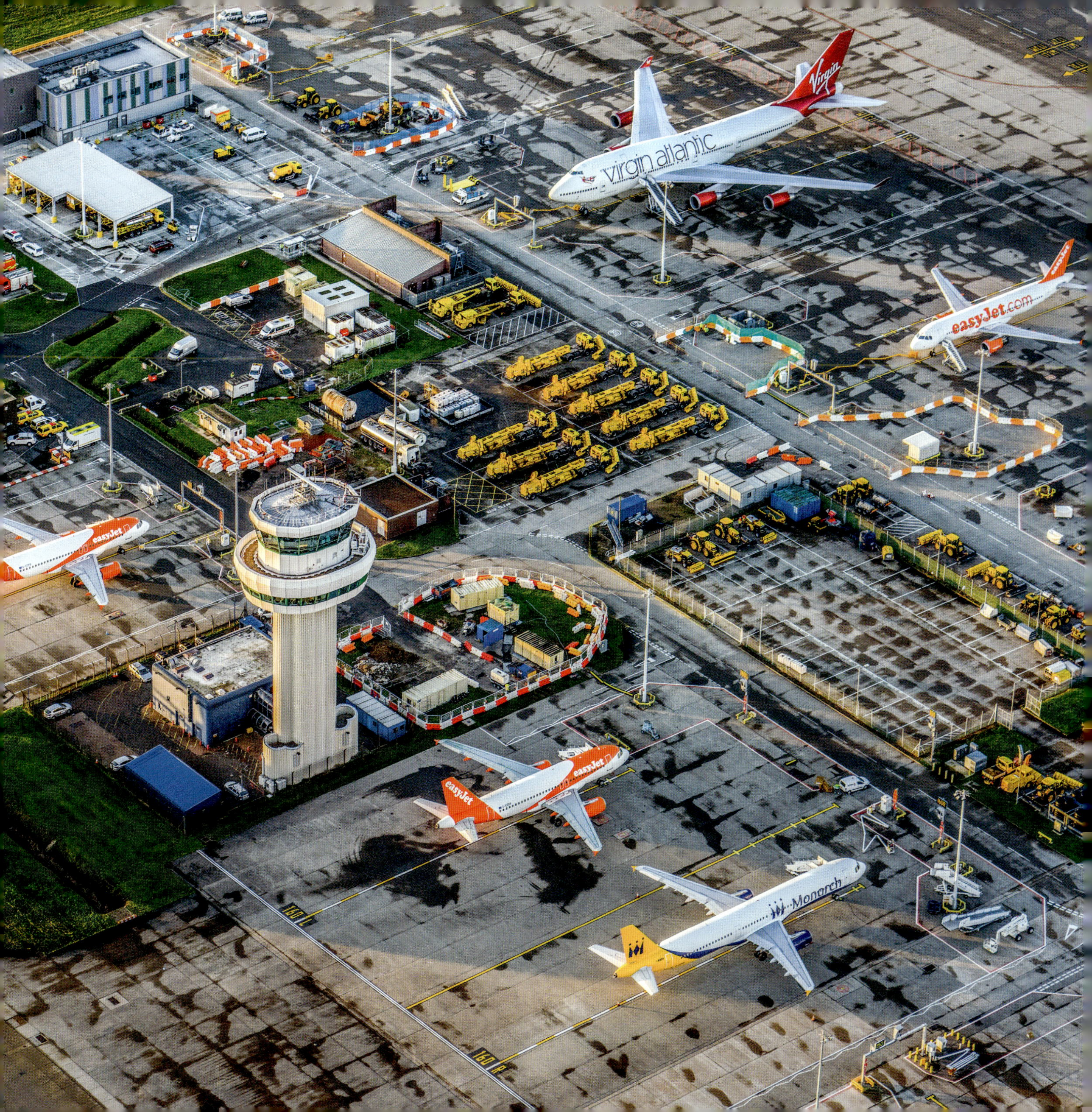
virgin atlantic
Virgin
easyJet.com
easyJet
easyJet
easyJet
easyJet
Monarch

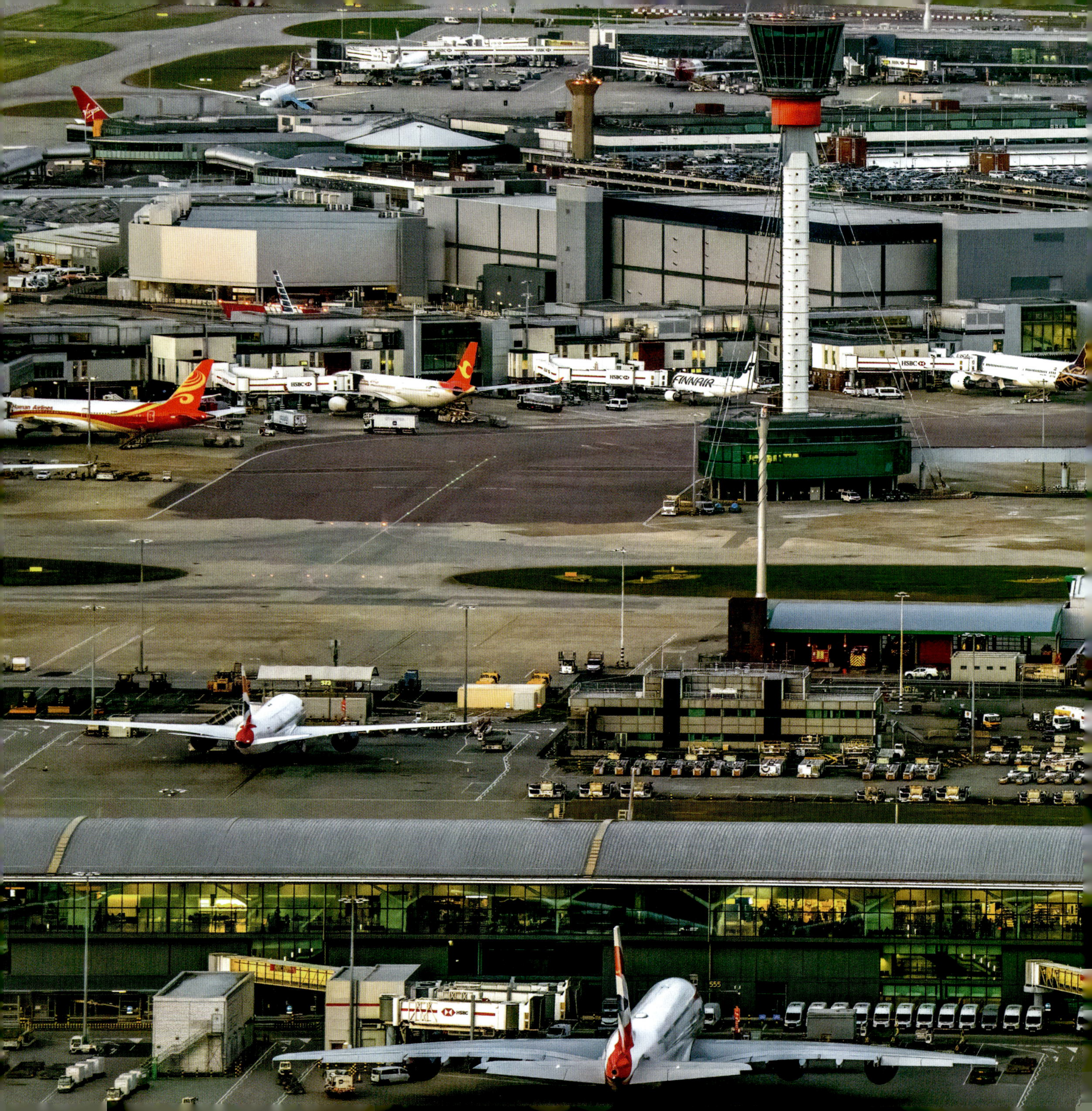
FINNAIR
HSBC

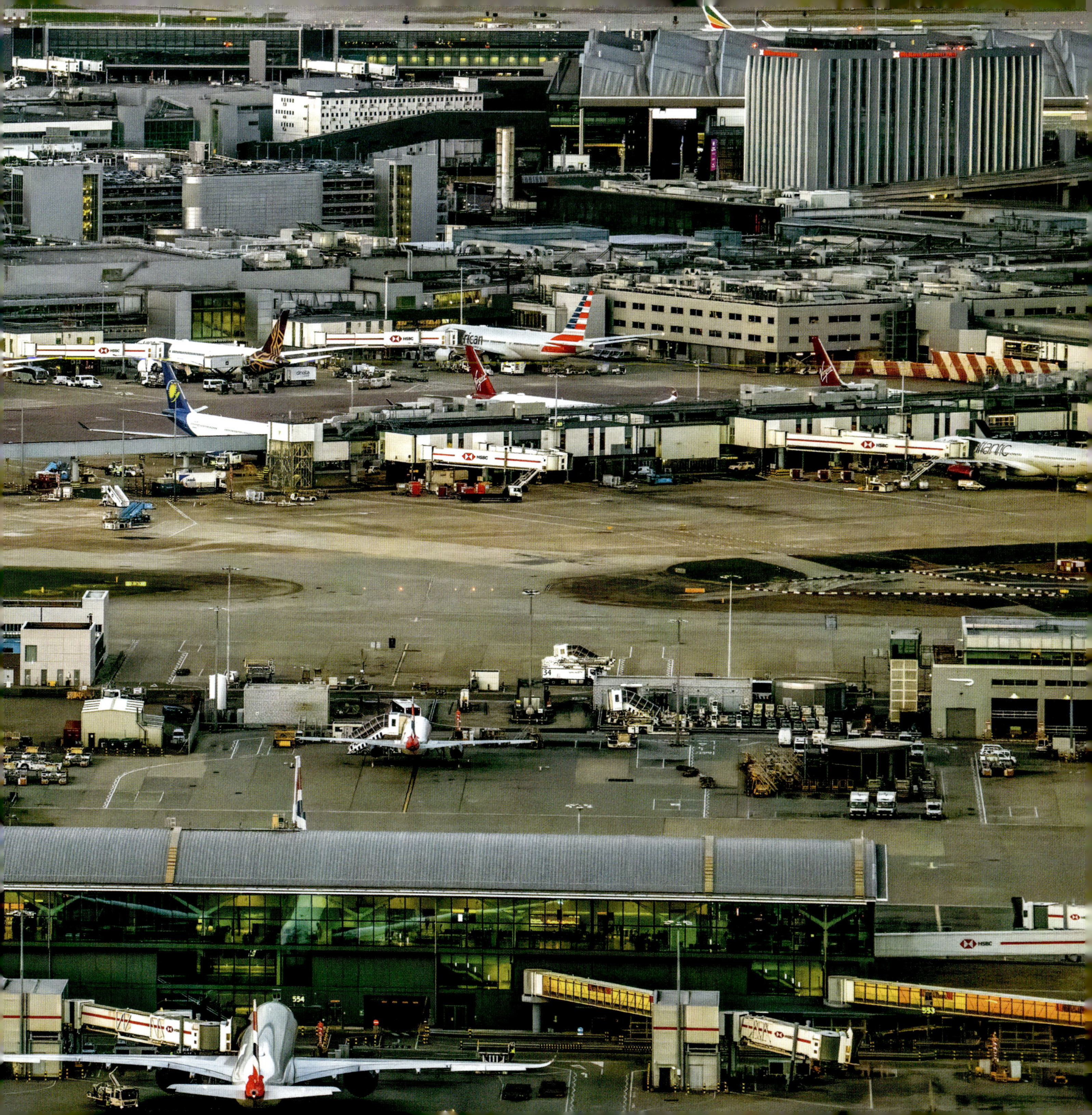

ARTIST'S STATEMENT

Jeffrey Milstein

Growing up in Los Angeles in the 1950s, my two interests were airplanes and drawing. I built all the model airplanes I could afford to buy and drew pictures of the stylish cars and jet airliners of the day.

In 1960, at the age of 16, I began taking flying lessons at Santa Monica Airport with money I earned from an after-school job. I passed my flight test on my 17th birthday (the minimum age). The flight school would give me an hour in a Cessna 150 in return for sweeping out a big hangar on Sunday mornings. I would fly over Los Angeles, taking pictures with an 8mm movie camera.

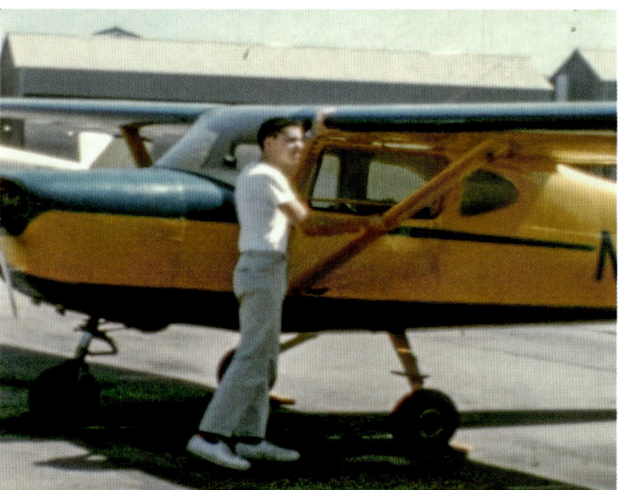

Seventeen-year-old Jeffrey Milstein performing a preflight inspection on a Cessna 150 at Santa Monica Airport in 1961

I loved seeing everything going on in the city below: cars driving downtown, people swimming at the beach, players running during a baseball game. I could see it all. It was thrilling to be piloting the small yellow-and-blue plane around the clouds, free to go wherever I wanted (this was a long time ago, before all the controlled airspace rules).

When I wasn't reading flying magazines, I was drawing and painting. In high school, I studied art with an influential teacher who taught us about the Bauhaus, where some of the foremost contemporary painters, graphic artists, and architects worked and taught. It opened my eyes to what good design looked like. After high school, I went to the University of California, Berkeley, where I studied architecture and art. As a student, I was required to get a 35mm camera and start documenting my work. I bought a secondhand Argus C3, the first of many cameras I would buy over my lifetime.

After graduating, I worked for an architecture firm in San Francisco before moving to New York City in 1969, where I earned my license. In 1975, I moved to Woodstock, New York, where I started my own firm designing primarily alternative build-it-yourself shelters and small solar homes. That same year, I coauthored a book with another architect called *Designing Houses*.

In 1983, I started a small design and publishing company called Paper House Productions. Over the next 17 years, the little company grew much larger, with an extensive line of note cards, many of which used photographs that I took. In 1996, I attended a workshop with photographer Jay Maisel. He inspired me enormously, and I decided that photography would be my third career. In 2000, I sold my company, set up a photography studio near my home, and began to photograph (what else?) airplanes.

My first photographic portfolio was of jetliners flying low overhead as they were about to land. My goal was to capture highly detailed photographs in perfect symmetry at the exact moment the planes were overhead. The images, which had the formal look of architectural or engineering drawings, were widely published, and in 2007, the collection became my first photography book, titled *AirCraft: The Jet as Art*. In 2011, the photos made their way to the Smithsonian National Air and Space Museum in Washington, DC, where I had a yearlong solo exhibit.

In 2012, more than 50 years after I had first photographed Los Angeles from a small plane, I decided to return to the air with the newest high-resolution digital cameras available to photograph cities once more. Over several years I made flights in small planes and helicopters over New York and Los Angeles, having other pilots do the flying while I concentrated on aerial shooting. My favorite type of image is the straight-down shot, a kind of architectural plan view, and over the years it has become a signature style of mine. It is more difficult to achieve because the pilot has to make steep, tight circles (not all of them like doing that) while I lean out the open door holding the camera. There is vibration from the rotor, added g-force from the tightly banked turns, and blowing wind. As I frame my photographs, I look for how the lighting is affecting the shot (my favorite time of day is during the last bit of sun), as well as the perspective angles, patterns, symmetry, balance, color, and framing. Eventually the photos of those two cities were published in a book titled *LA NY*.

Years later, I hoped to do a similar project over Paris, but I discovered that French authorities did not allow photographers to fly over the city, and only a small handful had ever received this permission. When I first contacted Helifirst, a Paris helicopter company, I was told I would have to be content with a circle around the city. I would not be able to get the straight-down photographs that had made my work in other cities so distinctive. I submitted an application, and eventually I was granted permission for two 45-minute flights over central Paris. With the photos from those flights and a few others around the outer ring and over Versailles, I created a book called *Paris from the Air*, which has since won several design awards.

My photographic interest in London began in early 2016, when I was asked by *Bloomberg* to shoot Gatwick Airport. Later that year, I was vacationing in the city with my college-age daughter, Lucy. She had flown in a helicopter with me before, one of the only passengers I've known who can take the steep turns without getting sick. She kept asking me to take her over London. I had a camera with me, so I finally agreed. It turned out to be a great flight, with many of the resulting photos appearing in this book, including the perfect overview of the Gherkin. The London controllers are very restrictive about the higher airspace over the city because of air traffic into Heathrow, but I really wanted that shot, so the pilot asked if we could get higher over the building. The controllers gave us four minutes, and luckily, I was able to nail the shot.

Years later, in late 2022, I had a show of my aerials at Messums Gallery in London. I brought a camera but had not planned an aerial flight, preferring warmer months for flying with the door open. But when we were walking around Piccadilly Circus at night we saw all the festive Christmas lights hanging above the streets. My girlfriend, Kim, said, "You should get a helicopter and photograph this from the air." With her help, I managed to line one up for the next day and the weather was good. The resulting colorful photographs make up the holiday section of this book.

In May 2023, I returned to London to photograph from the air for the fourth time to get what I needed to finish this book. In a very successful two-and-a-half-hour flight, I got everything I set out to get except Kew Gardens, which the National Air Traffic Services (NATS) controllers would not allow.

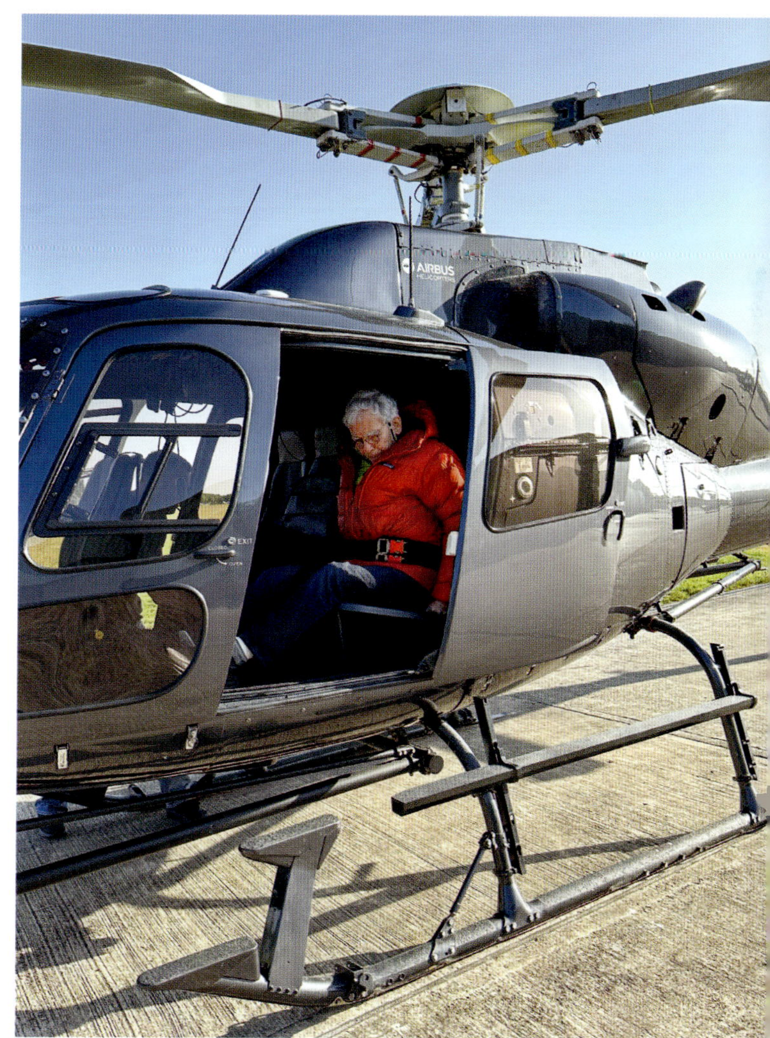

Jeffrey Milstein getting ready at Denham Aerodrome
for a flight over London in 2023

SELECTED NOTES

Robert Morton

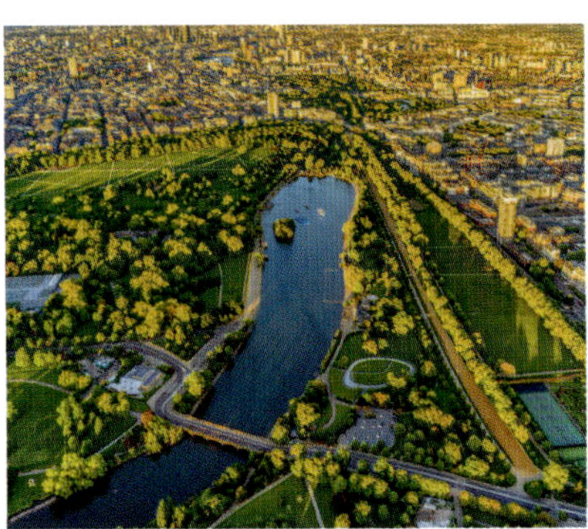

Hyde Park
Pages 2–3, 32–33, 34–35, 36–37 & 194–195

Hyde Park, a Royal Park and London's largest green space at about 340 acres, opened to the public in 1637, 100 years after Henry VIII took it from the monks at Westminster Abbey in 1536. Originally part of the manor of Hyde, the park may be so named from the Saxon word *hide*, meaning a unit of land large enough to support a household. Henry VIII used the tract for hunting, but later royalty landscaped it and finally made it into a public parkland. One of the park's distinctive features, the 40-acre lake known as the Serpentine, was created by George II's Queen Caroline, who enjoyed boating on it. Once supplied by water from the River Westbourne, which was dammed to create it, the Serpentine now fills from three deep, drilled wells. Available for swimming and boating, the lake has been used for many competitions, including events at the 2012 London Olympics.

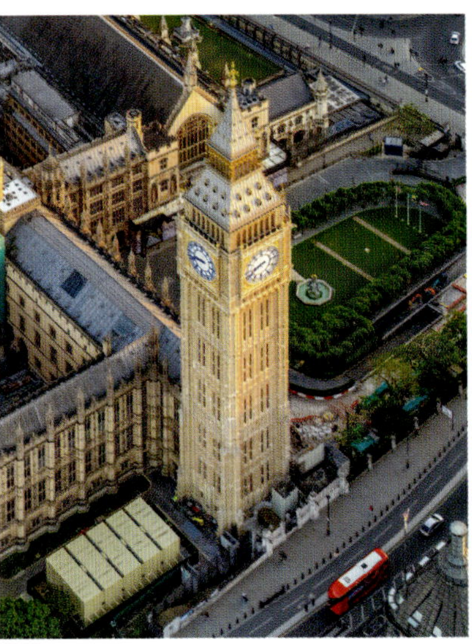

Big Ben
Pages 4, 168–169, 170–171 & 176

Like the Eiffel Tower in Paris, the most notable emblem of London is the great clock tower popularly known as Big Ben. But Big Ben refers to neither the clock nor the tower but rather the Great Bell, the largest of five bronze bells, four of which strike the quarter hours until the 3,000-pound Ben tolls the hours. The tower holding the bells and the Great Clock was renamed the Elizabeth Tower in 2012 at the Diamond Jubilee of Queen Elizabeth II. Finished in 1859, it was designed by Augustus Pugin in a Gothic Revival style and bears on its walls an array of shields referencing the four countries that make up the United Kingdom, as well as other emblems of English history. It is topped by a lantern above the belfry called the Ayrton Light, which illuminates when the House of Commons holds a session after dark.

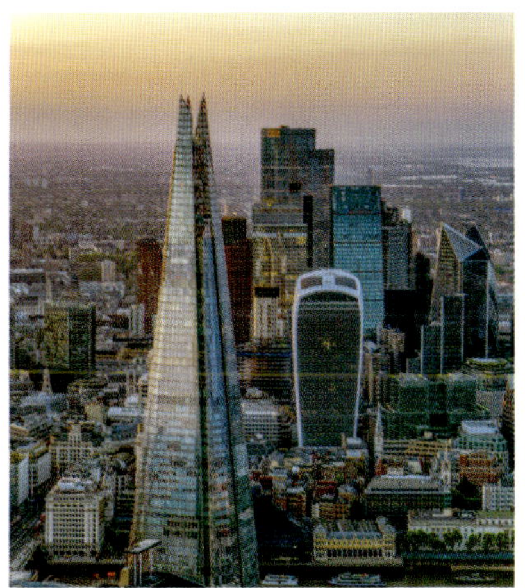

The Shard
Pages 6–7, 46–47, 130–131, 136 & 137

Rising like a giant sliver of glass above the London Bridge railway station, the tower known as the Shard dominates the South Bank. Opened formally in 2012, the pyramidal 1,016-foot skyscraper—the tallest building in the United Kingdom—was designed by the Italian architect Renzo Piano. It houses 26 floors of office space, a five-star hotel, three restaurants, 10 residential apartments—rumored to sell for $38 million—and a six-story viewing gallery with an open-air deck. Designed to be energy efficient even with its all-glass surface, the building has been structurally engineered to have a sway tolerance of 16 inches. Among the architect's inspirations were the many church spires seen in paintings of London done by the 18th-century master Canaletto. When Piano's plans were unveiled, English Heritage—the watchdog of monuments—claimed the structure would be like "a shard of glass through the heart of historic London."

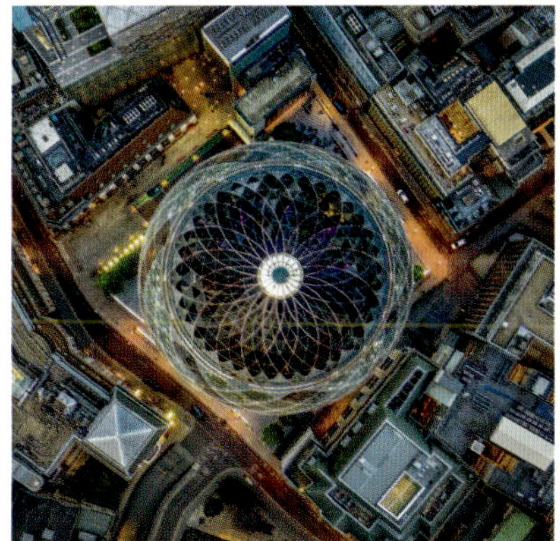

The Gherkin
Pages 8–9, 10, 52–53, 54–55, 56–57 & 60–61

Designed by Sir Norman Foster, the dome-topped, glass-walled skyscraper known as the Gherkin occupies an ancient site in the City of London whose street address and formal name—30 St. Mary Axe—refer to a 16th-century church of the same name. Constructed in 2003, the building's round shape suits its location on a small site bounded by narrow streets, where a rectangular structure's mass would appear too dominating. Its design specifications include passive solar and other structural features that save about half the cost of energy of a similarly sized tower. The Gherkin's 41 stories top out in a panoramic 40th-floor bar and viewing area known as the "lens," and a restaurant and dining rooms on the two floors below, which have made it a popular tourist attraction. In 2004, it won the Stirling Prize of the Royal Institute of British Architects by unanimous vote.

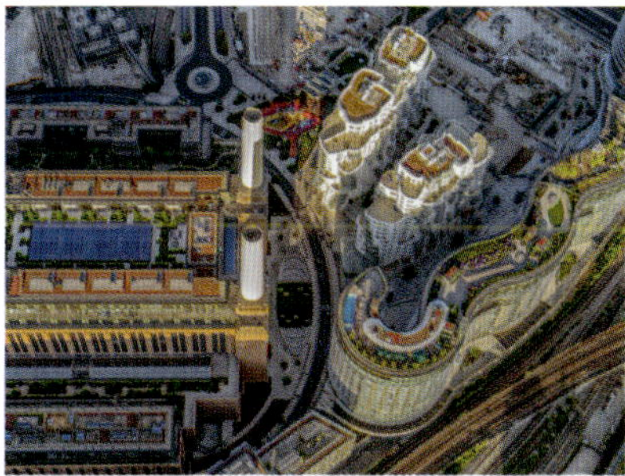

Battersea Power Station
Pages 12–13 & 134–135

Battersea Power Station on the South Bank produced one-fifth of London's electricity from the 1930s to 1983, when it closed. One of the world's largest brick buildings, it was also noted for its many Art Deco interior features. Once it was dormant, the plant was largely considered an eyesore, but because of its longevity and uniqueness it had earned a Grade II listing, meaning it could not be destroyed or substantially changed without government approval. Over the years numerous renovation schemes were proposed, including creating a theme park inside it. Finally, in 2013, plans were approved to create a new community of homes, shops, restaurants, and cultural venues at the power station and the 42-acre surrounding area. By 2023, there were 254 apartments inside the plant and about 100 retail outlets, including Apple, which moved its United Kingdom headquarters into the nearly 500,000 square feet of office space.

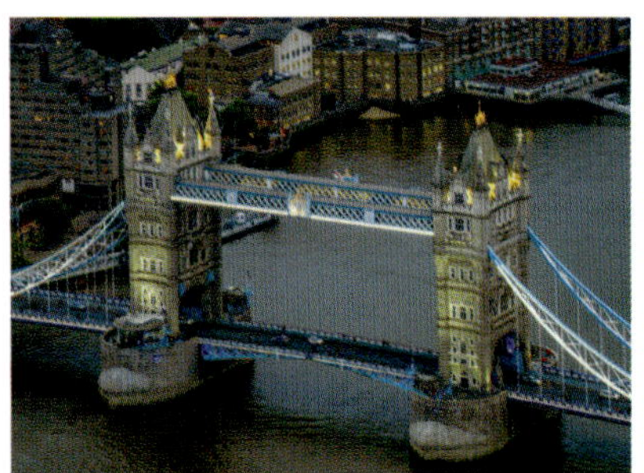

Tower Bridge
Pages 16–17 & 50–51

Tower Bridge—with its faux-Gothic towers, sturdy ship-like piers, and high steel-framed upper walkways—opened in 1894. It crosses the Thames just east of the Tower of London. A so-called bascule bridge, its central span opens at the center, each half rising to permit tall vessels to pass through, which happens about 1,000 times a year; opening and closing takes about five minutes. The cables and walkway struts were painted red, white, and blue in 1977 to celebrate the Silver Jubilee of Queen Elizabeth II and subsequently changed to largely blue and white. The bridge may be crossed on foot at the roadway level or on the upper walkway, where portions of the floors are made of glass. Crossing the bridge at street level costs nothing, but there is a fee for access to the exhibition and upper walkway. Paying visitors take an elevator to the walkway after entering the towers.

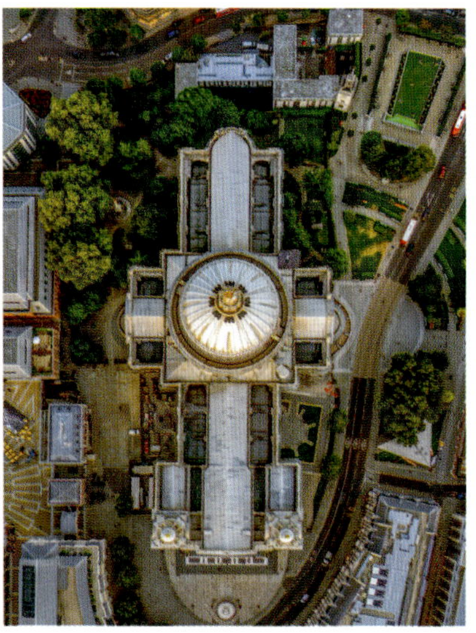

St. Paul's Cathedral
Pages 18–19, 66–67, 68–69, 71 & 72–73

St. Paul's Cathedral sits on Ludgate Hill, the highest point in the City of London, which has been occupied by churches dedicated to the Apostle Paul since 604. The immediate predecessor to the present church was so damaged by the Great Fire of 1666 that it was determined it should be replaced instead of rebuilt. Sir Christopher Wren did so spectacularly, creating a structure in a Baroque style with Renaissance and Palladian influences and a 365-foot dome that echoes St. Peter's Basilica in Rome. Wren was the first notable person to be buried in the church, which also contains tombs for the Duke of Wellington and Lord Nelson, as well as memorials to significant people ranging from the poet John Donne (who was dean of the cathedral for a decade) to Lawrence of Arabia to the 28,000 Americans who lost their lives in service connected to the United Kingdom.

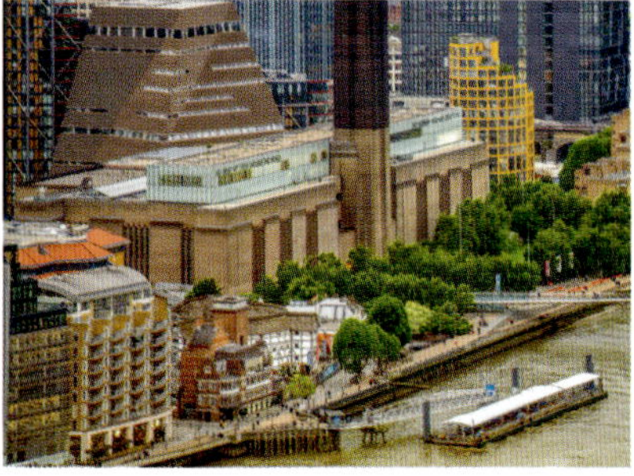

Tate Modern
Pages 18–19 & 142–143

Tate Modern began as a child of Tate Britain, which had been formed to display and collect British art and was initially funded by the sugar baron Henry Tate. It opened in 1897, but by 1992 museum trustees determined that modern art should have its own museum. As it happened, an abandoned industrial building on the South Bank was available for redevelopment. Some said that the hulking, red-brick power plant was hardly the model of an art museum, but with the Brutalist trend in architecture and the museum's focus, the site seemed ideal to the trustees. Money was raised, the Bankside Power Station was purchased, and a competition for its renovation was won by the Swiss firm Herzog & de Meuron. After removal of its giant turbines, boilers, and other equipment, the huge spaces—the entry hall alone measures 500 feet long, 75 feet wide, and 115 feet high—were ready for the public in 2000.

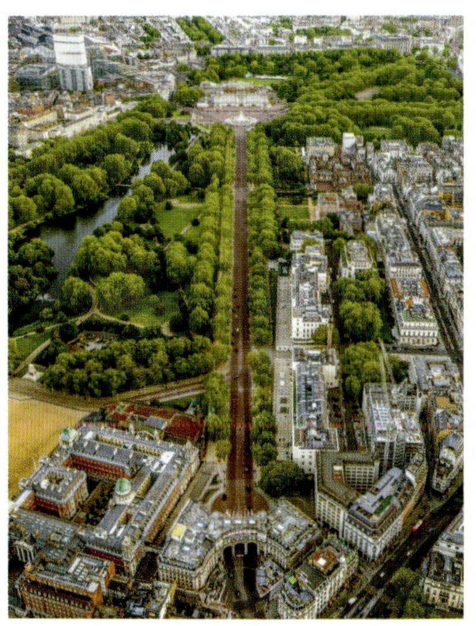

The Mall

Pages 20–21

The long, straight avenue that runs across the top of St. James's Park and leads to Buckingham Palace is called the Mall (pronounced *mal*). It was once used for playing a croquet-like game called pall-mall, then became a fashionable place to stroll, and finally was established as the ceremonial avenue it is today. Beginning at Admiralty Arch and ending at the Victoria Memorial, it runs just more than half a mile. Processions of the reigning monarch from the palace into the world at large proceed along this path. In the early 1950s, the minister of works had the idea of coloring the roadway as a kind of royal red carpet, and the application of a special blend of synthetic iron oxide to the pavement has been continued ever since. The Mall serves private cars, taxis, and buses on weekdays but is closed to traffic on weekends and all ceremonial occasions.

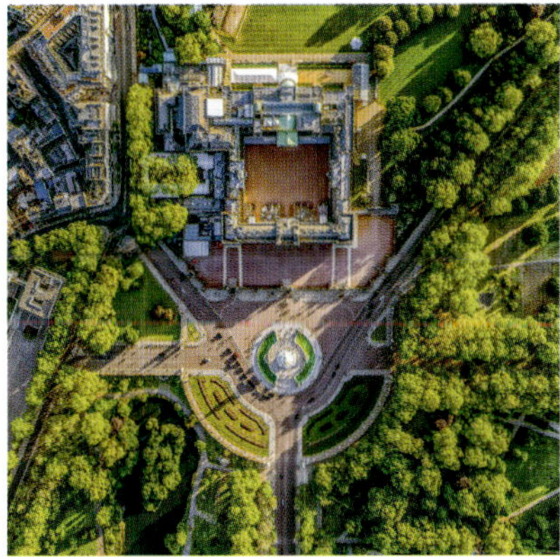

Buckingham Palace

Pages 20–21, 162–163 & 164

The palace that serves as a home to the reigning monarch and a management center for the monarchy was built for a duke of Buckingham in about 1710 and consisted of a relatively simple three-story, block-front structure with two service wings. George III bought it from the duke's son, enlarged and decorated it more lavishly, and then his son, George IV, filled it with an even more lavish treasury of paintings, sculptures, and decorative arts and had John Nash redesign the facades. After Queen Victoria took it over in 1837, she enclosed the three-sided structure with what's known as the East Front, facing the Mall. The palace contains some 775 rooms, as well as a movie theater, a swimming pool, a medical facility, and a post office. The grounds house some 40 acres of gardens and service buildings.

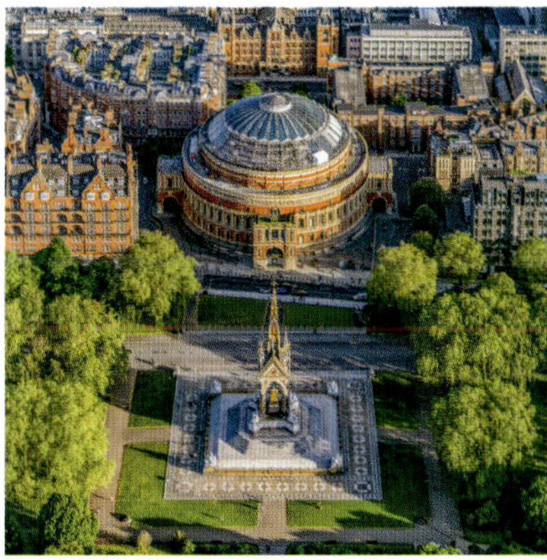

Albert Memorial and Royal Albert Hall

Pages 30 & 31

On the southern edge of Hyde Park stand the distinctive memorial to Queen Victoria's beloved husband, Prince Albert, and, across the road, the concert venue called Royal Albert Hall. Albert was not much liked by the English people at first, but his progressive ideas (he campaigned against slavery and for broad public education, the rights of women, and aid for the poor) and the queen's love for him eventually won them over. His prestige grew when he championed the Great Exhibition of 1851 that demonstrated Britain's leadership in science and engineering. Victoria was devastated by Albert's death at the age of 42 in 1861 and wore black until she died in 1901. The concert hall built in honor of Albert's passion for music opened in 1871. The memorial, a 176-foot ornate Gothic canopy, was erected in 1872, and three years later, a gilt bronze statue of the prince consort was inserted into it.

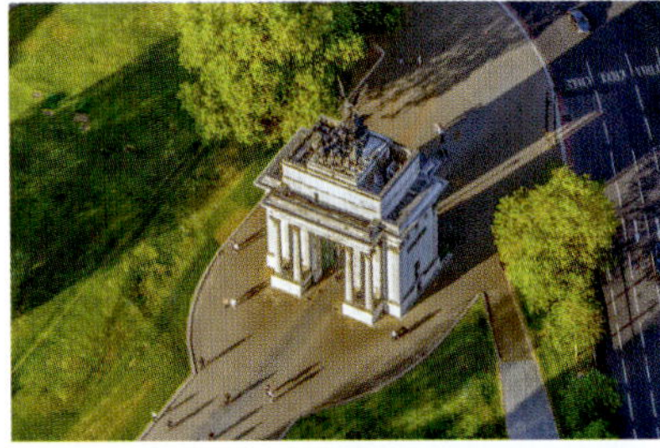

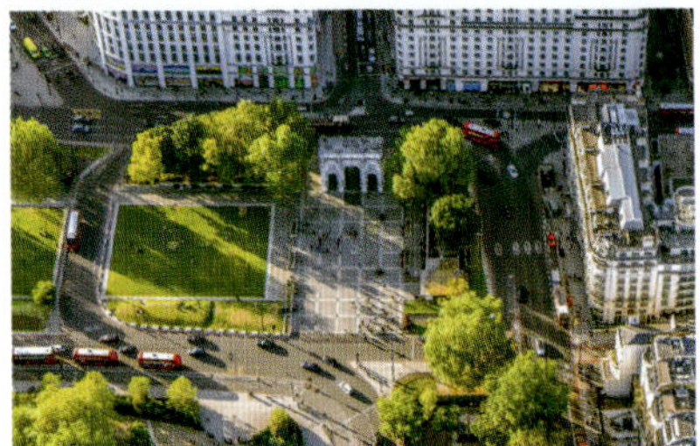

Wellington Arch and Marble Arch
Pages 35 & 36–37

Triumphal or ceremonial arches have been known in history since the Roman Empire, when a victorious general would be celebrated with a parade that passed through an arch erected in his honor. Hyde Park contains two such arches, Wellington Arch, in the southeast corner, and Marble Arch, in the northeast corner. Wellington Arch, finished in 1827, celebrates the Duke of Wellington's victory over Napoleon at Waterloo in 1815. In 1912, an Adrian Jones sculpture of Nike, the goddess of victory, riding a war chariot drawn by four horses (a traditional form known as a quadriga) was placed atop the arch, replacing a much-disliked equestrian statue of the duke. Neither arch was intended to be where it is today. They were designed as entrances to Buckingham Palace, but as the royal home was enlarged and remodeled in the mid-19th century, they were taken apart and reassembled in their present locations.

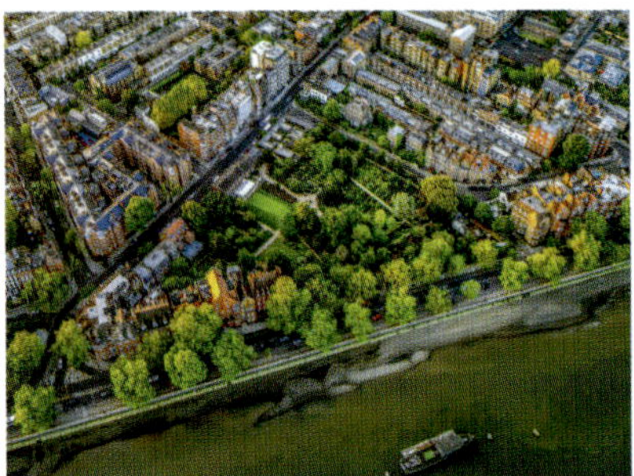

Chelsea Physic Garden
Pages 38–39

Belying its small size, only about four acres, the Chelsea Physic Garden has had an outsized influence on horticulture and medicine in Great Britain. Founded in 1673 by the Worshipful Society of Apothecaries, the garden cultivated medicinal plants for physicians. Directed by botanist Philip Miller in the middle and late 18th century, the garden imported millions of seeds and seedlings from all over the world and distributed them throughout the British Isles. Miller wrote a popular series called *The Gardeners Dictionary*. He also cooperated extensively with other gardeners, such as John Bartram, a Philadelphia horticulturist who supplied sought-after plant material from North America, especially the seedlings of certain trees that were desperately needed for the building of ships in Great Britain. Since its founding, the garden has been a center for botanical research, and in 1987 it opened to the public for the first time.

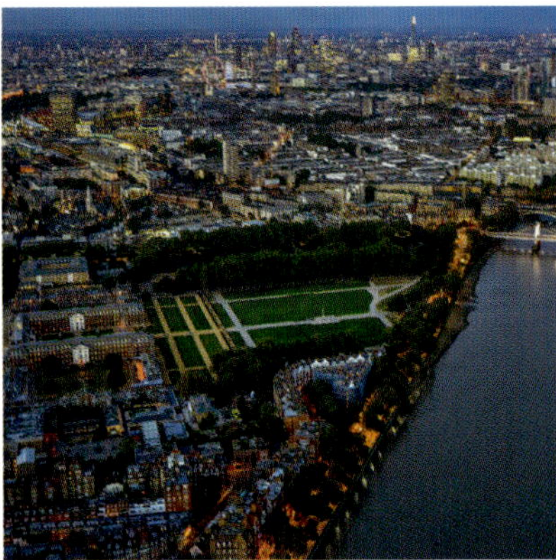

Royal Hospital Chelsea
Pages 40 & 41

Charles II determined that a place was needed to look after veterans of his army "broken by age or war," and in 1692 the Royal Hospital opened. Sir Christopher Wren designed the building, set in an 11-acre garden on the river in what was then the countryside in Chelsea. The facility no longer serves as a working hospital but provides a retirement and nursing home for aging soldiers, both male and female. They are called "Chelsea Pensioners" and wear a traditional red frock coat and black tricornered hat for ceremonial occasions. The grounds of the hospital have been used by the Royal Horticultural Society since 1912 for a show where a variety of highly prized medals are awarded for flowers and garden design. Open for five days in May, the show is a major feature of the London social season, invariably attended by members of the royal family.

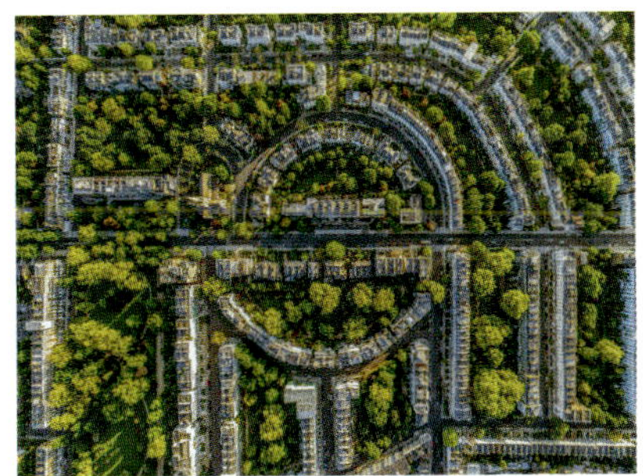

Notting Hill

Pages 44–45

Notting Hill was primarily a rural area known for brickmaking and pig farming until the 1820s, when land developer James Weller Ladbroke hired Thomas Allason, an architect and surveyor, to begin laying out plots for houses. Development of the area began seriously in the 1840s after the failure of a racecourse called the Hippodrome, which had a track that ran around the summit of the hill. Influenced by the circular geography and inspired to create communal gardens for clusters of houses rather than the usual straight-line, one-house-to-one-garden scheme, Allason laid out crescent-shaped roads with houses facing the street and backing on a large, grassy, tree-filled garden shared by all the houses. The area developed slowly, but by the end of the 19th century it had become a haven for upper-middle-class families. Elgin Crescent, Lansdowne Crescent, and Stanley Crescent addresses became synonymous with fine living.

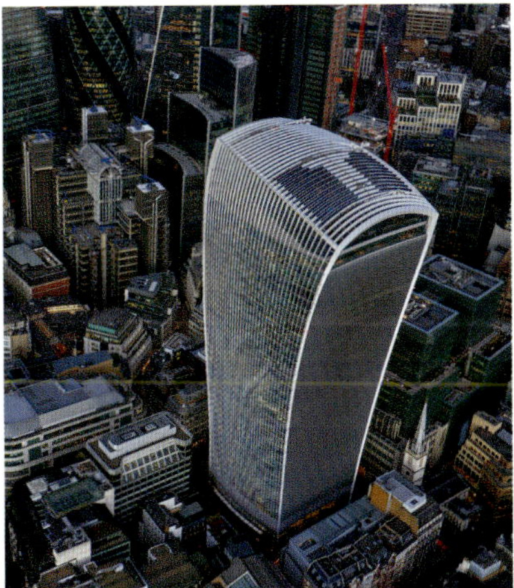

The Walkie-Talkie

Pages 46–47, 52–53, 60–61, 62–63 & 64–65

The skyscraper at 20 Fenchurch Street in the City of London was nicknamed the Walkie-Talkie for its resemblance to an old-fashioned handheld field telephone. Opened in 2015, the 37-story structure was designed by Uruguayan architect Rafael Viñoly and includes a sky garden that is three stories tall, with two restaurants, a terrace, a bar, and a viewing area. The building has been plagued by controversy, scathing reviews, and design problems, one of which was that the reflective surfaces of the forward-tilting upper floors mirrored intense sunlight into the street below, raising temperatures above 200 degrees Fahrenheit. That flaw has been corrected, but the wind-tunnel effect of those downward-curving upper floors occasionally disturbs pedestrians. Nevertheless, the quirky building has become a popular tourist attraction, especially for its wide-angle views over much of London.

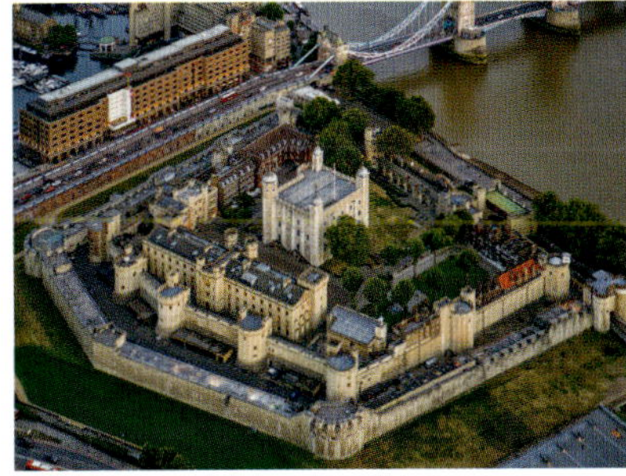

Tower of London

Pages 48–49

One of the icons of English history, the White Tower of the Tower of London dates from soon after 1066, when the French nobleman William, Duke of Normandy, took the throne by conquest and became William I. Variously a royal palace, a prison and place of execution, an armory, a menagerie, a chapel, and the treasury for the Crown Jewels, the tower incorporates part of the London Wall, a remnant of the defensive structure that encircled the Roman town of Londinium about 200 years into the Common Era. Encompassing about 12 acres and protected by two defensive walls, the complex includes the 13 towers that dot the two walls. Other buildings provide housing for the Yeomen Warders, composed of armed forces veterans. Nicknamed the Beefeaters, they ceremonially guard the tower and serve as guides for visitors.

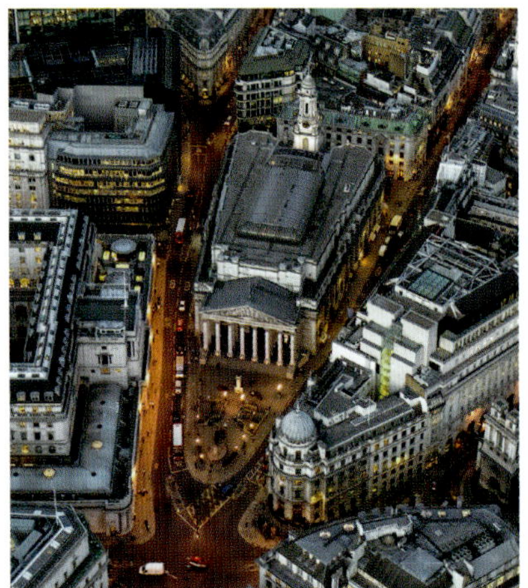

Royal Exchange, City of London
Pages 74–75 & 76–77

At the heart of the City of London, which by the beginning of the 18th century had become the financial center of the world, the classical facade of the Royal Exchange evokes all the wealth, power, and influence that once resided there. Opened initially by Queen Elizabeth I in 1571, it was destroyed by fire twice, rebuilt in its original form, and dedicated by Queen Victoria in 1844. No longer a home for stock trading or the insurance business that Lloyd's operated there for 150 years, the building now houses fashionable shops and dining venues, although the steps out front are still used for important state proclamations. Queen Elizabeth II's accession to the throne was announced there in 1952, and her death was proclaimed there on September 10, 2022, when King Charles III's reign was formally announced to the public.

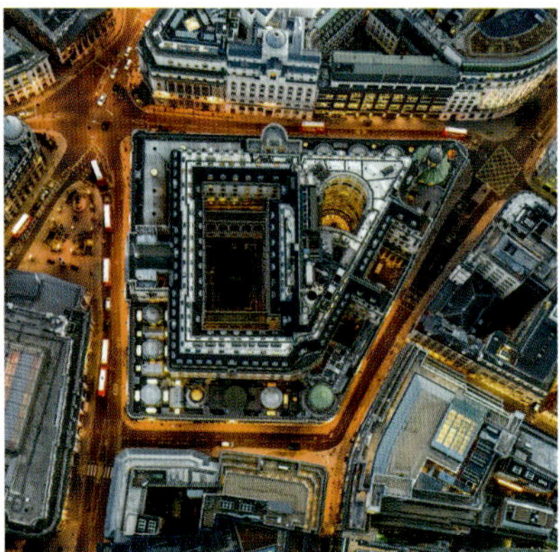

Bank of England, City of London
Page 78

The Bank of England, the large, rather anonymous-looking building across Threadneedle Street from the Royal Exchange, fills an entire city block. Established in 1694, the bank has occupied this space since 1734, where it has continued to act as the central bank of the United Kingdom, serve as one of the government's bankers, and issue banknotes exclusively in England and Wales and regulate that service in Scotland and Northern Ireland. The building itself has been renovated several times, most recently in the early 20th century when Sir John Soane's designs of the 1830s were substantially rebuilt, an act that the great historian Nikolaus Pevsner called "the greatest architectural crime, in the City of London, of the 20th century."

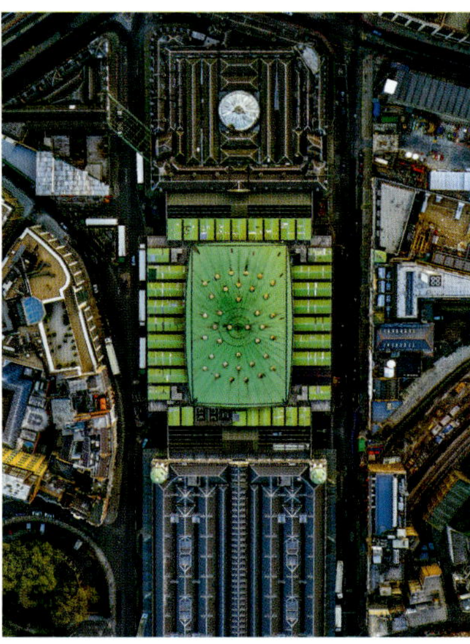

Smithfield Market
Pages 82–83

Unlike Covent Garden, a fruit and vegetable market that relocated out of the busy city center in 1974, England's largest wholesale meat market has remained doing business in the same place since medieval times, although the building that it occupies only dates from the late 19th century. Catering mainly to restaurants and grocers, the market's butchers also serve the public. Officially, the market is open from midnight to 7:00 a.m., but many stalls remain open through the morning. The area around the market has become popular as a tourist attraction and supports restaurants, bars, and nightclubs. The Smithfield name derives from its early description as a "smooth field" where horses were traded, games were played, and at one time executions were carried out. Wat Tyler, leader of the Peasants' Revolt, and William Wallace, the first campaigner for Scottish independence, were killed here.

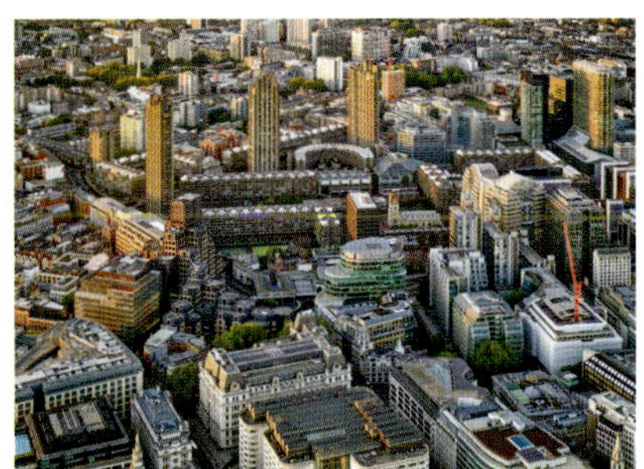

Barbican
Pages 84–85
The Barbican area of London, true to the origin of its name, sits just outside the Roman wall enclosing the city. By the middle of the 19th century, it housed some 14,000 residents. By the time German bombers got through with it in 1940, it was a ruin, and by 1951, only about 48 people remained. With almost no one to represent the area, it failed to attract redevelopment. Only in 1960 was a plan put forward by architects Chamberlin, Powell, and Bon to create a kind of utopian community with fine cultural facilities, along with the necessary schools, shops, and services. Construction began in 1965 and took 11 years to complete. Today, the 40-acre Barbican Estate finds some 6,000 residents living in 2,000 apartments. The extensive and vibrant arts complex hosts many groups, including the Guildhall School of Music and Drama, the Museum of London, and the London Symphony Orchestra.

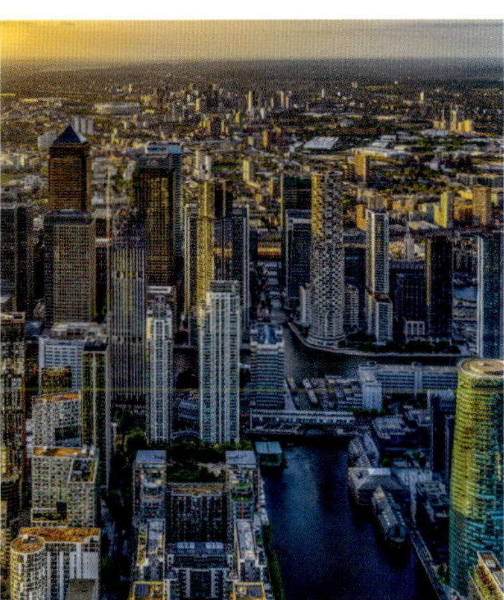

Canary Wharf
Pages 88–89 & 90–91
Probably named for the frequent trade Britain conducted with the Canary Islands in the Atlantic, where sugarcane was a dominant crop, Canary Wharf was once part of the docklands that made London one of the busiest ports in the world. The transformed area has become integrated into the City of London as an extension of its banking and financial activities since 1980, when the docks were effectively closed. Unusually, however, Canary Wharf's development has included much residential space. Some of the tallest towers are apartment blocks; one of them, called Landmark Pinnacle, rises 75 floors and is the tallest residential building in Europe. The streets beside the towers contain several large, grassy public squares, an assortment of bars and restaurants, a shopping mall, a public library, and two movie theaters. Not all the land was filled in, and two of the remaining areas of open water host marinas for private boats.

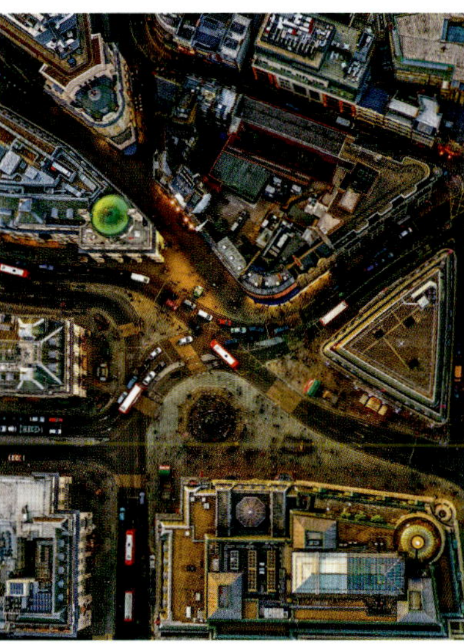

Piccadilly Circus
Pages 92–93, 110–111, 112 & 120–121
Piccadilly Circus did not exist until 1819, when it was created to access the new John Nash–designed Regent Street and provide a nexus for several avenues. Essentially a transportation hub, much like Times Square in New York City, the circus (after the Latin word for circle) connects the shopping venues of Regent Street with the theaters of Shaftesbury Avenue, the punky pleasures of Soho, and the many government offices in Whitehall and Westminster. Piccadilly runs east from the Duke of Wellington's Apsley House (known as Number 1 London) along the top of Green Park, past the Ritz Hotel, the Royal Academy of Arts, and the famous store Fortnum and Mason. Probably named after pickadils—cut-lace collars aristocratic men wore in the 17th century, which were made in the area—the street runs west to eventually become the M4 motorway, which goes all the way to southwest Wales.

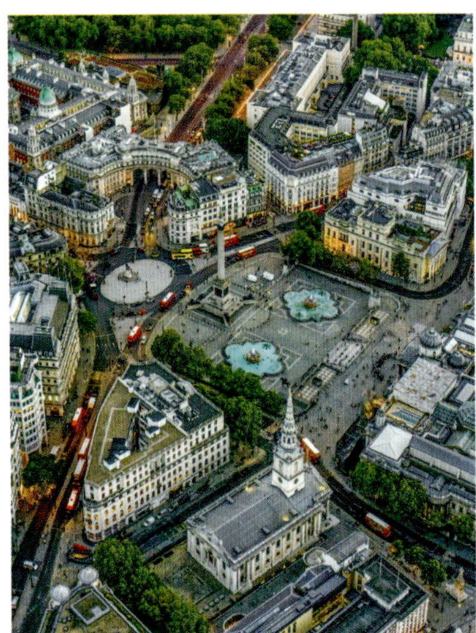

Trafalgar Square
Pages 92–93, 100–101, 102–103 & 226–227

Trafalgar Square commemorates the English victory over Napoleon's French-Spanish fleet off Cape Trafalgar in southern Spain in 1805. Flanked by a pair of fountains, the square's 162-foot column portrays Lord Horatio Nelson, the commander at Trafalgar. It was developed in the late 1830s when the National Gallery, which it faces, was being built. It was ornamented with Sir Edwin Landseer's four bronze lions at its base in 1867 and Sir Edwin Lutyens's fountains in 1939. The square links the Strand to the east (left side) and Admiralty Arch, leading to the Mall to the west. Historically, it has been the site of political demonstrations, antiwar and antinuclear protests, climate-change lobbying, an ongoing presence of buskers and other entertainers, and a hearty New Year's celebration. The square contains a marker from which every distance from London is measured, making it, in effect, the hub of the English world.

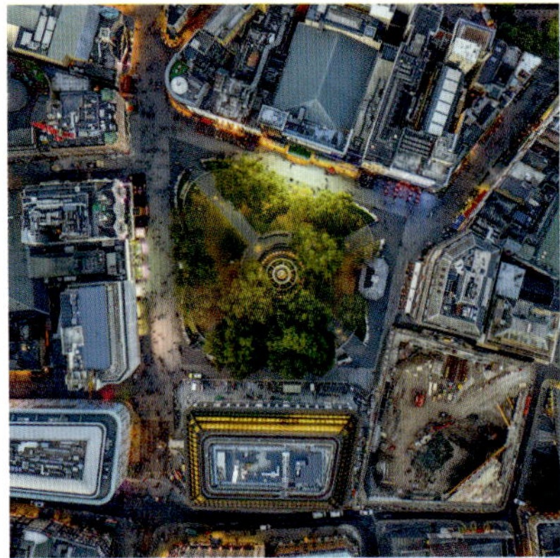

Leicester Square
Pages 92–93, 104 & 192–193

Leicester Square was privately owned from 1670 until 1874, when it was bought by a member of Parliament and donated to the local government. Named for nearby Leicester House, owned by the Earl of Leicester, the square had many notable residents in surrounding houses. Eventually, because of its location close to the National Gallery and the theaters of St. Martin's Lane and Shaftesbury Avenue, the square's residential component gave way to commercial pressure. In the 20th century, it became the locus for several of London's largest movie theaters, a venue for pop music, and a gambling casino. Since 1980, it has also hosted a booth called TKTS (modeled after the one in New York's Times Square) that sells half-price tickets for live theater and other entertainments. The square lights up at Christmastime with gift shops, food and drink stalls, a show called *La Clique*, and other events.

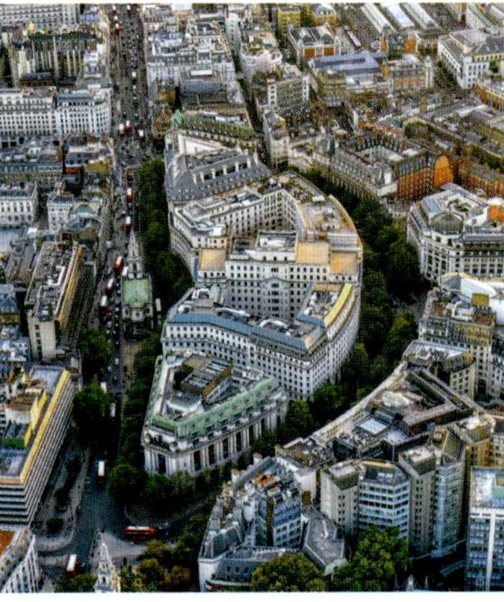

The Strand
Pages 94–95 & 96–97

The broad throughfare known as the Strand runs roughly east–west (top to bottom in the photograph) past the semicircular street called Aldwych that has the splendid Baroque church St. Mary le Strand tucked into its middle. Connecting the City of Westminster at Trafalgar Square with the City of London, the Strand changes its name to Fleet Street, Ludgate Hill, and St. Paul's Churchyard as it travels eastward. Close to the river (hence its name), the Strand has been the site of many aristocratic mansions (some, like Somerset House, have been transformed into other uses) and was later considered part of the West End's theater district, although only three working theaters remain. It has also been home to a host of distinguished writers, including most notably Charles Dickens, who lived nearby and often frequented a pub called Ye Olde Cheshire Cheese on Fleet Street.

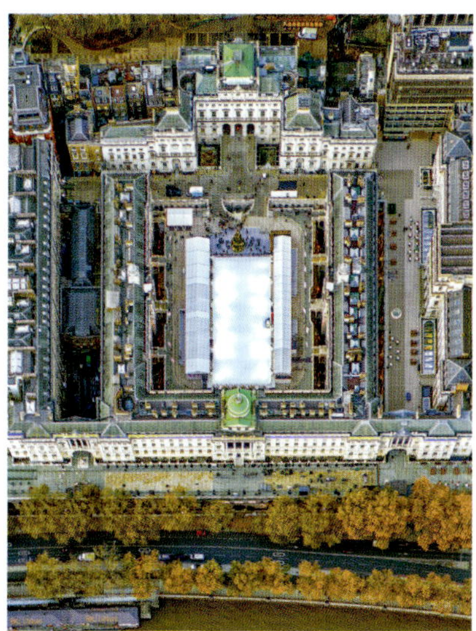

Somerset House
Pages 96–97, 98 & 197

Occupying a large block between the Strand and the Victoria Embankment along the Thames, the complex of handsome Georgian buildings called Somerset House, designed by William Chambers, has a long history in form and usage. Its original Tudor-style structure was remodeled in Renaissance designs by Inigo Jones in the early 17th century and refurbished by Sir Christopher Wren in 1685 before its last remodeling in 1856. It has housed key members of the reigning royal family, a long list of grace-and-favor residents, and most recently government offices and art institutions. It also hosts Photo London, an annual international photo fair in May. Today, a large part of the complex accommodates King's College London, whose Strand Campus lies just beside it. Somerset's cultural heritage continues with the Courtauld Institute of Art and Courtauld Gallery, as well as other similar institutions.

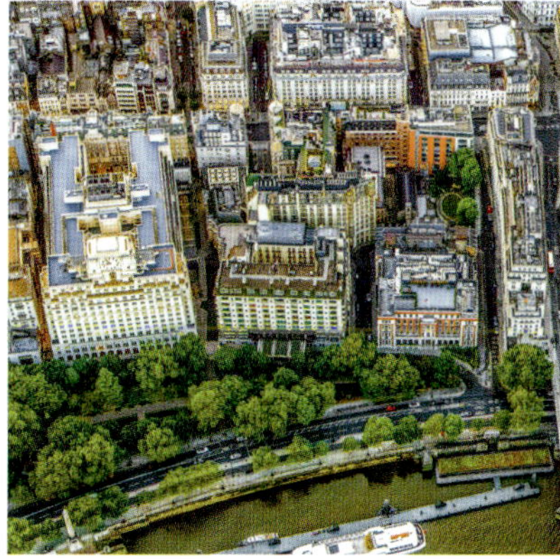

The Savoy Hotel
Page 99

Richard D'Oyly Carte, producer of the Gilbert and Sullivan operettas, built the Savoy Hotel on land between the Strand and the Thames that he bought in 1880, which had a long history of aristocratic owners from the Alpine region of Savoy. He decided that London needed a luxury hotel, and he set out to do it in true entrepreneurial fashion in the world's first building that was lit entirely by electricity. Uniquely, most of the hotel's 268 rooms had their own bathrooms with hot-and-cold running water, and they were reached by electric elevators, two innovations that after the hotel's opening in 1889 made the Savoy a showplace and a magnet for celebrities and artists. Sarah Bernhardt was a resident, Claude Monet painted views of the Thames from the windows, and, in subsequent years, Winston Churchill lunched there with his cabinet. The Beatles and Bob Dylan also stayed there, as did Whoopi Goldberg.

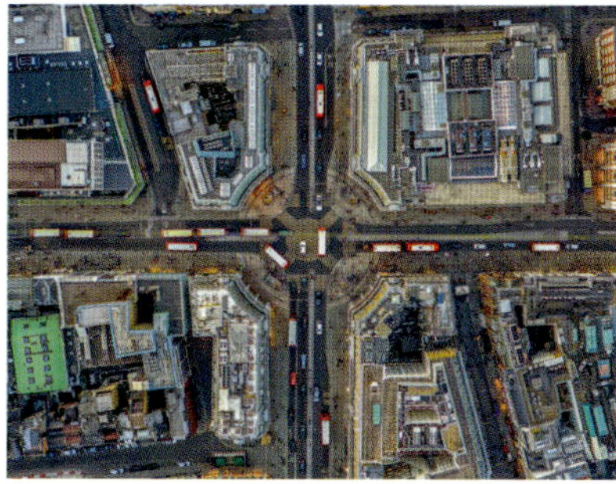

Oxford Circus
Pages 106–107 & 188

More geometrically precise than Piccadilly Circus, Oxford Circus serves as the junction between Oxford Street, which runs roughly east–west, and Regent Street, which travels roughly north–south. Developed in 1819 as part of John Nash's creation of the broad avenue named for the prince regent (the future George IV), Oxford Circus has been one of the busiest pedestrian areas in London, recording some 40,000 crossings per hour in recent years. One of the most popular shopping streets in London, Oxford Street is also shown on page 188 decked out in holiday lighting for the start of the Christmas gift-buying frenzy on Black Friday in late November. In about 2010, London merchants adopted the name and practice from the United States, where the Friday after Thanksgiving, usually a second holiday for most workers, has been a day of merchandise sales and special shopping since the 1950s.

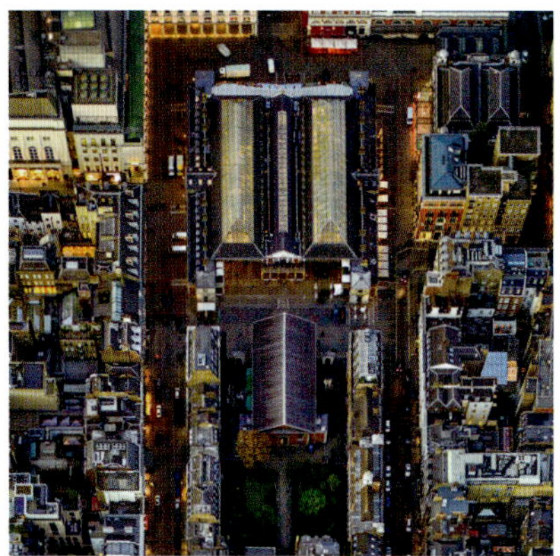

Covent Garden

Pages 109 & 190

Anyone who has seen the musical *My Fair Lady* will know that the Royal Opera House, where Professor Higgins first heard Eliza Doolittle's rich cockney accent, stands opposite what was once the busy fruit and vegetable market known as Covent Garden. The two are so closely linked that Londoners commonly call the opera house itself Covent Garden. The name dates to about 1200, when Westminster Abbey used the area for growing vegetables and fruit for a monastery and convent. After Henry VIII dissolved the monasteries, the area became private property, though the central square remained a marketplace. In 1830, a building was erected to house the stalls, including the large Apple Market. By the mid-20th century, street traffic in the area made its function untenable. The market moved away from central London in 1974, and the large building sheltering the stalls was converted to upscale food, drink, fashion, and other providers.

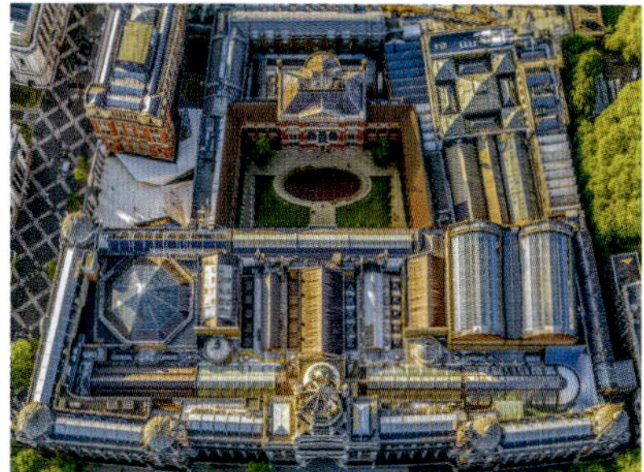

Victoria and Albert Museum

Pages 114–115

The Victoria and Albert Museum, best known as the V&A, had its origins in the Great Exhibition of 1851, which Prince Albert sponsored. The exhibition's focus on the world's achievements in the design and manufacture of textiles, glass, ceramics, jewelry, furniture, and other products inspired the idea to collect and exhibit those items in a museum. The V&A's first life was as the Museum of Manufactures, which opened in May 1852. After operating elsewhere, in 1909 it opened its present home in Kensington, designed by architect Aston Webb and underwritten by the Board of Trade. Covering 12.5 acres and with 145 galleries, the V&A has expanded its coverage to include fashion, photography, architecture, sculpture, and other arts. The collection of more than 6.5 million objects covers 5,000 years of history. Among its other distinctions, the V&A was the first museum in the world to offer visitors a chance to buy refreshments.

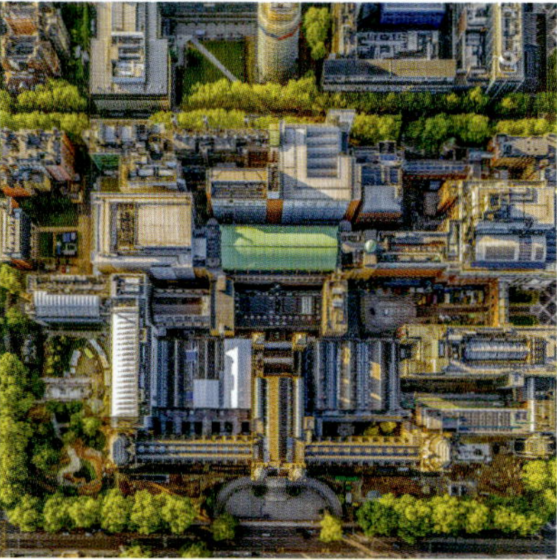

Natural History Museum

Pages 116 & 116–117

Sir Richard Owen, superintendent of natural history at the British Museum in 1856, decided that whales were too big for the BM, as it was called, and needed a home of their own. His efforts to create a natural history museum led to the purchase (with government funding) of a site next to the Victoria and Albert Museum that included a building to house the BM's collections. In 1881, a Victorian building clad in terra-cotta (which Owen believed would withstand the elements better than stone) was opened. For the longest time, the institution was called the British Museum (Natural History) until, finally, in 1992, its formal name became the Natural History Museum. More recent additions to the museum's 80 million items—covering botany, entomology, mineralogy, paleontology, and zoology—include a center dedicated to Charles Darwin and a collection of films and other media named for David Attenborough.

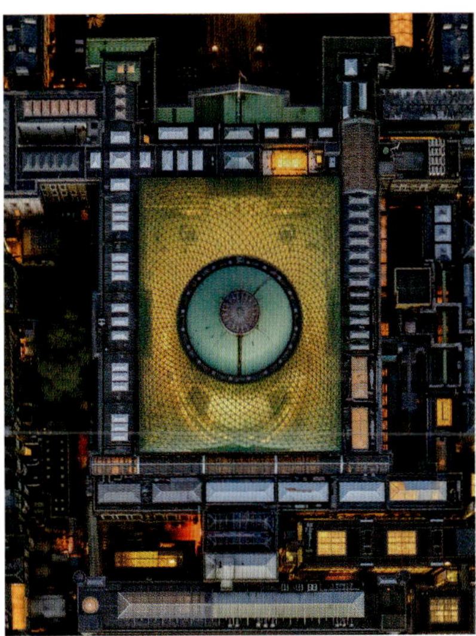

British Museum
Page 119

Contrary to the George Gershwin song, the British Museum has not "lost its charm," and remains the world's third most visited museum after the Louvre and the Vatican. The first national museum of its kind, it was founded in 1753 with some 71,000 books, artworks, antiquities, and natural history specimens owned by Sir Hans Sloane. In 1802, it received the Rosetta Stone, and in 1816, it acquired the Parthenon sculptures known as the Elgin Marbles. To gain space, the natural history collections were moved in 1963 to the Natural History Museum, and in 1997, the books were transferred to the new British Library at St. Pancras. At that point, Sir Norman Foster transformed the central quadrangle of the museum and roofed it with a glass ceiling consisting of 1,656 pieces, no two of which are alike. Called the Great Court, the new space opened in 2000.

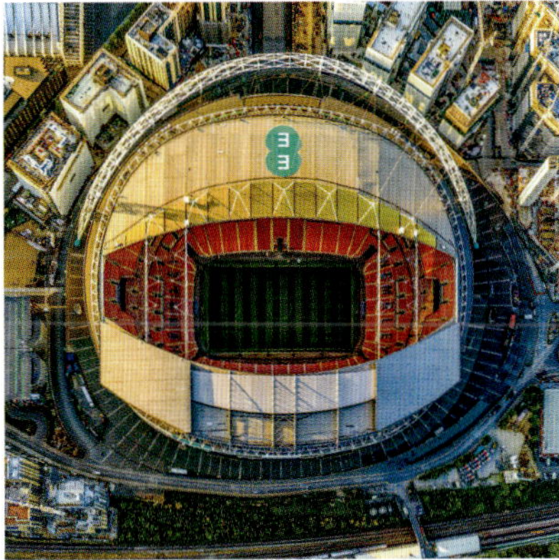

Wembley Stadium
Page 124

Owned by the Football Association, the governing organization of English football (soccer) and host to its championship, the FA Cup, Wembley Stadium seats 90,000 spectators. It is the largest soccer stadium in the United Kingdom. The original 1923 stadium was demolished in 2003. On its site, the new building, with its 440-foot steel girder arch, was designed by two firms—Populous and Foster + Partners—and opened in 2007. Much of the seating is covered by a partly retractable roof, but to maintain the grass field, the central portion stays open to sunlight. Located about eight miles northwest of central London, the arena has hosted the Olympics in 1948, the soccer World Cup in 1966, the Live Aid concert in 1985, and the women's soccer Euro championship in 2022. It has also been used for rugby matches, American football games, boxing and wrestling contests, and many different pop music concerts.

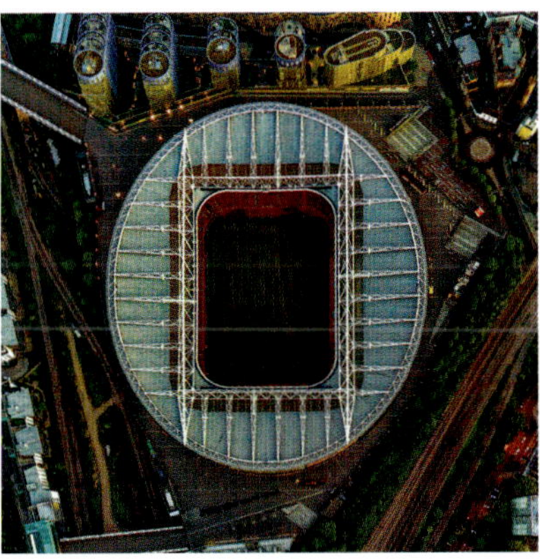

Emirates Stadium
Page 125

There are 20 football (soccer) stadiums in Greater London, and there may be as many as nine London-based teams that are likely to compete at the highest level in the English Premier League, though in the 2023–2024 season only seven qualified. Arsenal Football Club has competed in the first division since 1904, a dozen years after its founding. Nicknamed "the Gunners" because of the team's original location near a munitions depot, Arsenal played in Highbury from 1913 onward, but the team was denied permission to rebuild and enlarge the stadium as the millennium dawned so management sought a new site. Since 2006, the Gunners have played in a new stadium in Islington that seats some 60,000 spectators under a translucent roof only open over the grassy pitch itself. Designed by the architectural firm Populous, the stadium is sponsored by Emirates, the Middle Eastern airline.

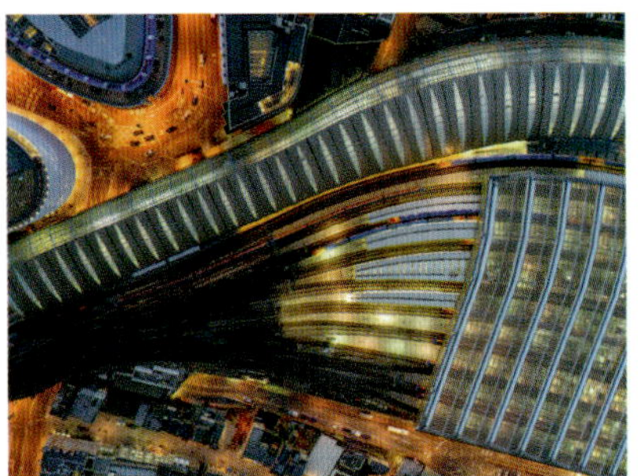

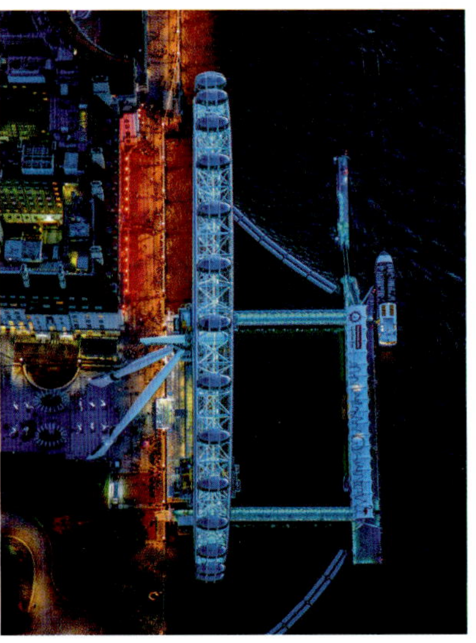

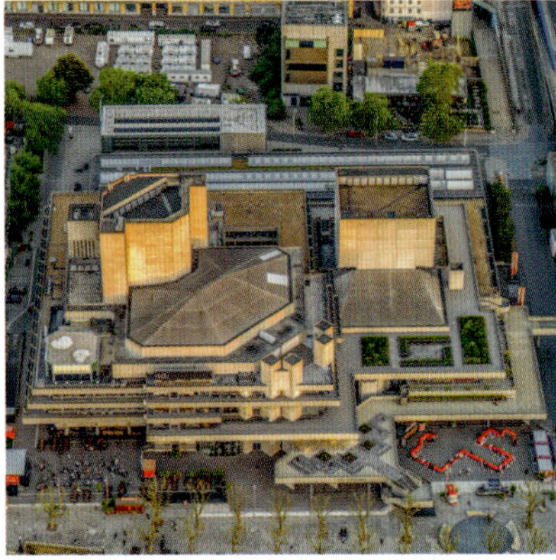

Waterloo Railway Station

Pages 132–133 & 138–139

Busiest of all the railway stations in the United Kingdom, Waterloo, on the South Bank, has served travelers from the south and west of England since 1848. The original station was rebuilt early in the 20th century and was the last station in London to accommodate steam trains. It was the first terminus for Eurostar trains coming direct from Paris and Brussels after the Channel Tunnel was completed in 1994 and Sir Nicholas Grimshaw's shiny, centipede-like International Terminal at Waterloo was ready to welcome foreign visitors. But the 1,200-foot-long, steel-and-glass-arched structure was made redundant in 2007, when Eurostar moved to the St. Pancras railway station across the river. In 2019, the international platforms were newly integrated into the other concourses, and Erik Behrens, design director of the project, said, "We reinvigorated a dormant beauty, one of the finest pieces of British high-tech architecture."

London Eye

Pages 132–133, 146, 147, 148–149 & 226–227

Rising 443 feet above the South Bank of the Thames near Waterloo railway station, the London Eye has become a premier tourist attraction since its opening to celebrate the millennium in 2000. Like the Eiffel Tower in Paris, it was intended to be taken down after a few years, but it proved so appealing that it has become a permanent fixture. The rotating wheel—with its 32 capsules, each holding up to 25 people, representing the Greater London boroughs—makes about one revolution every half hour, so passengers can usually get on and off without the wheel stopping. Designed by Julia Barfield and David Marks, the London Eye attracts more than 3.75 million visitors annually. In 2023, a half-hour ride cost about $50 for an adult, though prices are often combined with other attractions, such as boat rides on the Thames. A private pod can be rented for about $850.

National Theatre

Page 140

Theater has been a major part of British life since before William Shakespeare's time, and nowhere more vigorously than in London. Yet there was no national theater company with its own home until 1963, when the stellar Shakespearean actor Laurence Olivier founded one. Olivier's company had no home of its own and used a 19th-century theater in Waterloo called the Old Vic until 1976, when a permanent theater with three stages opened on the South Bank of the Thames. That building—in a style known as Brutalist for its rough surfaces, industrial materials, and sharp, angular aspect—was designed by Sir Denys Lasdun and Peter Softley. It has three performance spaces, one of them named for Olivier, each of which provides mechanical apparatuses and seating accommodations for different forms of theater, from traditional proscenium-arch productions to intimate chamber pieces and wildly experimental fantasies.

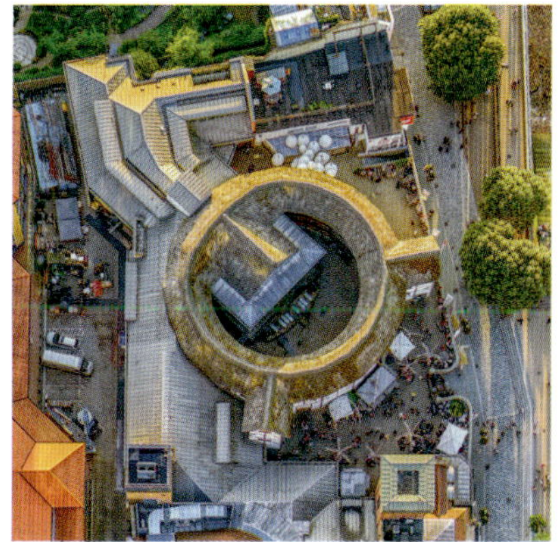

Globe Theatre
Pages 141 & 142–143

William Shakespeare wrote most of his plays for a theater called the Globe, roughly circular in form and built of oak beams with a thatched roof open to the sky in its center. Situated on the South Bank, the Globe could hold 3,000 spectators, most of whom stood on a dirt floor through the performance; nobility and the wealthy sat in a covered section above the thrust stage. The Globe opened in 1599, burned to the ground in 1613 while Shakespeare was still alive, was rebuilt, and then demolished in 1644–1645 by an act of Parliament that closed all theaters. In 1970, the American actor and director Sam Wanamaker, lamenting that the only trace of Shakespeare's theater in London was a small plaque, established the Shakespeare Globe Trust. For the next 27 years, he devoted himself to building a replica, and in 1997, on a site only about 750 feet away from the original, the Globe Theatre reopened.

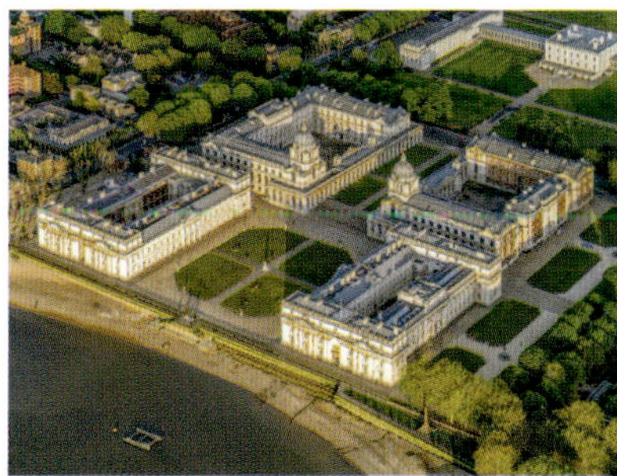

Old Royal Naval College
Pages 150–151 & 152

Perhaps the most beautiful and coherent assembly of architecture in London is at Greenwich on the South Bank. Designed by Sir Christopher Wren, the buildings originally served as the Royal Hospital for Seamen, finished in 1712. Until 1998, they served as the Royal Naval College, a training school. Since then, under management by the Greenwich Foundation, the Grade I–listed buildings have been scrupulously maintained but diverted to other uses. In 1999, some parts were leased by the University of Greenwich; a year later, Trinity College of Music became a tenant. On the grounds nearby are sites of great historical interest: the Royal Observatory, where the world standard of mean solar time, GMT, was established in 1884; the Queen's House from 1635, designed by Inigo Jones as the first classical building in Great Britain; the National Maritime Museum; and the famous tea clipper *Cutty Sark*.

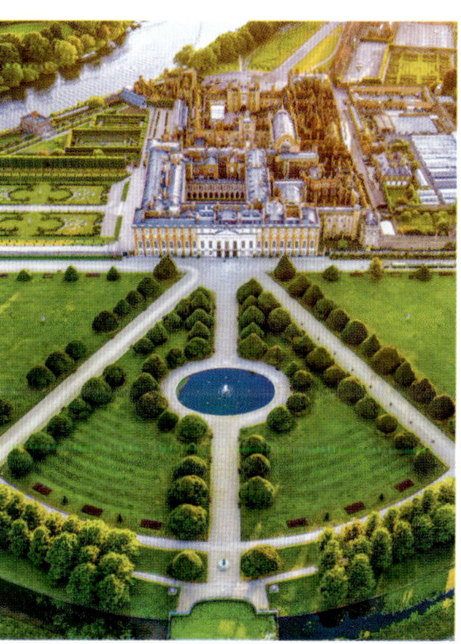

Hampton Court Palace
Pages 154–155, 156–157, 158–159 & 161

In the early 1500s, Cardinal Thomas Wolsey, Henry VIII's Lord Chancellor, bought a country estate beside the Thames and embellished it so attractively that his boss took it over. Henry VIII turned it into a lavish facility where his six wives and hundreds of courtiers were housed, entertained, and exercised. The four-walled Royal Tennis Court he built in 1530 is still used today. He also cultivated some 60 acres of gardens with fountains and ponds, a 750-acre parkland, and the world's first hedge maze. Henry VIII's Tudor palace became secondary to Kensington and then Buckingham Palace during the 18th and 19th centuries but was not unoccupied during those years. Its hundreds of rooms were used by aristocratic widows, retired military men, and other royal servants on a grace-and-favor basis. This practice continued even after Queen Victoria opened the palace to public visitors in 1838 and continued until 2017.

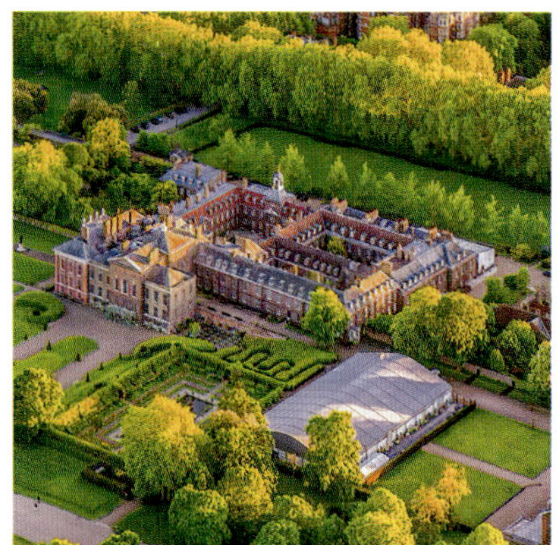

Kensington Palace
Pages 165 & 166–167

Kensington Palace, at the western edge of Hyde Park, has been a home for members of the royal family since William III and Mary II acquired the property in 1689. It was then a modest country estate that Mary believed would be better for William's health than the damp and foggy location of Whitehall Palace beside the Thames. Rebuilt and enlarged several times by Sir Christopher Wren, the main building and grounds eventually contained some 547 rooms. These were divided into apartments (some with as many as 20 rooms) and outbuilding cottages that variously housed several monarchs, numerous dukes and duchesses, and most recently Princess Margaret. The most famous resident, Diana, the former Princess of Wales, raised her two sons, William and Harry, here, and the new Prince and Princess of Wales, William and Kate, now call it their official residence.

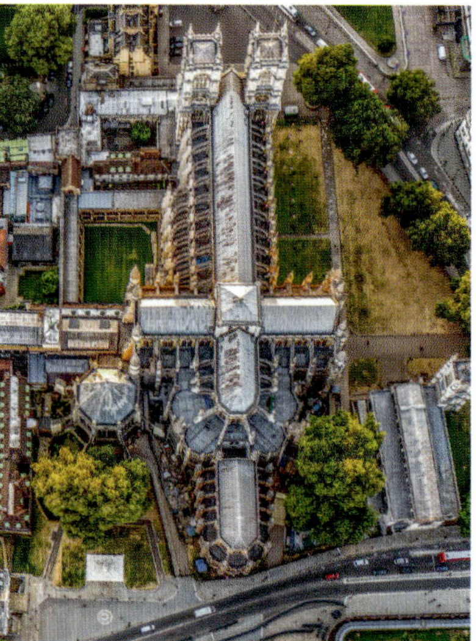

Westminster Abbey
Pages 172–173 & 174–175

Westminster Abbey and the precinct beside it, including the school founded by the monks of the original Dominican monastery, were established in about 785. Rebuilt several times, eventually in French Gothic style, the church found its present form when the western towers were added in 1745. If evidence is needed of its importance in British life, consider the following: 40 monarchs have been crowned here; 30 royals have been buried here, including 18 kings; at least 16 royal weddings have been performed here; Geoffrey Chaucer was buried here in 1400, Lord Byron was refused burial here in 1824, and Charles Dickens asked *not* to be buried here in 1870 but was anyway; in 1998, statues of 10 modern martyrs, including Dr. Martin Luther King Jr., were added over the abbey's west door; and a stained-glass window by David Hockney commemorating the reign of Queen Elizabeth II was installed in 2018.

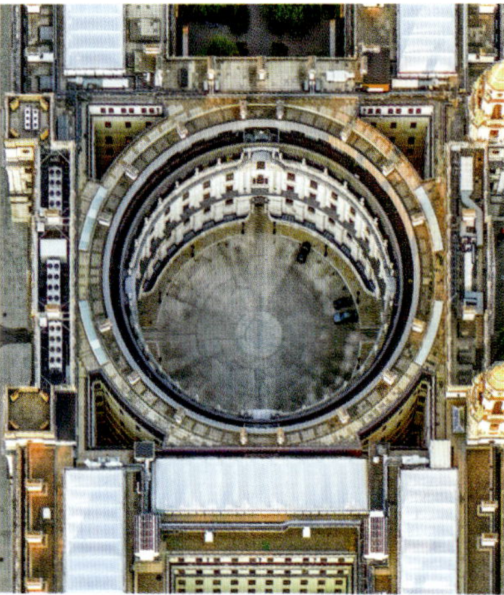

His Majesty's Treasury
Pages 177 & 178–179

The two enormous buildings diagonally opposite the Houses of Parliament shelter many important government offices. The one with the circular atrium began in 1940 to be the home for His Majesty's Treasury, sometimes referred to as the Exchequer. The treasury manages all government financial services—economic policy, taxation, customs and duties, investments, and coinage. The building provides little interest for the London tourist, but the Churchill War Rooms are in the basement. The rooms, where the prime minister and chief military commanders ran Britain's operations during World War II, are one of the most visited sites in the city. The almost equally substantial building next to it houses the Foreign, Commonwealth, and Development Office. Both buildings, clad in handsome neoclassical architecture, contain some spectacular interiors, with grand staircases and dazzling reception halls.

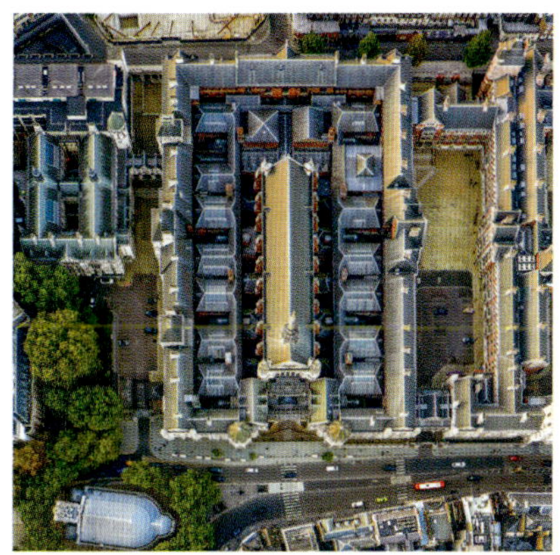

Royal Courts of Justice
Page 183

Just east along the Strand from Aldwych, where it meets Fleet Street, a large building complex houses the Royal Courts of Justice, which include a court of appeals, the High Court, and the Central London County Court, where a variety of noncriminal cases are adjudicated—matters of business law and probate, divorce, common law, and family or medical matters. Constructed in Gothic Revival style, the buildings, which look as though they date from centuries ago, were dedicated by Queen Victoria in 1882. The Inns of Court are nearby, as is St. Clement Danes Church (seen at lower left), designed by Sir Christopher Wren in 1682. Better known to the public in part because of the more sensational cases tried there and a popular television series about it from the 1970s, the Central Criminal Court, usually known as the Old Bailey, stands on the site of the historic Newgate Prison near Smithfield Market.

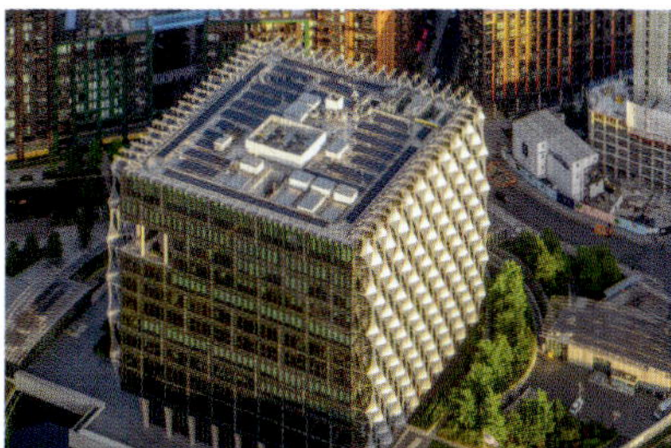

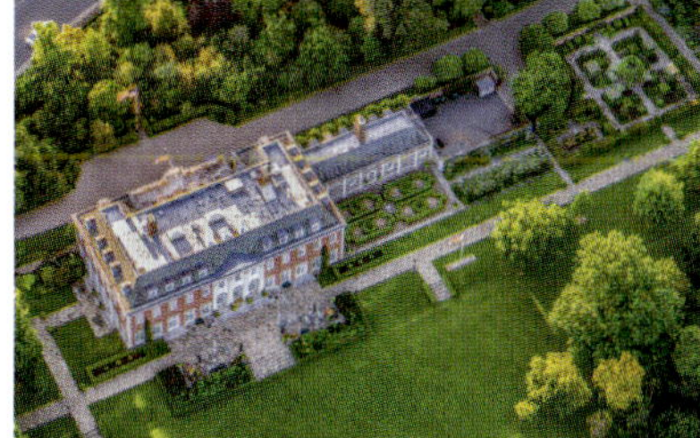

US Embassy and Winfield House
Pages 184 & 185

The US government announced in 2010 that a team led by the firm of KieranTimberlake had won the competition for a new embassy building on the South Bank in an area called Nine Elms. The winning design, a 200-foot glass cube raised on a hill set back 330 feet from the embassy's perimeter, has a semicircular pond on one side (called a "moat" by some). Construction began in 2013, and the energy-efficient building, surrounded by extensive green spaces and a housing development, opened to the public four years later. Designed for maximum security, the $1 billion structure's glass walls are six inches thick, formed from an elaborate sandwich of laminated sheets. A surrounding stockade of steel and cement bollards can withstand the collision force of an eight-ton truck. In contrast to the embassy's high-tech style, the ambassador's personal residence is a Neo-Georgian townhouse in Regent's Park.

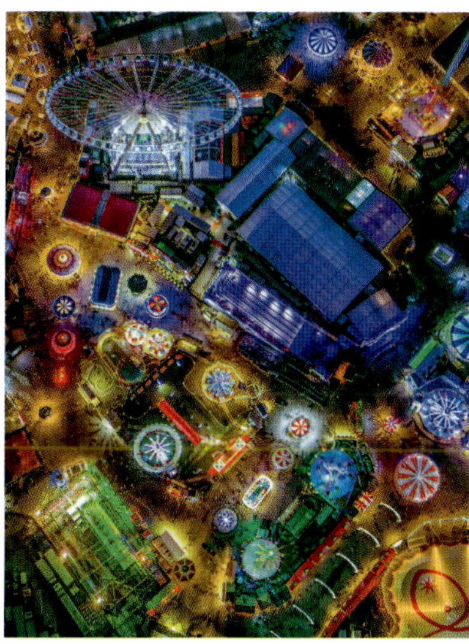

Hyde Park's Winter Wonderland
Pages 194–195 & 196

Since 2007, a large area near the Serpentine in Hyde Park has hosted the Winter Wonderland for six weeks each year from November to the following January. Under license from the Royal Parks, two event-planning companies put together a wide array of 100 or so rides and live entertainment options, plus food and beverage providers, market stalls, and an ice rink for skating. The Winter Wonderland includes a giant Ferris wheel, a roller coaster, and a freefall tower. Performances such as a circus, a comedy show, and an ice show are on offer, as well as Santaland with rides for children and Bavarian Village with a beer hall and music for adults. In its first 10 years, the attraction hosted more than 10 million visitors. Entrance is ticketed at peak times but free during certain hours.

ACKNOWLEDGMENTS

I want to thank all the people who have helped me create this book: Sir Norman Foster for writing a perfect foreword; Robert Morton, my friend, agent, and editor, who made the book so much better with his detailed and pithy descriptions and informative introduction; James Muschett, associate publisher, and everyone else at Rizzoli for their enthusiasm and support; Lori Malkin Ehrlich for her excellent design of the book; my partner and muse Kim Cantine, who helped with logistics and with her great eye for editing and was also a joy to travel with; my daughter Lucy, for encouraging me to photograph London; Jay Maisel, photographer extraordinaire, who inspired me to become a photographer; Jeff Hirsch of Foto Care, who supplies me with the latest photo equipment; and Helena Kaminski, my outstanding studio manager.

I'd also like to thank several helicopter companies and pilots—pilot Will Samuelson from Arena Aviation; Tom Aldcroft and pilot Miles Fletcher from A2B Aerial Filming; and Jeremy Braben and pilot Dougie Reid from Helicopter Film Services—as well as National Air Traffic Services (NATS) for airspace permission over London.

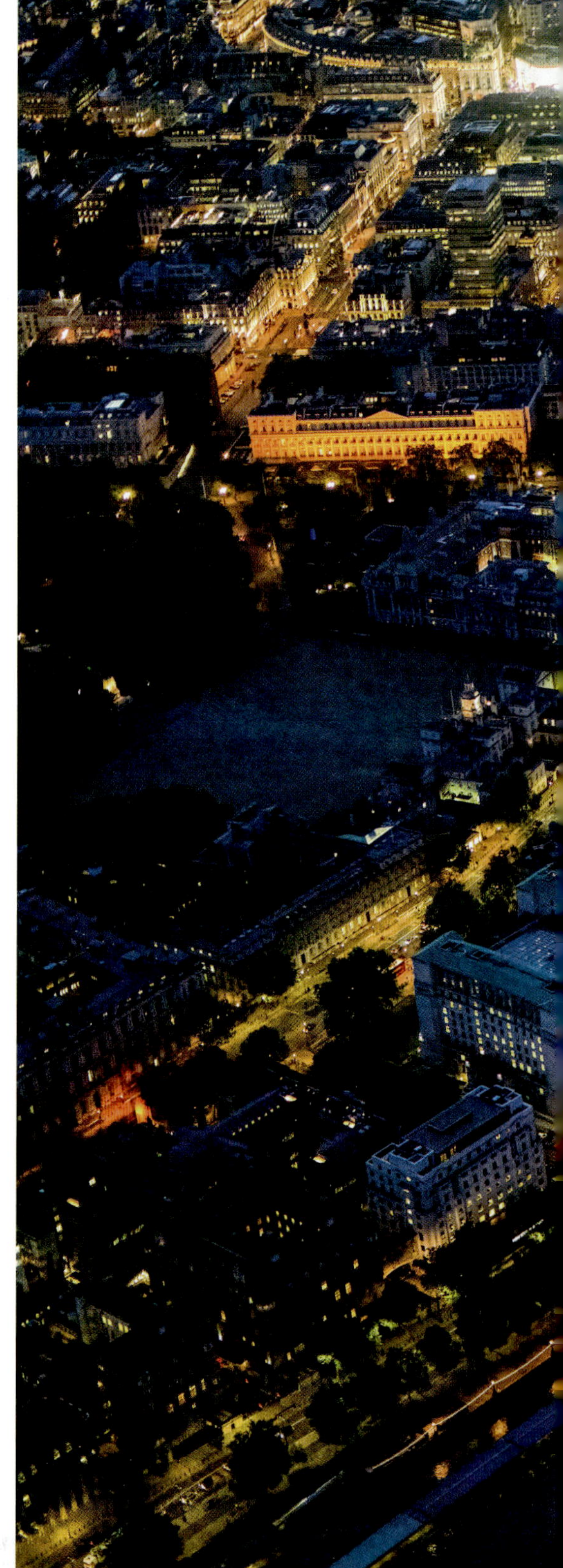

Looking over the London Eye toward Charing Cross railway station, with Trafalgar Square beyond

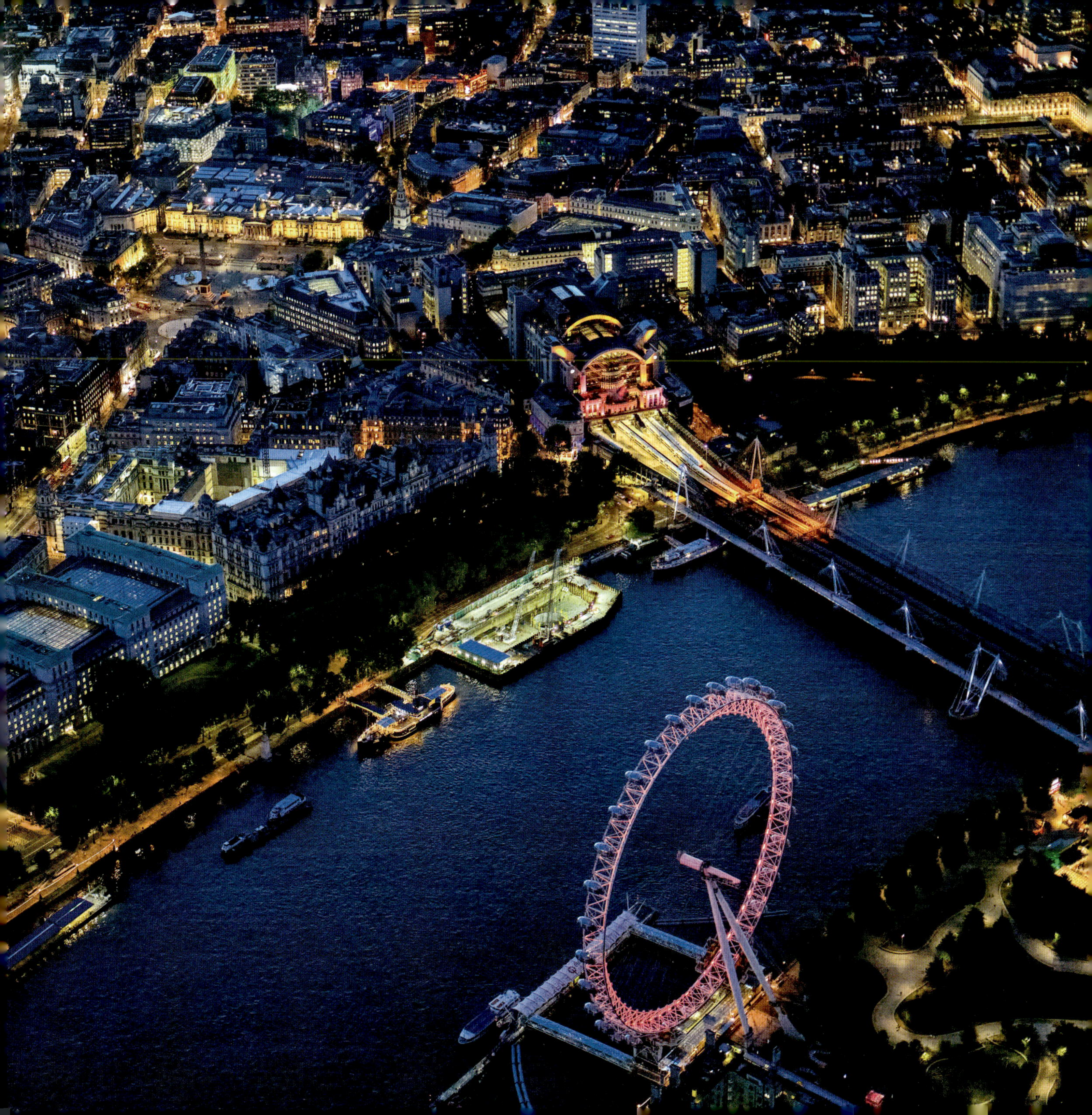

First published in the United States of America in 2024 by
Rizzoli International Publications, Inc.
300 Park Avenue South
New York, NY 10010
www.rizzoliusa.com

Publisher: Charles Miers
Associate Publisher: James Muschett
Managing Editor: Lynn Scrabis
Editor: Candice Fehrman
Design: Lori Malkin Ehrlich
Text: Robert Morton
Foreword: Sir Norman Foster

Printed in China

2024 2025 2026 2027 / 10 9 8 7 6 5 4 3 2 1

ISBN: 978-0-8478-9975-3

Library of Congress Control Number: 2023943532

Visit us online:
Facebook.com/RizzoliNewYork
Twitter: @Rizzoli_Books
Instagram.com/RizzoliBooks
Pinterest.com/RizzoliBooks
Youtube.com/user/RizzoliNY
Issuu.com/Rizzoli

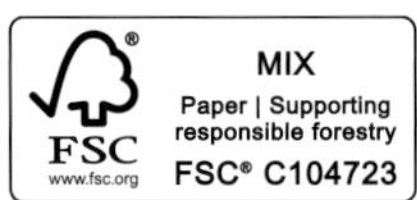

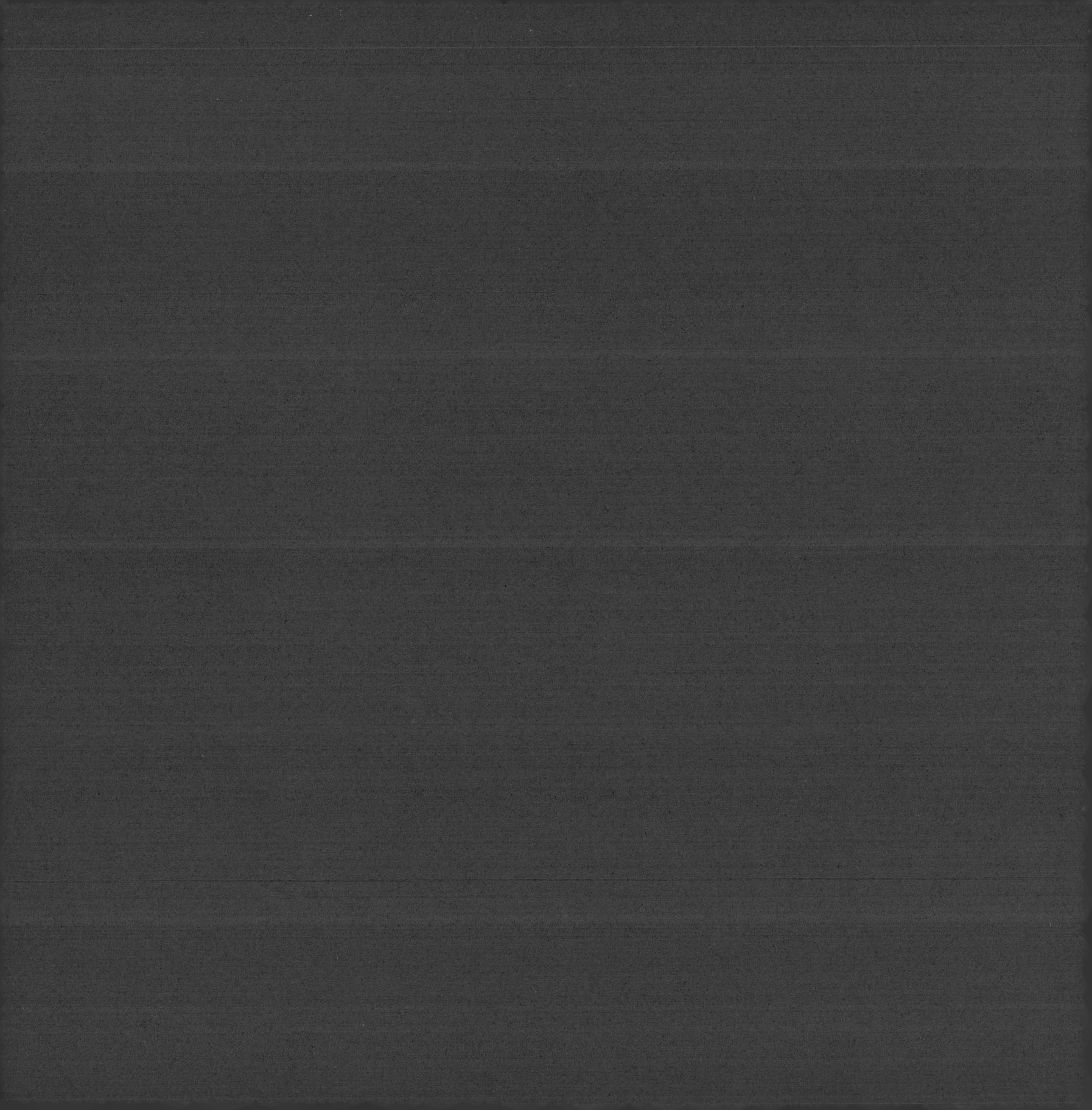